Queen Bee

Queen Bee

ROXANNE QUIMBY, BURT'S BEES, AND HER QUEST FOR A NEW NATIONAL PARK

PHYLLIS AUSTIN

TILBURY HOUSE
PUBLISHERS
THOMASTON, MAINE

Tilbury House Publishers
12 Starr Street, Thomaston, Maine 04861
800-582-1899 • www.tilburyhouse.com

Design by Lynda Chilton
BooksDesigned.com

First hardcover edition: June 2015
ISBN 978-0-88448-380-9
eBook ISBN 978-0-88448-420-2

Library of Congress Control Number: 2015939368

Printed in USA by the Maple Press, York, PA.

15 16 17 18 19 20 XXX 5 4 3 2 1

The photos on pages 1, 7, 22, 44, 78, 98, 114, 166, 186, 212, 231, and 335 are courtesy Bill Duffy, Northern Geomantics, Bradford, NH.
The photos on pages 53, 143, 244, 271, and 310 are from Great Northern Paper Company archives.
Map on page 365 courtesy Jym St. Pierre, RESTORE: The North Woods, Hallowell, ME.
Map on page 367 courtesy Bill Duffy, Northern Geomantics, Bradford, NH.
Map on page 368 by Daniel Coker, courtesy The Nature Conservancy, Brunswick, ME.

*For Anne Dellenbaugh, companion
on the longest unfolding path.*

CONTENTS

Looking northeast from Katahdin's Baxter Peak over Chimney Pond (foreground) toward North and South Turner mountains. Katahdin Lake is in the distance at right, with Deasey and Lunksoos mountains beyond it. (Bill Duffy photo)

Prologue

As Roxanne Quimby conducts me along the gravel road through the woods, it strikes me that returning to this place must evoke powerful mixed emotions for her. She recounts her history here on the banks of Salmon Stream in an isolated cabin outside the little town of Guilford, Maine. She speaks of the spartan existence, raising twin babies, divorce, and then hurling herself in a new direction—creating the phenomenally successful Burt's Bees natural skin-care company and ultimately opening the door to wealth, philanthropy, celebrity, and the means to finance a proposed new national park in Maine's mythic north woods.

It has taken me months to convince her to return to this patch of woods where she was a back-to-the-lander starting in 1975. I want to see where her Maine story began. I am hoping it will trigger memories that would be harder to tease out in her stylishly appointed West End home in Portland, where she is far removed, at least geographically, from that seminal period of her life.

As we walk along the trail that she first traipsed as a 25-year-old homesteader, Roxanne grumbles about the changes here. She still has strong feelings for this place. What was once a quarter-mile path off Andrews Road has been widened for easy vehicular access. The gash in the landscape is ugly, she laments, and it grieves her to see the land mistreated by subsequent property owners. She points to dry roots dangling from a gouged embankment, an old tub, scattered propane tanks, tattered blue plastic tarps, discarded household items, and strewn trash.

The charm of the place is gone, she believes. "I'm so disappointed," she sighs. "We went to great lengths to keep the land undisturbed. It was hard hauling all our belongings and supplies on our backs to preserve these lovely woods."

When Roxanne split her first cord of stove wood in 1975, the countercultural rush for things natural, organic, and environmentally friendly was just gathering strength in America. Not only did she walk the walk of that movement, she was a founding mother and leader of the transformative natural personal care products market. Burt's Bees literally sold the public—primarily women—on the use of healthy skin-care products made with simple beeswax and essential oils rather than the brew of toxic synthetics that most of the established brands contained. Her cult-like following saw Burt's Bees products as good for them and for the earth. The frugality she practiced as a back-to-the-lander guided her business decisions and, later, her land-conservations efforts.

The homesteading years remain her "magnetic north," she says, ambling around the old cabin. That lifestyle, she explains, gave birth to "guiding principles" that allow her to "feel right" with herself. The capital from her sale of Burt's Bees has given her the financial means to launch her national park campaign. She believes land conservation is a way of giving back to the customers who supported the growth and success of the company. "I feel like the universe guides me and leads me to opportunities because I'm on the right path. Why would the cosmic consciousness create obstacles for me if I'm doing the right thing, which is to preserve nature and to give the creatures of the earth some habitat where they are not threatened by mankind?"

I first caught up with Roxanne in 1994 as Burt's Bees was gaining traction in the natural care products sector. The eye-grabbing products associated with Burt Shavitz' unforgettable ornery, bearded face had become hot items. The way she packaged and promoted her goods made the brand seem at once elegant and reassuring, upscale and homey. There was a problem, however, and that was why I had contacted her.

Burt's Bees needed help to get through a critical growth period. Roxanne had sought assistance from the State of Maine but didn't receive a timely response. I was writing an article for the statewide weekly *Maine Times* about the company's predicament. My editor put Burt's Bees' plight on the newspaper's cover with a photograph of employees taking down the company sign from the Guilford headquarters as they were about to leave for greener pastures.

Soaring market demand told Roxanne she had a tiger by the tail, and the only way the enterprise could reach its potential was to move to a business-friendlier state. She chose North Carolina.

The dislocations incurred by her bold decision almost sank Burt's Bees. To survive, Roxanne had to reinvent the company. The little business ventures she had toyed with as a child had taught her the value of entrepreneurial experimentation and infused her with a capacity to think outside the box—and they had also taught her how bad it felt to fail. This time, she refused to let that happen.

Endowed with fabulous smarts, creativity, and instincts, Roxanne and a talented staff, including her two sisters, pushed Burt's Bees to breakneck sales growth. In the years between 1994 and 2003, sales rocketed from $4 million to $59 million, and Roxanne enthused publicly that her natural products would ultimately reach everyone, everywhere. The stovetop seat-of-the- pants enterprise that earned $200 in 1984 sold for hundreds of millions of dollars two decades later.

I caught up with Roxanne again in 2000, when she began pouring her Burt's Bees wealth into land for a proposed national park in the Maine woods. She became big news in Maine, attracting strong opposition to her park effort and sparking vehement personal attacks. While reporting on the national park controversy through the years, I grew increasingly puzzled by the unrelenting public campaign she waged. She could have hidden behind a business front for her conservation initiative and enjoyed a well-earned retirement, but Roxanne wasn't one to shy from those who saw her actions as audacious or even malevolent. Simply by being a woman in the male-dominated wheeling-and-dealing market of industrial forestlands, she rattled the status quo.

No other Maine philanthropist has ever been singled out by a muscular alliance of outdoor users, timber interests, private property advocates, and politicians for such aggressive vilification. Not even former Governor Percival P. Baxter, who received biting reproofs from northern Mainers when he purchased land for Baxter State Park and closed it to hunting, suffered the same degree of defiance and abuse. Rural storefront signs and pick-up truck bumper stickers howled "Ban Roxanne!" and much worse things were said about and against her on the Internet.

Who was this woman who wanted to buy, restore, and donate to the federal government tens of thousands of acres of timberland in the middle of the so-called working forest?

Eight years into her land acquisition and national park campaign, I approached her about writing a book, and she agreed to be interviewed extensively. For almost two years, she gave me a level of access no other writer has ever had, but then her cooperation ended. She couldn't tolerate being asked one more question about her life or work, and by 2011 she was feeling the need for less public attention, not more.

We first met face-to-face in late 2008. I found her unpretentious, likable, funny, and surprisingly open for someone so controversial. At 58, her dark, almost shoulder-length hair was showing gray streaks. She was physically sturdy, with the strong, weathered hands of a hard worker. Her round face, well-defined black eyebrows, and wide features hinted at her Russian ancestry. She had a hearty laugh that showed a line of straight white teeth. Although she had made a fortune producing beauty products for others, Roxanne hadn't given herself a cosmetics makeover, preferring a natural look without makeup, lipstick, or jewelry. Her standard garb was layered—she craved being warm— and as casual as it had been in her homesteading days. Comfortable loose sweaters, pants, scarves, and sandals made up her uniform. She still hung out clothes to dry on wooden racks rather than using an electric clothes dryer.

Beginning in early 2009, we met mostly in her Portland home, conducted dozens of phone calls, and exchanged many e-mails. Over time, interviewing more than a hundred additional people, I discovered that the whole Roxanne is much more complex and unpredictable than meets the eye. She is unapologetic for her abruptness, impulsiveness, and any other less-than-sunny aspects of her personality. Following her inner compass, she can reverse direction without explanation to those around her. Her years running Burt's Bees taught her to trust her instincts more than her advisors. She will not deviate from a path simply because it leads to conflict, but if her instincts tell her another path is better, she will not hesitate to abandon the one she is on.

Another of Roxanne's lesser-known traits is her self-styled spirituality, which is reflected in her opinions, decisions, and philosophy of life. Tarot cards, metaphysics, psychics, and meditation are among the paths she takes to reach her personal deep waters. They color her heart yet do not blunt the sharp edges of her personality.

She is admired, beloved, but also at times decried by people who have worked for or with her in business and in land conservation. Those I interviewed shared information on and off the record. Regardless of their personal feelings, almost everyone was impressed by how smart, shrewd, and purposeful Roxanne is. Some experienced how mischievous she is, and, at times, flirtatious.

Some key family members refused to talk about their relationships with Roxanne: her father, John Quimby; her brother, Rogers Quimby; her older sister, Renee Quimby; her former husband, George St. Clair; and her Burt's Bees co-founder Burt Shavitz. A number of past employees refused to talk about her on the record. Roxanne's philanthropic power seemed to be a contributing factor preventing leaders of nonprofits, among them conservation and environmental groups, from speaking to me candidly or at all.

There were numerous people, mostly former employees, whom I wanted to interview but couldn't find, as they had disappeared or died. This made it more difficult to verify stories that were told to me in different, sometimes contradictory versions.

Roxanne made available to me documents in her possession about Burt's Bees' early years, information that was critical to building the story of the company's origins. She gave me a confidential prospectus on the company sent to potential buyers in 2003 that revealed important financial data up to her sale of Burt's Bees to an investment group. I received nine years of her appointment calendars, from 1996 through 2004. Besides listing her meetings and travel schedules, these provided windows into private aspects of her life. She also gave me a twenty- page retrospective of her father's life, written by him.

All in all, telling Roxanne's story was the most difficult, frustrating reporting effort of my long writing career. Nonetheless, it was an exciting journey during the time she was interested in cooperating, and I felt and saw her charm and her ability to control events, as well as her vulnerability.

I look back with humor at an early Monday morning session in her immaculate kitchen in Portland, seated opposite her at a stainless steel table. Roxanne spooned oatmeal into her mouth, her head bent toward the bowl and her eyes glowering up at me as I asked detailed questions that seemed to make her weary. After that, I was wary of asking to meet her before late morning. It wasn't the last time she used silence to end my probing into her life.

Given Roxanne's fierce ambition to birth a new national park and her back-to-the-land credentials, I assumed when I started writing this book that she was a robust and dedicated outdoorswoman. I imagined she had hiked, paddled, and camped all over Maine, and that's why she wanted to allow some of the north woods to revert to wilderness. But she hadn't.

Yet in time I saw that she had been an outdoorswoman in the venerable Maine tradition. She had more or less *lived* outside during her homesteading years, and it was the memory of the wear, tear, and discomfort of that daily life in the elements that has caused her to gravitate toward indoor pursuits such as knitting and arts.

The driving force of Roxanne's interest in conservation is not only her commitment to land conservation but also her love of beauty—the same aesthetic sense that impassioned John Muir, wilderness hero and founder of the Sierra Club. "Everybody needs beauty as well as bread, places to play in and pray in, where Nature may heal and give strength to body and soul alike," he wrote in his 1912 book *The Yosemite*. In Roxanne's words, "There's never been anything made by a human that can approach the beauty of what is created by mother nature." An artist by nature and training, she said she has "never seen a work of art that has moved me like a natural landscape has."

One of the most memorable, stirring views a soul can encounter is the sight of the seemingly "forever" sea of dark-green forests and glimmering blue rivers and lakes rolling away on all sides beneath a small plane overflying the northern Maine woods. "The forest looked like a firm grass sward," wrote Henry David Thoreau, describing the view from atop Mt. Katahdin, "and the effect of these lakes in its midst has been well compared ... to that of a mirror broken into a thousand fragments, and wildly scattered over the grass, reflecting the full blaze of the sun." Roxanne has sat in many Piper Cubs, skimming close enough to the treetops to witness the reality of harsh impacts from industrial-scale logging and the resulting habitat damage threatening wildlife and fragile natural processes. I imagine her one day flying over the Penobscot River's East Branch watershed, where she has invested tens of millions of dollars of her Burt's Bees wealth to acquire 75,000 acres for a beautiful national park. I can see her smiling with the satisfaction of knowing those cutover woods are finally, safely, in the public domain, permanently protected, and recovering as a twenty-first-century second-chance wilderness. 🐝

Moon over Katahdin. (Bill Duffy photo)

The Maine Woods

From Roxanne's girlhood, Henry David Thoreau was a curiosity to her because his birthday was listed the day after hers on the calendar hung in the family kitchen. As she grew up, she fed her interest in him by visiting Walden Pond and reading his books. By the time she was a young woman, Thoreau was lodged securely in her psyche as a compelling spiritual influence.

Thoreau visited the north country in 1846 and was inspired to return twice more to record and experience its deep wilderness before civilization encroached. Roxanne felt a similar calling upon moving to Maine in 1975, and slowly realized that her purpose was to protect and restore the wilderness in the north woods.

Thoreau's fame rests partly on the books he wrote more than 150 years ago about his explorations to Katahdin and his excursion down the Penobscot East Branch. With Thoreau in the back of her mind, Roxanne began to purchase forestland along the East Branch for a national park and recreation area—the same riverlands where Thoreau paddled and camped in 1857.

By the time Roxanne entered the land conservation arena, almost a century and a half of efforts to protect the Katahdin region had gone by. That's a lot of history, and Roxanne was unaware of most of it.

When Thoreau first explored the Maine woods, what he found most striking was the vast, virtually uninterrupted forest. "It is even more ... wild than you had anticipated, a damp and intricate wilderness," he wrote in his 1864 classic *The Maine Woods*. The hidden dangers of the place for those not paying attention to the weather, wind, waterways, and trail conditions appealed to him. The roughness and remoteness of the mountain and lake country made his life back home in the pastoral, more populated landscape of Massachusetts feel tame.

Just how mesmerizing and exhilarating Thoreau found his three trips to the Maine woods came through in his writings.* "The kings of England formerly had their forests 'to hold the king's game,' for sport or food," he observed in *The Maine Woods*. "Why should not we, who have renounced the king's authority, have our national preserves ... not for idle sport or food, but for inspiration and our own true recreation?" Thoreau's idea of national preserves was extraordinary in its time and enormously forward-thinking given the reckless logging and killing of Maine's large mammals that was even then ongoing. By the mid-1800s, a third of Maine's forest had been cut over, and by the early 1900s almost all of the old-growth forest was gone.†

Meanwhile, woodland caribou, cougar, Canada lynx, coyote, Eastern timber wolf, and black bear were being hunted and trapped with abandon. "Maine, perhaps, will soon be where Massachusetts is," Thoreau warned, adding, "[A] good part of her territory is already as bare and common-place as much of our neighborhood." He believed that wild refuges were "essential for the long-term survival of American civilization," the earth's ecological sustainability, and human health and well-being.

Less than fifteen years after *The Maine Woods* was published, the sell-off of Maine's public forestlands to private owners was virtually complete, boosting the young state financially while ensuring unrestrained impacts on millions of acres owned for private profit. Protests rang out from a small number of those who today would be called preservationists or conservationists. They deemed the sale of state-owned land to speculators and forestry corporations for as little as pennies per acre a travesty, a massive transfer of public resources into private hands. Their response was to begin efforts to return some of the

*Thoreau made his trips into the Maine woods in 1846, 1853, and 1857.

†"Old-growth" in Maine generally refers to trees at least 150 years old in stands with little disturbance.

woods to the public domain. Much of the early focus was on the Katahdin area, as that sprawling mountain peak is the highest in Maine and has always been a focus of identity for Mainers.* The first pleas from Mainers, as well as from outsiders, focused on saving the mountain for tourism and hunting, and the story is significant enough to be the subject of a college class in Maine history or land conservation campaigns.

In 1861, state geologist Charles Hitchcock and noted agriculture advocate Ezekiel Holmes proposed a carriage road and hotel at Chimney Pond, below Katahdin's summit, to accommodate visitors who would have access to the peak via foot or horseback. In 1895, the first statewide organization to get involved in the conservation movement, the Hotel Proprietors' Association of Maine, put forward a 576,000-acre state park proposal centered on Katahdin. Proponents feared the region was in jeopardy of being "devastated by lumbermen, fires and a squatter population." Maine Inland Fisheries and Game commissioner Leroy Carleton advanced an idea in 1899 for establishing a "game preserve to include the caribou grounds on and around Katahdin."†

More substantial calls to preserve the Katahdin area arose at the beginning of the twentieth century. In 1901, the *Bangor Daily Commercial* newspaper urged the formation of "a great public reservation." That same year, business journalist Francis Wiggin of Portland delivered an address to the State Board of Trade proposing a "reservation ... [encompassing] the twelve townships that would include our highest elevation Mount Katahdin, and the beautiful West Branch lakes."

Author George Kimball of Hampden picked up on the national significance of the region and was quoted in 1905 as saying, "Had I the influence and eloquence I would seek the country's ear and tell of another National Park extending from Ambajejus on the south to Churchill's Lake on the northeast, and to Chesuncook and the Allagash on the west; while Katahdin rearing its glorious head and flinging down its shadows on half a thousand lakes, should dominate all."

---

*Katahdin was revered and feared by the Wabanaki ("Dawn Land People") long before Europeans arrived in America.

†Woodland caribou were native to Maine, and Katahdin was the "last stronghold" in the eastern U.S. Overhunting resulted in the big mammals' extirpation by the early 1900s. A reintroduction using caribou from Newfoundland was tried in 1963 but failed for unknown reasons. More caribou from the Canadian provincial island were reintroduced to the Katahdin area in 1990 but died from multiple causes, including brainworm disease and bear and coyote predation.

Just when park opponents might have wondered if the pleas for protection would ever stop, some influential Republicans joined the chorus. Between 1910 and 1916, U.S. Representative Frank Guernsey, a Republican from Dover-Foxcroft, initiated efforts in Congress to protect the Katahdin area as a national forest or national park, garnering support from the Maine Inland Fisheries and Game Commission, the Maine Sportsmen's Fish and Game Association, and the Maine State Federation of Women's Clubs. The Maine Legislature even supported it, but a national preserve was doomed because the forest industry had developed a political stranglehold on the region and was not about to tolerate federally owned lands in their backyard. Still, University of Maine professor Lucius H. Merrill, in a passionate talk to the Bangor Historical Society, predicted that protection of Katahdin by the federal government "cannot be doubted." The area was "a great natural asset which has never met the appreciation which it deserves," he said.

Between the 1870s and 1916, no one did more than Piscataquis County native John Francis Sprague of Dover-Foxcroft to beat the drums for a national park. A Republican lawyer and writer,* he had a seat in the state senate, published a popular history magazine, *Sprague's Journal of Maine History*, and presided over a statewide sportsmen's group as well as the North American Fish and Game Association. "If a portion of Maine's northern wilderness could be set apart for this purpose where moose, deer, bears, beavers and all of the animals, and all of the song birds of our woods could forever remain unmolested and be possessed of a real home safe and secure from vandals and destroyers, what a wonderful national park it would be in the years of the future," Sprague wrote in the June 1916 issue of his history journal.

One of Sprague's colleagues in the Maine Senate was Republican Percival Baxter of Portland, who took up the effort to preserve Katahdin. The stars lined up behind Baxter, albeit slowly.

Percival Baxter's "Forever Wild" Park

Percival Proctor Baxter—or "Percy," as he was known—was born in 1876 to a patrician Portland family. His father, James Phinney Baxter, had

---

*Maine politics and government were dominated by Republicans in Sprague's day, and the GOP was not then the anti-environmental party it would become at the end of the twentieth century. Democrats were not only scarce, they were often the more conservative party. Things had changed dramatically by the time Democrat Edmund Muskie won the governorship in 1954 and led his party's upsurge.

co-founded the Portland Packing Company and earned considerable wealth from it. James then became a student of Maine history and served as president of the Maine Historical Society for 30 years. He also served six terms as Portland's mayor. Following in James's footsteps, Percy attended Bowdoin College, where he played varsity football; edited the college newspaper; studied politics, civic leadership, and philanthropy; and graduated Phi Beta Kappa in 1898. His dog, Deke, lived with him in his dormitory and accompanied him to classes.* After graduating from Harvard Law School in 1901, he returned to Portland to manage his father's real estate investments. Although he had seven siblings and three older brothers, the family's fortune went largely to him.

Percy made his first visit to the Katahdin region during a 1903 fishing expedition. Firming up his ideas for a state-owned park while in the Maine House in 1917–21, he proposed in 1919 that the state spend $20,000 to purchase 115,000 acres of cutover woods for a Katahdin preserve. His house colleagues balked at the expenditure; it's reasonable to suppose that they couldn't envision a threat to Maine's vast north woods.

Baxter had never stood on Katahdin's summit until he joined a group of friends and politicians climbing the mountain in August 1920. He was then 43. After crawling across the scary Knife Edge between Pamola and Baxter peaks, he said, "I wouldn't do it again for a million; I wouldn't have missed it for a million." The climb reinforced his desire to protect the area.

After winning a seat in the Maine Senate in 1920 (having served an earlier term in 1909–11), Baxter was elected senate president in early January 1921. By the end of the month he was Maine's new governor, succeeding Frederick Parkhurst, who had died of a heart attack. Suddenly Baxter found himself with a higher bully pulpit from which to advocate for a Katahdin park, and he used it. "Mount Katahdin Park will be the state's crowning glory," he declared, "a worthy memorial to commemorate the end of the first and the beginning of the second century of Maine's statehood. This park will prove a blessing to those who follow us, and they will see that we built for them more wisely than our forefathers did for us."

But he was again beaten back by his most powerful opponent and Maine's largest landowner, Great Northern Paper. Neither its president, Garrett

*While at Bowdoin in 1896, Baxter accompanied classmates to Bath, where William Jennings Bryan, Democratic presidential candidate, was speaking. (Bath was the hometown of Bryan's running mate Arthur Sewall.) The young men were disruptive enough to get themselves arrested, but Baxter was able, with his father's help, to avoid a police record.

Schenck, nor Schenck's chief assistant, Fred Gilbert, had any use for Baxter or his goal to establish a park around Katahdin. Baxter was not easily deterred, however. He had money, friends in high places, and seemingly unlimited patience.

Once back in private life, preserving Katahdin became Percival Baxter's overriding goal. He wanted to give the people of Maine a wilderness legacy they would treasure forever. After Schenck's death in 1928, William A. Whitcomb became CEO of Great Northern. He and other company officials admired Baxter and opened the door to meetings and negotiations over land purchases to protect Katahdin. As the country plunged into the Great Depression in 1930, Baxter purchased 6,000 acres—including Mt. Katahdin—from Great Northern for $25,000,* then donated it to the state to become the nucleus of a park. His proviso was that the land "shall forever be used for public park and recreational purposes, shall be forever left in the natural wild state, shall forever be kept as a sanctuary for wild beasts and birds, that no road or ways for motor vehicles shall hereafter ever be constructed thereon or therein." The name Baxter State Park was adopted the following year.†

Baxter faced an unexpected challenge of federal interference in the 1930s, as President Franklin Delano Roosevelt's New Deal proposed establishing national forests and national parks across the country to help reverse the economic distress of the Great Depression. Maine Governor Louis Brann (1933–37)—the only post-World War I Democratic governor in Maine until Ed Muskie was elected in 1954—proposed a million-acre Roosevelt National Park around Katahdin, believing it would boost the Millinocket area's economy, which was completely dependent on the two big Great Northern paper mills. At Brann's request, the National Park Service conducted a reconnaissance survey of the region straddling two counties (Penobscot and Piscataquis) in 1934–35, and in 1936, Dr. E. A. Pritchard, an associate recreational planner at the National Park Service, asked Baxter how he felt about the park service buying land contiguous to Katahdin or taking over Baxter State Park as part of a larger national park.

Baxter, who had made three land purchases by then and steadfastly opposed a national park (not trusting the federal government), wrote to

---

*Equivalent to $500,000 in 2015.

†By 1962, Baxter had enhanced the park with 28 additional donations of land to be held in trust for Maine citizens, creating a 201,018-acre preserve. Today the park contains 209,501 acres.

Pritchard on August 15, 1936, saying, "If your Park Service wants a National Park in Maine there is available much land and many lakes and streams in Washington and other counties, with no state Park to restrict and limit your purchases." He implored Pritchard to let his state park go forward without interference from the federal government. "Do allow me, with the assistance of old 'Father Time,' to handle this matter as I have planned, for what has been accomplished here has been done only after a long and tiresome contest, absolutely single-handed and in the face of abuse and bitterness that you would not believe possible where a man is merely trying to do something worthwhile for his Native State."

Nevertheless, in 1937, the National Park Service reported that an area of at least 500 square miles (320,000 acres), including Katahdin, merited the status of either a national park or a national monument,* prompting Maine's Republican U.S. Congressman Ralph Owen Brewster to introduce a bill to create a Katahdin National Park. Baxter was livid at Brewster's initiative, which was supported by the Appalachian Mountain Club and championed by Maine native Myron Avery, head of the Appalachian Trail Conference.† Baxter successfully pressured his connections in Washington to defeat the bill. One of his allies in that effort was his old adversary Great Northern Paper, which didn't want a federal presence in timber country. Another was the newly formed Wilderness Society, which was opposed to major tourism developments in the Katahdin area. Then, as ever, politics made strange bedfellows. Brewster's national park attempt in northern Maine was the last for more than 50 years.

Over the decades, Baxter met strong hostility from Katahdin-area residents because he banned hunting on lands he acquired. By the time he had accumulated 142,000 acres, George Barnes, a Republican from Houlton who was speaker of the Maine House of Representatives in 1945–46, had begun working against further expansion of the no-hunting park. "Fish and game

*The recommended area included the townships bordering the East Branch of the Penobscot River where Roxanne would acquire lands for her proposed national park some 60 years later.

†Brewster was a controversial figure with a long political career. He served as governor in 1925–29, but his reputation as a populist who often took on the power companies and other big business interests was tainted by the election support he received from Maine's Ku Klux Klan. He and Percival Baxter were on the same side on one major issue of the day, exporting the state's hydropower; both opposed it. Otherwise they were enemies, and Baxter publicly accused Brewster of KKK sympathies. Brewster's reputation took another hit after his election to the postwar U.S. Senate when he allied himself with Wisconsin senator Joe McCarthy. Brewster and Senator Margaret Chase Smith, also a Republican, became adversaries over McCarthy's communist witch hunt.

clubs in the area feel as strongly as do I," Barnes told the *Bangor Daily News*, naming prominent northern Maine businessmen who were on his side. Baxter acknowledged that it was "not pleasant to be criticized" but that he had to "bear up ... and carry on." Like Roxanne Quimby decades later, he was forced to make pragmatic retreats from his initial vision of a strictly wilderness preserve, settling for "forever wild" and "wildlife sanctuary" designations in parts of the park while allowing hunting in two areas and "scientific forestry" on 29,584 acres. He felt a strong sense of possession of the lands he fought so hard to acquire, asking visitors, "How do you like my park?"

A Yankee blue blood and a lifelong pew owner at Portland's State Street Congregational Church, Baxter was also a social and political maverick, an outspoken leader in the progressive causes of women's suffrage and animal rights. As governor he ordered the State House flag lowered to half-mast when his dog died, angering veterans' groups. He went against the state GOP to fight the export of Maine's hydropower, and he broke party ranks to vote for Democrat John Kennedy in the 1960 presidential election. Before he died a bachelor in 1969 at age 92, he requested that there be no funeral service. The last words his grand-nephew Rupert White heard from him were "Jesus, I'm coming." His ashes were scattered in Baxter State Park.

The Modern Campaign for a National Park

The rise of the national conservation movement in the 1960s prompted efforts in Maine and nationwide for expanded protection of diverse wildlands and wildlife habitat. Along the way, the idea of restoring cutover lands (that is, acreage that has been cleared of trees) gained favor. Wilderness could be restored by nature's healing hand if left alone. More than 150 national park system units encompassing 53 million acres were created between 1961 and 1981, doubling the acreage of public lands administered by the National Park Service. The movement stalled during Ronald Reagan's presidency, and it was years before national parks and monuments, historic places, and other units in the National Park Service once again began to increase.

In 1988, nineteen years after Percival Baxter's death, the National Parks and Conservation Association, an independent, nonpartisan advocacy organization, renewed the pressure for a federal park around Baxter State Park. Several other calls for large parks in northern Maine followed. In 1989, The Wilderness Society recommended a 2.7-million-acre Maine Woods Reserve. In their book *The Big Outside,* environmental activists Dave Foreman and Howie Wolke upped the ante with a more ambitious proposal for a 10-million-acre wilderness preserve stretching north from Baxter Park to include the St. John River and the Allagash Wilderness Waterway, which had been designated as a U.S. Wild and Scenic River in 1970. Maine's largest environmental advocacy group, the Natural Resources Council of Maine, floated the idea of creating a North Woods Conservation Area of several million acres in 1991, and the Northern Appalachian Restoration Project proposed a five-million-acre Thoreau Regional Wilderness Reserve in 1994.

Also in 1994, RESTORE: The North Woods launched its drive for a 3.2-million-acre Maine Woods National Park and Preserve. This proved to be the campaign that wouldn't go away. Wilderness advocates had founded RESTORE in 1992 in response to the epic ongoing upheaval in the longstanding paper company ownership of millions of acres of Maine's commercial timberland. The privately owned region in northern Maine known as the "north woods" was the largest remaining forest in the Northern Appalachian region and one of the last vestiges of backcountry east of the Rocky Mountains. This legendary territory included 10.5 million acres of land—almost half of Maine's entire landmass—that had never organized a local government. Although much of it was heavily networked with logging roads and scattered development, it was virtually empty compared with most anywhere else east of the Mississippi. Only 8,000 people lived in this sprawling territory—a fraction of the number of moose and bear. Along with Maine's granite coastline, the north woods defined the state in the eyes of its residents and the nation. RESTORE's Jym St. Pierre described the north woods as the "last big landscape in play" in the eastern U.S.

RESTORE promoted its proposed park as an extraordinary opportunity. The land within the mapped boundary of the future park was the heart of the north woods. Despite damage done by logging, pesticide spraying, and more than 25,000 miles of logging roads built after the mid-1970s, much of the land still had the look and feel of wilderness: free-flowing rivers, clear lakes, towering evergreens, scattered old-growth spruce and maple, alpine-like mountain summits, deep gorges, delicate orchids, bald eagles, Atlantic salmon, blue-spotted salamanders. It was enough to make biologists and naturalists fumble for adequate descriptions.

Within RESTORE's proposed boundaries were the Appalachian Trail's Hundred Mile Wilderness, the headwaters of five major rivers (among them the nationally designated Wild and Scenic Allagash Wilderness Waterway), and Native American travel routes. Such a seemingly endless territory could provide "wilderness recreation on an Alaskan scale," RESTORE pointed out. RESTORE advocated acquiring park land from willing sellers at fair market value, eschewing the unpopular approach of taking land by eminent domain. Before any land could be purchased, however, RESTORE needed citizen support for a federal study of the feasibility of establishing a park. Garnering that support was about as tough a project as anyone could attempt in northern Maine, where the federal government was distrusted and private property was considered sacrosanct.

The park plan, as RESTORE explained it, could provide an economic alternative for a region going downhill fast. The group's pitch was that the long-relied-upon woods industry was weakening quickly in the face of global competition, financial losses, aging mills, environmental rules, conflicts with employee unions, and faster tree growth in the South and overseas. Ecotourism, service-sector jobs, and small, diverse manufacturing enterprises offered a more stable future than an economy overly dependent on forest products, RESTORE argued.

The organization gained attention with a brochure called "Proposed National Park & Preserve: A Vision of What Could Be." Looking like the brochures for existing national parks, the publication made the case for saving "America's Crown Jewel," noting points of interest and providing tips on recreational opportunities. The brochure included a map of the imaginary park, color photographs, and an enthusiastic narrative that made the proposal seem doable and worthy, spotlighting what could happen to the wildlands if they were left in the hands of timber liquidators and developers. The brochure pointed out that 70 million urban residents lived within a day's drive of Maine's north woods, creating an enormous temptation for developers to convert the landscape into vacation enclaves, resorts, and exclusive hunting club reserves.

Many people in the politically conservative Greenville-Millinocket-Patten area—along with state and local sportsmen's groups—were instantly opposed to the proposed park. In addition to the specter of federal ownership, taking land out of commercial forest management was viewed as a threat to local jobs and the culture of the region. Park opponents imagined outsiders calling the shots in their backyard, imposing recreational restrictions, and putting up more gates with access fees. They pictured a loss of their freedom to hunt, fish, and ride their snowmobiles and ATVs on all that paper company land they treated more or less as theirs. Their response reflected a divide between area residents—who were frequent three- or four-season forestland users—and "people from away" who visited occasionally, mostly in the warm months.

By the 1990s, it seemed that the tradition of public access to Maine's corporate-owned forestlands by foot and vehicle was a recognized right. In reality, public use of these vast lands—constituting half of Maine's 10.5-million-acre unorganized territory and almost a quarter of the entire state—could be shut off at any time on the whim of the owners.

In fact, locked and unlocked gates had been installed in the north woods in the late 1960s as the river drives of logs were coming to an end, and one large landowner had begun then to charge access fees at a few gates. In 1971 a consortium of thirty forest companies established North Maine Woods Inc. (NMW) to oversee access and manage campsites on their 2.5 million acres. Checkpoints were built, and recreational users were charged a fee. Great Northern Paper's one million acres of timberland were not in the NMW system when the company began charging a day-use fee in 1987.

Paying for access that had been free for so long created long-term resentment among area residents.* By the 1990s, free foot access was guaranteed on less than five percent of the unorganized territory—the portion owned by the public—and some of that was roadless.†

A month after Jym St. Pierre opened RESTORE's Maine office in Augusta on Earth Day, April 22, 1995, the Sportsman's Alliance of Maine announced that it was joining battle against a national park. Executive director George Smith, an influential lobbyist in Augusta, charged that RESTORE's proposed park "would be the death of the Maine Woods for us—the death of hunting and trapping, timber harvesting, jobs, access, and our outdoor heritage."

This was just the latest Sportsman's Alliance offensive against RESTORE. Previously, the alliance had opposed RESTORE's initiatives for wolf recovery and protection of the endangered Atlantic salmon. RESTORE's park proposal

*In 1993, the Millinocket Fin and Feather Club signed an agreement with Great Northern Paper (GNP) to withdraw opposition to relicensing of the company's hydropower dams in exchange for free day use of GNP lands. In 1999, the new owners of GNP placed the so-called West Branch lands under North Maine Woods recreational oversight, initiating a fee to access those one million acres. The club filed a lawsuit but lost all the way through the Maine Supreme Court.

†Maine's unorganized territory, consisting of over 400 townships covering 14,052 square miles, has no local municipal government.

presented the financially troubled alliance with a great fundraising opportunity. Smith pressed members to contribute generously, up to $1,000 apiece, for an all-out campaign against RESTORE.*

Millinocket's Fin and Feather Club also joined the anti-park forces. Formed in 1951, the club had decades of experience fighting efforts to ban hunting and snowmobiling in Baxter State Park. Members considered a national park "the same way we would regard a thief in the night or a con-man," said club stalwart Jimmy Busque. He claimed the federal government "would erect gates and charge a fee." (In fact, RESTORE had proposed just the opposite, eliminating private paper company gates and fees.) "They would destroy roads and would not permit snowmobiling, hunting, or trapping," Busque asserted. (Again, RESTORE had proposed the opposite, a guarantee of snowmobiling, hunting, and trapping rights in designated national preserve areas.) Not wanting facts to get in the way of a good fight, the club started selling bumper stickers that read "Keep Maine Free—No RESTORE for ME."

On the other hand, RESTORE's proposal received a positive response from the *Maine Sunday Telegram*. On June 12, 1994, editorial page editor George Neavoll called for a "fair hearing" from people, given how badly beaten up the industrial forest was. "Sadly, much of what Thoreau saw from Katahdin's flanks—and much of what RESTORE envisions—does not exist today," he wrote. "The 'Maine Woods' west of Katahdin and north along the Allagash, in the heart of the proposed national park, simply are no more. They have been cut from horizon to horizon right up to the western boundary of Baxter State Park." Beyond the waters of the Allagash and the screen of riverbank trees was a moonscape made by clear-cutting, he said. The situation gave rise to the phrase *beauty strip,* used by environmentalists in reference not only to the Allagash but also to other rivers, streams, and lakes where industrial-scale clear-cutting was occurring beyond a narrow waterfront zone—with no laws against it at the time.

Huge clear-cuts were the industry's response to salvaging spruce and fir trees ravaged by spruce budworm, which had reappeared in the late 1970s.

---

*Smith received a 12.5 percent commission on income from the Sportsman's Alliance of Maine's fund-raising efforts, which amounted to about $8,000 in 1994. He said in 2010 that the Sportsman's Alliance had to have opponents such as RESTORE. "You can't write a letter and say everything's going great, send us money. You have to say everything is going badly." After he left the organization in 2010 to devote more time to writing and co-hosting a weekly television program (he had been writing a weekly column and other work for more than 20 years by then), Smith endorsed Roxanne's park proposal but continued to express doubts about RESTORE's larger vision.

(Recurring infestations were part of a natural cycle in northern spruce-fir woods but were rendered more virulent by timber-company monoculture.) The enormous scale of the clear-cutting prompted extensive publicity and statewide public outrage, generating unsuccessful attempts in the mid-1990s to ban such abusive harvesting practices.

Amid the budworm outbreak and environmentally damaging salvage operations, GreatNorthern Paper disclosed dire financial problems that would necessitate laying off a third of its 3,000-member workforce in the coming years. On the heels of this downsizing announcement, the state was shaken by an avalanche of land sales by the big timber barons—Great Northern, Bowater, International Paper, Champion International, MeadWestvaco, Inexcon, Nextfor, Hancock Timber Resources Group, and Scott—and by the real estate frenzy that followed.* The camel's back had been broken in the north woods, but many northern Maine residents refused to see it. Unable to take in the reality that the vibrant age of paper manufacturing was over, they were horrified by the notion that the Katahdin region could become a huge park and tourism hub. Many closed their eyes and minds to the fast-moving changes.

Speculators scoured the north woods for wilderness lots to sell as vacation retreats, and "kingdom buyers," a new breed of landowners, sparked statewide concern as they acquired large lakeshore fiefdoms. Liberty Media billionaire John Malone emerged as the biggest of these. In 1998, Malone bought 7,400 acres around the southern end of five-mile-long Spencer Lake, near Jackman, from Plum Creek for nearly $3.5 million, or about $456 an acre. In 2000 he purchased the remaining 8,000 acres surrounding the lake, paying $10 million, or $1,330 an acre, to the investment firm GMO LLC. In 2011 he would purchase 900,000 acres sprawling across the state, making his Maine holdings five percent of the state's entire landmass—nine times the size of Roxanne Quimby's holdings and twelve times the size of the national park she was then promoting against unyielding opposition.

Unlike Roxanne in years to come, Malone would not be decried or derided for buying such a huge chunk of the woods that it made him the largest landowner in Maine. He continued harvesting timber. He continued to allow

*Great Northern sold to Georgia Pacfic, which sold to Bowater, which sold to Inexcon—all the same land. Scott sold to SAPPI, which sold to Plum Creek Timber. SAPPI's announcement of its intent to sell marked the first time one of the major landowners had put land on the market without having already lined up a buyer.

public recreational access to the land. His kingdom was not within the proposed national park, and he kept to himself any thoughts he had about setting aside land for conservation and wildlife protection in the future.*

As large forestland tracts shifted into new hands, RESTORE's executive director Michael Kellett weighed in with an urgent message. The cutting in the Maine woods during the spruce budworm infestation of the previous two decades had been the most intensive in history, but the woods were "still intact enough to be restored," he wrote in the Summer 2000 issue of *Wild Earth* journal. "In Thoreau's day, Americans had the luxury of not creating a 'national preserve' in the north country. We no longer have that luxury. We need a Maine Woods National Park and we need it now, before the opportunity is lost forever."

It was into this polarized debate and weighty saga of north woods conservation proposals and endeavors that Roxanne Quimby injected herself in 2000. The long history of the park idea had infused its supporters with a sense that it was not a matter of whether a national park would happen, but where, when, and how. On the cusp of the twenty-first century, Roxanne seemed to be the angel who, finally, could breathe life into the vision.

She had no reason to doubt that she could be successful. Despite her business talents and experience, however, she was naive in this new role. She greatly underestimated the historical, political, and cultural changes taking place in the Katahdin region in the wake of massive forestland sales and paper mill downsizings and bankruptcies, increased restrictions on recreational access to woods and waters, camp leaseholders being forced off private lands, and the threat of large vacation subdivisions. Area residents were angry, fearful, and defensive, and Roxanne was a convenient target upon which to unleash pent-up emotions. The opposition leveled at her was far more intensely personal than that encountered by Percival Baxter a half century before, and she didn't see it coming.

On the other hand, national park foes also greatly underestimated never-say-never Roxanne, just as competitors and doubters had done when she built Burt's Bees from a tiny backwoods start-up selling candles and honeybee gifts

*An unpaid director of the libertarian anti-tax think tank Cato Institute since 1995, Malone was described as "congenitally averse to paying taxes" in a November 2014 Bloomberg article. The article described how Malone (whose net worth was $7.5 billion) avoided several hundred million dollars of taxes in 2014 by shifting Liberty Global's corporate address from Colorado to London.

to an internationally known natural skin-care products corporation. Anyone who thought Roxanne would back down from something she deeply believed in didn't know her story. 🐝

Wassataquoik Stream—see map, page 367. (Bill Duffy photo)

Origins

R oxanne Quimby is the quintessence of a self-made woman, but the character of her self-making was molded by her domineering father, John Arthur Quimby, and her doting, big-hearted maternal grandmother, Thais ("Baba") Willens. They are the keys to understanding Roxanne's storied rise from poor back-to-the-lander to business superstar.

As experienced entrepreneurs, John Quimby and Thais Willens created the immediate family culture, class, and circumstances that developed little Roxanne into a clever and creative merchant before she entered first grade. Extreme differences in these elders' personalities and beliefs provided the yin and yang in Roxanne's early world, affecting her emotional makeup and her earliest aspirations.

That these close family influences should be so contrary is not surprising considering their dissimilar origins. Thais Willens's ancestors came from European Russia's rural Ukraine and Belarus. Their dramatic and exciting history included a brave exodus from their native home to strange new towns and foreign cities. Civil war and Jewish pogroms chased them eastward, first to Vladivostok in eastern Russia, then to Manchuria and on to Shanghai, China. On the other side of the family, the Quimbys experienced a comparatively less hazardous diaspora, leaving England on a direct Atlantic route for America in 1638, possibly because of political or religious reasons. Still, a transatlantic voyage in a wooden sailing ship entailed substantial hardships in that age. Like the Willenses, the Quimbys met whatever challenges faced them and survived.

Though headed in opposite compass directions, both families were searching for a better, more prosperous life in a free society. They gambled that their quests would succeed, not end in disaster. Risk-taking was a characteristic passed on to Roxanne in abundance, and it became her trusted ally when push came to shove in her personal life or in the business world.

Roxanne often attributes her success to the business fundamentals she learned from Thais Willens and to John Quimby's failed entrepreneurial schemes. Her mother was a loving presence but had little time to dote on Roxanne, having given birth to three more children in quick order after Roxanne appeared. Besides the unending demands of raising four little ones, Rebecca Quimby's other consuming responsibility was relocating the family time after time. John Quimby's frequent career changes uprooted them from one state to another until Roxanne was in high school.

John Quimby was a stern, demanding father. Young Roxanne rebelled against his power over her but respected his tireless efforts to "make a million" outside his day jobs. His refusal to give up despite repeated failures would later be an inspiration to her.

Thais Willens, who ran a seasonal fast-food stand at a resort beach, taught Roxanne about money in a very different way. Warm, loving, and gentle, she instructed her preschool granddaughter in the basics of earning a living from a small, simple business. From "Baba," Roxanne learned the value of negotiation to get the lowest prices at the farmers' market and make a fair profit from customers.

The Vilenskys

Roxanne knew her mother's family name as Willens, but that surname had been Vilensky in Ukraine, the ancestral homeland in the southwest corner of the Russian empire. The Vilenskys lived in the infamous Pale of Settlement established by Catherine the Great in 1791, which comprised about 20 percent of European Russia, including large swaths of present-day Ukraine, Poland, Lithuania, Moldova, Belarus, and western Russia. Although the government decreed the Pale to be a safe haven for Jewish settlement, it was, in effect, a corral.

Discrimination by non-Jews in the Pale sometimes burst into violence, and pogroms devastated Jewish communities there in the last years of the nineteenth century and the first years of the twentieth. Roxanne's grandfather was born in 1894, the year Tsar Nicholas II ascended the throne. As a young man, Benjamin Vilensky witnessed the reverberations of the Russian Revolution of 1917.

While much of Russia was torn apart by the fighting of the years following the revolution—in which the Bolsheviks' Red Army was opposed by the powerful but loosely organized anti-Bolshevik White Army—Jews in the Pale suffered particularly from the White Army's anti-Semitic pogroms. At that time, "the Yids were considered 'game' to be hunted, caught and killed whenever the Cossack [White Army] warriors ... entered the villages and towns," wrote Liliane Willens, Roxanne's maternal aunt, in her 2009 memoir *Stateless in Shanghai*. The book documents those harrowing times, providing most of what Roxanne knows about the Vilensky/Willens lineage in Russia, the escape to China, and the immigration to America.*

In 1919, Roxanne's grandfather, Benjamin, and his younger sister joined thousands of other Jews leaving European Russia for the country's Far East—a territory that spread out from Lake Baikal in central Siberia to the Pacific Ocean. Travel to the frontier was rough and often terrifying, but the exodus provided Jews some reprieve from harassment, military recruiters, and the fighting between Whites and Reds. The Vilenskys ended up in Russian-controlled Harbin in Manchuria in northeast China. But job possibilities were limited there, and within a year, they headed for cosmopolitan Shanghai.

Shanghai, sitting at the edge of the East China Sea at the entrance to the Yangtze Valley, was widely known at the time as the Paris of the East because of its vibrant East-West commerce. With wealth came upscale shops, clubs, fashion, and other signs of luxury. Treaties signed in the mid-1800s by the Chinese gave British, French, and American expatriates special privileges.

---

*The book is based on tape recordings Thais Willens made about her early years in Russia and letters from Roxanne's grandfather, Benjamin, to her grandmother, Thais, when he was stranded in China. It also includes the diary of Thais's sister Jacqueline concerning the final years of the Japanese in Shanghai, and discussions with family, friends, and others familiar with the Willenses' personal history and the political upheavals of the times. Thais Willens often talked to her children about her childhood and close relatives in Russia, but Benjamin didn't discuss his Russian past.

Most important was the notion of extra-territoriality, which allowed foreigners the right to live and do business outside the Chinese legal system and answer only to Western authorities and courts.

These concessions paved the way for the Europeanization of Shanghai. Foreigners, with Chinese approval, became concentrated in areas of the city known as the International Settlement and the French Concession. In the 1930s, approximately 10,000 British, 5,000 American, and 1,500 French nationals lived in the two settlements. British and American ex-pats lived and socialized mostly in the International Settlement. The French Concession was known for its social distance from the others, protecting its inhabitants' culture from Anglo-American influences.

Settling in the French Concession, Benjamin Vilensky wanted first and foremost to be a translator, or, failing that, an office clerk. In his quest to make himself employable, he made a momentous decision upon arriving in Shanghai in 1920, hiding his Czarist Russian origins by anglicizing his family name to Willens. Benjamin Willens listed his place of birth as Chisinau, in Romania's Bessarabia.

Benjamin's wife—Roxanne's Baba, Thais Vinokuroff—also called Russia home. Thais, the most influential of Roxanne's four grandparents, was born in 1902 in Novonicolaevsk, Siberia. As a young girl she worked in her grandfather's bakery, which was eventually taken over by her father, Lithuanian-born Samuel Vinokuroff. Although discrimination against Jews was less prevalent in the Far East, there are family stories of classmates harassing Thais and her brother, Boris.

When she was 16, the shifting fighting fronts of the civil war began to threaten Novonicolaevsk, and Samuel decided the family should move. He sold their house and bakery—using the proceeds to buy jewelry, a portable form of wealth that was recognized everywhere—and they found refuge in Harbin, which was filled with Jewish émigrés. There he used some of the jewelry to buy a small rooming house to rent to the stream of refugees fleeing Russia. But since most of the renters were poor or penniless, the rooming house venture failed. Samuel became impoverished when he lost his last valuables to jewelry swindlers. With job prospects dim in Harbin, the Vinokuroffs— like the Vilenskys—traveled to Shanghai in 1920.

Benjamin happened to live in the same boarding house as the Vinokuroffs and met Thais one evening at dinner in June 1924. In her book, Liliane Willens described her father then as "handsome ... light brown hair with a streak of white in the middle, green eyes and … 5'10" tall. Her mother, Willens wrote, was "a petite 5'2" young woman with black hair, brown eyes, high cheekbones, very white skin and a warm smile." They married four months later, in October. It was a prosperous time for Shanghai, with much new foreign business giving rise to considerable construction. Benjamin's success and steadily increasing income allowed the Willenses the privilege of a middle-class life—a significant financial and social step up for both sides of the Russian family. He became a top agent for Sun Life Assurance, and the young couple rented a larger apartment in a new building on Rue Paul Henry, bought a car, and hired a cook and a houseboy. The couple had three children: Roxanne's mother, Rebecca (born in 1925), Liliane (born in 1927), and Jacqueline (born in 1932). When the girls were old enough, they went to prestigious schools for foreigners and spent summer vacations with their mother at the beaches or in the mountains away from stifling Shanghai.

Benjamin lost his job when Sun Life closed its offices after December 7, 1941, the "Day of Infamy" for the U.S. at Pearl Harbor. At that time the Japanese military confiscated all Allied properties and firms in Shanghai. This was a difficult period for the family, but after the war, Sun Life reopened its Shanghai office and rehired Benjamin. Buying insurance policies became affordable again, especially for foreigners, and Benjamin eventually accumulated enough cash to invest in a nightclub with two friends. The club became a popular watering hole for foreigners and eventually generated enough profit to enable Benjamin to become a joint owner of a rental apartment building in the former French Concession.

Thais too expanded her business ventures, developing a small import-export business with her sister Brania, who had immigrated to San Francisco in 1937. Brania shipped Thais goods such as nylons and plastic handbags that were in high demand among Shanghai women.

The Quimbys

Roxanne's paternal ancestors, the Quimbys, left Surrey, England, and landed in Salem, Massachusetts, in about 1638, arriving in America more than 300 years before the Willenses. By the end of three years, William Quimby and his sons Thomas and John had moved south to Stratford, Connecticut, where they were among the first seventeen families to settle. Robert, the youngest, remained in Salem and later relocated to Amesbury for work as a shipbuilder.

During the Amesbury massacre of July 7, 1677, Symon, a Massachusetts Native American who was living with Robert's family, turned on the Quimbys, killing Robert and seriously wounding his wife, Elizabeth. In 1694, during King William's War, Native Americans kidnapped their second son, William, when he was 34 years old.

The year prior to his abduction, William Quimby had fathered a son, also named William. When the young William was old enough to make his own way, he struck out for New Hampshire, taking the Quimby heritage farther north. He fathered a son, Ebenezer, who fought against the British in the Revolutionary War in 1775 and survived to marry Hannah Colby of Amesbury. In 1808, Ebenezer and Hannah Quimby moved from Salisbury, New Hampshire, to Maine.

The Maine landscape in those years was not the undisturbed wilderness one might imagine it to have been. In a shift to market hunting brought about by European influence, Native Americans had disturbed parts of the old-growth forest, killed its wildlife, and harvested its native plants long before settlers like the Quimbys arrived. Later, European settlers altered the ecosystem further to make room for farms and villages. Fire, sometimes started by lightning and at other times set accidentally by settlers, left a black mark on the land that Roxanne Quimby would one day want to see restored to a wilderness-like state.

Ebenezer and Hannah's fifth child, Eben E. Quimby, moved to Sebec in the Piscataquis River valley and married Sebec-born Charlotte Bunker on March 25, 1822. After being married to Eben for eight years, Charlotte died in 1830, leaving three children. Eben then married Rhoda Packard on May 29, 1831, and they had four children. The last one was John Colby Quimby, Roxanne's great-great-grandfather and the first of her family to be a native Mainer.

Born on June 15, 1838, John Colby Quimby began his adulthood in the sawmill industry. He joined thousands of young men who worked in the hundreds of sawmills on the Penobscot River in the Old Town–Bangor area. The outbreak of the Civil War caused Quimby, then 23, to leave his mill job to enlist on April 30, 1861, in Company K, Regiment 2 of the Maine Infantry. In 1863 he requested a leave of absence and returned to Maine to marry his sweetheart, 25-year-old Roxanna Goldsmith Kendall. Six months into his marriage, he returned to the war. There is no record of whether he left before the birth of his son, Carroll, on January 7, 1864, in Abbott.

After the war, in 1866, John Colby Quimby gathered up his wife and son in Abbott and resettled seventeen miles south in Dexter, where he had purchased 66 acres for $1,700. They later relocated to Lewiston, where John was hired by a lumber dealer and in a couple of years became Lewiston's city marshal. After a year in law enforcement, he worked for the city as a lumber surveyor.

In 1882, at the age of 44, Quimby packed up the family again and headed for Sheboygan, Wisconsin, where the furniture business was growing. In doing so, he joined the many Maine loggers and war veterans who migrated before and after the Civil War to the greener pastures of the Midwest and California. He held jobs in Sheboygan as superintendent and foreman of a sawmill and later worked as a city lumber inspector. He moved once more after the death of his wife, to the National Soldiers' Home in Milwaukee. There he died at the age of 78, eight months after the passing of Roxanna.

Carroll worked his way up from a bookkeeping job to executive positions in the Sheboygan furniture industry. He and his wife, Carrie Rogers, whom he had married while in Lewiston, Maine, became ensconced in the business, social, and religious communities of Sheboygan and were held in great esteem for their leadership. They had three children—John Alvan, Frank Kendall, and Arelisle—all of whom graduated from college and built professional careers.

John Arthur Quimby

John Alvan Quimby, Roxanne's grandfather, married Margaret Genter on June 3, 1922. Margaret's education was in speech therapy, and after marrying John Alvan, she added to the couple's income by giving elocution and singing lessons in the family living room. John Arthur Quimby, Roxanne's father, was born on August 12, 1923, and was brought up in tight financial circumstances. When of school age, he rode his bike or walked more than a mile to his classes. Receiving no weekly allowance from his penny-pinching father, he did odd jobs to earn pocket money, picking dandelions from the Genters' yard to sell to neighbors for dinner salads and setting pins at the local bowling alley.

As a youngster, John was inspired by his mother's brother, Harold Genter, a successful entrepreneur. Harold had made a risky investment in a new contraption called the Toastmaster, becoming a partner in a company formed to manufacture inventor Charles Strite's pop-up electric toaster. The venture was financially lucrative and encouraged John Arthur to believe that he too could invent a gadget that would make him rich.

John took his father's advice to go into engineering. In the fall of 1941, he began a five-year work-study program at Northwestern University's new Murphy Technological Institute in Evanston, Illinois. In his second year, with the U.S. at war, he enlisted in the U.S. Navy to take advantage of the government's offer to pay the rest of his college education. He received his ensign bars and mechanical engineering degree in late spring 1944, and the navy sent him to Cornell University in Ithaca, New York, to train as an engineer for steam-powered ships. He was shipped out in the spring of 1945, just after the death of President Franklin D. Roosevelt on April 12.

John saw an opportunity in the navy to make money during supply trades between ships. He and a few buddies acquired a carbonated water dispenser and traded ship items for soft drink syrup. They set up a "happy hour" soda fountain and made a lot of money that later had to be handed over to their superiors. John's navy crew was decommissioned in Shanghai, and while awaiting orders, he took work in modest jobs for the United Nations Relief Association and the Chinese Navy, which kept him from returning to the U.S. with his fellow sailors. As part of his job, he was given the services of a Chinese translator, Manford Chang, who asked him to have dinner with his family, and on that occasion John met Chang's married sister, Gladys Muller, a secretary at the U.S. Army base. Later Muller asked John Quimby to accompany her and a co-worker to an army picnic in the Shanghai Hills outside the city. The co-worker was Rebecca Willens.

John's Chinese superiors, graduates of the Massachusetts Institute of Technology, told him that he would be promoted to an administrative position at the dockyard if he would obtain a graduate degree from the Harvard Business School. John's Harvard application was accepted in the spring of 1948, and he and Rebecca decided to marry and go to the U.S. together.

The immediate problem for the couple was announcing their plans to their families. They expected a strong reaction from the Willenses because he was an American and a "goy" (not Jewish), but Rebecca's parents were surprisingly quiet and practical about the match. They recognized that John Quimby was a fast ticket out of China for Rebecca if the pair were married, and the whole family was feeling an urgency to get out of the country. The end of the Sino-Japanese war in September 1945 hadn't brought peace to China. Rather, it merely unleashed more energy and resources for the civil war already in progress between the forces of Chiang Kai-shek and Mao Tse-tung.

Finding a minister to marry the interfaith couple wasn't easy. No Orthodox rabbi at the time would marry a Jewish woman to a Christian man. Finally an American Baptist missionary agreed to perform the ceremony on April 12, 1948.

In May 1948, John and Rebecca sailed to the U.S. When the couple arrived in San Francisco, they were met by Rebecca's Aunt Brania and her family. They stayed there for a week before flying to Chicago, where John's parents waited at the airport to meet their new daughter- in-law. The newlyweds spent the summer of 1948 with his parents. In September, they moved to Allston, Massachusetts, a Boston neighborhood, before the start of Harvard's college semester. In October, John learned that the job in China he had expected to have after graduation had evaporated with Mao's victory over Chiang Kai-shek. At about the same time, newly pregnant Rebecca had a miscarriage.

The newlyweds both worked to pay the bills while John was still in grad-uate school. During the summer, he was a door-to-door salesman peddling storm windows; she worked at the MIT Coop.

As the civil war escalated in China, Rebecca's family wanted to immigrate to the U.S. Thais and her daughter Jacqueline departed Shanghai in March 1949, two months before the fall of Shanghai to Mao. Benjamin remained behind because of his Romanian passport and was stranded there for almost another year.

Benjamin Willens was 56 and Thais almost 50 when they finally restarted their lives in America. The Willenses could afford no more than a second-floor apartment about a half-mile from the shore in Revere Beach, a working class town north of Boston. Thais opened a fast food stand on Ocean Avenue sell-ing hamburgers and hot dogs to tourists. Benjamin didn't work. Their circum-stances would never return to the upper-middle-class status and privilege they had known in Shanghai.

Blue-eyed and bald, Roxanne arrived on July 11, 1950, at Cambridge City Hospital, weighing a hefty 10 pounds-plus. Rebecca named her after the lead-ing lady of the romantic tragedy *Cyrano de Bergerac*, one of Thais's favorite plays. Little Roxanne was born into the idyllic postwar era, an America of middle-class ascendency.

A month before becoming a father for the first time, John Quimby grad-uated from Harvard Business School with a degree in business management and a job with Babcock and Wilcox, a major provider of boilers to the U.S. Navy during World War II. The job required the Quimbys to move to Bronx-ville, near New York City, where Renee was born on August 29, 1951.

The Quimby family began to fit the popular notion of a nuclear family. John was the sole breadwinner, and Rebecca, the good wife and mother. A house in the suburbs was in their plans, as were additional children, all of whom were expected to go to college.

Soon B&W sent Roxanne's father on the road to handle management issues at various plants. In February 1952, the family relocated from Bronxville to Akron, Ohio, near B&W's main plant in Barberton. After working to improve quality control at the Akron plant, John was assigned to the drafting department at the same location.

At B&W he befriended a colleague who made wine at home, and John's entrepreneurial interest was triggered again. Under his friend's guidance, he borrowed a grape press and bought grapes and a keg with the idea of becoming a vintner. Spreading a sheet in the Quimby family's living room, he cajoled young Roxanne and Renee into helping him de-stem the grapes and put them in the press. He then strained the juice through cheesecloth and stored it in a cask. Impatient with the length of time the juice needed to ferment and age properly, John lost interest in that enterprise.

Employee strikes at B&W prompted him to become more interested in employee relations, and he started an employee stock club to get more workers involved with company affairs. It wasn't long before company management let him know that they weren't happy with the stock club effort. His punishment was a salary cut. John was so offended that he quit, a reaction he would repeat throughout his work life when reprimanded or stymied.

Dipping into his savings, John jumped into the home construction business and bought 24 acres in Bath, Ohio, about five miles from Akron. He and a B&W co-worker did some of the work on the first house, putting Roxanne and Renee to work as go-fers. Roxanne recalled her father telling the girls that they had to be good or he would put them in the foundation cement slurry.

When the first prospective buyer fell by the wayside, John ran out of money, and the family was forced to sell their own small dwelling and move into the unfinished spec house. At this point John had four children to support. A third daughter, Rachelle, had been born on October 2, 1953, and was followed by a son, Rogers, on June 2, 1955. With bills mounting, John took night work at McNeil Machine Shop, manufacturing tire molds for Goodyear. The job lasted only six weeks before he was terminated for refusing to join the union, but Goodyear then hired him to work in their tire design department. He was transferred to Syracuse, New York, in the late 1950s to train as a salesman.

The Quimbys purchased an old two-story home in Watertown, where John set up a Mr. Frosty franchise with a friend, but the business was short-lived. Goodyear had new plans for John in the company's Albany, New York, district.

The family resettled in Kingston, New York, but John soon left Goodyear for a sales job at Hilti, then left Hilti to become a sales manager at American Machinery and Foundry's friction welding division in Stamford, Connecticut. Subsequently he was assigned to the AMF office in Des Plaines, Illinois. There, the Quimbys rented an apartment rather than buy another home. One of John's memories of that time was that all the children but Renee had braces on their teeth, and he was pleased to get a discount for dental services.

During Roxanne's time in Des Plaines, her father came up with the idea for U DO VooDoo dolls. The idea was to sell the dolls to sports pep clubs for their fundraising efforts. The dolls were made of Styrofoam in the shape of football or basketball players and were painted in the opposing team's colors. Roxanne recalled helping her father fashion a mask for herself so she could spray-paint the VooDoo dolls in two colors. A sticky label was put on the back of each doll's head, where the score of the game could be recorded. The purchasing club received pins to stick in the dolls as a way to weaken the opposing team (mimicking Haitian "black magic" voodoo spiritual rites). When the scheme failed, John Quimby spent years getting rid of the dolls.

After a year in Des Plaines, Quimby was fired from AMF when he criticized the company's decision to move its Stamford operation to Shreveport, Louisiana. He then moved the family to Lexington, Massachusetts, in 1964, where he worked for Bellofram, a manufacturer of fabric-reinforced diaphragms that provided a leak-proof covering for pistons and cylinder seals. As a sales manager, Quimby was again on the road much of the work week. After a run-in with the president of the company, Quimby lost that job too.

One of the entrepreneurial schemes he worked on in Lexington was Mulligans, an automatic coin-operated golf net. He thought it would appeal to golf enthusiasts to practice their driving shots. He placed one of the units on the car roof and drove to Florida to try it on real golf courses. That effort failed for lack of golfer interest.

After her youngest years, Roxanne came to see her father's ideas as doomed to fail. When she was at the top of her game at Burt's Bees, she would say that he failed because he was too "full of himself" to understand the mind and desires of the consumer. Despite her father's entrepreneurial flops, however, she was energized and inspired by his unrelenting efforts to make something happen. Her siblings were also shaped by the "risk and initiative" efforts of John Quimby, which created an atmosphere of ambition in the household. All three of them would one day go to business schools and work in the financial sector. Roxanne credited John Quimby with being an exemplar of hard work, self-sufficiency, and inventiveness.

With her father constantly on the road and moving his family to so many relocations, life in the Quimby household was trying at best. Roxanne's mother was overwhelmed with caring for her brood of young children while managing daily chores and household maintenance. By necessity, because her mother was so busy with her younger siblings, Roxanne had to entertain herself. She learned to depend on herself emotionally and not to ask much from her mother.

John Quimby wasn't a patient man; he demanded order in his household and set firm rules for the children's behavior. Roxanne thought of him as a drill sergeant who demanded efficiency in all things. There wasn't much room for spontaneity. Roxanne noted that her father had "eight planets in Leo, so astrologically he was a hyper-Leo and [that is] why he had to reign over his domain, controlling his little subjects."

At age five, Roxanne was informed by her father that she needed to start earning and saving money and should not expect to rely on him for financial help after she finished high school. He promised to match the amount of money she had in her bank account when she started college. From then on, she would sink or swim according to her own capabilities. "Wow, I thought, I'd better get busy," Roxanne recalled. She and Renee wondered how they were going to earn so much money by the time they were 18 years old.

As the first-born, Roxanne felt the weight of her father's rule most keenly. She first rebelled at age five, according to her later memory. Her parents were going out to dinner and hired a neighborhood girl to look after the kids. Roxanne threw a fit because she felt she was trustworthy enough to care for her three siblings. She told her father she knew the telephone numbers of the police and fire department and could do just fine overseeing her siblings. He reacted with humor and hired the babysitter anyway, which increased rather than ended Roxanne's pushback.

Roxanne honed her resistance to her father as she went through grammar school and into high school. "If you did something against his moral code, you'd be punished for it," she recollected. "He was a man of extremes, and it was clear to us as children that when he was punishing us, he was withholding love."

Renee, according to Roxanne, tried "to be under the radar," hiding behind her older sister and their mother to avoid being a target. (She was also a Virgo like their mother, with a personality similar to Rebecca's, Roxanne said.) The youngest siblings, Rachelle and Rogers, received relatively small doses of harsh treatment, Roxanne remembered, because her father grew weary of being a disciplinarian.

The most frequent punishment was being forced to stay home or to do things that were tedious, boring, or plain abusive in Roxanne's mind. John Quimby forced the child who asked for more ice cream at dinner to eat the whole half gallon. The child who asked to watch television past the regular bedtime hour was made to sit up until the wee hours of the morning. "It was like torture for a little kid," she said. "I remember being in front of the television at 2 a.m. watching a science fiction show, and I was scared out of my mind."

Her husband's disciplinary tactics put Rebecca Quimby between a rock and a hard place. She acceded to her husband's authority when he was at home. When he was away, she rarely initiated punishments of her own. When highly frustrated by Roxanne, Rebecca would pretend to run after her daughter with a raised hairbrush but never caught her, the chase being more of a game than anything else. Roxanne felt her mother's love in the interaction.

The family's frequent moves meant leaving pals behind, but John Quimby belittled the importance of maintaining childhood friendships, according to Roxanne. When she cried, her father told her it was over "nothing." He pointed out that he didn't have any friends from childhood, and she would forget hers, too. "My sadness at leaving those little relationships was not acknowledged, and it hurt," she said.

Whenever John Quimby returned home from a road trip, tensions in the household mounted. Rebecca Quimby tried her best to please him. She spent most of her time in a house dress or pants scrubbing, cleaning, and cooking. She had no time to maintain a vegetable or flower garden, or to keep up with women's fashions, or to have much of a social life with her husband. Roxanne resented how her father dominated her mother. "Like, wow, how did he get all the power in the family?"

Sometimes John Quimby took Rebecca out for an evening on the town, and Roxanne saw her mother in a different light. Rebecca Quimby was simply gorgeous to her oldest daughter—green eyes, dark wavy hair, white teeth, a knock 'em dead smile, and a svelte figure. Roxanne watched her mother put on lipstick, pearls, and an off-the-shoulder evening dress and transform herself to model-like beauty. Years later, that memory would influence one of Roxanne's critical decisions about expanding Burt's Bees' product lines.

Rebecca Quimby's children felt their mother's innate kindness, love, and service to the family. Her daughter Rachelle recalled her as "an angel." But as Roxanne became more her own person, she lost respect for her mother for awhile. "She wouldn't stand up for herself," Roxanne said. "I think my father had no respect for her." Roxanne's view evolved, however, when she became an adult and understood the psychological dynamics at play in marriage and family. She began to appreciate how hard her mother had tried to be positive and helpful to reduce the tension and disharmony created by John.

Rebecca Quimby convinced her husband to allow the children to attend free summer camps, but the youngsters didn't have dance or music lessons because John didn't want to pay for them, and the kids couldn't save for them because they didn't get allowances. Roxanne and Renee joined a Brownie Scout troop in Kingston, New York, but had to drop out after a time because they couldn't pay the dues.

Yet there was one special pleasure for Roxanne that was non-negotiable for Rebecca. Roxanne declared at an early age that she was going to be an artist when she grew up, and Rebecca—seeing that her daughter drew constantly and was very creative—took her seriously and purchased poster paints, brushes, a wooden easel, smocks, and other art materials. Later Rebecca facilitated Roxanne's going to summer camp, where she would sit in the art room all day with paints and clay instead of participating in other activities. If an art museum was nearby that offered Saturday art classes to children, Rebecca made sure Roxanne participated. Roxanne felt her mother's validation of her talent as an invaluable gift.

In grade school and high school art classes, Roxanne learned the techniques of perspective and shading and was wowed by artistic techniques for creating horizons and vanishing points. Her art extended to making scrapbooks from movie tickets, postcards, and souvenirs collected during trips and visits to restaurants.

The Quimby children enjoyed the childhood activities of postwar America. Bicycles provided the possibility of adventure and a taste of freedom from parental oversight. The kids had roller skates, the old-fashioned kind with a key. They played dodgeball and read *Archie and Veronica* and *Superman* comics.

Roxanne was taken with the popular 1960s television series *Dr. Kildare* and joined the Richard Chamberlain fan club, receiving a photo of the handsome star. Hula hoops were big. John Quimby talked about them a lot, wishing he had invented them because they were so cheap to make and were sold at a high profit. Roxanne thought she was better at hula hooping than her siblings.

The children were allowed to have a hamster and a turtle but no dogs or cats. "My mother didn't quite get the concept of living with an animal in the house," Roxanne recalled.

Thais "Baba" Willens

In the summers of the mid-1950s, young Roxanne was shipped off to stay with her grandparents at Revere Beach for three or four weeks to give her mother some rest from child care. Baba took Roxanne under her wing, training her in the fundamentals of small business.

First, Thais introduced Roxanne to the fruit and vegetable market at Scollay Square, now the site of Boston's Government Center, where she learned about buying, selling, and price negotiation. She watched her grandmother carefully look over the fruit to see if it was ripe and if the vegetables were freshly harvested. Thais haggled with vendors over prices, trying to get items for 50 percent off.

In a ledger book, Baba recorded every item she purchased and what she sold it for. She even noted the daily weather so that she could follow its impact on sales from her food stand. Roxanne was allowed to study the green-cloth ledger and was fascinated by it.

The food stand was a small, white-painted wooden structure with red trim. It had a counter, a Fryolator, a refrigerator, a cash register, and open shelves stocked with ingredients and supplies. A metal grate was pulled down over the front of the stand at night to protect it.

To Roxanne, accompanying Baba to the beach was like going to work. Baba taught her basic arithmetic and let her make change from the register. One of Roxanne's tasks was to keep count of how much penny Bazooka bubble gum was sold. The gum, kept in a large glass jar, was tempting to little Roxanne. She couldn't keep herself from unwrapping the occasional piece of gum and eating the odd candy or ice cream bar.

Seeing this, Baba explained to Roxanne that eating the goods ate into profits, and despite her young age, Roxanne understood her grandmother's counsel. Frugality in personal finances and in business was a basic ingredient of money management that Baba imparted to Roxanne. Roxanne saw her grandmother's philosophy practiced in the simplest ways, such as washing used paper towels and hanging them to dry for reuse. Baba's business practices revealed a way of making a living that Roxanne never saw or understood from how her father "brought home the bacon."

Baba softened her admonitions with a Russian term of endearment, *dovochka maya*—"my little girl." She knew how important it was to be patient and kind with Roxanne and her siblings, especially when "educating" them about their behavior. She never raised her voice and never harshly reprimanded Roxanne—the opposite of John Quimby's approach. Roxanne knew that Baba was no saint, however. She heard her grandmother mutter impolite Russian words when customers tried to get more cheese on their burgers or a second cup of coffee without paying more.

Roxanne received her first lessons in customer service from Baba, too. She was encouraged to observe what customers wanted and didn't want, particularly noticing which items sold best. Baba taught Roxanne that the quality of the food was critical for repeat business and that hard work was fundamental to success. Roxanne witnessed Baba's disciplined labor not only in the long hours the food stand was open (8 a.m. to 10 p.m.) but also in the many hours her grandmother spent planning, gathering, organizing, and preparing the items she sold; the peeling of potatoes for the French fries, the making of Kool-Aid–flavored ice to hand-shave for slushies sold in Dixie cups, and on and on.

During those formative years, Roxanne knew how much her grandmother cherished her. Baba whispered many times in her thick accent, "Don't tell the other grandchildren, but I love you the most." The deep affection went both ways. Her doting grandmother was Roxanne's "good adult," the one she wanted to emulate. Benjamin Willens was quiet and undemonstrative, Roxanne later remembered.

When the children visited, Baba made special dishes from the old country—pelimeni, piroshki, blintzes with sour cream, and strudel—and told enchanting stories of bygone days in Siberia when all the wives got together to make noodles and ethnic dishes. "My mom was into Kraft macaroni and cheese because she was a '50s housewife," Roxanne recollected. "Grandmother was this exotic cook. If she was making strudel, she'd make the dough so thin you could see through it." When making the Russian version of raviolis, the wives would make hundreds and hundreds of them, divide them up, and put them in the barn for the winter to freeze. "Little did I know I was going to live that lifestyle years later," Roxanne said.

Baba told her granddaughter of the troikas—horse-drawn sleds—and brutal winter weather of Siberia. "At times the snow was so deep, Baba's family would be able to see only the tops of horses riding by their home," Roxanne remembered. "She cuddled me close and taught me nursery rhymes she had learned as a child. I think it was just as much fun for her as it was for me. I doted on her."

When the Willenses spoke Russian to each other, Roxanne didn't know what they were saying but loved the rhythms and complexities of their language. "I listened more to the sounds than the meaning, because what they spoke wasn't English," she explained. "They had very kindly ways of speaking to each other, so I loved the way they talked, whatever the language." If Baba became overwhelmed when all four Quimby children were visiting, she would simply say, "What am I going to do?" Such a low-key reaction was "really different from the judgment going on in my family," Roxanne remembered. "I loved being around my grandmother because she was so accepting of who we were just the way we were."

Baba made sure that Roxanne knew her life in Revere Beach wasn't as luxurious as it had been in China. "I think she was embarrassed by [her circumstances]," said Roxanne. But Roxanne was proud of her grandparents' Siberian background; their story seemed exotic. "They had a history caught up in this global revolution, and they played a direct part in that," Roxanne noted. "I was pretty interested in what they experienced and the story of how my mother got to this country."

Her grandparents' origins made Roxanne long to be from someplace far away. In the meantime, she carried around an image of Siberia in her mind. "Maybe that's why I would be comfortable living off the beaten path in my twenties," she said.

Young Merchant

Eighty-six years old in 2011, John Quimby readily recalled when he first saw "the little merchant" in Roxanne. She was no more than six years old when they were living in Bath, Ohio, on a farm with an apple orchard. Roxanne helped gather apples for the cider her father sold in plastic gallon jugs.

The cider was placed on a table by the side of the farm driveway and a bucket was set out for payment by the honor system.

Roxanne, mindful of the work she had done to get the cider to "market," was worried that people would take the jugs without paying. She hid behind a tree at the cider stand and finally saw one person stealing cider. Roxanne ran home crying that a terrible injustice had occurred—the family had been robbed!

The cider business was the springboard for little Roxanne to launch her own money-making pursuits. Having learned from her father that money was power, she wanted both. Between the ages of six and twelve, she developed quite a childhood business résumé. She was the chief executive officer and president of all operations, and she had three younger "employees" (her siblings) to do her bidding.

Her first venture was selling SweetHeart Soap. She hand-painted the embossing around soaps with pinks and purples to enhance their attractiveness. Roxanne tapped Renee to be her assistant, and Rachelle was the sales agent, dutifully ringing neighbors' doorbells to see if any housewives would buy the gussied-up soap.

Roxanne tried hawking yarn dolls and stuffed cloth animals she made, but those efforts were not half as much fun as her cookie business. When she was eight years old, she and Renee solicited cookie orders according to Roxanne's scheme. They called up prospective neighborhood customers and sang a Roxanne-created jingle: "Annee's Bakery is the best, whether you travel east or west. Call us up and don't be late. 322-3698." (The bakery name was a combination of both sisters' names.)

Roxanne bought rolls of flavored dough from the grocery store to make chocolate chip and other kinds of cookies. Customers had to pay in advance before the Quimby sisters would stick the dough in the oven. Without Baba on hand to remonstrate, however, Roxanne couldn't stop herself from eating into the cookie profits. Renee became angry, shouting, "No! No! Don't eat that. It's for Mrs. Smith," but since Roxanne was the boss and loved sweets, she taste-tested to her heart's content. Blood didn't run deep when it came to selling cookies. Aunt Liliane, her mother's sister, wouldn't buy cookies from her nieces because, she said, they looked like "mud pies."

A mail-order catalog was Roxanne's most complicated childhood endeavor. The publication was printed by a legitimate mail-order company. She wrote her name on it as the local seller and mailed it to prospective customers, but received only one order. The merchandise arrived to the customer in broken pieces, and she had to refund the customer's purchase price from her own pocket. Her father had talked her into getting into the business, and when it crashed right out of the gate, she vowed not to let him talk her into any more schemes. She also found out how bad failure felt—a lesson she would never forget.

By the time she was a teenager, Roxanne was old enough to babysit on weekends. She needed to build up a savings account for college to receive as much matching money from her father as possible. She also was pressured by her father's declaration that she wouldn't be allowed to continue living in the family home after high school, whether or not she went to college.

Roxanne lied about her age to get a job at Margie's Bridal Shop in Niles, Illinois, when she was fourteen or fifteen. Her job was to "run dresses" back and forth from the stockroom to the fitting rooms. Later she worked for Howard Johnson's restaurant in Lexington, Massachusetts, serving ice cream.

Thrifty and creative by nature, Roxanne loved her home economics classes in school. In high school she made her own A-line skirts, wrap-around shirts, pleated skirts, and dress suits with jackets.

Throughout childhood, Roxanne was the top dog among her siblings. Her younger sisters and brother were not as strong-willed, and she could coax and intimidate them into doing her bidding. "The whole theme of obedience was driven into our little heads by my father," Roxanne said. "My father taught me he was the boss, but I was second in command. I kinda' required the same obedience from my sisters and brother. They were pretty compliant."

Roxanne described Renee as the "worrier" of the siblings and Rachelle as the "noisier" one who screamed and hollered to get attention from their mother. As the only boy, Rogers was treated like "a little wonder" by her parents, in Roxanne's opinion. He got into his fair share of childhood trouble, but Roxanne's memory is that John Quimby was more tolerant of Rogers' misbehavior than hers.

The three sisters shared a bedroom, and as they grew into their teens, they talked about their looks. Rachelle remembered the siblings looking in a mirror to determine who was the ugliest, and in Rachelle's memory it was always her. "I was the lowest in the pecking order," she recollected. "They did anything they could to pick on me."

Yet the siblings were grateful for one another whenever they moved to a new city and entered a strange school where they knew no one. They walked to school together and felt the reassurance of one another's companionship until they made new friends. Repeated adjustments to being "the new girl" in school augmented Roxanne's sense of self-sufficiency, she later believed.

Roxanne experimented with a shortcut to studying—putting her school-books under her pillow so that the information could infuse her brain by osmosis while she slept. "So what if I flunk the test. Who cares?" she thought to herself. "I always managed to do okay," she later recalled. "Academics were just not that important to me. I made a decision to get by and take a lot of art courses, which was what I really wanted to do."

She amused herself with mischief-making, from passing notes around when the teacher wasn't looking to tearing "fairy loops" from the backs of classmates' shirts. She made fun of Renee, who was the proverbial good student, diligent about her homework (and a Phi Beta Kappa in college). Rachelle considered herself not as good academically as her sisters.

In her early teens, Roxanne was in love with the beauty and glamour of lipstick, shadow gloss, eyeliner, mascara, face powder, and blush. John Quimby didn't want his daughters wearing makeup. If any of the girls appeared at the breakfast table wearing eye makeup, their father would make them wash it off before going to school. Roxanne's response was to stuff the makeup in her book bag and primp in the school bathroom. Then she would wash it off before her father came home from work.

Like many teenagers, Roxanne could draw out phone conversations with friends for an hour or more, but John Quimby set a maximum call time of three minutes, saying that anything needing to be discussed by phone could be done within that time. He used a stopwatch to enforce this rule, and at the end of three minutes would take the receiver away from Roxanne or her siblings and hang it up. She remembered him saying, "You spent the whole day with these kids. How come you have to talk to them on the phone after school?"

Another sore point between father and daughter was the can't-drive-with-a-teenager-in-the-car rule. It provoked Roxanne into outfoxing her father by stuffing her bed with pillows and crawling out the second-story window to meet her girlfriends with driver's licenses. When she was sixteen and had a boyfriend with a car, she sneaked out the window to meet him, and John Quimby was never the wiser. He caught Renee a few times slipping out for dates and skipping school.

Roxanne remembered feeling embarrassed and angry when she brought new friends home. Her father would grill them about what their fathers did for work. "He'd ask them too many questions and make them uncomfortable to the point of almost ridiculing them." It was another way he made it more difficult for her to cultivate friendships among her peers.

John Quimby's position on religion was yet another difficulty for the family. He came from a Congregational background, although he wasn't an active Christian. Still, he and the family observed Christmas and Easter. When the children were very young, he took charge of getting a Christmas tree and Easter baskets, but he drew the line there on religious observances. He would not allow Judaism to be practiced in his household, despite the fact that Rebecca was Jewish.

Roxanne felt that her father's opposition to the Jewish faith was rooted in his discomfort with Rebecca Quimby's immigrant background. "They had a war over religion," she said. They yelled, and her mother cried. Roxanne recalled that one time after a fight, her father bought Rebecca a bouquet of flowers as a way to apologize.

Ultimately, Rebecca Quimby took a stand against her husband on the Jewish issue. She thought it was important for her children to be raised in the tradition of their Jewish elders. Leaving her husband behind, she took the children to observe Hanukkah and Passover at her parents' home in Revere Beach. Rebecca's sisters, Aunties Liliane and Jacqueline, joined them for those observances.

"This was a big deal for her to go against my father," said Roxanne, "but her grandfather's father and sister had been murdered for being Jews. Taking responsibility to ensure we were connected with our Jewish heritage was a way of respecting the family that hadn't been able to escape the mayhem in Russia."

Roxanne learned that the Willenses were "definitely unhappy" about the marriage of Rebecca and John Quimby because "he was a non-Jew, was arrogant, and made fun of their accents," Roxanne said. Her father's reaction to the Willenses' faith and accents led her to develop a strong sense of justice. "I thought my father was unfair for putting them down because of their accent or heritage," she said.

Another large influence on Roxanne was Henry David Thoreau. Every time she looked at the household calendar for July to count the days until her birthday on the 11th, her eyes shifted to July 12, where Thoreau's famous name was printed. "I felt we were soul mates," she reflected.

In high school she began to learn who Thoreau was—poet, naturalist, essayist, philosopher, and transcendentalist—and why he was important. Her class took a field trip to Thoreau's world-renowned retreat on Walden Pond in Concord, where he had built a one-room wooden cabin overlooking the water and spent most of two years—from July 1845 to September 1847—living alone efficiently, observing the seasons, and writing about his experiences and insights. Walking around the pond, Roxanne thought she felt his spiritual presence, and she was enthralled to stand inside the cabin, even though it was a replica of the original, which had been torn down. She was so inspired by him that she visited Walden by herself. She enjoyed being inside the abode, contemplating Thoreau's enduring legacy. She read some of Thoreau's most revered works touting simplicity and self-sufficiency and his classic essay "Civil Disobedience," which urged individuals to resist government in the face of unjust actions. The messages impressed her.

During the late 1960s, Roxanne was aware of civil disobedience in action in nearby Boston, New York, and other U.S. cities over the Vietnam War, civil rights, women's rights, and other social issues. Her generation was fed up with war-mongering and money-obsessed American power structures and took out their anger and frustration in protests and sit-ins on college campuses. In the spring of 1968, student demonstrations over the war shut down Columbia University in New York. Students at Harvard, Boston University, and Radcliffe went on a four-day hunger strike to protest the war.

By the time Roxanne graduated from Lexington High School in June 1968, she was sure she didn't want to live by her father's values and mainstream conformity. "His value system was very superficial, not applicable to who I was," she said.

Yet, at the same time, she wasn't going to rid herself totally of all he represented. John Quimby had taught her that she could be self-sufficient at a young age and make her own way in the world. "He was a really good role model in his entrepreneurship, even though he failed," she said. "He never stopped trying, and he always believed in himself. His next new gadget was going to be as big as the hula hoop, and he was going to be a millionaire. His unbridled optimism, although somewhat naïve, was something you have to have a healthy dose of if you're going to be in business."

Stair Falls on the East Branch of the Penobscot River. (Bill Duffy photo)

Heading West: San Francisco, 1970

B y the time she was ready for college, Roxanne's bank account totaled $5,000. John Quimby made good on his word and matched her savings. In June 1968, immediately after high school graduation, she entered the University of Massachusetts (UMass) at Amherst, the system's flagship campus in the Connecticut River valley.

Because the university could not accommodate all the students who wanted to attend, Roxanne was offered a "swing shift" schedule: attend the summer session, skip the fall semester, and resume classes at the start of 1969. She lived at home in the fall and waitressed, waiting to pick up her coursework at UMass.

Back on campus in January, Roxanne was assigned to the dorm named for her high school inspiration, Henry David Thoreau. She embraced a completely new world at UMass—a more demanding academic environment and the "make love, not war" culture of the Sixties. The youthful radicalism she encountered was appealing to her, as she was ripe for rebellion from her parents. She started wearing long cotton dresses, smoked marijuana for the first time, and discovered psychedelic music. Her favorite bad boys were The Doors and their wild lead singer, Jim Morrison.

Reveling in the independence from her family, Roxanne decided to get a dog. She had always wanted one, but her parents didn't want dogs or cats in the house. She found Sid, a golden retriever, through a local newspaper classified. (The name was short for Siddhartha, the Buddha's name.) "I wanted someone to love," Roxanne said. "I fell in love with that dog."

She also fell in love with a classmate, George Walker St. Clair Jr., a senior from Newton, Massachusetts, who was majoring in psychology. They became involved romantically in the winter of 1970. She was attracted to him, she remembered, because he was taller than she and had a pony tail, a guitar, a nice voice, and drove a Volkswagen. While he looked like a hippie, Roxanne didn't think he was the real McCoy. It didn't matter to her, since she didn't know exactly who she was becoming, either.

George was the oldest of George and Mary Gena St. Clair's three children. His parents had met in Bethlehem, Pennsylvania, while both were working at Bethlehem Steel. George Sr. was transferred out of the metallurgical department into sales after World War II, accepting a transfer to the Boston office. He handled sales in Maine, and two of his customers were Bath Iron Works, the big navy shipbuilder, and Bangor-based Snow and Nealley, producer of high-quality tools for farm and home. The St. Clair family established a summer place on Parker Pond in the Belgrade Lakes region north of Maine's capital, Augusta.

After graduating from UMass, George Jr. was intent on having a California experience. Throwing caution to the wind, Roxanne decided to go with him, find a good fine arts school for herself, and eventually pursue a professional painting career. California would get her far away from her parents, satisfy her touch of "Go West" fever, and spice up her budding adult life with adventure.

Heading West

Having researched the most interesting art schools, Roxanne decided to try avant-garde San Francisco Art Institute (SFAI). The hedonistic environment of San Francisco in 1970, three years after the Summer of Love in Haight-Ashbury, was a magnet for hippies, gays, and runaways looking for freedom, love, and nirvana. Women's libbers espoused women's rights in issues from abortion to pay equality, and peaceniks demonstrated against the war in Vietnam.

Roxanne's parents were worried about her leaving for California with a virtual stranger. John Quimby disapproved of George St. Clair because he had no money to speak of and no prospects for a lucrative career. The young adventurers didn't care what John Quimby thought, because they were moving 3,000 miles away. Nonconformity and self-determination were what mattered to them.

Roxanne and George packed Sid and their belongings into George's gray VW Beetle and spent a month driving cross-country. They first headed north to Vermont and crossed the border into Canada, passing back into the U.S. in the Midwest. Along the way, they pitched their tent in Badlands National Park in South Dakota, Grand Teton National Park in Wyoming, and Redwoods National Park in California.

This was Roxanne's first experience of national parks. The beauty and majesty of the wild landscapes awed her, making deep emotional and spiritual impressions. At the park campgrounds, friendly retired RVers invited Roxanne and George to share hot meals with them. Roxanne never forgot how "cool" the older people were in their kindnesses.

Although she didn't know it at the time, one of her relatives by marriage loved public lands too. Aunt Wilda, the wife of Roxanne's uncle, Frank Quimby, played a key role in national forest conservation in Wisconsin in the late 1930s. She was a leading advocate of making conservation education compulsory in Wisconsin public schools. During the effort to pass legislation toward that goal, she came up with the idea of creating a School Children's Forest within Nicolet National Forest in northeastern Wisconsin. She envisioned that it would bring children closer to the natural world.

The national forest service liked the idea, agreeing to plant and protect one acre of land for every $2.50 contributed by a school. A certificate was given to the participating school by the regional forester, as well as a map so that pupils could visit "their" plantation forest. Thanks to Wilda Quimby, a Children's Forest was located west of Anvil Lake in the national forest and expanded to 200 acres.

Wilda Quimby, a garden club leader and officer of the Wisconsin Conservation League in 1940, was fortunate to hear forester and ecologist Aldo Leopold speak at the league's first annual meeting. Professor Leopold, of Madison, would later be regarded as the father of the wildlife conservation and wilderness preservation movement in the U.S. Roxanne would admire him greatly a half century later when her own interest in conservation blossomed.

San Francisco

SFAI was one of the oldest art schools in the U.S. and an easy one in which to enroll. Admission was a matter of walking into the administration building and paying a semester's tuition, which was less than $1,000 because there was no residential campus to maintain and only a few classroom buildings.

Roxanne was shocked by how freewheeling and radical SFAI was then. Academic requirements were minimal, courses were pass/fail, and attendance was optional. The school's only requirement for a Bachelor of Fine Arts degree was to pass the art history class, while the state of California required that students take an English course. There were no personal conduct rules that she could remember later. She witnessed students using cocaine in the bathrooms.

When Roxanne arrived at SFAI, the school was aflutter with experimental, conceptual, and performance art, even altering the language of art. It was "busting open the whole idea of art," she said. Roxanne relished the innovation and experimentation. She thought her teachers and classes were very good, especially in studio drawing and critiques. She wanted to learn art's classical techniques from the ground up, but a lot of that was left to her own initiative. "No one supposed you should paint on a canvas," she explained, as that was old school. She had to figure out some of the basics for herself, such as stretching and preparing a canvas, measuring watercolor paper, grinding and mixing paints, and which brushes were the right ones to use.

Her attempts to blend what SFAI could teach her with what she could do for herself caused her to feel shaky about her education, wondering what tools and techniques she was missing that were important to develop her art potential. She worried that she should have gone to Pratt Institute in New York or another more traditional arts college.

Roxanne experimented with how far "out there" she could take her subject matter in oil painting class. Shadows, symbolisms, and illusions excited her. "I was interested in capturing the fantasy and netherland of 'is this real or not,'" she said. She used the Italian chiaroscuro technique—the blending of light and shade—to create the illusion of depth in her paintings.

Roxanne remembered a pastiche class in which she picked a work of art to replicate. It took her 70 hours to complete. The process taught her the discipline of looking and the difference between intentional looking and superficial seeing. She studied great women artists but was never "turned on" by them. Rather, she was drawn to the Dutch masters, such as Vermeer and

Rembrandt, and the more modern Edward Hopper and Winslow Homer (the latter two having painted in Maine).

A dutiful, steady student, she remained at school after classes to paint because there was much more space and light there than in her apartment. One teacher told her that she could spot East Coast students because they were usually the ones who attended class regularly and completed assignments. Roxanne was determined to take full advantage of what she had paid for. She had inherited a high regard for thriftiness from her father and grandmother.

Roxanne and George lived in an apartment on 24th Street and Guerrero in Noe Valley, on the edge of the Mission District and not far from The Castro, the working class neighborhood that had turned into a gay village. The modest Mission District was made up of Latinos and senior citizens, with rents afford-able enough to attract newcomers. Roxanne and George's studio-plus apart-ment had a tiny kitchen, a living-dining area, a bathroom, and a bedroom. The rent was just $90 a month.

Roxanne found part-time work as a waitress in neighborhood restaurants to help raise the few thousand dollars of income she needed to contribute to the annual household budget. Although George had a degree in psychology from UMass, he took a job with a modular home company that made prefab-ricated houses and found a second job as a waiter.

For convenience, and because she had no driver's license, Roxanne either rode her new bike or took the city's trolley to SFAI classes. She enjoyed taking Sid on the trolley for walks at Ocean Beach, adjacent to Golden Gate Park.

Six months into their San Francisco sojourn, the phone rang at 5 a.m. in their apartment, and George answered it. At the other end of the line was John Quimby, who came to the rapid and correct conclusion that Roxanne and George were living together. He hit the roof because the couple wasn't married, and from "his big moral high horse" told Roxanne she was throwing her life away in San Francisco studying art instead of getting an MBA and a good job offering financial security.

John Quimby then cut off all further communication with her. "I didn't really care," she remembered. "[He was] done telling me what to do." The estrangement would last eighteen years, affecting her in untold ways. John forbad Rebecca from calling their daughter, so Rebecca called Roxanne secretly from a pay phone, letting the phone ring once and then hanging up, the signal for Roxanne to return the call to her mother.

"I was her daughter, and she wanted to stay in touch," recalled Roxanne.

"It was so sad. I thought she had the right to call me if she wanted." Her mother sent money to Roxanne to pay for their calls, unbeknown to John Quimby.

For an impressionable, defiant, coming-of-age 20-year-old like Roxanne, San Francisco was over-the-top in a fabulous way. Roxanne was ripe to be personally and politically transformed by the city's many influences, to find out where her edges were and what she really believed in. She embraced alternative spirituality and feminism and became a vegetarian. "It was full-on Buddhism, astrology, Tarot cards, psychic fairs, and Maharishi Mahesh Yogi," she said. "I just got blown open in terms of alternative spirituality. I probably had a yearning to believe in something ... to find meaning for being here."*

Roxanne was open to most everything alternative and liberating as long as it broke with the societal institutions that represented her father's philosophy and politics. Like many people her age, she rejected middle-class values of material wealth, social respectability, and emphasis on family, traditional education, and authority. Her rule of thumb in San Francisco was that trying anything was okay on her journey to bring about changes in her innermost being.

A neighbor, astrologer-herbalist Joyce Yoshioka, was the first to read Roxanne's astrology chart. Roxanne mulled over how she fit the prescription for Cancers as home-oriented, possessive, moody, changeable, and good at gardening and cooking. She thought of herself as capable of seeing potential where others might not and wondered if that knack was typical of Cancers. It was all so fascinating that she took astrology classes so she could dabble in the practice herself. "George called astrology astro-garbage," she recalled.

She also discovered the Theosophical Society and attended local meetings of the esoteric organization. She read the prolific works on Eastern philosophy by Alan Watts and took to the New Age spiritual teachings of Ram Dass, author of the 1971 counterculture bible *Be Here Now*. She set up an altar at home with candles and objects that were meaningful to her.

At UMass, Roxanne had started ditching traditional feminine standards, substituting a hippie appearance. Besides wearing peasant skirts, she threw away her bras and no longer fussed over her looks. She let her hair grow longer and braided it, stopped shaving her legs and underarms, and didn't wear jewelry. "I sort of looked like a gypsy," she said. George, recounted Roxanne,

---

*The Maharishi ("Great Seer") developed the Transcendental Meditation technique and introduced it to the U.S. and elsewhere around the world. He was guru to the Beatles in the late 1960s.

wasn't into the counterculture lifestyle as much as she was. "It didn't affect his core as it did mine," she believed.

Roxanne never experimented with hard drugs because the pot she smoked was so strong "that it drove me crazy." She figured that if she ever tried a substance that was highly addictive, she might not be able to stop.

House plants became important to her. With no yard of her own, she potted indoor plants to make the apartment attractive and "green." She joined the Bromeliad Society, even though that family of plants was not her favorite, because the meetings were held at a convenient time and provided an entrance into the greater world of flora. "It was a big, big, big thing for me because plants, including trees, became an enormous influence in my life later." She became so attuned to plants that she couldn't be in a room with a plant that she intuited was "suffering" without trying to help.

Despite the history-making protests going on in the city, taking to the streets was neither Roxanne nor George's cup of tea. Neither did they participate in the first Earth Days. Roxanne concentrated on her studies and her personal transformation; George worked to keep the bills paid.

On the other hand, the counterculture's folk music and books were influential forces on both of them. In the early 1970s, a tidal wave of songs and books hailed the importance of personal freedom and spoke to the wonders of rustic life. Three Dog Night's "Out in the Country" and John Denver's "Country Roads" were instant hits, strongly affecting disenchanted young people who were wondering what to do with their lives and where to go. The media popularized communal living, especially in the West, and the notion that life was best enjoyed through baking one's own bread and growing one's own food to connect the self, spirit, and earth.

Roxanne sang the protest and freedom songs and pondered their messages about living peacefully, healthily, and close to the earth. She came across Helen and Scott Nearing's classic book *Living the Good Life* and Maurice Greenville Kain's *Five Acres and Independence: A Handbook for Small Farm Management* and was impressed by their philosophy of self-sufficiency, living lightly on the land, and providing inspiration for others. "They were among the early thinkers in ways of mixing politics and a sustainable lifestyle and coming up with something that worked on so many levels," she said. "I felt their simplicity regime was excellent. It was real inspiration."

Frances Moore Lappé's *Diet for a Small Planet* convinced her to become a vegetarian. "I was shocked at the cruelty and resource unsustainability around meat production," Roxanne remembered. "The world could get away from the cruelty to animals and eat rice and beans and be perfectly healthy and not have starvation—if we could join together and make those changes happen." The books of pioneer nutritionist Adelle Davis played a role in furthering Roxanne's awareness of the importance of nutrition and eating healthily.

She embraced composting, organic gardening, and living sustainably as best she could in the city. "I was totally onboard because I felt that it was time—socially, environmentally, and economically—to make revolutionary changes," she said. "And the revolution had to start with me. I remember Voltaire saying cultivate your own garden ... that your own lifestyle needs to demonstrate solutions to social issues if you want them to change."

When Roxanne graduated in June 1973, her parents didn't attend the ceremony. She and George stayed in the city for another year. She waitressed, painted canvases she hoped would sell, sewed clothing, and laid all her handmade goods on a blanket on a sidewalk or at local parks and craft fairs. She still believed that she was going to make a living as an artist, although no one bought her paintings and drawings.

The day Roxanne realized that she was finished with San Francisco is etched in her mind. The feeling had been building as the population grew, rents jumped, and she and George found it increasingly difficult to earn enough money to stay in the city. She had once been excited about the opportunities abounding in San Francisco, but now she was depressed by urban life. "I couldn't figure out how I could afford to live there comfortably or be close to nature," she said. Their rent had just been raised to $120 a month—an increase of $30.

One day she was sitting in their vehicle waiting for George to run an errand when she noticed garbage in the street. "Like, if you had the choice of being somewhere, why would you live where the refuse of civilization is all over the place?" she asked herself. Suddenly she revolted against the ugliness and filth of the city.

In that moment, Roxanne decided to join the back-to-the-land movement and leave behind the suburban materialism of her parents' generation. She would go to the woods, live off the grid in a self-built cabin like the Nearings, and immerse herself in nature. She would be part of the solution to the ills of society and the planet. Her lifestyle would mirror her personal politics and philosophy, and it would be affordable.

Roxanne didn't have to convince George to make a sharp right turn. From halcyon times at his family's camp in Maine, he could easily envision it. At Parker Pond, he had helped his dad and a local man build the cabin where his family spent many summers vacationing, fishing, and paddling on quiet waters.

In the spring of 1975, Roxanne, George, and Sid packed up their worldly goods in "Big Red," their VW van, and headed north along the coastal highway. Finally, Roxanne was actualizing her generation's dictum to "turn on, tune in, and drop out," the slogan popularized in the late 1960s by Dr. Timothy Leary to describe his LSD experiences.

Camping or staying in cheap hotels, the couple drove through redwood country and small rural communities of loggers, hippies, and homesteaders. Roxanne and George liked the open space, brightness, and upbeat feeling of northern California, and they would have put down roots there if they could have found affordable land. But their joint nest egg was just $3,000, and even in 1974, that wasn't enough to buy what they wanted—land near the coast.

They drove on into Oregon and Washington State. Although both states were beautiful, the farther north they went, the more uneasy Roxanne became. She didn't like the Seattle or Portland areas with their cold weather, dreary rain, and absence of that California spark. In Washington State, the van broke down. Fate had caught up with them. 🐝

Long logs arriving at Great Northern's Millinocket mill, 1970s.

Back to the Land: Maine, 1975

hile Roxanne and George waited for their car to be repaired, they came to an agreement to shuck the West and return to the East Coast. Something was telling both of them to return to a part of the country that was familiar. Again they took their time driving cross-country, camping most of the way back.

The first place they stopped to check out land prices was Vermont. The Green Mountain State enticed them with its picture postcard landscapes of dairy farms, rolling hills, and mountain summits. Vermont was where Scott and Helen Nearing had created their version of a simple, sustainable lifestyle in the early 1930s, during the Depression. Twenty years later, the Nearings had wanted a more out-of-the-way place to live organically—a place that wasn't the vacation destination for tourists and winter skiers that Vermont had become after World War II. In 1952 they moved to out-of-the-way Harborside on the Maine coast, where they perfected their signature good life.

Vermont in 1975 was too expensive for Roxanne and George. "By then, Vermont was already gone," Roxanne said. Wealthy New Yorkers had discovered it for second homes and recreation. A realtor advised Roxanne and George to head for Maine with their $3,000, because that was the only place where they would find land they could afford. The Pine Tree State's scruffy, sparsely settled interior had plenty of parcels selling for $100 an acre.

Driving over Route 2 through New Hampshire's imposing White Mountains, Roxanne and George entered Maine through Gilead and Bethel in the western part of the state. Roxanne had never been in Maine, the state known for its stoic, independent Yankee character, vast forestlands, and stunning coastline. She had an eerie feeling she was "called" to Maine, that there was "something I was meant to do."

From Bethel, she and George traveled 250 miles east across central Maine, picking up Route 9 to coastal Lubec, the small Washington County fishing village where the sun first hits the continental U.S. All the way across Maine, they passed through the forest industry's domain, although there were no signs announcing they were in the "paper plantation." A controversial Ralph Nader Study Group report had recently labeled Maine "a land of seven giant pulp and paper companies imposing a one-crop economy with a one-crop politics which exploits the water, air, soil and people of a beautiful state."

Lubec, on the eastern edge of Georgia-Pacific's vast timberland holdings, was a destination for Maine coast tourists because of its easternmost U.S. landmark, the West Quoddy Lighthouse station, and the bridge to Campobello Island, site of the former summer home of President Franklin D. Roosevelt. Although property prices were low in Lubec, they were still too high for Roxanne and George. The couple didn't even bother to follow the coast west and south, knowing that prices would only climb as they got closer to the resort towns of Bar Harbor, Camden, and Boothbay.

Instead they headed north toward Maine's farthermost county, Aroostook, whose economy was rooted in potatoes and wood products. As they drove hour after hour on Route 1 north, Roxanne's thoughts turned to Henry David Thoreau and to the Nearings, who also held Thoreau in high esteem. She liked thinking about their ties to Maine, especially remembering Thoreau's three expeditions to the Katahdin region, west of where she and George were driving. Thoreau had been captivated and put on edge by the "primeval, untamed, and forever untamable Nature" he encountered on Maine's mountain sentinel, the 5,270-foot Katahdin. Roxanne felt a mysterious magnetism at work in her psyche, a kind of power she couldn't articulate.

At the same time, she felt spooked while passing through small villages and towns full of houses nearly two centuries old and dotted with cemeteries. "There were so many lives lived in those places, and the houses' windows looked like eyes staring out," Roxanne recalled. "It felt otherworldly, especially compared to 'sunny, anything goes' California. Maine looked very serious, with not a lot to laugh about and not a fun place at all."

The couple's explorations finally took them to rectangular-shaped Piscataquis County with its large geographic footprint in central and northern Maine. Piscataquis had long been known as the poorest, least populated, most forested, and most dyed-in-the-wool Republican bastion among Maine's sixteen counties. But it also offered backwoods parcels that Roxanne and George could afford and enclaves of hippies already established in the surrounding area. In Dover-Foxcroft, the county seat, Roxanne and George heard the news they had been waiting for. "I've got just the place for you for $3,000," a realtor told them.

The parcel he showed them was not remote, but it was off the beaten track, about halfway between Dover-Foxcroft and the mill town of Guilford (on the Guilford side of the town line), an hour west of Bangor. Roxanne and George purchased it more or less on the spot. "It was $100 an acre and the first thing we could afford from the time we left California," Roxanne said. The town valuation for the 30-acre lot was only $780; the annual property tax was a mere $18.72.

Roxanne was positively impressed by the real estate agent's friendliness and that of his family. The realtor's office was in his home in Dover-Foxcroft; his wife served them hot corn muffins, and the two daughters seemed pleasant too. From this first impression, Roxanne and George assumed the area was welcoming enough to put down roots.

Maine in general was considered friendly to back-to-the-landers, so much so that the young in-migration of the 1970s reversed the earlier loss of the state's under-35 population of the 1950s to a net gain. United Farm Agency, a real estate concern, peddled farms nationwide, touting cheap farms in central Maine. *Mother Earth News*, founded in 1970, was a do-it-yourself national primer providing essential information to anyone wanting to build their own house, run a farm, grow their own food, and provide themselves with home-based energy. In Maine, George and Karen Frangoulis of Blue Hill published *Farmstead*, another how-to magazine that reached out to the flood of young folks heading back to the land.

Guilford splayed out on both sides of the Piscataquis River. Its population was about 1,800 when Roxanne and George arrived. Despite the influx of newcomers into Maine, Piscataquis, the second largest county in the state, had shrunk to a population of 16,667 souls because of a dearth of jobs. Per capita annual income was only $4,555 due to the low wages on farms and in the textile and wood mills. Many families scraped by from month to month on state welfare subsidies. The county was economically depressed by any measure.

Guilford, however, prospered more than surrounding towns because it was the primary center of job opportunities in the county. There were three local manufacturers of woolen goods and wood products. In 1975, the town's largest employer was Guilford Woolen Mills, which produced textiles and other woolen products. Pride Manufacturing made wooden golf tees, ice cream sticks, cotton-top applicators, and wooden cigar tops. Hardwood Products produced coffee stirrers, skewers, and other wooden items. Together, the manufacturers accounted for 1,000 jobs.

Some Guilford residents—both natives and homesteaders "from away"—commuted to education and counseling jobs in nearby Dover-Foxcroft. The state was in the process of deinstitutionalizing Maine's major mental health hospitals in Augusta and Bangor and had opened day treatment centers outside the big cities. The change offered the possibility of jobs in outlying places, such as Dover-Foxcroft. For back-to-the-landers with appropriate college degrees, that was good news. Some, however, wanted only low-end jobs that required little commitment while providing the minimum cash they needed.

Guilford was surrounded by outlying villages that typically comprised barely more than a town office, post office, and general store serving a few score to several hundred households. The outlying area was dotted with dairy and chicken farms, sugar maple "bushes," fields, and woods. Much of the county was owned by Scott Paper, one of the seven giants of the pulp and paper industry. While the company contracted out logging jobs locally, the best-paying Scott jobs were in the company's paper mill 55 miles south, in Winslow.

Outside the paper company empire, there was inexpensive land to be had, and word spread in the hippie communities that Piscataquis County was a good place to find parcels for $85 to $100 an acre. Some wanted to buy; others weren't interested in owning property and found a cheap rent, such as an old unused hunting camp.

Some in-migrants came from middle-class or well-to-do families who were willing to help out financially, but not all parents provided that assistance for their wanderlings to try a subsistence lifestyle. Richard Garrett, who had grown up on a farm in Vermont before moving to Maine, noticed that most of the newbies had no real skills to work a place and thus had to learn as they went. "Some made the transition in spectacular fashion," he said.

The newcomers were a mixed bag politically and socially. There were self-described left-wing radicals who had been involved in political protests. The opening of a new McDonald's in Dover-Foxcroft prompted a few radicals to talk about blowing it up. Others, like Roxanne, talked peace and love and "being groovy" but didn't have an activist history.

Some back-to-the-landers were social joiners; others were not, preferring to keep to themselves. Most everyone smoked pot or grew it on the sly and shared with friends. Free-spirited sexuality was enjoyed behind the scenes among some couples, married or otherwise.

Entrepreneurship sprouted with the arrival of the in-migrants. They opened small businesses in Dexter and Dover-Foxcroft that offered massage, health food products, organic produce, and organic clothing. "Unless you made your own opportunities, you were working at low-paying jobs, destitute, or on relief," said Garrett, who homesteaded in nearby Wellington and practiced freelance photography.

A Homestead

Roxanne and George's Andrews Road property was not much more than a stone's throw west of the historic Lowe's Bridge*over the Piscataquis River and just under five miles east of the center of Guilford. The half-mile gravel access road to their parcel bisected an old narrow-gauge railroad and crossed a short cement bridge over Salmon Stream before dead-ending at a farmstead owned by Dr. Don Underwood, who kept cows in the pasture.

The woods, a mix of birch, pine, spruce, and fir, bordered Salmon Stream, which meandered into the nearby Piscataquis. In 1975, the trees were low enough for a pleasant view of the Sangerville hills in the distance.

Roxanne and George soon realized the downsides of purchasing land without frontage on Andrews Road or the state highway. The utility companies wouldn't run electric or telephone lines to the property unless the couple paid for the work themselves. Roxanne and George couldn't afford it, so they did without electricity. The postman wouldn't deliver mail to their door, so

---

*Built in 1857, this covered wooden bridge was washed away in the April Fool's Day flood of 1987. A modern facsimile replacement was built on the original abutments in 1990.

they had to walk to the highway to check their box. The town plowed Andrews Road up to the doctor's place in winter, leaving Roxanne and George to figure out how to get through the snow to their property.

With no way to drive to their land, they parked their VW van, Big Red, in a cleared space off Andrews Road and made a trail from the parking area to their plot. Everything had to be carried on their backs or by sled or cart—kerosene, groceries, building supplies, and, eventually, twin babies.

With youthful enthusiasm and idealism, the couple rolled up their plaid shirtsleeves, picked up bow saws, and set about clearing trees for a cabin site. They'd decided the best spot was in the middle of the 30-acre lot, a choice flat area that bordered the stream. They kept the opening in the woods small so as to disturb the land as little as possible.

While working on their own place, they rented a farmhouse without heat and plumbing in Dover-Foxcroft, driving daily to their land to work. Roxanne had no ax or bow saw experience. George had acquired construction skills while helping his father build the family's Parker Pond cabin, but cutting down trees to clear a site for a house was a new experience for both of them.

As Roxanne toiled and sweated, her thoughts turned again to Henry David Thoreau. She recalled his similar labors building his Walden Pond hermitage and his mantra of "simplify, simplify, simplify." The harder the labor, the more she focused on Thoreau, recalling such quotes as, "If one advances confidently in the direction of one's dreams, and endeavors to live the life which one has imagined, one will meet a success unexpected...."

By early fall, the rudimentary site work was completed, and it was time to quit until the spring of 1976. Roxanne and George had spent all their savings to buy the land, so they had to find winter jobs to pay for a new dwelling. They figured they would need $2,000 to build a one-room board-and-batten cabin with a loft. In October 1975, the pair left Guilford for Boston to find work that paid better than the available jobs in the Guilford area. Roxanne was hired as a unit secretary-receptionist on the psychiatric ward at Harvard Medical School's teaching hospital, Beth Israel. She spent hours with patients, listening to their concerns and complaints. She studied their medical records and learned their astrological signs, thinking she could better grasp their problems with such knowledge. Roxanne lost respect for Western medicine during that winter.

One of the psychiatric nurses, a skilled knitter, helped advance Roxanne's own knitting abilities. By the time Roxanne left the Beth Israel job, she could knit complicated patterns of outerwear, from socks to cardigans. Years later, she would rely on knitting to get her through hours-long business meetings.

Roxanne and George were married before returning to Maine. George's parents hosted the May 1976 ceremony in their Newton, Massachusetts, backyard. Roxanne's mother and her Aunt Liliane attended, but John Quimby, still not speaking to Roxanne, didn't come with them. In deference to both families' faiths (Christian and Jewish), the ceremony was nonsectarian, with no mention of God or Jesus. Roxanne made her own blouse and skirt for the wedding. She and George spent their honeymoon on Cape Cod.

While in Massachusetts, they bought new ten-speed Peugeot bicycles. Roxanne wouldn't hold a driver's license until 1981 and relied on George for her transportation. A bike gave her another way to get around in Guilford that was easier than walking or thumbing if George couldn't drive her.

The concerns of both families followed the couple to Guilford. Roxanne and George had chosen a hard lifestyle outside the middle-class culture in which they'd been raised—but her father was the only parent openly opposed to what she and George were doing. He saw his daughter going backward, rejecting the progress and upward mobility that the Greatest Generation had worked hard for and believed in. "Going back to the tundra" was his reaction, Roxanne later remembered.

Rebecca Quimby's immigrant history enabled her to understand Roxanne's attraction to a pioneer life. She supported whatever her daughter wanted to do. "My mom put me in a category of independent artist, so she didn't judge or disapprove of me," said Roxanne. "She wanted to send me a vacuum cleaner, but of course I had no electricity." Their concerns aside, the St. Clairs were sympathetic with George and Roxanne's decision because they valued the rustic summer life they had created at Parker Pond.

In June, before Roxanne and George started building their 20- by 30-foot home, they constructed a screened-in shelter for a little enjoyment and relief from summer's pesky black flies and mosquitoes. It also offered a good place to camp while they constructed the cabin.

The cabin itself proved challenging. Unable to afford a cement foundation, the couple purchased 12-foot-long posts from a mill in Clinton and three-quarter-inch sheathing boards from a mill in Willamantic. Big Red was big enough to transport all the wood. A half-dozen new friends helped haul the lumber to the building site.

Getting the posts into the ground was the first order of business. Roxanne and George first tried digging post holes with a shovel—a tough way to get down six feet. Fortunately, a farmer neighbor offered to lend them his post-hole digger.

It took half the summer to get the long, heavy posts set into the holes. The posts rose right to the roof line—a way to avoid having to build load-bearing walls. The building was tied together with floor joists hooked to the posts. On many mornings, Roxanne pulled out star-nosed moles that had fallen blindly into the post holes.

Roxanne called the construction period "a trying time" because progress was slow, the bugs were awful, and it was a wet, rainy summer. "A lot of times we sat around wondering if we were crazy," she said. "It was a lot harder than we thought—physically and mentally demanding. I remember a lot of complaining." They also feared not being able to roof and sheathe the cabin in time to beat the coming cold and snow.

It was November before the cabin was finished enough to move into, and even then the building had no insulation or finished floors, but only a spruce subfloor. Because the floor was 18 inches above the ground, the winter winds swept underneath, making the cabin difficult to keep warm. It would be a few years before they could afford to lay a tongue-and-groove finished floor.

The couple spent the winter insulating the cabin. Roxanne sewed padded window quilts from scraps and decorated window curtains with crewelwork. She braided a large rug for the floor and made furniture. The picnic table that served as the dinner table was a housewarming gift from the St. Clairs.

Except for the spruce subfloor, the inside of the cabin was all pine. Roxanne and George built the cabinets themselves and bought a used black iron sink for the kitchen area. Two woodstoves provided heat for boiling water and preparing meals. One was a large Atlantic cookstove; the other was a knock-off of the popular Jotul brand. They cut their own firewood with a cross-cut saw and an ax.

Because the house had a high ceiling, the temperature in the living area was frequently less than 55 degrees, even with the two stoves roaring. Kerosene lamps and two wall-mounted gas fixtures provided light in the evenings. Two stone steps, eventually replaced with wooden ones, provided entry to the front, the cabin's only door. A woodshed, a two-holer outhouse with composting barrels, and a root cellar behind the cabin rounded out the little compound.

Vegetarianism became a financial as well as an ethical choice for Roxanne and George. They dug up rocks and roots to clear a space for a garden. Although there would never to be enough sun in that spot for ideal growing conditions, the garden produced plenty of beets, turnips, rutabaga, and zuc-chinis. Unlike some of the other homesteaders, the couple didn't keep animals for milk, food, or wool.

Once a week, Roxanne and George drove to Dover-Foxcroft to shop for things they couldn't grow or make themselves. They became involved in the Food Mill Co-op that operated out of an old potato barn. Roxanne helped organize the food deliveries to a central warehouse and participated in the distributions.

The couple cooked most everything from scratch, using a lot of oatmeal, bulgur, and spices and creating many rice and bean dishes. They made their own bread, grinding wheat into flour by hand. Without refrigeration, they kept limited fresh produce except what they could grow or buy in bulk from the co-op. Their small root cellar was cool enough to store milk and cheese, and anything fresh was consumed quickly to prevent it from spoiling. If they got a crate of oranges, they ate them all in days, not weeks. They supplemented their meals with milk powder and nutritional yeast. Their favorite sweet was no-bake carob nut balls, a forerunner to today's protein bars.

Roxanne and George dug out and rocked a natural spring behind the cabin for their drinking water supply. For bathing, they bought a portable galvanized tub called a hog feeder from the Agway store in Dover-Foxcroft. The tub was so small that they had to sit with their legs hanging over its sides. They carried buckets of water from the stream or spring into the house for daily use, hauling as little as possible to conserve their energy for other things. In winter, walking across an icy path with freezing water was not only tiring but sometimes dangerous.

Homesteading represented Roxanne and George's commitment to leaving a light footprint on the earth, similar to the Nearings—conserving resources, producing as little waste as possible, and turning their backs on capitalism. Roxanne didn't want to participate in mainstream society's consumption that was "wrecking the planet." She went so far as to take an "informal vow of poverty." And as she went about the demanding work of her new life, she prayed for peace.

As Roxanne remembered later, "At first, it was all very liberating and exciting. I didn't have the income or resources to buy a house, and yet I owned a house. I felt really secure. This is my house, our house. No one could tell us to move out. No one could take away the land. But to have that, I had to trade out a few things—running water, electricity, and the convenience and comfort of driving the car up to a garage and stepping into the house. No mortgage, no rent. I thought it was amazing that I could have that, so it all seemed like a really good trade." She also wanted children at some point and "wanted to raise them in a place where I didn't have to warn them about the dangers of walking out our front door."

Curious neighbors, most of whom had grown up on farms and knew the basics of cooking, canning, and planting, stopped in now and then to see how Roxanne and George were getting along and to drop off home-cooked food. Roxanne imagined that these native Mainers equated what she and George were doing with their grandparents' lifestyle and were quietly thinking that "maybe we could pull this off." She was pleased with their interest and felt that small-town Mainers were not hostile to newcomers with California license plates who wanted to build a house in the woods; people out West had not seemed as welcoming.

In truth, Guilford residents were divided in their response to the influx of hippies and homesteaders. Some considered the newcomers political lefties who smoked pot and probably enjoyed free love. Paul Davis, however, had a sense that once long-time residents got to know the back-to-the-landers, they liked them.* Older farmers benefited from the labor offered freely by the homesteaders at haying and harvest time.

When Roxanne closed her pine door at night, she felt safe from the pressures of mainstream life and the potential terrible events that might destroy the country. If there was a nuclear attack from Russia, she thought, she and George and other back-to-the-landers might survive in the woods of central Maine.

Living on the Land

Roxanne put herself in a situation to receive the kind of education that only nature can give.

"Mother Nature is totally unforgiving, totally impartial," she said. The physical demands were unrelenting—breaking ice in the stream with an ax to get water, walking across the snowy, icy path with five-gallon buckets of the freezing liquid, and heating the water on the stoves.

---

*A native of Dexter, Davis was a Maine state trooper at the time and moved to Sangerville by the 1980s. The Republican later became a state legislator, serving two terms in the state senate (the second of which was ongoing as of this writing) and four in the Maine House of Representatives.

This daily routine became second nature, requiring sturdiness, practicality, patience, and careful husbanding of the resources at hand. It built backbone in Roxanne, forging a steely resolve to conquer whatever stood in her way. She basked in the blessings of morning birdsong and the sights of fox, rabbit, or deer running past the cabin. The ever-present sound of the rushing stream close by their cabin was another blessing bestowed by the land.

Roxanne was outdoors so much that she considered it "the biggest room in my house. I became intimate with my natural surroundings. Nature gives such intrinsic rewards to anyone who is willing to stay outside long enough that it changes you." It made her a nature lover, a transformation that would express itself twenty-five years later in ways unimaginable at the time.

Roxanne's neighbor Tom Staley, an artist, remembered Roxanne's dedicated and accomplished housewifery. The floor of the cabin, once finished with tongue-and-groove spruce boards, was polyurethaned with a shiny coating, and Staley remembered it as the first place he was ever told to take off his shoes when he entered. Roxanne followed visitors around with a cloth to wipe the floor of any debris they carried in.

Whatever the day's demands, Sid the dog continued to bring joy to Roxanne. When she opened the front door in the morning to let him out, he was free to roam. He "was in his glory" in the woods, she remembered. He would charge out the door and chase rabbits to his heart's content. She was happy that he would never have to be constrained again, as he had been in California during his puppy years.

There were young couples with small children within a short distance of Roxanne and George who also were homesteading, and they provided support and a sense of a like-minded community. Rita and George Corbin, who were building their off-the-grid cabin in the woods of Dover-Foxcroft, were helpful friends from the start.

The Corbins met Roxanne and George through the food co-op and pitched in to help build the cabin. Roxanne and Rita became best friends. Rita Corbin recalled that Roxanne was "a one-track-minded person" who gave her all to anything she was involved with, from homesteading to knitting.

"Roxanne and George seemed like a good couple," said Tom Staley. "They had a sense of humor." He recalled that his friends managed to laugh about the time when some of their cabin loft's ceiling squares fell in on them while they were sleeping, peppering them with squirrel droppings.

Joanie White was another close friend who socialized with Roxanne and

George and later worked for both of them at different times. She remembers Roxanne as "fun-loving and game ... light-hearted and free."

Making Ends Meet

Roxanne had thought she would earn enough income from selling her paintings to cover the costs of her non-materialistic life, but she couldn't find buyers for her art. Both she and George had to find part-time jobs to pay the property taxes, buy household and personal essentials, and keep food on the table. Endowed with a rich speaking voice, George found work at a radio station in Guilford. Roxanne applied for a stitching job at the Hathaway Shirt factory in Dover-Foxcroft but, amazingly, failed the manual dexterity test. She returned to her old standby—waitressing—and other low-paying work. She worked at Dottie's, a diner-type eatery on Guilford's main street, the Covered Bridge, and Tony's at the Dexter Motor Lodge.

Roxanne liked waitressing because she could augment her salary with tips, and it gave her more control of her time than other jobs might. She didn't hold a waitressing job for long, however. She often dashed in to work at the last minute or wanted to leave early. One day she showed up at the Dexter Motor Lodge restaurant with a shaved head. She was a fan of Irish singer-songwriter Sinead O'Connor, and what was good enough for Sinead was good enough for her. Her employers were not amused.

When the old VW bus gave out, Roxanne and George were too poor to have it fixed. Instead they rode their bicycles or walked where they needed to go. Fortunately, the Covered Bridge restaurant was within walking distance of the cabin. In mud season, Roxanne wore knee-high black rubber boots for the slog through the wet woods to work; in winter, she snowshoed back and forth from the cabin to the restaurant. One holiday season, perhaps 1977, she worked for Hall's Christmas Tree Farm making balsam fir wreaths. Cynthia Hall, who hired her, recalled that she was "very enterprising." After the wreaths were finished, Roxanne gathered up the needle remnants to make sweet-smelling sachets and spruce oils and sold them at various venues.

Most of the homesteaders in the Guilford area knew one another. Besides the Corbins, Roxanne and George became friends with several other couples and returned the favor of helping with their building projects. These neighbors gave them their earliest social connections, but Roxanne and George were on the fringe, not the center, of the back-to-the-land community.

Bruce Tibbetts met Roxanne and George at Bob's Farm, Home and Garden in Dover-Foxcroft. The store had been opened in 1974 by Tibbetts's father-in-law, Louis Smith, who also ran a health food shop in Bangor. "When the hippies came in smelling and reeking of pot, Lou didn't want to keep the store anymore, and I took over the place," said Tibbetts. Roxanne and George bought whole grains and organic products at Bob's. His memory of them was that they were "truly granola."

The 1970s were rife with political issues that impassioned back-to-the-landers, such as abusive forest practices, pesticide spraying, and recycling. Roxanne was not a member of an organized environmental group, although she identified herself as an environmentalist by virtue of her day-in, day-out lifestyle. But she became interested enough to participate in a hotly debated statewide initiative to ban throwaway cans and bottles—her first activist effort.

Aimed at reducing roadside litter and promoting resource conservation, the proposal appealed to her so much that she donated to the cause, tacked up posters, and circulated flyers in favor of passage. The bill making its way through the Maine Legislature against the determined opposition of the beverage industry required grocers and other retailers to pay deposits to the distributors from whom they purchased beverages—five cents for most bottles and cans and 15 cents for wine and liquor bottles. Retailers were then to collect equivalent deposits from consumers, who would redeem the deposits upon returning their empty cans and bottles. Enacted in 1976, the law became effective in 1978 and was hugely successful, resulting in a 90 percent return of discarded containers.

Eighteen months into their homesteading years, Roxanne became pregnant. She was 27 years old, wanted to be a mother, and planned to have her baby born at home, not in a hospital. She took Lamaze classes with George at the local adult education facility and lined up a midwife to assist her. She attended the home birth of her Parkman homesteader friend Ellie Daniels's first child, at which no midwife was present.

Anticipating more costs when the baby was born, Roxanne signed up for the state WIC (Women, Infants, and Children) program and began collecting food coupons. (She never applied for the federal surplus food program.) WIC was a supplemental nutrition program for pregnant women and women with small children. The coupons could only be spent on specific items—cereal, milk, and some forms of protein. Roxanne drank a lot of milk and ate liver, since those items were inexpensive and on the approved WIC list. She stuck with it out of financial necessity.

Her first visit to her pediatrician, Dr. Lee Ann Berry, was in May 1978, just three weeks before her due date on June 4. An ultrasound confirmed what Roxanne already suspected. She and George were going to have twins. Dr. Berry was displeased that Roxanne hadn't had earlier pregnancy checkups and worried about what might happen in the event of a breech birth, but Roxanne insisted she could take care of herself.

The doctor ordered Roxanne to rest, and then, upon seeing the expectant mother riding her bicycle into town on June 1, insisted that Roxanne check into the Dover-Foxcroft hospital by 1 p.m. that day or find another doctor. Roxanne acquiesced.

Welcoming the Twins

At 6 p.m. on June 2, 1978, Lucas Robin, about eight pounds, and Hannah Bess, a little over five pounds, were born. Hannah was named after Roxanne's maternal great-great grandmother, while Lucas was named by his father for a television star he admired, Lucas McCain of *The Rifleman*. Hannah was given Roxanne's last name; George's surname was bestowed on Lucas.

The day Roxanne arrived back at Andrews Road, she began marching to a different drummer, practically and spiritually. The two tiny infants required almost round-the-clock work, especially in a cabin without running water and lights. Sleep deprivation was a given, and she now had to accept more limits on her personal time.

Roxanne borrowed two wooden cradles from friends. She breast-fed the newborns—in part so there would be no bottles to wash—and to avoid constant nursing, she fed them simultaneously. Sitting cross-legged on the floor, she positioned a baby in the crook of each arm and at each nipple. Ellie Daniels, who witnessed the feedings, thought Roxanne was amazingly adept at managing so efficiently.

Roxanne used cotton diapers rather than disposable ones that would end up in the local dump. She boiled the soiled diapers once a week in large wash pots on the cookstove, then hung them outside to dry unless it was so cold they would freeze on the clothesline. She bathed the babies in a wash tub, and their carriage was a wooden garden cart.

Roxanne's mother and sister Renee traveled to Guilford to see the twins when they were six weeks old. Rebecca Quimby wanted to make sure her daughter and grandbabies were alright. "She was totally amazed that I wasn't feeding them anything but mother's milk," said Roxanne.

The visit was Rebecca Quimby's first look at Roxanne's living situation. She was curious but not judgmental about how her daughter managed. Rebecca and Renee stayed at the hotel in Guilford; there was no room at the cabin. Her mother made another visit or two while the twins were young.

Mildred Mauthe, who owned the Covered Bridge Restaurant and Motel, knew Roxanne was living a hard life. "Her mother used to come up to visit from Boston and refused to stay over there," she said. "She'd use the motel, just come in and shake her head. She'd say, 'I'm not going to take a shovel to go out to go to the bathroom.'"

From the get-go, George was a hands-on father. "The only thing he didn't do was nurse them," Roxanne said. "He would get down on the floor and interact with the babies at their level. My reaction was, 'Oh my God, how can you spend so much time doing nothing?' But he was doing something really important, and thank goodness for it. He was a good dad—he got that role right." As an adult, Hannah confirmed that "Dad was the traditional mom figure. He was nuts for babies and little kids."

For a while, Roxanne was part of a women's consciousness-raising group that met at Jody Worden's house to share the joys and difficulties of homesteading, marriage, and children. But not long after the twins were born, Roxanne dropped out, and some of her friends lost touch with her, assuming that she was too overly stressed with motherhood and the labor of homesteading to continue to attend.

Roxanne's memories of the twins' first years make her smile. "They were hooked into each other from the start," she said. "They had total communication. They seemed to understand things on a level that wasn't available to adults. They'd babble to each other for hours, and George and I were left wondering what in the world they were saying."

The twins were entertained by simple things. Roxanne gave them a metal lunchbox with two buckles and a few spoons inside. They spent hours exploring the box and the sounds. The thick Sears catalog was another favorite toy. The twins tore page after page from the catalog, fascinated with the ripping. To make sure the catalog lasted for many playtimes, Roxanne let them rip up only one section at a time. The babies also found the cushions of the couch fascinating amusements.

When they were ready for toys, virtually all of them, except for metal Tonka trucks, were made of wood, cloth, or paper, in keeping with their parents' philosophy of "natural is best." Roxanne made the children an outdoor sandbox and a wooden rocking horse with a face of stuffed socks. One morning she saw a fox snatch a toy from the sandbox and run off with it into the woods. She relished living so close to wildlife that she could see such animals at close range.

George invented stories for the children such as the Great Ugli Mooglie and The Muffin Man, and the Giant Snard. "The twins fell asleep listening to the sonorous sound of his voice," Roxanne said. "It was simple and effective."

With no babysitter, Roxanne and George had to take the twins with them on outings or errands. Winter was especially challenging. Roxanne would bundle up the twins for the walk through the woods and across the cold, windy field to their vehicle. "They stiffened right up and gasped for breath" when the wind hit their faces, she recalled.

Roxanne's own birthing experience made her interested in becoming a midwife. After attending Rita Corbin at the birth of Corbin's first child in 1979 to see what the responsibility might entail, she decided not to pursue midwifery but did become a Lamaze coach for a short time.

Creativity and Materialism

When the twins were two, Roxanne learned that the Whitney Museum in New York City was mounting an Edward Hopper retrospective. Rebecca Quimby, sensing how important it would be for her daughter to see it, sent her $200 to cover the cost of the trip. "That gift from my mother showed so much support for me," Roxanne recalled. "She knew that George and I didn't have $1.30 between us."

After purchasing a plane ticket, Roxanne had $40 left and kept the cash in her hand while in New York to make sure she didn't lose it to a pickpocket. When a museum guard at the Whitney noticed that Roxanne was clutching the cash, he advised her to put it in her pocket to avoid attracting attention.

Roxanne spent "every waking minute" at the museum studying the Hopper paintings, some of them painted in Maine. The conditions of human loneliness and isolation, hallmarks of most of Hopper's best paintings, resonated with Roxanne as she took in Hopper's "outsider" view of life. After her brief visit in such a major locus of art as New York, Roxanne once again felt hopeful about her own painting.

From then on, despite the demands of caring for the twins, she made sure she had time to paint. When the babies napped, she painted. She needed to paint in the daylight because the cabin was so dark at night, with its dim oil and gas lights.

Roxanne set up her materials on the indoor picnic table. For convenience, she used watercolors instead of slow-drying oils, which could be messy. She worked on a 24- by 18-inch piece of watercolor paper tacked to a slightly larger piece of plywood. It was easy to put away the piece when she had to stop to care for the twins or prepare dinner.

Roxanne's Maine paintings were mostly surrealistic. She painted a series called the *Seas of the Moon* landscapes, which showed her fascination with rooms, doors, walls, wallpaper, and the perfect lines of windows and clapboards—à la Edward Hopper. She painted the night sky as seen through a window, with the moon appearing so close that the craters were visible. She was never able to achieve the art of subtle blending from light to dark for which she strove, but the success she did feel in controlling pigments gave her confidence in her creative expression.

During the winter of 1979–80, Roxanne painted at Alan Bray's studio in nearby Wellington once a week in the evening with a few other local artists. Bray, emerging then as an artist of note, recalled that Roxanne's watercolors were sophisticated and well designed. It was obvious to him that she had talent, and her work reflected her art training. The four participants talked about one another's works, said Bray, who later gained a national following for his magical landscapes, but the gatherings were more for support and sharing than serious critiquing.

Roxanne tried entering paintings in the Portland Biennial Art Show at the city's art museum, but they weren't accepted. She showed her *Seas of the Moon* series at the Dover-Foxcroft library, but none of the paintings sold.

She then turned to drawing, an art form she hadn't learned much about at the San Francisco Art Institute. In 1979, Betty Edwards published *Drawing on the Right Side of the Brain*. The book was revolutionary for artists in its eye-opening brain science, allowing them to understand that the right hemisphere was the creative center and key to unlocking one's art and intuitive gifts. Roxanne was so inspired by it that she set about teaching herself to draw using Edwards's book as a guide. Using pencil and paper, she made one drawing after another with the same intensity she used in all her endeavors. Roxanne showed her portrait drawings to fellow artist Tom Staley for feedback.

"The drawings got better over time," he said. Roxanne briefly taught drawing at the Charlotte White Center in Dover-Foxcroft.

Roxanne wasn't the only one in the family who was imaginative. George loved writing. He wrote down his dreams in the morning and kept a personal journal. He composed poems and penned fiction when he had a moment to himself. Years later, he would read one of his poems at Lucas's wedding.

Their part-time jobs meant that at least one parent could always be home with Hannah and Lucas. Roxanne and George eagerly introduced the twins to the outdoors. The children were bathed in Salmon Stream when Roxanne didn't want to go to the trouble of heating water on the woodstove. She dunked them in the cool waters, believing it wasn't bad to "toughen them up."

The twins learned to swim in the stream, pick berries in the bushes, and gather wildflowers and rocks along the woods paths. An indelible memory for Lucas and Hannah was being free to run around naked and dirty. Another memory they shared with Roxanne was running into a hornet's nest while raspberry-picking and having to run for their lives into the stream.

One of Hannah's first memories was a bloodsucker attaching itself to her leg. She went screaming to her father. She also recalled the gingerbread cake that Roxanne baked for her fourth birthday. It was so hard they ended up gleefully smashing it with a hammer.

One of Lucas's favorite stories is how he and Hannah crawled under the stairs to the loft and helped themselves to the crunchies in the dog's food bowl. Sid, in turn, helped himself to their birthday cakes. Whatever mischief he and Hannah got into as kids, Lucas thought his parents "were pretty easy on us."

George's dedication to ensuring that the family had dry stove wood made an impression on young Lucas. So did his dad's bread baking and his mother's handmade house decorations. Lucas recalls that Roxanne insisted on keeping things very clean. "We never lived anywhere that people could keep their shoes on indoors," he said.

Necessity made Roxanne and George disciplined spenders. She knitted clothing for the twins and was glad to receive hand-me-downs for them from George's family. Roxanne herself made do with a scant wardrobe of well-worn sweatpants and wool sweaters. She took advantage of free and low-cost opportunities in the area. For instance, they shopped at the Helping Hands Thrift Shop in the basement of the Methodist Church.

Conscious of the comforts she had known as a child, Roxanne pondered the question of whether she was depriving her kids by raising them in defiance of middle-class materialism. But she concluded that life at Salmon Stream provided an enriching childhood to the twins. "It was a gift to be able to give my kids the freedom and safety of being in a place that was basically benevolent," she said. "They received a depth of understanding about nature, day and night, and the seasons. I thought they could get the more materialistic things later if they wanted them."

Self-Employment

By the early 1980s, Roxanne realized that she was not going to be a successful painter. She hadn't sold a single painting, and time was moving along. So she simply stopped painting. "It had been a way for me to explore my own psyche, but I was getting more desperate to make a living, so I put the art away," she said. "I was definitely okay about it. I saw giving it up as a necessity." She fell back on selling second-hand goods.

In the early 1980s, flea markets, rummage sales, and craft fairs were popular in towns across Maine. On Fridays and Saturdays, Roxanne poked around looking for interesting, low-priced items she thought she could resell at higher prices on Sundays. She relished scouting for deals and discovered that she was good at business speculation. "One time I came across a box of Wedgwood china that was marketed for 10 cents a plate," she remembered. "The next day I sold them for $30 a plate. The sellers were people who were probably emptying out Grammy's old house, didn't want the dishes, and didn't know it was a valuable kind of china."

In short order, the $150 a week she made in good weather made her realize she could give up waitressing and be her own boss. Self-employment offered her the kind of control that meshed with her desire for as much independence as possible. "Working for myself was really what I wanted to do for a long time so I wouldn't have to punch anyone's clock," she said.

Once, at a flea market in Abbot, Roxanne came across a small silver cup with the initials JQA—almost her father's initials, JAQ. "Okay, that's weird," she thought. "It was a dime, so I bought it. I didn't know we had any connection there, but there was a Quimby Pond nearby." She later discovered that she had paternal grandparents and great grandparents from nearby Sebec and Abbot. "It made me feel I was coming home in a way that I didn't even understand then," she said.

George was cautious about Roxanne working for herself, she recalled. Their income needs would only increase as the twins grew up. He questioned whether Roxanne could meet her financial obligations while being a small-scale entrepreneur.

George was a "steady type who wanted a paycheck every Friday and needed that security," Roxanne elaborated. "He didn't like the unknown. But I loved the unknown—not knowing what's going to happen. That's why I liked business. It's a lot like fishing. You throw the hook in and sometimes you just can't believe what you caught. Sometimes you go home with nothing."

Virginia "Gini" Anderson, who lived near Roxanne and George, was among the first to see how enterprising Roxanne was. Anderson ran a redemption center in an old nineteenth-century potato barn on Route 15 near Lowe's Bridge over the Piscataquis River. In the summer of 1982, she changed the business and began selling second-hand items. Roxanne brought used goods to the barn to sell.

Anderson remembered Roxanne as being "very good at selling ... good at anything she did." Tom Staley, who was married to Anderson at the time, said Gini and Roxanne haggled together over goods, even when there were no customers. "Roxanne would almost spit she was so excited," he said.

One of the local flea markets was at the North Dexter Grange on the North Dexter Road. Some sellers didn't like working there because the market was outdoors in all kinds of weather, but Roxanne didn't mind. She plied her trade there on Sundays and learned the value of patience in selling.

One seller in her eighties offered used margarine plastic tubs for 25 cents. No one bought them, said Roxanne, but the woman was undaunted and sat at her table each Sunday, ever hopeful for buyers. She intrigued Roxanne, telling her that everyone in the world was crazy but the two of them, then adding that sometimes she wondered about Roxanne.

Another venue for selling goods and entertaining the twins was the East Sangerville Grange, about three miles from Roxanne and George's place. The Grange was declining because its older members didn't want to run it anymore. Local farmer and state representative Don Hall, a Democrat, became the driving force to revive memberships and activities in order to prevent the Maine State Grange overseers from shutting down the post. He recruited young in-migrants as members even though their politics and lifestyles were radically different from the older, straight-laced, conservative membership, and they saved the day. "We upstarts rebirthed the Grange as a country club," one such recruit, Theresa Boetner, later recalled. Members organized craft fairs, contra and square dances, pot lucks, community suppers, a winter carnival, a Halloween haunted house, and movie showings. Bands, folksingers, and storytellers performed regularly. At Easter gatherings, the adults poured Bloody Marys for members and made pancakes for the children, according to Boetner. "We were family for each other," she said.

Roxanne and George participated in the Grange activities, viewing it as a chance to give their children interesting rural-style entertainment. One year, Roxanne sold used goods at a Grange fair. She and George never joined the Grange, and that rankled some of their peers. But most everyone knew Roxanne and George had no money for membership dues.

Roxanne's Aunt Liliane Willens later summed up her niece's homesteading years this way: "[She] was living a life of conservancy, as an anti-capitalist, with her nose in the air and nothing in her pocket."

One of the summer highlights for the twins was visiting George's parents at the Parker Pond cottage. There, Lucas learned pole fishing and spin casting, a pastime that became one of his passions as an adult. George also began teaching the twins to paddle canoes.

Changed Living Arrangements

By 1983, Roxanne was restless, bored, and feeling the increasing responsibilities brought on by growing children. Her own life seemed stalled. She knew she wasn't going to save the world or leave a legacy by hauling water and chopping wood. The belief that she should make a contribution to society began to hound her.

The work and experience of homesteading had been extremely valuable and soul satisfying to Roxanne. She and George had proven they could take care of themselves with the barest of necessities. She had developed a great appreciation for the rhythms of day and night, where her water came from, where her food originated, how hard it was to heat a house if the hand-sawn wood was green, how much work it took to haul and stack firewood, and how everything she used had to be replaced through physical labor.

Now, however, self-sufficiency felt like drudgery to Roxanne. Frozen laundry and the fatigue of poverty tarnished the luster of the Nearing-inspired lifestyle. The isolation of the cabin prevented friends from dropping in, and she didn't have a phone with which to call anyone. There was no television for entertainment or distraction. Saving dirty dishwater to scrub the floor and chopping ice off the spring in order to draw drinking water got old. They had no money to waste on owning or running a car, and thus no mobility beyond riding a bike or hitch-hiking. On and on it went like that.

The hard life magnified the differences in Roxanne and George's personalities and needs. Roxanne noticed this especially. She thought George was too negative and too fixed in his ways, although friends saw him as thoughtful and responsible. She believed her mercurial temperament and impulsive and whimsical nature were too much for him. She chomped at the bit, feeling a need for experimentation and independence. She concluded that there was "no way he was able to flex enough for me to be happy in the marriage."

She wanted to strike out on a new, more expansive path. It seemed impossible for her to be hobbled any longer by poverty or by another person. Her poverty wasn't something she could immediately shed, but her marriage was. She told George she was leaving and wanted a divorce. They explained to the twins as best they could that their living arrangement was going to change. Although Lucas recollected being upset about his mother leaving, he said, "It wasn't a big deal at the time."

In January 1983, Roxanne gathered her personal belongings and left. "I had a sense of really leaving my old life behind," she said. "I felt fortified." She was not alone in giving up on the back-to-the-land way of life and divorcing her mate. Homesteading was hard on relationships. Couples were worn down by the constant work, grew sick and tired of being poor, and needed rejuvenation in a more mainstream way. Roxanne and George were among the first couples in their extended circle to break up, but they were not the last. Time led to other splits, and folks moved out of the area or out of state.

Roxanne hit the open road without the children but relocated only 20 miles away to Garland. She didn't worry about the twins because George was such a good father. She felt it was inappropriate to take them with her before she was ensconced in new quarters. In her mind, she and George had agreed to share custody.

She moved into an unoccupied cabin as rustic as the one she had just left. The owner, a woman friend living on the Maine coast at the time, had not left behind any firewood. Roxanne took out her trusty bow saw, gritted her teeth, and spent hours cutting dry limbs for the woodstove. It was going to be a cold winter.

Some of Roxanne's friends, such as Rita Corbin, were saddened by her move. They understood that she wanted to be a free, wild spirit. Friends rallied around George to help support him and the twins while Roxanne was getting resettled.

George and the twins moved to the Covered Bridge Motel, and after a short time, George bought a three-bedroom house in town near the Dover-Foxcroft hospital, and he and the children settled there. Besides working at WDME radio, he held down a shift at Ames Department Store. The children loved having hot showers, electric lights, a flush toilet—and a kitchen where young Lucas taught himself how to make pastries following Martha Stewart recipes. George continued to feed the twins' imaginations with new stories and characters invented especially for them. Sometimes he would tell the stories while sitting in the doorway between Lucas and Hannah's bedrooms or sitting on their beds as they were falling asleep. Hannah begged her father for stories even when he was tired. "He was always persuaded by our pleas and would tell the stories until his words were nonsense because he was falling asleep," she said. George eventually bought a television for the kids and allowed them to watch one program a day.

Despite Roxanne's expectations, custody of the twins became a battleground. George wanted full custody, but Roxanne was not about to give up joint custody. After heated arguments, they agreed that the twins would spend a week at a time with each parent. By the end of 1983, Roxanne and George were legally divorced.*They sold the homestead for $20,000.

In the spring of 1983, Roxanne moved out of her friend's cabin. To save money, she decided to camp out for the summer at Wassokeag Lake in Dexter. In effect, she was homeless. To provide room for the twins during the weeks they were with her, Roxanne set up two tents at the campground, one for sleeping and storage and one for cooking and hanging out. Even though it was summer, Hannah recalled that the temperatures were so cold she needed "tons of blankets" over her to stay warm in the thin-walled tent.

On the twins' fifth birthday on June 2, 1983, Roxanne sustained a heartbreaking loss. While she was hosting a birthday party for Hannah and Lucas, her beloved 15-year-old dog, Sid, disappeared. Regularly spooked by thunderstorms, he retreated into the rainy woods during a storm that day and didn't return. Roxanne never found his body.

---

*Neither had remarried by late 2014.

She was glad she didn't have to see him dead or bury his body. She came up with the notion that he chose "to walk off into the woods while I had ten little children celebrating the twins' fifth birthday. He was so accommodating to me."

To get to town and work, and to transport the kids, Roxanne purchased a used Rambler for $300, calling it "Midnight." Once that summer, a thunderstorm swept over the lake, frightening Roxanne and the twins, who bolted from the tent to the car for safety. The wind was so strong it picked up the "living area" tent and blew it into the lake. Roxanne was horrified, but the twins thought it was an exciting adventure.

Before their teen years, the twins took their life of joint custody with its frequent uprootings in stride. They remember the peripatetic lifestyle of that period as one of luxurious freedom and interesting experiences, from flea markets to Grange socials and camping out with their mother.

In the fall of 1983, Roxanne found a house-sitting/low rent arrangement. The old farm property, on Route 150 in Parkman, was for sale by owners Allen and Pam Bell. In addition to a 150-year-old gambrel-roofed shingled house, the property had a large barn, a greenhouse, and other outbuildings. The Bells, who helped start the Maine Organic Farmers and Gardeners Association (MOFGA) in 1971, had run a greenhouse business there, selling seedlings, perennials, ornamental bushes, and fruit trees. Roxanne understood that she could stay only until a buyer came along.

Running water, electricity, and a bathroom made caring for the twins much easier. There was no central heat, but Roxanne was long-accustomed to making do with a woodstove. The outbuildings and woods provided the children and their friends with plenty of opportunities to play and explore. Roxanne liked sitting in the sunshine in the greenhouses during cold weather. The years she had spent living in the cabin had instilled in her an intense dislike of feeling cold.

The driveway off Route 150 gave Roxanne a convenient place to set up a mini-flea market to supplement her income from waitressing at the Dexter Motor Lodge. She also bartered for goods, exchanging firewood for heating oil from neighbor Tris Manchester and letting him graze his Jersey cow in her pasture in exchange for milk for the twins. She planted a larger vegetable garden than ever before to save on food costs.

There was a dark cloud hanging over the Bells' place however; a girl in her late teens had committed suicide in the closet of an upstairs bedroom. To change the energy of the room, Roxanne set up an altar there with candles and items that had meaning for her.

Within a year, Wynona and Eric Boothroyd of Guilford expressed interest in buying the house, and they completed the purchase in August 1984. Wynona Boothroyd didn't know Roxanne until she and her husband looked at the house in June, but she had seen her around town, at the food co-op, the contra dances, the flea markets, and the fairs. She knew Roxanne sometimes took a waitressing job at the Dexter Motor Lodge. A future employee of Roxanne's, Wynona Boothroyd noticed that when Roxanne wasn't waitressing, "she took to wearing army fatigue pants and white 'wife beater' tee-shirts" and that summer had shaved off "her very long beautiful thick dark brown hair."

On the day the Boothroyds closed on the property, Roxanne moved to another cabin, this one near the Dexter airport. The dwelling had electricity and a woodstove but no plumbing. Around that time her old car died on the side of the road, and she left it there. Without a vehicle, she began hitch-hiking to and from town.

One of her neighbors down the road was Burt Shavitz, who lived alone in a converted turkey coop. She had seen him selling honey at the grocery store parking lot in Dexter. In the spring of 1984, she was hitch-hiking from her cabin to the town post office, and Burt gave her a lift. 🐝

Katahdin, from Deasey Mountain. (Bill Duffy photo)

Burt and the
Bees: 1984

Born on May 15, 1935, Burt Shavitz was fifteen years older than Roxanne and a frequent topic of local talk. He was viewed as an eccentric and independent cuss, an outlier. Burt's untrimmed bushy gray beard and mustache, long graying hair, and piercing blue eyes gave him a wild look. He was six feet tall, bony, disheveled, and usually wearing a blue-and-white-striped railroad cap. "He was quite the local color," Roxanne recalled. He had a reputation for talking a blue streak to people he knew, and he was infamous for not caring what anyone thought of him.

Roxanne was intrigued by edgy characters because they were just as apt as she was to thumb their noses at social conventions. Thus, despite Burt's rude behavior, she was romantically attracted to him.

During the ride to downtown Dexter in the spring of 1984, Burt chattered away to Roxanne about keeping bees and chickens—his chief interests at the time. Not wanting to stress himself, he confined his "earning a living" efforts to selling honey on weekends between July 4 and the beginning of the fall hunting season. During that period, Burt was a roadside fixture on Route 7 in Dexter. He stationed his old, beat-up yellow Datsun pickup in the parking area of Fayscott Machine Shop, flipped down the tailgate, and waited for passersby to buy his gallon jars of honey for $12 each. The containers—empty mayonnaise and relish jars—came free from local restaurants.

By the time Burt delivered Roxanne to the local post office, she was tingling with excitement. She had surmised from their conversation that he "really knew his truth," as she felt she knew hers. She wanted to see more of Burt Shavitz.

Burt's Dexter persona as "the Bee Man" gave no hint of his life before Maine. If the Internet had been invented then, Roxanne might have found a website mentioning Burt Shavitz, notable New York photographer. A native of Manhattan, Burt was the older of two boys born to actor Ed and sculptress-painter Natalie Shavitz. The family moved out of the city to Great Neck, Long Island, when Burt and his brother, Carl, were young, and Ed went to work in his father's graphic design business. Burt was more interested in his dog, his bicycle, and his camera than school and socializing. "I never went to a dance in high school or grade school," he said. "I didn't go to basketball games or baseball games—that didn't interest me. I was an outcast … because I was not real social."

He endured a couple of years of college before the draft caught up with him in the 1950s, sending him to Germany with the U.S. Army's Third Infantry Division. In the military, his boyhood interest in photography caught fire. He wound up as the official photographer for the Third Medical Battalion.

When his army stint was done, Burt turned his back on the family business—which he said his grandfather wanted him to run—and instead entered photography school and moved to Manhattan. There he found fascinating subjects to freeze on film, including the city's Bowery bums and antiwar protests. He wandered the streets with several cameras around his neck, snapping photos of scenes and people.

For awhile he took photos for a Jewish weekly, then used his burgeoning portfolio to wrangle himself a stringer job with *Time-Life*. Among his prestigious assignments were President John F. Kennedy's inaugural address in 1961, the 1963 civil rights march on Washington, and Malcolm X's funeral in 1965. His published photos also included some of the decade's celebrities, such as poet Alan Ginsburg and flamboyant New York attorney Roy Cohn, chief counsel to U.S. Senator Joseph McCarthy during the notorious Communist investigations of the early 1950s.

In 1970 (when Roxanne was headed to San Francisco), an arts grant took Burt to rural Ulster County in southeastern New York State. Liking the quiet rural area, he decided to stay, and took a job as caretaker of a Mohonk Lake cottage at the ritzy resort of Mohonk Mountain House, a seven-story Victorian castle near the village of New Paltz. It was there that a friend taught him how to raise honeybees.

According to Burt-lore, his frugality gave rise to an interest in bees. As the story goes, the local grocery store charged more for honey than Burt wanted to pay. He figured that if he kept bees and collected the honey, he could have free honey and make money selling it. "It was a realization," he said later, that "I never had to look for a job again—as long as I led a low-key existence."

After his beekeeping apprenticeship, Burt looked for a cheaper and more reclusive place to live than Mohonk and landed in the central Maine town of Dexter, population 3,951. Having inherited some money, he was able to buy 10 acres on the Dunn Road. Local beekeeper and farmer Ellsworth Perkins gave Burt an old pig house, and Burt fixed up the tiny quarters enough to live in, bought a flock of chickens and a pony, and set out beehives in fields and woods around Dexter and Guilford. He stenciled "Burt's Bees, Dexter, Me.," on the wooden hives to identify them as his.

Burt "moved up" in living quarters when Corinna farmer Harry Hatch gave him an 8-foot-square turkey coop. Eventually Burt was keeping twenty-six hives and earning about $3,000 a year in cash from the honey sales, enough to pay his property taxes, annual vehicle registration fee, and light bill and to buy food. He had no ambition to grow his enterprise further because he liked an unhurried daily routine doing just what he wanted. "No one ever accused me of being ambitious," he said later.

Burt's first wholesale honey customer was Bob's Farm, Home and Garden in Dover-Foxcroft. He delivered the honey in five-gallon tin pails. There were mixed opinions on the sanitary qualities of Burt's honey, with some folks calling him "Dirty Burty" behind his back. Patti Dowse of the tiny Somerset County town of Cambridge was one who wouldn't buy the honey because she was convinced that Burt peed outside the hives to provide the bees with salt to ingest. But Bob's store owner Bruce Tibbetts thought the honey was clean and remembered no complaints from customers.

The state bee inspector for the Dexter-Guilford area, Bob Egan, later recalled, chuckling, that Burt tried hard to prevent him from getting a good look at the hives. Burt "yapped ceaselessly at me," Egan remembered. "He had a way of giving you a migraine. He jabbered and jabbered so much I had to stick my head in a cool stream."

At the time Roxanne met Burt, she was waitressing at the Dexter Motor Lodge restaurant and bar. Burt began stopping in to chat with her, calling her "Roxi"—a nickname she let few use to her face. A mutual chemistry developed, and they became lovers.* Burt was 49 and Roxanne was 34, but neither cared about the age difference. During the summer of 1984, Roxanne took the first step toward ensuring that they would see each other regularly by asking Burt if he would teach her about beekeeping. She offered to work free, and he was glad for her help. Roxanne had come along at just the right time, because Burt had a bad back and poor eyesight, and lifting the five-gallon honey buckets was a repetitive chore that had become painful for him. Roxanne was younger, stronger, more energetic, and had better vision, and her fingers were nimble enough to handle the bees. Burt would instruct her a little while Roxanne watched. "He was an expert on beekeeping," she said. She viewed his bee yards as "a little lab" to learn the art of beekeeping.

There was no aha moment over the prospect of inviting bees into her life. The winged creatures were interesting, but Burt was the main attraction. Looking back on the Burt she fell in love with, Roxanne said later that she thought she had found "a diamond in the rough." She was intent on "taming" him but not marrying him; one marriage had been enough. Burt remembered that "a little voice spoke to me and said 'Wow, here's a woman who can do it all.'"

Burt was "slightly rude" and "unaccommodating" from the beginning, she said, but she didn't hold that against him. "It was just how Burt was," she explained, recalling that he wouldn't even offer to clean the trash or remove the oily tire chains from the truck's passenger seat when she rode with him.

Roxanne was concerned about introducing Burt to her six-year-old twins. Lucas's introduction took place at the cabin in Dexter that Roxanne was renting. "I had fallen through a hole in the floor," Lucas said. "I remember looking up and seeing Burt standing there and thinking, 'Who are you?'"

---

*A documentary on Burt Shavitz called *Burt's Buzz*, produced by Canadian filmmaker Jody Shapiro, debuted at the annual Toronto Film Festival in September 2013, triggering considerable coverage from the Internet to the *New Yorker* magazine. Shapiro sold the film rights to a DVD distributor, which released it in 2014. A number of "opening nights" were held from Waterville, Maine, to Los Angeles, and media reviews ranged from "shallow and boring" to "a charming portrait of a curmudgeon-turned corporate celebrity." The documentary was a coming-out vehicle of sorts for Burt, who had shied from publicity. In an interview for a *New Yorker* magazine article at about the same time, he said that when he and Roxanne met in 1984 after she had left her husband, she was "man hungry, and she and I, by spells, fed the hunger."

Learning to Keep Bees

When Roxanne came into Burt's life, his hives were spaced miles apart so the bees would have enough range to forage for pollen. It took almost a full day to make the round of the hives, during which time Roxanne learned the practical aspects of the operation.

She didn't worry about being stung, believing she could avoid it by "being aware of the mood of the hive." Thus, she harvested the honeycombs on days when the bees were busy outside the hives and not paying attention to her. Besides, she knew that bees pay for stinging with their own death, a trade she figured they were not prone to make easily. When she did receive the occasional sting, she slapped mud on her skin to reduce the inflammation.

Upon learning that the bees were less irritated by white cotton than synthetics or wool, Roxanne began to wear a white, long-sleeved cotton shirt that buttoned at the neck and wrists. She tucked her shirt into cotton khaki pants and pulled her white socks up over the pant cuffs. She also wore a bee hat. Sometimes Burt wore white coveralls over his other clothes.

Each colony had a queen bee, and a queen's wings must be clipped to prevent her from leaving the hive with the primary swarm. Roxanne wore gloves for this delicate task, proceeding with a surgeon's care to avoid inadvertently squashing the queen. She loved the fact that a bee hive is a female monarchy. The queen rules the hive, at least for a time. Worker bees, also female but without full reproductive capability, gather pollen for the hive and keep the temperature on an even keel, especially in the brood area where the baby bees develop. A cadre of males called drones has one job—to fertilize the queen, who is about twice as large as the worker bees.

In two or three years, a hive's queen reaches old age or is killed. Sensing the need for a new queen, the worker bees secrete a nutritional substance called royal jelly and feed it to a few chosen larvae. The jelly causes these larvae to develop ovaries, which will enable them to lay eggs—the key characteristic of a queen. The first of these female bees to emerge kills the others so that she can dominate the hive without competition.

The bee season ends in autumn. Because the store of honey is too small to feed all the bees through the winter, the drones, who aren't needed by the queen when she is not reproducing, become expendable. The workers drive all the drones out of the hive to die in the cold. Because the drones resist, two or three worker bees are needed to force out each one.

The hive maintains a "skeleton crew" in winter, and these bees consume the honey to keep from dying. They mass themselves in a solid sphere around the honey, then rotate positions, with the cold bees in the surface layer crawling toward the middle, while the ones in the middle gradually work their way outward. If there is a shortage of honey, the bees in the most favorable interior positions pass food outward to the cold and starving bees on the perimeter, thus ensuring that all the bees get some nutrition. Bees always do what is best for the colony.

When Roxanne grasped how bees worked together, it was like looking under a microscope for the first time or seeing the moon through a telescope. It was an "oh, my God" moment, she said. The bees' cooperation struck her as a metaphor for how humans should live and care for one another.

The twins accompanied Roxanne and Burt to the hives during their weeks with their mother. Knowing the bees could get riled, Burt gave Lucas and Hannah small chores to busy them away from the hives. Roxanne recalled that one job was to gather rocks into a pile. The twins also set up a roadside lemonade stand, hoping to make a little money from passersby.

The honey had to be extracted from the combs before cold weather thickened it. When the season was over, Burt and Roxanne wrapped the hive boxes in black tar paper to protect them from the winter chill.

Between October and May, there was repair work to do in the bee yards and regular inspections to guard against bears breaking into the hives. Roxanne made garden seed packets during the winter to sell in April. Mostly, though, the winter months meant time off from beekeeping.

School for Hannah and Lucas

After attending Head Start in Sangerville and kindergarten in Parkman, Hannah and Lucas entered the first grade at Mayo Street Elementary School in Dover-Foxcroft in the fall of 1984. In 1985, however, they transferred to a new alternative school, Wassookeag, in Dexter, founded by homesteader couple Bev Crockett and Sam Brown.

Roxanne thought the twins could get a better education at Wassookeag, which practiced an amalgam of the Montessori and Waldorf educational philosophies with an emphasis on hands-on learning. The school partly subsidized the twins' tuition. In Roxanne's later estimation, Wassookeag was a pivotal experience for the kids. Their every capability was nurtured, she said, and they easily learned to read and write. Hannah became a vegetarian at the school. Roxanne and George participated in numerous parent and parent-children gatherings, and Roxanne taught the students beeswax candle-dipping and papermaking.

In 1986, transportation problems forced Roxanne and George to withdraw the twins from Wassookeag and enroll them for third grade in the elementary school in Parkman. They transferred to Guilford for the fourth grade in 1987, and then to Dover-Foxcroft's SeDoMoCha Middle School for the fifth through eighth grades. It was hectic and disruptive for the whole family. The only trouble Lucas remembered getting into during that time was lighting fires in the woods with friends and playing minor pranks.

Some of the stories her children brought home from school worried Roxanne—stories that focused on their poverty-line situation and caused the twins social embarrassment. Some of Lucas's classmates looked down on his family's backwoods lifestyle. It was the first time he had thought of himself as "odd." Hannah and he were picked on for wearing the same clothes two or more days in a row. Schoolmates also made fun of the twins for eating "weird" foods such as bulgur instead of cheeseburgers.

Roxanne had made a lot of the twins' clothes when they were little, then switched to buying things at thrift and second-hand stores as the children grew up. One of Hannah's relatives sent her hand-me-downs. Lucas was more interested in his skateboard than his clothes.

Roxanne pondered the problems caused for her children by her lack of money and her chosen lifestyle; she wanted to do better for them. At the same time, she wanted to model wise money management. When shopping, she drove home points about frugality, practicality, and environmental consciousness. Once when Lucas bought a plastic ruler for school, Roxanne made him walk back to the store and return it for a wooden ruler that was "more natural" and wouldn't break easily.

Seeking a peek into whether her fortunes and finances would change for the better, Roxanne frequently read Tarot and Angel cards and her astrological horoscope—her favorite occult paths for accessing information about the present and future. She "pulled cards" and examined the twins' astrological signs to explain their personalities and lives. She wanted to foretell the years ahead. She felt it was important to share this expression of her spirituality with the twins to expand their understanding of the ethereal realm.

Making Candles

When Burt met Roxanne, he had been keeping hives for more than ten years in Maine, storing the beeswax in buckets at a friend's barn in Exeter. He had accumulated at least 200 pounds of unused beeswax by 1984, and he suggested that she try her hand at making candles with it.

Roxanne instantly saw an opportunity waiting to be harvested. The beeswax could be turned into value-added products such as candles, and the honey could more profitably be sold as a gift item than a food. She could put the sweet stuff into small, decorative jars with attractive labels and make much more money than the same volume of honey sold in plastic gallon containers. She thought this could take the bee business to a higher value-added level and lift her out of her chronic financial woes.

With the Christmas holidays approaching, she set to work preparing a test run. Burt did not share her enthusiasm for ramping up the business—"I already had what I wanted," he said later—but he encouraged her anyway.

Roxanne's new path would be unorthodox and unpredictable. That was how she operated, and the way she developed Burt's Bees into a bona fide business would prove the crowning achievement of her approach to life and enterprise. She got out her pens and paints to make jar labels and fired up her kitchen woodstove. She melted the beeswax in pots and then strained out the dead bees. Each candle required thirty dippings, a labor-intensive and time-consuming process even after she devised a wooden rack that allowed her to make and hang up to 144 candles a day.

In late November 1984, Roxanne took her honey and candles to the eighth annual Christmas craft fair at SeDoMoCha Middle School in Dover-Foxcroft. She set up a table and spread out her products, charging $2 for a jar of honey and $3 for a pair of candles. By the end of the day, she had pocketed $200. "I just couldn't believe it," she recalled. "I thought, this is it, I am in the money." The income seemed promising enough for Roxanne and Burt to invest $400 from their meager funds to purchase items needed to jumpstart the little enterprise. They bought a supply of wicks, a couple of grosses of honey jars, candle dyes, and a stainless steel boiler for dipping candles.

Roxanne was not afraid to gamble on the enterprise; she had little to lose. She was getting older, worn down by living so close to the bone, and was determined to do right by her children financially. She calculated that if she could reach $10,000 in annual sales, the enterprise would support herself and the twins more comfortably.

Her timing was dead on. The hippie and back-to-the-land movements had spawned a new generation of small-scale entrepreneurs who were invigorating the previously weak American market for natural and organic products. These homesteaders and farmers-turned-entrepreneurs infused tremendous energy into festivals and fairs all over New England. The events connected producers not only with consumers but with one another, enabling them to see the wonderful items being dreamed up by others and to size up their competition.

More than any other venue, the Common Ground Fair provided huge support for nascent ventures like Burt's Bees. Roxanne loved the three-day annual fall event. Back-to-the-landers, organic farmers, and food co-op enthusiasts formed the backbone of the Maine Organic Farmers and Gardeners Association (MOFGA), which had founded the Common Ground Fair in 1977 to celebrate healthy and sustainable lifestyles. The fair drew about 10,000 people in its early years, despite the fact that burgers and soda were banned. Soon attendance jumped to 50,000, and the trendy event, originally in Litchfield, had to move to the larger Windsor fairground and then, later, to land in Unity to accommodate the crowds.

In 1985, Roxanne and Burt began going to festivals, craft shows, and fairs beyond Maine, in New Hampshire and Massachusetts. The business was first named Make Peace Chandlers, not Burt's Bees, and Roxanne called herself "Electra Make Peace." Her change in name, she said, was an expression of "throwing off the patriarchy." She knew nothing about branding, but she would learn fast.

Susan Blaisdell, a weaver and owner of Skowhegan Handwovens, met Roxanne at the Yarmouth Clam Festival where they were both selling goods. She recalled that all Roxanne had to show was honey, candles, and a few craft items under a plastic tarp held up with metal poles. Some of the other vendors scoffed at the Make Peace Chandlers products and name, but Blaisdell was impressed with Roxanne's creativity and cleverness.

Roxanne pored through Burt's vintage collection of beekeeping books and journals, seeking ways to improve her candle making and ideas for other, easier-to-make beeswax products. A. J. Root's *American Journal of Beekeeping* triggered her imagination. Her production space was cramped in the Dexter camp kitchen, but she made do. She added beeswax polishes and Christmas ornaments to her product offerings and continued to diversify her candle line with rolled beeswax and novelty candles. She collected pollen and sold it as a health potion to mix with orange juice or use as a food supplement.

From the beginning, her guiding principles were to keep things simple, make no more products than she could sell, avoid debt, and make a profit. Reflecting on that time later, she said she didn't want debt because then she would be beholden to someone else. "I love being on the edge with no predictability, no one to report to. Anyway, there was no way a bank would have given me the money to start Burt's Bees. I could just see myself with some banker trying to explain, 'I've never had a job or anything, but could you give me some money because I have this idea about beeswax.'"

Her idea was to play to peoples' nostalgic yearnings for a down-to-earth, more reassuring way of life. She was confident that the high quality and homespun nature of the products she created would keep customers returning for more, like bees to flowering blossoms.

It wasn't long after the Yarmouth Clam Festival that Roxanne stopped calling herself Electra Make Peace because, she said, "[I] couldn't get anybody to call me that." She also stopped calling the business Make Peace Chandlers, and thenceforth it was Burt's Bees. The name had been there all along—stenciled to the sides of Burt's hives—and it was catchy and had enough alliteration to entice people to repeat it, which she thought might draw their attention to her products. She created a pen-and-ink drawing of an old-fashioned, dome-shaped beehive, called a skep, for the product label.

Happenstance brought Roxanne together with woodcut artist Tony Kulik at a crafts fair in Camden in 1985. Kulik remembered Roxanne as a "backwoods hippie" with long hair. She wore a granny dress, thick socks, boots, a couple of layers of sweaters, and a stocking cap, but her business sense was obvious to anyone who talked to her. On the other hand, Kulik viewed Burt as "an aging, unlikable" odd duck.

Roxanne was impressed by Kulik's artistry, and in a move to better present Burt's Bees products, she asked him to make a woodcut of the skep drawing on her product label. Kulik took the job, charging her only $35, a steep discount from the usual $600 to $1,200 he commanded from other commissioned woodcuts. She was delighted with the result, consequently hiring Kulik for woodcuts of other products. Kulik later recalled Roxanne telling him that she'd make him wealthy, "which she didn't quite do, but it came pretty close."

Kulik's second etching was the now-famous face of big-bearded Burt with his old railroad cap. Kulik worked from a photo provided by Burt's mother, and Roxanne experienced an epiphany upon seeing it: She now had a "face" and a brand in Burt, one that definitely stood out from the competition.

Using Burt's face as a logo was a gamble, but Roxanne was willing to bet that people would see it as humorous, friendly, and unpretentious. Moreover, having a living person for the "face" of the company opened the door to creating a personality who could interact with the public. She daydreamed that Burt could become a cult hero similar to Jerry Garcia, the Grateful Dead guitarist and songwriter, or Ben & Jerry's Ice Cream founders Ben Cohen and Jerry Greenfield.

Roxanne was right. Consumers were smitten with Burt's face and Burt's Bees products. Burt's humble-looking character and the brand's old-timey plain woodcut presentation provided a positive marketing punch. Using Burt's visage could be seen as a feminist move, too, one that Roxanne hoped would send a message to women that real beauty wasn't on the outside, as the major brands proclaimed, but rather came from within.

Burt's face was splashed on promotional literature and displays, but the bee skep was featured on product packaging in the early years. Not until the mid-1990s would Burt's full-bearded visage begin to adorn such "Burt's Bees Bedazzling Brands" as beeswax face soap, moisturizing crème, pollen night crème, and royal jelly eye crème. And in the early years, Roxanne used mostly honey, cream, and beige shades to promote the earth-friendly nature of the products. (The exceptions were colored candles and some labels.) Over time, however, bold colors, especially bright-yellow and red, would become trademark Burt's Bees hues.

While it was important to make products that would sell, Roxanne thought packaging—labels, wrappings, and containers—counted equally as much in attracting consumers. "She knew it was important to have a good product but always thought the packaging closed the deal," recalled Sol Solomon, a New Hampshire–based sales manager who once represented Burt's Bees. Stylish designs and packaging materials, including raffia and Japanese rice paper, were another way to distinguish Burt's Bees products as more than just countrified stuff from the boonies. The sophistication in the packaging glowed.

Connecting with Customers

Roxanne started making beeswax products without much idea what consumers wanted to buy. She had lived without newspapers and television for so long that she was out of the loop. "By the time I went into business, consumers were like a different species than I had known years before," she said.

To figure out those yearnings and desires in the mid-1980s, she had to get into peoples' heads. Roxanne couldn't afford to hire someone to divine consumer preferences or assemble a focus group, and anyway it wasn't her style. Instead, when showing her products at craft shows and fairs, she studied her customers closely, evaluating their body language and listening for comments to see how they made decisions. "I equated their responses with primate behavior, and I had to be totally open to watching this species behave as a consumer and understand what the trigger or need was," she recalled. "Customers can't outright tell you why they buy something or don't. The answer is deep-seated. It has to be intuited."

What first caught her attention was the regularity with which shoppers turned Burt's Bees candles upside down to look at the bottoms. She believed they wanted to see how the candle was finished as a way of assessing its quality. Her response was to make sure the candle bottoms were perfectly smooth.

"Getting someone to part with their money is an incredible thing to do because money is their security, and people want to hold on to it," she observed. "Ninety percent of people have anxiety about buying things, even little purchases. I could see the house mortgage and their kid's education running through their minds as they pondered whether to buy something from me." Watching customers, Roxanne thought of her father's unsuccessful entrepreneurial attempts. She was sure he failed because he wasn't customer-oriented. He wanted to produce what interested him, and he never changed that approach.

While Roxanne's method of customer research was unscientific and anecdotal, she didn't have to justify her way of doing things to anyone, even Burt. Her technique became a source of strategic wisdom that worked amazingly well throughout the time she owned Burt's Bees. It instilled in her a deep belief in her innate business acumen and her ability to "read" consumers.

By the end of 1985, its first full year in business, Burt's Bees grossed $10,000. In 1986 she would double that. Hannah Quimby, eight years old by then, remembered being very pleased that she could buy new clothes at Reny's Department Store in Dexter and cast off some of her hand-me-downs.

Even though Burt's Bees was growing enough to entice a bank to loan them start-up capital, neither Roxanne nor Burt pursued that route. They had no credit history or credit cards. Their only option was to spend earnings to expand the company, and to Roxanne, this still felt like the best and safest way to go.

Ambition

Roxanne made the business decisions because Burt's Bees was a sole proprietorship—hers. Though technically a co-founder, Burt was never an equal, active business participant with Roxanne. He sometimes helped with craft fairs and farmers' markets because the effort was fun and different for awhile. But he was in his early fifties and had been set in his ways for years, and he had no desire to relaunch himself as a business phenomenon or extroverted pitch artist. "A good day is when no one shows up and you don't have to go anywhere," he said later.

Roxanne, on the other hand, radiated ambition. The first sweet taste of success left her craving more, even if it meant turning toward the capitalistic world of her father that she had once rejected. Ambition drove her to take to the road, weekend after weekend, driving throughout New England with or without Burt. It was hard and sometimes scary when she was alone with little spending money in her pocket.

One time she panicked when her used Ford Econoline van broke down on the Massachusetts Turnpike and she had less than $5 in hand. She managed to get the vehicle off the highway and to a mechanic. Telling him she was broke, she showed him the jars of honey she was taking to a nearby craft fair, promising she would make more than enough money to cover the repairs. Trusting her, the mechanic fixed the cranky alternator, and Roxanne, good as her word, returned to pay the bill.

Because she couldn't afford a motel room, she slept many nights in the back of her van or Burt's pickup truck. There were "midnight of the soul" times when returning home to Dexter from a trip in winter, having made little money. Arriving in the wee hours, she would find the cabin stone cold—as cold inside as it was outside. She couldn't warm up in a hot bath because there was no plumbing. Waiting for the woodstove to heat up, she would fall into bed with her clothes on, exhausted. When it was all too much, she soothed herself by meditating on her belief that success was about picking herself up one time more than she fell.

Road trips felt easier and more fun when the twins went along. Hannah and Lucas recalled that, when they were about seven or eight years old, they loved getting up at 5 a.m., stopping in Dover-Foxcroft at a convenience store to get gas, and being treated by their mother to a sweet goodie. By helping her to load and unload products, they could make two or three dollars at the fairs and shows, and they made friends with the children of other vendors. Accompanying their mother on a road trip was a lark for them, even though Roxanne was working, giving most of her attention to customers and sales. As Hannah and Lucas grew older, they were allowed to make candles, label boxes, and pack items for shipment.

Roxanne was gutsy enough to do whatever it took to best position her products at sales events, even if it meant pushing the envelope. Tony Kulik recalled Roxanne and Burt being blacklisted from the 1985 fair in Camden after it was discovered they had slept in their tent booth to save money. The two were banned from other fairs after leaving early because their sales were slow.

Kulik laughed at a memory of the couple trying to depart stealthily from a Directions Crafts Fair at the New Meadows Inn in Brunswick. The Burt's Bees booth was situated at an outside window near Kulik's booth, and he watched as Roxanne handed company products through the window to Burt. While taking down the Burt's Bees booth canopy, however, Burt poked a hole in the ceiling, presumably incurring the wrath of the organizers. "Roxanne's M.O. was uniquely hers," he added.

Roxanne confirmed that she was "always in trouble" with the managers of the craft fairs. "I was challenged by the prevailing limitations and wanted to check to see if they were real or not," she explained. "Sometimes I found out they were real."

Burt's Bees bottled honey was such a good seller that Burt couldn't keep up with the demand. He stopped keeping bees in the late 1980s and sold them off. Roxanne said the bees were getting the varroa mite, which required a beekeeper to use antibiotics to save the hives, and Burt didn't want to do that. They started buying honey and beeswax, first from Florida and eventually from as far away as Ethiopia.

Roxanne's candle sales were increasing too, but candles were a seasonal item. Sales spiked around Christmas and then fell off. Roxanne believed that she needed more product diversity to build a viable year-round business and better support herself and the twins, and she kept going back to the old country journals for ideas.

The ingredients she had to work with were beeswax, essential oils, and herbs. In addition to the candle and honey products, she began making beeswax boot, furniture, and stove polishes, seamstress beeswax (to lubricate hand-sewers' thread), and one-ounce blocks of pure beeswax for household uses such as preventing windows and drawers from sticking.

Perusing old farm catalogs and remaining keenly aware of what her competitors were doing, Roxanne began developing selected skin-care products and contracting others. Over the next few years, Burt's Bees would start offering a beeswax face soap, royal jelly eye cream, pollen night cream, and moisturizing cream.

Her research showed her that skin-care products had once come in small tins, which seemed another way to evoke a homespun feeling in customers while enabling a higher retail price per volume sold. She began packaging the polishes in little lithographed tins.

A natural at experimentation, she tinkered with one product or another in the early stages of the business. It was inexpensive, and she wasn't discouraged by mistakes, some of which blossomed into new ideas for products. "Okay, let's try that," she would tell herself.

Packaging considerations married her nature-based ethic with her artistic and design talents. She used birch bark, shredded parchment, and raffia ties to enhance the visual and tactile quality of the honeycomb, beeswax, and herb candles. She was mindful of having each item express "a lot of humility" and reflect a message of goodness. She believed that the aesthetics that went into the design of her creations would cause consumers to feel they were discovering a fresh, different, healthy choice.

To describe the products, Roxanne used catchwords like "natural," "pure," "healing," and "nourishing." Her guiding vision of what constituted a "natural" product was the items she remembered in her grandmother's kitchen cupboard—ingredients that were unprocessed, such as peppermint and almond oils, comfrey, and oatmeal. The Boot Food polish was "an all-natural mixture of beeswax and lanolin," and Beeswax Moisturizing Crème was "an all-natural skin care product containing beeswax, sweet almond oil, oil of rose, aloe vera gel and other healing ingredients." The ingredients in Burt's Bees products were not only natural but easy to pronounce, not the strange, multisyllabic words found on the product packaging of most competitors, words only a chemist could decipher. This was yet another mark of Roxanne's shrewdness, building on the Burt's Bees image of integrity and credibility. "If you were going to evoke the 'natural' brand imagery, you couldn't then contradict it with your ingredients," she said. Ingredient labels weren't legally required during the early years of Burt's Bees, but they were good for business.

Roxanne couldn't afford to advertise much. Burt's Bees relied mostly on word of mouth and visibility at craft events. Fortunately, the "green movement" was building a customer base and creating a buzz about natural and organic products. Whole Foods, the largest organic foods company in the U.S., was expanding, as were other health food stores and small boutiques, and all were seeking earth-friendly items like Burt's Bees products for their shelves. Natural and organic products cost more, but health-conscious shoppers felt better about buying them, even if they didn't know all their ingredients.

Roxanne didn't see price as a big factor in attracting customers. She believed in the quality of Burt's Bees products, and she was convinced that consumers would pay a premium if they shared that belief. In fact, she thought the price made Burt's Bees items more special to many. As the product line evolved, fragrance became a critical marketing factor. "I thought it was a great place to work the magic of selling because smell evokes an emotional response from people," Roxanne said. "A lot of smells are related to food and trigger sensations of comfort, such as vanilla and butter."

At her fair booths, she put out a product tester for customers to try. Women, especially, liked to dab fragrant cream onto their skin and then smell it. "That's how I learned that smell is an amazing way to get inside someone's head without their permission," she said. She believed that the olfactory sense in the brain's hypothalamus is "a very primal place. If you're trying to elicit a positive buying decision about your product and go beyond a person's 'oh, I can't afford to buy that,' smell is a good way to do it because the mind doesn't control the olfactory."

Roxanne had a good nose for fragrance, and she cultivated this sense until she could trust it above anyone else's. She held sole control over Burt's Bees' use of fragrance-based essential oils. Concerned about the petrochemical residue left in commercially available essential oils, she used only oils that had been extracted with alcohol or carbon dioxide under pressure and contained no residue. She was determined to keep Burt's Bees in line with the values and philosophy she had established at the company's beginning

While relying on intuition and instinct, she was also pragmatic. She didn't hesitate to discard slow-selling products and try something different. She figured there was a lot of trial and error with a new company. It was up to her to minimize the mistakes and limit the financial costs.

Patti Dowse, who operated a handbag manufacturing business in Cambridge, Maine, knew Roxanne and Burt when they were selling honey out of the back of their truck. She thought the two were "nuts." She recalled that Roxanne wore combat boots, camouflage shirts, and a beret to "make a statement." As Burt's Bees evolved, Dowse found herself on the same fair circuit as Roxanne, and she was curious about Roxanne's creations.

Typically the fairs and other country venues sold "a lot of loving hands work," said Dowse, referring to items such as bed quilts and crocheted clothes and goods. "Roxanne's creations stood out from the rest. They were different and eye-catching. She could take something humble or everyday functional, like a candle, and make it into something incredible and sophisticated, even luxurious, with the packaging. Roxanne had real talent."

She was also impressed by Roxanne's aspirations. None of Roxanne's cohorts on the fair circuits had ambitions like hers, according to Dowse, who had been in business herself since 1971. Another important factor evident to Dowse was how Roxanne "was so careful of the money part, careful of every nickel she spent."

Dowse viewed Burt as a drag on the business, irritating to some who worked the fair and Grange circuits and downright offensive to others. Theresa Boetner said the first time Burt's Bees wanted to sell items at the East Sangerville crafts fair, Burt was the one who showed up with the goods. Although the vendors were limited to an eight-foot-long table, Burt appeared with a display so oversized that Boetner told him he couldn't use it. After the fair, Burt was told he couldn't participate again. Roxanne, however, was allowed to sell products at later Grange events.

In Burt's Bees' early years, it wasn't easy to find the products outside fairs and craft shows. Not only did the company do no advertising, it had no phone number to call, and neither Roxanne nor Burt had a home phone. Roxanne convinced Hillier Artman, owner of the Harvest Moon Emporium in Dexter, to act as a go-between, taking messages and ordering items for Burt's Bees.*

---

*The Harvest Moon Emporium was mostly a store for cooks but also sold herbs, spices, and cheeses.

A New Homestead

With sales slowly but steadily increasing, Roxanne saved enough money to buy inexpensive land and establish a new homestead. On July 18, 1985, she purchased 40 acres of fields and woods on the North Dexter Road in the town of Parkman (population 780), five miles south of Guilford center, from local farmer Orland Smart for $30,000.

There was little to distinguish Parkman from the surrounding country-side. The village center comprised the town office, the Baptist Church, the Grange Hall, and a country store. The tiny town had declined substantially from its heyday in the late nineteenth century, when it was economically, politically, and religiously vigorous. Agriculture had once predominated, but had been overtaken by lumbering. Overburdened log trucks bound for nearby mills rumbled along Harlow Pond Road, which intersected the North Dexter Road. Hall's Christmas Tree Farm and dairy farms with modest Cape-style homesteads were about the only landmarks. A few mobile homes were scattered along the roadside, which was hugged by spruce, fir, and deciduous trees. Borestone Mountain, a rugged two-peaked summit just under 2,000 feet, could be seen in the distance to the north, beyond Guilford.

Roxanne didn't build on her new property immediately, because her mother was ill with cancer. Her parents had moved to Florida while their two youngest children, Rogers and Rachelle, were still in high school. When Roxanne heard what a dire situation her mother was facing, she flew to Clear-water to be with her, planning to stay several weeks. John and Rebecca were separated at the time.

Pain in Rebecca Quimby's leg had alerted her to what was diagnosed as a cancer of the lymph glands that had metastasized throughout her body. She decided against chemotherapy. "Mom was pretty stoic about the whole thing," said Roxanne. "Her attitude was 'these things happen.'"

While sitting at her mother's bedside, Roxanne painted honeybees on hang tags and labels for Burt's Bees products. She reflected on the trip arranged by her mother the previous year. Rebecca had taken all four Quimby siblings with her to Israel, planning and paying for the trip as a celebration of their Jewish heritage.

The family had visited Tel Aviv, Jerusalem, and Haifa. Roxanne was inter-ested in Israel not just because she was Jewish but because she had become more open to a diversity of beliefs and practices. At Galilee in northern

Palestine, she felt what she termed "the Jesus vibration, the presence of the Messiah." She wanted to visit the Wailing Wall in Jerusalem's Old City, but women were not permitted access at the time. It was the only overseas trip that all four Quimby children had ever undertaken with their mother. Roxanne later thought it was her mother's last burst of energy.

The entire family gathered around Rebecca near the end of her life. Her mother was in a "Buddha state, peaceful," Roxanne said. Rebecca Quimby died on January 28, 1986, at the age of 59. It was a memorable day for the nation, too, because the space shuttle *Challenger* exploded, killing all seven people aboard.

Faced with a great deal of food preparation on the day of the funeral, Roxanne pulled out one of her mom's favorite recipes. Although Roxanne didn't consider herself much of a cook at the time, the sour cream cake turned out perfectly. "Mom was looking out for me," she said. "It was the first time I felt her presence from the other side, and it was very reassuring to me that she was making contact with me so quickly. So I remember her death as a positive experience."

Before her death, Rebecca made Roxanne promise to keep the family together and told her daughter that if there was anything she could do for her from the "other side" to help Burt's Bees become successful, she would. "I was like, whoa, that's really great because who knows what she could do, especially a mom for her own kid," Roxanne said. "There might be some strings she could pull for me."

Roxanne returned to Maine in early February 1986. The following summer, she pitched an army tent to live in and hired a local carpenter to help her construct a house.

The final structure was a small saltbox with wooden clapboards. It had one room downstairs and a loft above. A basin and a tiny gas stove in a corner of the room passed as a kitchen. A woodstove filled another corner of the room. There was no running water or electricity for awhile; an outside well with a hand pump sufficed. An outhouse completed the homestead.

Roxanne moved into her new home in October 1986, having spent about $3,000 to construct the building, the same amount she and George had paid for their land on Andrews Road eleven years before. In 1987, she paid $497 in property taxes; the property was valued at $29,420—$16,720 for the structures and $12,700 for the land. The taxes increased later when she built three small additions to accommodate a separate kitchen, two more bedrooms, and two bathrooms and added gas heat, electricity, and running water.

The exterior modesty of the cabin belied the artistic flourishes within. The floors were rectangles of clay tiles in various shades of red; wide, fancy moldings were used around the floor edges. Roxanne hung dried herbs, flowers, and pretty baskets from the decorative tin ceiling. There were arched windows along one outside wall. Outdoors, in front of the house, she planted a garden of thyme.

Although Roxanne was earning more money, Lucas recalls that nothing was wasted. Hannah and he ate oatmeal "every day for a year," he said. "There was never a time we didn't have enough to eat, but things were pretty hand-to-mouth."

Having fun at her house was easy. The eight-year-old twins drove Roxanne's Civic sedan up and down the driveway, helped build a treehouse for themselves, and loved sliding down a snowy embankment in winter. They were allowed to build fires in the driveway. They also spent hours biking around the area on country roads. Roxanne wasn't worried about strangers bothering the children in this rural community, and she allowed them a freedom to explore that they wouldn't have had in a city.

Shortly after Roxanne moved into her new abode, the Maine Department of Transportation determined that Burt's property in Dexter, at the end of the local airport runway, was the best site for a new wastewater treatment plant. The state took Burt's 10 acres by eminent domain and evicted him. The law required the state to pay Burt a fair market value for his property so he could rebuild elsewhere. He would be required to install electricity and running water to meet the building codes of the day.

Burt hauled his turkey coop to Roxanne's land, placing it at the head of the driveway, then used the state money he'd received to begin constructing a small Cape-style house between the turkey coop and Roxanne's cabin.* His property taxes increased from $90 to $1,000 a year.

Roxanne and Burt never lived together. It was important to her that the twins not be confused about who their father was. She wanted them to think of Burt as the neighbor next door. Lucas was sure that Burt "couldn't stand children," but living a stone's throw away, he was a regular presence in the twins' lives when they were staying with Roxanne. He took them canoeing and cross-country skiing and helped them learn to float on their backs in local waters. 🐝

*Although Roxanne continued to live in her cabin, she put the land title in Burt's name on April 29, 1987.

Undercast from Deasey Mountain. (Bill Duffy photo)

Backwoods Entrepreneur

As Burt's Bees grew, Roxanne needed more space for the business than her kitchen provided. She didn't have to look any farther than the end of her driveway. There, on land adjoining her property, sat an empty one-room schoolhouse. It too was owned by Orland Smart, the farmer from whom she had purchased her land. In late 1986, he agreed to rent the schoolhouse building to Roxanne for $150 a year, the cost of the annual insurance premium.

The schoolhouse was a mess. Its rotten wood and broken windows invited rats, squirrels, and porcupines, and it had no electricity, running water, or toilet. But the rent was too cheap to refuse. The critters were shooed out, broken windows were patched with cardboard, and the chimney was repaired. A pot-bellied woodstove was installed for heat and a gas range for melting beeswax. Kerosene lamps supplemented the daylight that shone in through the windows. The schoolhouse operation was makeshift, but it was a step up from Roxanne's cabin kitchen.

One day Bev Crockett, a friend from the twins' Wassookeag school days, stopped by "corporate headquarters" to see if she could help with anything. "Things smelled delicious because she was dipping candles at the time," Crockett remembered. Because Crockett kept the books for Wassookeag, the two talked about Burt's Bees business issues. Roxanne had no company bank account, preferring to pay bills from her personal checkbook. Invoices were skewered on a nail sticking up from a board. Crockett suggested a business checking account and other bookkeeping improvements, and soon after, Roxanne hired her as the company's part-time accountant.

When state bee inspector Bob Egan visited the schoolhouse in 1986 to see how Roxanne and Burt were doing, Roxanne was in bare feet while melting beeswax on hot plates. When he told her she would never make a living with such a bare-bones enterprise, "She looked at me all-knowingly, like, 'What do you know?'" he said. Egan laughs now at how much he underestimated her talent and drive.

Roxanne was in the schoolhouse only a short time before she needed additional space to produce products for a greater number of craft and country fairs. Burt scouted for condemned mobile home trailers and found a brown-painted one for $1,500 in 1987. By 1988 there was enough cash to buy two more old trailers, a red one and a blue one, for about $1,000 each. Burt tore out the plumbing and built-ins from all three, and a carpenter made tables and shelves for Burt's Bees operations and storage.

As soon as she had the trailers, Roxanne hired some women who lived close by to help out. Her all-female crew wasn't just coincidence. "I needed productive, committed, efficient workers, and my best bet was women," she said. She hired seven, all of whom started at minimum wage,* and she gave small raises to those who performed well.

Each of the trailers had a designated use: one was for production and packaging; one for packing and shipping; and one for inventory and storage. Burt's turkey coop was called "the honey house" because the honey was stored there, and it also served as an office for a time. None of the trailers would have passed sanitary regulations under the manufacturing rules of the day, according to employees, but messes and dirt didn't bother them, said Wynona Randall, "because we all lived that way. Our houses were all that way."

Other conditions, however, presented challenges for the women. It was often too cold or too hot in the trailers, only one of which—the production trailer—was heated. If Roxanne or Burt failed to start a fire in the woodstove early enough on a winter morning, it took time for the trailer to warm to a comfortable temperature. Nor was there any air conditioning for hot summer

*Maine's minimum wage was $3.55 in 1986 and rose to $3.65 in 1987.

days. Because there was no loading dock, the women had to lug heavy pack-ages down the steps from the shipping trailer to the waiting UPS truck. Finally, the sympathetic husband of one of the women built a loading platform.

There were other restrictions on the workers as well. Roxanne didn't want them to talk or play the radio while on the job, although, Hilde Bensheimer recalled, they did when she wasn't on the premises. In Joanie Slamm's opin-ion, the women suffered too because of "Burt's personality." Slamm relates that she became "the go-between Burt and the girls because he could be so abrasive."

Roxanne was willing to accommodate her crew's personal needs. When Joanie White found working in the production trailer too hard on her body, she was allowed to take materials home for assembly. Linda Luellen, who had small children, also did piecework at home so that her thin paycheck was not consumed by daycare costs.

Despite the makeshift nature of operations, the little company's potential was apparent even to the first group of workers. "Roxanne worked at least 12 to 16 hours a day and was always creating," said Slamm. "Even when she was taking care of the twins, she was working in the production trailer until 10 at night and would be back at 8 a.m." Linda Luellen was impressed that Roxanne never asked any of them to do a job she wouldn't do herself.

Lip Balm

Because Roxanne was so inventive, it was perhaps inevitable that she would consider making a natural beeswax-based lip balm. Lip balms had been popular for decades and made a lot of money for their manufacturers, and the leading American brands—ChapStick and Blistex, which had first been marketed in the 1880s and 1940s, respectively—were not natural; they contained petroleum-based ingredients such as mineral oil. Roxanne thought she could make a synthetic-free lip balm that could compete with the old brands. It would be inexpensive, easy to make, and weigh virtually nothing, thus making it cheap to ship. She experimented with various mixtures of beeswax, essential oils, and herbs.

Hers would hardly be the first natural lip balm; in all likelihood, the first natural lip balm was human earwax. Native Americans had made lip protectors, according to Deb Soule, founder of Avena Botanicals in Rock-land, Maine. Europeans had brought natural salves to the New World, and

New England pioneers and farmers had concocted various versions. Lanolin and beeswax, readily available in farm communities, were the basis for healing remedies for lips and hands chapped and cracked by cold, harsh winters. Soule herself learned how to make a pure lip balm with beeswax and olive oil when she was a teenager studying with renowned herbal elder Adele Dawson.

With Burt's Bees' available production space already occupied by candle making and other handcrafting, Roxanne pondered where to find room to make lip balm. Happenstance gave her the answer when Sharon Cloud, an herbalist from New Hampshire, called her out of the blue to inquire about purchasing beeswax. Their conversation set in motion an agreement between the two women for Cloud to produce Burt's Bees lip balm in Concootook, New Hampshire, and package it in small tins, something the big lip balm companies had never tried.

At the time Cloud, who had founded Cloud Works ten years previously, was making several natural products on her kitchen stove: a beeswax-based herbal salve, a moisturizing cream, and several scented body oils. Roxanne shipped cases of 1,000 tins to Cloud, who recalled being paid six cents for each filled tin. The lip balm was a liquid when it came off the stove. The size of the tins made them difficult to fill by hand even with a little measuring cup.

The vintage look of the tins matched the homespun image of Burt's Bees that Roxanne wanted to convey. She had also designed what turned out to be the perfect label for the tin: a bee with bright white wings and two black bands across its orange body. She felt that the happy-looking design would lure consumers, and its simplicity was on-message with the unpretentiousness of the Burt's Bees image. She gave a sunny yellow background and red lettering to the lip balm label, promoting it as "a soothing, healing mixture of beeswax, comfrey, Vitamin E, almond, and peppermint oil."*

Cloud made Burt's Bees lip balm for two years, but as sales of the product increased, Roxanne wanted to move production to Guilford, where she could have closer oversight of quality. Cloud was offered a job at Burt's Bees but didn't want to relocate. Her working relationship with Roxanne ended.

The lip balm was one of several products Roxanne outsourced. Lacking the space, employees, and equipment to make everything she marketed, she purchased products from other manufacturers to complement Burt's Bees line.

---

*Sharon Cloud recalled using all these ingredients plus coconut oil in the lip balm.

Fire

To fill orders for honey products, Roxanne kept a generous supply of honey in five-gallon Dunkin' Donuts pails inside Burt's house, where it wouldn't freeze. In January 1988, a fire broke out on the first floor.

Roxanne believed that the blaze began after Burt laid his oil-saturated work gloves on the kindling pile beside the woodstove. Roxanne and Burt, along with several employees, were only 50 feet away in the trailers. One of the women smelled smoke, and Roxanne rushed over to the house, opened the door, and saw burning timbers dropping charred pieces of wood onto the floor. An aluminum ladder laid against the loft had softened from the extreme heat. The most startling sight was honey flowing across the floor from melting plastic containers.

Roxanne called the fire department, but the fire truck drove past the driveway. Hearing the sound of the siren decreasing in volume as the truck went on down the road, Roxanne ran out to the road hollering. The vehicle backtracked and found the driveway, but valuable time was lost.

Firefighter Alvin McDonald, who responded to the emergency call, said there were no big flames coming from the house. The building was so well insulated that the fire was mostly smoke and heat. He remembered the honey mess because the firemen's boots were quickly covered in it.

"When they turned on the hose, they slid backwards in the honey," said Joanie Slamm, who witnessed the event. As the fire crew sprayed water, Burt insisted that they not break any windows so he would be saved the cost of replacing them. He seemed anxious to get back inside, and once permitted to do so, he crawled up the ladder to the loft, where he opened a chest to see if the contents had burned. According to two of the firefighters, the chest was full of cash, all intact. Roxanne explained that Burt liked to stash cash for quick access.

After the fire, the honey was stored in plastic barrels outside the production trailer.

The 1988 Catalog

Roxanne's summer of 1987 was busier than ever. Burt's Bees had booths at thirty-nine New England craft fairs between May and December that year.

The company's budding success was apparent in its two-page 1987 financial statement. Total gross income jumped from $20,000 in 1986 to $80,011 in 1987. After expenses, the 1987 profit was $16,574. The best-selling items were seven-inch candles, which brought in $7,325. Stove polish brought in $7,007; beeswax ornaments, $6,922; Teddy Bear honey jars, $5,538; and one-ounce blocks of beeswax, $4,854.

Roxanne paid herself $2,800 that year. Employee wages totaled $5,887 (ranging from $1,102 to $1,248 per worker), while Bev Crockett earned $386 for accounting services.

Expenses included $9,120 for packaging; $9,030 for fair fees; $8,694 for purchased beeswax; $5,068 for craft wax; and $8,209 for travel expenses, including upkeep of the van. Roxanne spent only $546 on advertising. For the next decade, she stopped advertising altogether to put dollars into other business needs.

Roxanne's attention to her growing enterprise was interrupted when she learned that her grandfather, Benjamin Willens, had died on May 1, 1988, at the age of 94. He was buried at the Agudas Israel Cemetery in West Roxbury, Massachusetts. His wife, Thais, would outlive him by a decade.

While grieving the loss of her grandfather, Roxanne was developing a small catalog for Burt's Bees retail store buyers. It was a strategic move. This first catalog gave her a vehicle to display all of the company's products in color and to begin the written story of the company, something that would help Burt's Bees achieve iconic status in the years ahead.

Publication of the catalog, which is now a prized collector's item among Burt's Bees fans, was a joint effort by Roxanne and two employees of Graphic Design in Fairfield, Ralph Lazotte and Alan LaVallee. Lazotte was a designer, and LaVallee, who worked in quality control for Graphic, was a professional photographer on the side.

Lazotte's first impression upon meeting Roxanne and Burt was that they were "certainly unique characters." He remembered that Roxanne appeared to be wearing "about 25 wool coats. She looked like she lived in a cave." As he began working with her, however, Lazotte was startled by her business savvy. "Talking to her was like talking to a Philadelphia lawyer," he recalled, "and she was a perfectionist. She knew what she wanted—the best."

Lazotte's job was to design Burt's Bees labels and hang tags, while LaVallee photographed the products in his basement studio. It took numerous sessions to complete the photographic work.

Roxanne wanted the catalog's inside cover shot to be a bee skep in a flower garden. For that shot, LaVallee placed a skep in a cluster of yellow, orange, and white autumn flowers at the garden of the Waterville Humane Society. The catalog project left him with an indelible memory. The night before a scheduled shoot for the Maine honey jar page, he came down with a bad flu. He couldn't cancel the shoot because neither Roxanne nor Burt had a phone in Parkman. He showed up, but they didn't. An hour later, they called to say their vehicle wouldn't start in the –20° F weather. They went on to explain that they expected the temperature to warm up and would get to Waterville by noon.

LaVallee protested, saying he was so sick he could barely stand up. "Roxanne became angry at me for suggesting postponement because she had paid someone $6 to bake biscuits to be used as props with Burt's Bees fruit-flavored honey." LaVallee relented.

Roxanne's temperament during the project left a lasting impression on Lazotte. "If you wanted 'nice,' you didn't get it," he said. Burt accompanied Roxanne to Graphic's office now and then. "He sat like a deaf mute," Lazotte said. "But if she was not around, he was an engaging fellow."

The bold colors of the catalog cover were a visual exclamation—Look at us! The background design, a beeswax pattern of cherry yellow, would become the company's primary logo and hue. The name of Burt's Bees was lettered in equally bright red and green. The bee skep engraving was sandwiched between "Burt's" on the top and "Bees" on the bottom. Lazotte remembered the engraving as a "clip art" illustration provided by Roxanne.

A short introduction inside the catalog, written by Roxanne, struck a winsome note, homey and humble. It romanticized the rural, earthy roots of the company, its connections with nature, and the purity of its products. Roxanne aimed at making it all irresistible to consumers:

> In a very small town in rural Maine, a town so small that it has no sidewalks, traffic lights, post office, or even its own zip-code, Burt's Bees, for the past several years, has been creating ornamental, functional, and whimsical beeswax products of superior quality and design. We derive our inspiration from our surroundings, which are as pure and simple as can be found in the United States. Within fifty yards of our office and workshops, which sit on fifty acres of woods and fields, we have been visited by deer, moose and fox, skunks, rabbits and bear, hawks, blue heron and Canada geese. We believe that our daily interaction with nature's rhythms keeps our vision fresh, our ideas innovative, and our service friendly and caring.

The products, she wrote, reflected the smells, colors, and sights of her rural backyard, "which we believe to be healing and nurturing as well as beautiful." Beeswax, honey, pollen, royal jelly, herbs, and other botanical ingredients were the basis of Burt's Bees' "kitchen cosmetics" recipes. The products exhibited "simplicity, purity, and a commitment to a healthier, calmer life style. We know you will be delighted with their originality and craftsmanship. And please know: we want your business and we'll work hard to earn it."

Almost anyone perusing the catalog would have found the message and the items appealing. The offerings included beeswax and herb candles and a vial of essential oils to refresh the fragrance of each candle. Honeycomb candles were tastefully wrapped in Japanese rice paper, birch bark, and raffia, then decorated with sprigs of winter oats and nested in a wooden box filled with excelsior. Along with "Roll Yer Own" honeycomb candle kits was a selection of novelty candles and votive and pillar candles. Jars of Maine honey were offered in "delicate" raspberry and strawberry flavors.

Other products in the catalog included beeswax ornaments and a beeswax nativity set; various polishes for furniture, boots, and woodstoves; and one-ounce blocks of pure beeswax for household uses such as tight windows, zippers, and irons.

The last page of the catalog presented Burt's Bees' first collection of skin-care products—lip balm, moisturizing crème, night crème, royal jelly eye crème, and face soap. They were all in small containers to encourage consumers to use them before the short shelf life of the natural products, without chemical preservatives, expired.

The eye-catching item that shared the final page was an herbal body oil and perfume called "Roxanne," which she had created on a whim as "a decorative, gifty-type thing." It was destined to be the only product to which she would affix her name, and it was available for only a short time. The perfume and body oil contained real flowers and herbs suspended in mineral oils, giving the liquid a very clear appearance. The lightly scented perfume came in three small sizes in imported Italian glass bottles.*

The end page made a forthright statement about why Burt's Bees would not use ingredients often included in mainstream skin-care products—chemical and potentially toxic ingredients that Roxanne felt were bad:

*Mineral oil was a petroleum product, the use of which Roxanne soon disavowed.

We believe that what you don't put on your skin is as important as what you do. That's why we leave out the mineral oil, stearic acid, propylene glycol, glycol sterate, cetyl, alcohol, magnesium aluminum silicate, dimenthicone, methyl-paraben, carbomer 934, terra sodium EDTA, diazolidinyl urea, etc. Our skin care products contain only the purest, most natural ingredients we know of. They are the products of sea and earth, flower and fruit, farm and field. Our list of ingredients include honey, royal jelly, pollen, clay, seaweed, flower oils, herbs, apricot and almond oil, beeswax and vitamin E. We ask that you try them once; their healing and nourishing qualities will make you a devoted fan.

There were no prices in the catalog. A separate flyer—a glossy yellow sheet printed on both sides—listed the cost of each item. Continuing the inviting commentary about Burt's Bees offerings, the flyer thanked buyers for their interest. Roxanne promised they would "be delighted with [the products'] originality, craftsmanship and natural beauty." All orders had to be prepaid or paid on delivery by UPS. Instead of an impersonal machine, Burt's Bees products "are made and packaged by human hands," the flyer emphasized in bold lettering.

The best-selling candles, a pair of 12-inch rolled honeycomb ones, sold for $27 per dozen. Packaged in mauve and white boxes with clear covers hot-stamped in silver, they came in a dozen colors from Williamsburg blue to Christmas red. The rolled honeycomb "minnies," a smaller version of the longer candles, were tied together with velvet or satin bows and had a $9 per dozen price tag. Because the $21 "Roll Yer Own" honeycomb candle kit was a favorite with children, Roxanne had printed fun "bee facts" on the back of the package. Watermelon candles, strung on jute, were hand-painted and fruit scented. They came in three sizes and were priced from $15 to $30 a dozen. The cinnamon-scented apple candles, at $21 for a dozen pairs, were strung on continuous wicks, while the cinnamon-scented heart candles were strung on jute.

The beeswax tree ornaments—a cow, Teddy bear, sheep, corn, rocking horse, cat, rabbit, moose, chicken, heart, and scissors—sold from $13.50 to $21 a dozen, depending on the ornament. The ornaments were strung on gold threads and packaged in clear Ziploc bags. A twelve-piece nativity ornament set nestled in shredded parchment cost $8.

The little tins of lip balm sold for $12 a dozen; the moisturizing crème was $27 for a dozen one-ounce jars; stove, furniture, and boot polish were priced from $21 to $24 per dozen canisters; and tins of beeswax for seamstresses were $6 a dozen.

Burt's Bees turned Maine honey into soft, creamy honey butter in an original way, as promised in its catalog: it was whipped with a workbench drill. Customers paid $30 for a case (24 eight-ounce jars) of regular Maine honey. For a case of Maine honey butter, they paid $54, making the product the most expensive item Burt's Bees sold in 1986 and 1987.

The catalog advertised bee skeps, made of rush and rattan, for gardens or patios. Roxanne and Burt had discovered the skeps during a rare vacation to the Caribbean island of Haiti. Immediately taken with them, Roxanne bought and shipped truckloads to Parkman. Wynona Boothroyd recalled that the skeps were highly profitable; they were purchased wholesale for about $2.50 and priced for American buyers at $12.50 to $20.

Sales hit $130,000 in 1988, and Roxanne expected the new catalog to send them higher.

Going Wholesale

Roxanne was excited to display her growing line of products at MOFGA's Common Ground Fair each year. It was the one fair she wouldn't miss, because it spoke to her soul as well as her pocketbook. The fair brought together the community with whom she identified personally and professionally.

For three days, she and like-minded colleagues shared healthy home-grown food, information, music, and an opportunity to meet the newest entrepreneurs engaged in sustainable living. At the 1988 fair she met Danielle Smith Bouthot, an employee of Tom's of Maine, who would become her pal and eventually her employee.

Tom's of Maine, Nature's Gate, and JASON Natural Products were small entrepreneurial enterprises founded in the 1970s to produce healthier, safer personal-use and skin-care products. Tom's, based in Kennebunk, Maine, had become the most recognized name in the personal care aisle of health and natural food stores across the country. It had expanded from non-phosphate laundry detergent (ClearLake) into toothpaste, deodorant, mouthwash, shaving cream, and other personal care items. The company began selling to mass market chains in 1983 and grossed more than $2 million in 1989.

Roxanne and Danielle were hawking their respective products in the crafts sections of the fairgrounds when they began talking. What immediately impressed Danielle was that Roxanne ran her own booth and was a hands-on person, constantly rearranging her displays to attract passersby. She was also "very hippie-looking" and carried a red satchel of Angel Cards on a string around her neck, but that wasn't off-putting to Danielle, who had grown up in a back-to-the-land household.

As Roxanne picked Danielle's brain for marketing and sales ideas, Danielle noted Roxanne's intuitive grasp of business matters and was amazed that Roxanne avoided using focus groups and marketing studies to guide her business decisions, relying instead on her own sense of what people wanted. Danielle was so eager to help Burt's Bees grow that, with Tom Chappell's approval, she started selling Burt's Bees seconds at the Tom's of Maine factory outlet in Kennebunk. Chappell didn't object because the two companies were not competitors at the time. Rather, he recalled, their product lines complemented each other.

Until 1988, Roxanne had sold to individuals at craft fairs, farmers' markets, and flea markets and to small gift stores. The travel was exhausting, and the market penetration of Burt's Bees was restricted to the places Roxanne could visit with her goods.

That year she jumped out of the retail sector into the wholesale trade, a move that was favorable and timely. It cost more to get into trade shows than consumer shows, but the big gift expos and trade shows brought retailers to Roxanne, enabling her to limit her travel. She also began hiring commissioned sales representatives to peddle Burt's Bees products to stores.

The downside was that the wholesale price for a product was only half its retail price, which meant that Burt's Bees had to sell twice as much product to earn the same income. That in turn meant ramping up production and hiring more employees.

Roxanne's wholesale strategy was a risk, but she had to be a gambler to achieve her ambitions, one of which was to become a millionaire. That desire had been imprinted on her from childhood by her father's unfailing though unsuccessful notion that his first entrepreneurial million was waiting just around the corner. The twins were still in grade school, and Roxanne wanted Burt's Bees to reach $1 million in annual sales by the time they were in high school.

Believing that she first had to visualize herself as a millionaire, she found the help she needed at Reny's Department Store in Dover-Foxcroft in a basket of self-hypnosis audiotapes selling for 99 cents each. She bought a cassette on prosperity, placed it in a tape recorder at her bedside, and let it play all night, hoping to absorb the positive teachings and information while she slept. The man pictured on the cassette case looked seedy, but his instructions provided effective guided visualizations with which to open a mind. He invited listeners to "go into the elevator and go up to the twelfth floor, open the door, and find yourself in a new room."

His goal, he said, was to convince his listeners that abundance would arrive. He said that all the negative messages about money we receive as children—such as the one about money not growing on trees—cramp and constrain our adult reality. He offered ways to retrain the brain to be positive about money, wealth, and prosperity.

Once Roxanne realized that the tape worked for her, she tried tapes on a variety of subjects, such as improving memory and meditation. "Our biochemical processing center has hard-wired beliefs," she later reflected, "and we either operate on those beliefs for our whole lives or at some point we challenge our operating instructions and replace them with others. If we do change old thinking, it usually has to be done with repetition and discipline."

It was difficult to remain certain that Burt's Bees would be a success in the face of daunting statistics about the high failures of entrepreneurial ventures. "I had to have a complete conviction that it was going to be a great success, and, on the other hand, I was always taking risks," she recalled. "Risk implies you don't know if things are going to work out. So you may not be sure in the short run, but you can believe in the long run everything's going to work."

Since Hannah shared a bedroom with her mother, she had to listen to the tapes too. Roxanne wondered if the tapes would help Hannah become a wealthy woman in her own right.*

Envisioning great riches ahead, Roxanne considered how she would spend her money responsibly. With dollar signs in her head, she drove to Portland to talk with a rabbi about what she would do with Burt's Bees profits after setting aside an inheritance for the twins. She wanted to know what the Jewish faith and ethics had to say about money. She was told that donating to charities was important, and after the visit she made a $5,000 charitable gift. When Burt's

---

*Roxanne noted that Hannah was the more frugal of the twins, accumulating a healthy savings account by her early thirties.

Bees received an unexpected large order soon after, Roxanne was sure a higher power was at work.

New York Success

In 1989, the outlook for Burt's Bees shifted dramatically. At a gift show in West Springfield, Massachusetts, the owner of the trendsetting New York City boutique Zona stopped by the Burt's Bees booth. Louis Sagar didn't speak to Roxanne at the time, but he bought a teddy bear–shaped candle and put it in his Soho store window.

Zona, one of the first "lifestyle" stores, had a loyal following, and Sagar's customers liked the Teddies as much as he did. The candles sold so well that Zona was soon ordering shipments of a hundred Teddies at a time—a large order for Burt's Bees. The buzz over the candles was loud enough to attract the attention of competitors who kept an eye on the Soho store for the latest hot item. Soon Brookstone, a specialty retailer for hard-to-find and useful home and office items, put in a big Burt's Bees order. Next the tony Manhattan store Henri Bendel got wind of the interesting little Maine company, and the secretary to Bendel's president called Roxanne directly, insisting that she fly to New York to make a presentation the following day at the Fifth Avenue store. Burt's advice was, "Well, Roxi, that's a good address." He sensed an exciting opportunity.

Roxanne gathered up a canvas bag of product samples and flew to New York with visions of what might come of the trip. She first visited the Henri Bendel flagship retail store at 10 West 57th Street. When she walked around the corner to the store's business office, she thought she was followed by a store detective because she was wearing a baggy wool coat, boots, and looked "sort of homeless."

She was agog upon meeting Henri Bendel's president. "She was such a beautiful, gorgeous woman with red hair and wearing a suit that was very expensive," recalled Roxanne. The company president said to her, "I've been waiting all my life for a line like yours."

Henri Bendel not only bought Burt's Bees entire line but displayed the products on two round tables at the store's front entrance, the prime spot in the building. "It was low-end stuff for Henri Bendel," said Roxanne, but Bendel's would keep Burt's Bees in that high-traffic location for more than two years, giving it free advertising exposure to shoppers.

Burt's Bees was on a roll, and Roxanne believed the Universe was delivering her a message. "I had a tiger by the tail," she effused again and again. Burt's Bees was not only an emerging entrepreneurial phenomenon, but, Roxanne realized, the company was ahead of the curve in a new era of natural and organic care products.

Another small miracle for Burt's Bees was the company's unexpected invitation to display at the New York International Gift Fair in August 1989. This was one of the major wholesale trade shows in the country, and space was allotted by states, with only a certain number of businesses per state receiving an invitation. Roxanne was told early in 1989 that it might take four years for a spot to open up. She applied anyway, with fingers crossed.

When another Maine company suddenly dropped out, Burt's Bees was offered the slot. With only six weeks to get ready, Roxanne was overwhelmed by her good fortune as well as the amount of necessary preparation.

A top trade show in a big city convention facility was wholly different from showing at a craft fair. It meant being indoors for days, dealing with stronger competition, and incurring higher expenses. Instead of paying $100 for a table on the village green in a small New England town, a vendor had to pay several thousand dollars for a 10-foot by 10-foot booth. Union employees carrying merchandise into the trade show building charged $90 an hour.

After weighing the costs and the effort required, Roxanne decided that she wasn't ready to grasp this opportunity, but Burt said, "Go!" So she headed to Bangor to have her hair coiffed and to purchase a taupe suit (which she still owned 26 years later) and paper pads with blue carbons for writing orders.

Burt's Bees attracted a long line of buyers at the show, and Roxanne wrote $5,000 of orders, a record for the company at one trade show. Gift store owners soon saw that Roxanne's lip balm, candles, soaps, and gifts flew off their shelves, and reorders flowed in. Back in Parkman, Roxanne received phone orders from leading department stores. She recalled taking an order from Bloomingdale's with mitten-covered hands because it was so cold in the Parkman trailer office.

Without a business degree, flying by the seat of her pants, Roxanne had reached an impressive point five years after starting Burt's Bees. Her pre-tax earnings were about 25 percent of sales—a rate she would maintain as long as she owned the company. She wanted to increase that, of course, and she thought the way to do so was to maintain or even further toughen her already-tough terms of trade.

Roxanne refused to pay slotting fees, trade allowances, or co-op marketing fees to secure or increase her shelf space in a store.* She also adhered to strict credit and payment policies. A new customer's first three orders were to be paid by credit card or money order, and no credit was extended until the fourth purchase. She would not give buyers a "deal" no matter how prestigious they were, and she required a high minimum order. Everyone paid the same price for the same products. She wouldn't let cases of products be broken into smaller ones. She charged for samples and testers instead of giving them away. She offered no free shipping. These practices—along with zero debt, no market research, no sales forecasting, and virtually no advertising—made Burt's Bees unique and solidly profitable. Roxanne's strict selling terms may have dampened sales growth, but given the way sales would later outpace production capacity, a damper on growth was probably not a bad thing at the time.

Craving an objective professional assessment of her enterprise, Roxanne contacted the Small Business Administration in May 1989 and was referred to SBA contractor John Sanders, an associate professor of accounting at the University of Southern Maine in Portland. Roxanne's most urgent question was whether Burt's Bees was a sustainable operation rather than a passing market fancy. Meeting with Roxanne to explore that question, Sanders was immediately impressed. "Her mind was going a mile a minute," he recollected. "She was the most creative person I had ever seen."

He was bowled over by her products and their packaging. "They looked like they came from Fifth Avenue instead of old trailers in a field in little Parkman," he said. Sanders was astonished that Roxanne could live on almost nothing, support two children, and be debt-free in the early stages of developing a small business. At the same time, it didn't take him long to realize that Burt's Bees was a learn-as-you-go operation.

In Sanders's opinion, the company needed to improve its recordkeeping. Troubling to him was a failure to follow "generally accepted accounting principles"; that is to say, Roxanne was not conforming to standard bookkeeping and financial practices. He noted Roxanne and Burt's minimalist lifestyles,

*Slotting fees are paid to retailers for routine shelf placement. Trade allowances are discounts in excess of standard trade discounts offered to retailers in exchange for promotional retail prices to stimulate sales to consumers. Co-op marketing fees are paid to retailers in exchange for endcap, table, catalog, or other favorable placement of a product or products. Retailers often abuse such devices, treating them as profit centers. Manufacturers commonly decry the practices, but few have the fortitude to refuse to participate.

lack of business training, and inability to borrow capital. Burt's Bees had little choice but to operate strictly on cash from sales. He also recognized "personnel problems" stemming from Burt's relationship with employees.

Roxanne's seat-of-the-pants product pricing caught Sanders's attention, but he recognized that it didn't harm cash flow, which was "overall positive," especially after Christmas sales. He mentioned several glaring inefficiencies: the manual system of record-keeping; operations from three trailers instead of a central facility; no inventory system; filling orders on an as-needed basis; and inadequate storage.

Asked about his assessment years later, Sanders reflected that Roxanne had been receiving her business education on the job—a hard, sometimes overwhelming way to learn. What few records the company kept were mostly cash receipts and cash disbursements. No fixed assets or capital balance records were maintained. There was no way to track cash flows and other financial data. Cash flow balances didn't match checkbook balances because not all transactions were deposited or disbursed through the bank account.

"Roxanne's strongest point is her creativity and common sense in business dealings," Sanders wrote in his report to her. "She has packaged an attractive product and maintained low overhead … on a pay-as-you-go basis." From their discussion of the product lines, it appeared to him that Burt's Bees was "trying to be too many things to too many people." He suggested a reduction in the number of products to allow Roxanne to concentrate on bestsellers and raise prices and profits. He recommended systematizing the accounting to avoid duplication and to include product costing; changing the sole proprietorship in Roxanne's name to a partnership or corporation; generating monthly or quarterly financial reports; retaining a certified public accountant and attorney; and using a market study to assess distribution channels and pricing.

Sanders estimated the book value of Burt's Bees in 1989 at $106,683 based on its inventory value ($37,648), fixed assets (including the trailers), product and brand value, and liabilities (which were minimal). Seventy percent of income was generated from trade shows such as New York City and Los Angeles, 15 percent from sales representatives, and 7.5 percent each from mail and telephone orders. To the central question of whether the company was viable and sustainable, his answer was yes. Years later, with the benefit of hindsight, he called that an understatement. 🐝

Traveler Mountain from Haskell Deadwater, on the East Branch of the Penobscot. (Bill Duffy photo)

Burt's Bees Moves to Main Street

Not long after receiving Professor Sanders's assessment of Burt's Bees, Roxanne moved the company from the trailers in Parkman to the center of Guilford. In a hurry to find an empty building, she purchased the J. K. Edes & Sons building on Water Street, the main road through downtown Guilford along the Piscataquis River. The two-story 1860s-era brick building was empty except for mice and rats. It lacked air conditioning and a working bathroom, but its oil heat and electric lights were a step up from the trailers.

Roxanne and Burt purchased the building for $40,000, paying half at closing from the Burt's Bees checking account. The company was doing well enough to secure a mortgage for the balance from the Bank of Guilford.

The Edes building had originally housed a dry goods store that sold everything from ladies' gloves to frying pans. An 1891 exterior makeover had left the structure with an Italianate façade, including brick corbelling and rounded Romanesque windows on the second story, giving it an architecturally distinctive appearance. J. K. Edes sold the building in 1920, and it subsequently hosted various businesses including an IGA grocery store. By the mid 1980s it was owned by a local partnership who installed a bowling alley and pool hall. After five years of high maintenance costs and low patronage, the owners called it quits and sold the building to Burt's Bees.

Once the purchase-and-sale documents were signed, Roxanne hung a self-designed large, multicolored wooden BURT'S BEES sign over the front door. After painting the walls and laying a new floor, she held an open house on May 4, 1990.

Bev Crockett was among the locals who showed up to see the new digs. The entry, she later recalled, was set up as a showroom for Burt's Bees products, with items displayed in attractive wooden cupboards. Behind the entry area was the production space, with tables designated for handcrafting, assembling, wrapping, packaging, and shipping. The second floor, accessed by a side stairway, was used as office space and an area where Roxanne could plan, create, tinker, and formulate products. The attic was used for storage.

The Guilford town office was within a stone's throw of the Edes building, and Bob Littlefield, town manager for 17 years, took a keen interest in the newly arrived business. He had heard a lot about Burt, who "was such a character," and he knew Roxanne because she had worked at the Covered Bridge Restaurant at the same time as Littlefield's youngest daughter. Littlefield remembered Burt borrowing a broom and a shovel from the town office and not returning them, and using the town's front-end loader to transport heavy items for the business.

With Roxanne's ambitions surging, she tacked a paper banner over her desk that made her goals perfectly clear: "Elizabeth Arden, Watch Out." The banner referred to the internationally famous Arden, who, along with her archrival Helena Rubenstein, gave birth to the cosmetics industry, convincing women they should use makeup to be classy and beautiful. Arden was of particular interest to Roxanne because her exclusive 1,200-acre Maine Chance Farm was located 50 miles southwest of Guilford, in Rome, near the Belgrade Lakes. The estate was not only a race horse stable but a posh health spa that attracted a host of celebrities, among them actresses Judy Garland and Ava Gardner and First Lady Mamie Eisenhower.

Hiring Workers

Roxanne's first challenge in her new quarters was increasing production to meet the sudden increase in orders from Zona, Henri Bendel, and other new clients. She began operations in Guilford with a half-dozen employees, a few of whom had worked for her in Parkman. They churned out candles, polishes, honey, honey butter, lip balm, and moisturizing crème as fast as their hands could move. More employees were required as the orders increased, and the workforce ramped up to 20 in 1990.

Roxanne spread the word that she welcomed job applications from women of all stripes, including those who had minimal education or were on food stamps or welfare. "I wasn't going to be hard-nosed about hiring and getting side-tracked by peoples' résumés," she reflected. Guilford was a staunchly Republican town, and she was unsure whether local women would work for a countercultural liberal Democrat. She was hoping a paycheck would matter more than politics, and she was right.

She interviewed prospective workers at the riverside King Cummings Memorial Park, across the street from Burt's Bees.* Virtually all of the available jobs were entry-level handcrafter jobs that paid $3.75 an hour.† Merit raises, applicants learned, were possible for outstanding job performance. Two or three supervisory jobs offered the highest pay, which one supervisor later remembered as no more than $1 an hour above the minimum wage.

The only unwelcome job seekers were smokers. Roxanne culled them from the applicant pool. Flammable beeswax and oils in the workplace made it imperative that workers be safety conscious and above all not light cigarettes, especially in closed spaces.

Before deciding whether to hire an applicant, Roxanne meditated at the altar in her bedroom, first lighting candles of various colors and placing objects on the altar to invite an answer. Taking note of the applicant's birthday, she would write the name on a piece of paper and place it on the altar. She leaned heavily on intuition, astrology, and Tarot cards to guide her subconscious to an answer. "With this method, I could gauge everything about [applicants] without knowing anything about their credentials," she said. She could sense if someone would be arrogant or of the wrong mindset, and she was even interested in how applicants dressed. "I had to see all that stuff to make a final decision on women," she remembered. To consult about business as well as personal matters, she worked with a woman psychic in Skowhegan.

*King Cummings was a wealthy Maine businessman and philanthropist who ran Guilford Woolen Mills from 1945 to 1985. He was also the board chair and leading stockholder of the Sugarloaf Mountain Corporation (a ski company) in the 1980s and early 1990s.

†In 1989, Maine's minimum hourly wage increased by 10 cents an hour to $3.75, which at that time was in line with the federal rate. The wage increased to $3.85 in 1990 and to $4.25 in 1991 (again in line with the federal rate), where it remained until 1996.

Not wanting others to think she was bizarre, she kept these astrological and spiritual practices to herself.

The kind of workers Roxanne wanted would get along with each other, excel at their jobs, and, importantly, do her bidding without pushback. Despite her best efforts, she made plenty of hiring mistakes. "People were unpredictable and hard to read," she said. During Burt's Bees' four years in Guilford, she "went through 100 people" to build up to and maintain a crew of 44 or fewer. The way a new hire set up her work station and the time it took for her to understand her job signaled whether she was a keeper or not. One woman lasted only 15 minutes, according to the supervisor who fired her.* Roxanne fired another woman after a couple of days because the employee couldn't count wrapped soap fast enough.

She was unwilling to compromise on her employee production standards because it would hold back the momentum of Burt's Bees. "Firing was like weeding carrots," she said. "As the baby carrots struggled to come up, you'd have to weed them or none would be good." She also said by way of explanation, "I thought it was worse to slowly saw through someone's arm than take a really sharp knife and get it over with in a second. There was simply no gain to keeping on a person on artificial respiration when they weren't making a contribution to the company."

Roxanne would later acknowledge that she was "abrupt" in lowering the ax on some people, and she trained her supervisors to be similarly disciplined and focused. Word got around that she was mean and hard-nosed, but she didn't care. "If I really had a chance to be the best company in America, which I thought I did, I needed A-plus people. I thought if I had the right team I could get anything done."

It wasn't easy. Guilford had only one grocery store, so Roxanne would sometimes run into a woman she had fired. It was awkward knowing that without the Burt's Bees job, the woman might not be able to make her next mortgage payment. Moreover, the constant training of replacements was expensive, and when Roxanne fired someone, it demoralized others who knew and worked with that person. There was an "am I next" worry among staff, she recalled. "But I felt it was more expensive to put up with people who were not right for the job than to get someone better."

One supervisor recalled a "tremendous pressure" on workers due to the

---

*The supervisor asked not to be identified.

high volume of orders and limited production space. In her opinion, the Edes building was too small from day one. Needing more space, Roxanne eliminated the showroom and converted the entrance of the building into an office with a land-line telephone and fax machine.

Production employees found the work physically demanding. They had to stand at their work tables and were told not to talk to each other. One employee described her 3½-year stint at Burt's Bees in the early '90s as the worst work experience of her life. She recalled that Roxanne set the heat in the drafty building at 50 degrees and put a lock on the thermostat, but the workers used a tool to unlock it when Roxanne wasn't around. (Roxanne flatly denied ever locking the thermostat at a low setting.)

Roxanne and Burt's romance had begun to taper off two years after they'd met. "He was interesting and fun, but there wasn't room there for a partnership," said Roxanne. "Once I understood that, I dropped it." But they continued to work together at Burt's Bees and lived on the same property in Parkman. Burt supported Roxanne's determination to grow the business. From his days as a national media freelance photographer, he knew the good feelings that came from success. He wasn't interested in the production line—the making of candles or other handcrafted items held no appeal for him. ("My mom in a lot of ways dragged him into this company," Roxanne's son, Lucas, would say years later.) Yet, at times during the busy seasons (late summer and pre-Christmas), Burt helped pack and ship products. He went with Roxanne or sometimes on his own to trade shows to promote the products. Most of the time, however, he was willing to be "finder, fixer, and facilitator," Roxanne said.

The job she thought he did best was bill collecting. Trade customers were given 30 days to pay, and if they were late, Burt was on them like a hound dog on a scent, calling, cajoling, demanding. Customers would pay up just to stop him from calling.

Employees worried about Burt's Bees' ownership. It was obvious that Roxanne ran the business. Why then was Burt's name on the company, they asked her; why not Roxanne's Bees? "I'd always say, 'My name's on the check. That's all I care about, the money, not that Burt's name is all over the signs or tags,'" she recalled. "They'd say, 'OK. We see.'"

Orders piled up for beeswax and other handcrafted products, and Roxanne smiled every morning when she looked at her Elizabeth Arden banner. Arden's company had been sold to Fabergé for $657 million in 1987.

Because Bev Crockett hadn't followed Roxanne to Guilford, there was no one to oversee a growing backlog of bookkeeping needs, and Roxanne wasn't about to outsource that function to an expensive accounting firm. Instead she called Guilford High School and explained the assistance the company was looking for, and a guidance counselor recommended 14-year-old Paul Daigle, a math whizz and member of the math team. Roxanne knew Daigle's family, and when Paul assured her that he could do accounts receivable and accounts payable, she gave him a brief tutorial and put him to work. With five sisters at home, he fit in well in a woman's workplace.

Years later, Daigle remembered Roxanne's flowing hair, ankle-length dresses, and sandals. She impressed him as being a penny pincher through and through. "She rarely took money out of the checking account for herself," he said. "I knew what was in the account, so I knew the amount she had access to."

Three months after starting the bill-paying job, he was put in charge of payroll, signing paychecks with her stamp. He later recollected that Roxanne never checked on him to make sure he was paying the correct amounts to employees. (Roxanne said that she did in fact review his work for accuracy and that he never gave her a reason to doubt his honesty or capability.)

Daigle worked for Roxanne for three years, until the end of his junior year. Years later he remembered starting at $2.75 an hour and ending at $3.10 an hour when he left Burt's Bees. (The state minimum wage was lower for minors at the time.) Each Friday he walked over to Guilford Key Bank to make a deposit, and Roxanne recalled vividly that he wore a suit to work on Fridays because he wanted to be dressed like a business representative. He carried the Burt's Bees deposit in a little zippered cash bag. "He was so cute, a little nerdy kid who wore big glasses," Roxanne said.

Daigle was perplexed that Roxanne wouldn't hire a professional manager to oversee the expanding business, especially as Roxanne and Burt weren't around all the time. When Roxanne was absent, Burt was the go-to person, and when both of them were away, one of the supervisors acted as manager. Sometimes it was Daigle. "I was put in charge at times but not really in charge," he recalled, noting his age and lack of experience. While he was temporary manager, the employees, mostly in their thirties and forties, would ask Daigle to resolve issues. "I would show up at work after school, and these employees would ask me what to do about things that had accumulated during the day," he said. "My reaction was 'What? You guys are ridiculous asking me. You're 40 years old, and I'm 15.'"*

In addition to his bookkeeping responsibilities, Daigle helped with whatever else was needed, from taking orders to shipping packages. He remembered "upselling" a customer who called to order lip balm; by the end of the call, the customer had purchased display cases and dozens of products to fill them. Roxanne was shocked that a young teenager could handle a sales call so adroitly, he said. After a summer of working over 40 hours a week, he asked Roxanne for a raise, and she gave him one—but only 10 cents an hour.† He didn't complain but never forgot how crushed he felt.

Burt's Bees had sales of $500,000 in 1990, more than twice the previous year. Paul Daigle provided a temporary answer for day-to-day bookkeeping—accounts payable, accounts receivable, wages, and inventory management—but the company needed a full-time bookkeeper. "We kept missing [income withholding and unemployment tax] deadlines that the IRS felt were really important," Roxanne acknowledged. She advertised in the *Boston Globe* for a bookkeeper, to no avail.

Roxanne's Formulas

Roxanne personally created and controlled the formulations of all new personal care products such as face crèmes. Acting as a pseudo-chemist, she experimented and tested ingredients, believing that what came out of her makeshift lab on the second floor of the Edes building was completely safe for consumers. There were no scientific trials before products were marketed‡— nor was she the only entrepreneur in the 1970s and 1980s who was concocting potions in the age-old, self-trained herbalist tradition. Fortunately, most

---

*Paul Daigle began working at Burt's Bees before there were production supervisors. Before he left, Roxanne hired supervisors to handle issues, training, and questions that sometimes had fallen in his lap. But Roxanne remained Burt's Bees' quality control manager because she didn't want to spend money to find and hire one from the outside. She sought to create a culture of quality by drumming her production values into the heads of employees. Her workers, in turn, taught the quality requirements to new hires.

†Daigle said that he wasn't allowed by law to work over 40 hours a week but did anyway. "We kept it off the books," he said. "I banked some of that time, and Roxanne allowed me to take a 'paid' vacation" with the comp time.

‡No safety trials were or are required of personal care products if the ingredients used are on the GRAS ("generally recognized as safe") list, as the ingredients used by Burt's Bees were.

Burt's Bees products were anhydrous (lacking water) and thus not subject to mold or bacteria. But the crèmes were "wet," and with only natural preservatives staving off contamination, they could grow mold or bacteria given sufficient warmth, humidity, and time. According to Roxanne, no contamination issues came to her attention in Maine.

At the Edes Building, Roxanne created a simple laboratory on the second floor equipped with a table, a chair, and small bottles of the essential oils—such as peppermint, lavender, and rosemary—that gave fragrance to her personal care products. She achieved a desirable fragrance by adding a scented oil drop by drop to glass vials. When the fragrance was just what she wanted, she counted the number of drops to know how many parts per hundred she would need for large batches of a product. "I was trying to provoke a certain kind of behavior with the fragrances—the buying behavior," she remembered. "I thought that was really, really important." Increasingly, she favored yellow and gold for product packaging, colors she hoped consumers would associate with honey, sunshine, and *National Geographic* magazine. The red lettering she used on the bright-yellow labels of the skin-care products—a practice she had begun with lip balm and various polishes in 1987—was designed to grab customers' attention more effectively than the earth tones she had once favored.

Because Roxanne's crew could produce only a limited number of handmade goods daily, she expanded her purchases of gift products from her Haitian supplier, Ace Wood Craft. Order slips from March 1991 showed the purchase of 5,000 willow birdhouses, 1,597 wire bird feeders with lids, and 15,060 minimum-glazed pottery pots. Rush and rattan rugs, rush beehive baskets, and rustic metal candle boxes filled out that month's order, and there were many more such purchases over time.

Given the *de facto* military rule in Haiti, armed guards were present at the Ace factory when weekly paychecks were handed out to several hundred workers. "The country was a wreck," Roxanne remembered later, and the living and working conditions there worried her. She disapproved of the island nation's government but believed that doing business there helped provide factory jobs for the poor.

Consumers began to favor the lip balm over the polishes and other products, and customers expressed their increasing love for Burt's Bees in letters sent to General Delivery at the Guilford Post Office. Some letters were hysterically funny, according to Roxanne, who kept a few for the company's archives. Correspondents gushed about lip balm, some decorating their letters with illustrations of flying bees. One man wrote that he suffered dry mouth and lips after smoking pot, and lip balm was the perfect cure. Another reported that his rashes had been incurable until he used Burt's Bees lip balm on them.

Perhaps the most lavish praise came from a customer in Toronto who wrote, "In all my eighteen years of glorious lip injuries, never have I grown so fond of a lip balm, as I have to yours. Those dry winter nights when I'd wake in a cold sweat, lips cracked, mouth dry, I'd find myself in a trance, whispering, 'Burt, Burt!', and every night I'd find myself thanking this eminent savior from Guilford. Well, the winter days are over, but the lips still suffer. My lips have seen a spring of abundant solar radiation, and Burt still heals." When the customer used up his tin of the "divine substance," he couldn't find more and sent $25 to Burt's Bees for as much lip balm as that amount would buy.

Not all of the letters were bubbling with praise, but complaints didn't bother Roxanne. She felt that any handwritten letter was a sign of success, because a customer had taken the time to pen an opinion. Her ultimate measures of success, however, were sales and profits. "People will say a lot of stuff, but if they actually buy something, that's the acid test," she said.

Business Suitors

The business world began to take notice of Burt's Bees as a promising investment in the early 1990s, and two or three unsolicited investors showed up each year to inquire about buying the entire enterprise or a share in it. From her earliest stabs at making money as a child, Roxanne had loved the feel of cash in hand. To her, selling products and amassing money in the high-stakes marketplace was exciting and satisfying. She couldn't get enough. But she knew she would sell Burt's Bees in a second for the right amount of money. Holding on to the enterprise for the sake of history or legacy meant nothing to her.

She toyed with prospective buyers to educate herself about negotiating a sale and evaluating the company's worth. She viewed the exploratory meetings as "dates ... and I dated a lot of guys," she said. Usually there was just one date per interested party—either Roxanne didn't like the suitor (always a man) or his offer was too low. The most unusual of these was a former executive of a cosmetics company who brought along his male lover and a woman who claimed to be a princess. Roxanne remembered the executive as incredibly well-groomed, manicured, and wearing a luscious camel-hair coat that might have cost as much as her yearly salary.

The trio arrived on a cold February day on their way to visit a friend at a Maine ski resort. They drove a large vehicle carrying azalea topiaries as a gift to their friend and left the engine running during the meeting to keep the plants from freezing. That irritated Roxanne, who deemed it wasteful and polluting. The meeting, though pleasant, ended without an offer, but the man in the camel-hair coat called later to ask Roxanne what she wanted for 100 percent of the business. When she told him $5 million, the suitor was so outraged he wrote a scathing letter advising her that the next time she wanted to sell the business, she should get a broker who could give her a reality check on the company's value. She didn't bother to answer him.

Roxanne knew that prospective buyers figured they could get Burt's Bees inexpensively because it was a backwater company hungry for capital. They didn't figure that Roxanne had their number before they walked in the door. The only exception was Stuart Kauder, a television ad salesman from New York and self-described addict of lip balm since his teen years. "I had tried every [lip balm] that existed," he later said. One day he saw a Burt's Bees lip balm tin on an associate's desk, tried it, and loved it. He was dismayed that the only stores in Manhattan that sold the product were Zona's in Soho and Eat, a boutique on Madison Avenue.

Kauder phoned Roxanne in 1991, gushing with passion for lip balm and asking if he could help promote it. The discussion led Roxanne to invite him to Guilford to see the company operations and explore a partnership.

It seemed the perfect time to bring in someone with Kauder's advertising background and enthusiasm. Exhausted from unending work, Roxanne wanted more time for the creative end of the business. She proposed that if they could work amicably together, she would sell him one-third of the business for $30,000. If not, because he would have to quit his job in New York for the trial with Burt's Bees, she would give him a default payment of $20,000. They signed a contract with those terms.

Kauder took a room at a Guilford bed-and-breakfast. His first impression of Roxanne was that she was talented and a fast learner. "She was always thinking of ways of staying ahead of the curve," he said. "At the time, there was no natural lip balm like hers in the [U.S.] mainstream personal care business."

He was struck by how well Burt's Bees was doing, given Roxanne's loose business practices and limited capital. The first floor of the Edes building was "like a big kitchen," with employees churning out lip balm, candles, and all the other products with pots, spoons, and blenders. Kauder viewed the production side of the business as unsanitary, a characterization Roxanne later strongly refuted. He wanted to put lip balm in dispensers across the country, and he proposed that she either purchase a stainless steel mixer to produce the lip balm more sanitarily or outsource the formula to the manufacturer of Blistex in Illinois.

Roxanne nixed his ideas, and after working with him three months, she informed him that their deal was off. An angry Kauder told her, "You'll never be more than a little company," echoing the conclusion of state bee inspector Bob Egan in 1985. Roxanne took his statement as a challenge. Back in New York, Kauder founded a natural products business that made Moiststic, his version of Burt's Bees lip balm. He succeeded in getting the product into organic grocery stores such as Whole Foods and Fresh Fields before selling the business in the mid-1990s.

Expanding

In 1991 and 1992, Roxanne began developing a new line of pet products, starting with Burt's whole-grain dog biscuits. Needing space outside the Edes building to make them, she negotiated with Patti Dowse to rent part of the old Foley Boot Company factory in Cambridge, on Route 172, eight miles south of Parkman. Dowse used part of the single-story building for her handbag manufacturing operation, Erda Leathers.

Dowse agreed to rent 11,000 square feet to Roxanne for $450 a month, later recalling that Roxanne used a measuring tape to lay out the exact area she needed and not one square inch more. Dowse wasn't surprised; word had gotten around what a penny-pincher Roxanne was.

The dog biscuit baking process produced a great deal of smoke, which drifted into Dowse's part of the building, threatening to ruin the fabrics stored there. According to Dowse, when she asked Roxanne to turn on the building's exhaust fan (which was located in Roxanne's space), Roxanne refused because doing so would incur a higher electrical bill.

Dowse had given jobs to many poor women in the area and was sympathetic to Roxanne's struggles with an undercapitalized business. As she got to know her tenant better, she concluded that Roxanne suffered more than most entrepreneurs because she had "intense expectations" of her employees.

Burt's Bees had been a sole proprietorship for its first several years, with

Roxanne owning 100 percent of the company. In 1991, the business filed as
an S corporation, which enabled Roxanne to shield her personal assets from
potential lawsuits against the company.* With incorporation, Roxanne agreed
to give Burt a one-third share of the business. He wanted it, especially after
Roxanne had almost sold a share to Kauder. She considered her willingness
to share ownership with Burt as "fair … and somewhat generous on my part."

Driven by her sense that she was going to make it big, Roxanne pushed
her employees hard to get products out the door. Shirley Ellis went to work
for Burt's Bees in mid-September 1991, pouring honey. She started at $4.25
an hour and after a couple of months received a raise to $4.50 an hour; in
another couple of months, she received another raise to $4.75. "I proved I
could show up on time and could get along with people," she recalled. Her
jobs changed too, such as stringing rope through the Burt's Bees aprons and
putting together hand-molded fruit and vegetable candles in gift baskets for
L.L. Bean and Neiman Marcus. In February 1992 she was earning $5.00 an
hour, and her last raise, almost a year later, moved her to $5.50 an hour. She
also received paid holidays, sick days, and vacation.

Roxanne took care to show her appreciation to workers. When Burt's Bees'
sales hit $1 million in 1991 (a year in which full-year revenues reached $1.5
million, triple the previous year), she hosted her first Million Dollar Breakfast
at a local restaurant. She also treated employees to an annual Christmas party
with a turkey dinner and gifts, and she brought in ice cream on hot summer
days. She also arranged summer day care for a dozen or so children of her
employees, renting a school building for this purpose.

One reason for the continued growth of Burt's Bees was the company's
increasing participation in wholesale trade shows around the country; each
show reached many buyers. Roxanne's sister Renee, though not yet on the Burt's
Bees staff, covered some of the largest shows in cities such as New York and Los
Angeles and gave Roxanne feedback on how to run a better booth operation. In
a May 30, 1992, memo, Renee advised teaching employees how to read body
language, such as posture and eye contact, and how to better handle complaints
about Burt's Bees products. Buyers' most frequently asked questions concerned
credit terms, order minimums, discounts, and delivery time frames.

Roxanne offered retailers a 50 percent discount off recommended retail

*The profits and losses of an S Corp pass through to the income tax returns of the person or
persons who own the business.

prices, and she required advance payment by credit card on the first few orders from a new account, after which the terms were "net 30"—i.e., payment within thirty days of invoice. Those terms followed the industry norm. But she also charged for shipping, refused to fill orders for partial case quantities, and required stores to pay for product samples. Renee reported that buyers for big retail accounts objected to those conditions.

It was at this point that Sol Solomon became Burt's Bees' national sales manager. An industry veteran with a sales brokerage company in Bradford, New Hampshire, Solomon had founded Truly Natural Marketing in 1990 and had sales representatives pushing natural care products across the country. He had seen Burt's Bees products at gift stores and major trade shows and knew right away that the "ingredients, integrity, and unique packaging" had tremendous potential. Roxanne was one of the few vendors he ever pursued, and he worked with her for two years, establishing Burt's Bees in the natural care products sector, or "natural," as he called it. He viewed her as "a creative genius" despite her attire (which he described as "layers of wool") and her disheveled look (like someone who "came out of a cave"). At the time there was "nothing like her products" in the market, he said. "Roxanne had the three necessary criteria for success in natural: clean ingredients, attractive packaging, and reasonable price points." Plus there was "the cool name and image of Burt as a beekeeper ... and something that was just intangibly alluring about her products."

Solomon was convinced that a move into natural product outlets would lead Roxanne to mass market potential, but she would have to soften "her onerous terms of doing business to match what was customary in natural." He pitched a deal to Roxanne, and she agreed to hire him as her sales broker and to loosen or eliminate some of the rules that worked against sales, such as charging for testers and shipping. "[It] was a constant battle," he said.

Using his reps, Solomon quickly established Burt's Bees with natural and specialty food stores and national health food chains such as Whole Foods, Wild Oats, and Fresh Fields. Working with Roxanne "was like riding a rocket ship, the products were so insanely popular," he said. "On several occasions [she] called me to complain about how many orders we were sending in! I've never had a vendor express that sentiment since. She thought our success was going to threaten her business in other classes of trade, such as gift and department stores. I repeatedly told her the products should be sold everywhere." Solomon remembered Roxanne as "boisterous" and "a person of extreme contrasts," and she fired him after a couple of years. "There was no pleasing her," he recalled.

During that time, Joe Marks, sales manager for Baudelaire, Inc., an importer of high-quality soaps and body care products, was a "friendly competitor" of Burt's Bees. He liked Roxanne's Birkenstock sandals and crew socks and remembered that she was known as "the bag lady" and someone who "marched to her own drummer." Yet he had the same impression as others in the natural products business: Burt's Bees had something special. Roxanne was getting somewhere not just by accident, luck, or being in the right place at the right time, but by clever business decisions, he said. "She had sizzle."

Roxanne crowed in the media about the success of Burt's Bees and its future potential. "We're growing at the rate of computer chip companies," she told the *Bangor Daily News*, projecting growth to soar to $4.2 million in 1992, up from $1.5 million in 1991. By 1991, Burt's Bees was doing well enough that Roxanne could start paying bonuses, and her records show that in 1991 and 1992 she paid bonuses of $50 to $1,000 to various employees, the highest ones going to supervisors.

In 1992 a representative of the U.S. Department of Labor's Wage and Hour Division office in Portland arrived in Guilford to assess Burt's Bees' compliance with the federal Fair Labor Standards Act. The investigator—whom Roxanne thought "had a real chip on his shoulder" about Burt's Bees—spent a couple of weeks looking at employment and wage records and eventually alleged several wage irregularities and child labor violations between March 1990 and March 1992. Visiting the homes of the women who did home-based piecework for Burt's Bees, he asked if their kids ever helped. When several answered affirmatively, he concluded that the kids were working, which was contrary to the minimum age standards codified in law.

The case brought against Burt's Bees referred to a dozen boys and girls of ages four to fifteen, seven of whom were children of employees. One employee told the investigator that she had allowed her five-year-old to take tissues out of a box that held layers of honeycombs. She estimated that her child helped 15 minutes per week. Another mother had allowed her three kids, all under ten years old, to separate sheets of tissue paper from the rolled beeswax candle material.

Addressing each charge, Roxanne discussed the youngest children first. Removing sheets of tissue paper from wax could not possibly be considered real work, she argued. "It was just play, just like a young child helping make cookies, weed a garden, or wash the dishes," she insisted. "At most, it was a learning process." Roxanne maintained that Burt's Bees "had no knowledge or reason to believe the children were involved in working with the materials to roll candles." As for the kids who removed wax Christmas tree ornaments from molds after they cooled, she said Burt's Bees was not aware they were engaged in the process and, in any event, did not consider it work.

Roxanne acknowledged that one fifteen-year-old boy had helped with handcrafting gifts for two weeks, but that, she said, did not constitute working in "the manufacturing process" as the complaint charged. Such work "is not a valid violation of any labor law," she protested, nor was it a violation that the boy had climbed two feet up a stepladder to change a light bulb. The allegations, she said, were absurd. The three school days the boy had worked were exam days, not class days, and he had no exams scheduled on the days in question. Similar charges were filed with regard to Paul Daigle, and Roxanne's response was similar, as it was in the case of two teenagers who allegedly helped their mother on the production line.

An assistant district director of the Wage and Hour office notified Roxanne on March 30, 2002 that Burt's Bees owed wages totaling $1,372 to twelve employees, and a civil penalty would be assessed for the violations. Roxanne paid the back wages, but she was "very, very angry about it," and she was "furious" upon being notified in July of a $9,700 fine. "I could not believe this," she said. She contested the fine, and the matter was automatically referred to the chief administrative law judge.

Roxanne's response to the fine was a passionate denial of "all alleged allegations." She questioned the department's efforts to inform small businesses such as her own about regulations they were required to follow. In a letter of July 22, 1992, to the Wage and Hour Division administrator in Washington, she stated that Burt's Bees had "made every effort to comply" with all municipal, county, state, and federal laws. Small companies such as hers couldn't afford hundred-dollar-per-hour lawyers to ferret out regulations that were not made readily available to the business community by the agency assigned to enforce them. Her company relied "in good conscience" on the advice of local high school administrators and state labor department officials, she said. "We were led to believe that we were subject only to [state] regulations, and we followed these to the letter."

Other business owners "were shocked to learn that such regulations even exist," she claimed. One of her employees had tried to locate a copy of the law Burt's Bees had allegedly violated, and the only place it could be found was at a Depository of Federal Documents office. The regulations were so well concealed "and hidden in the shadow of state regulations" that they didn't exist "for practical purposes," she said. She suggested that inspectors were going after small businesses looking for "an easy kill."

She was souring on state regulators as well, having fended off several discrimination, worker compensation, and equal employment opportunity cases by 1993. The two discrimination cases filed with the Maine Human Rights Commission included a 1991 allegation of sex discrimination that was dismissed for lack of reasonable grounds, and a 1993 disability complaint that was thrown out for administrative reasons.*

Other allegations of discrimination went to the Equal Employment Opportunity Commission, including a woman who claimed that she'd been fired because she was pregnant. Roxanne, who attended all the hearings, believed the complainants were "playing the system" and using up a lot of her time and energy. All the cases were dismissed.

A New Catalog

Another expansion of company operations occurred about this time. Burt's Bees purchased a Victorian house on the hill across the Piscataquis River, primarily to handle the candle-making production. The Oak Street building, which cost $40,000, was in a residential neighborhood, but Guilford had no zoning ordinance to restrict commercial or manufacturing activities there. Interior walls were removed to create more open space for production, and some twenty people eventually worked there, increasing the total Burt's Bees workforce to about forty. Later the Oak Street facility was also used for silk screening tee-shirts and sewing Baby Bee clothes. The finished products were sent to the Edes building to be packaged, inventoried, and shipped.

At about 5:45 on the morning of June 3, 1992, the first employee to arrive at the Oak Street facility saw flames through a window. She made a hasty call to the fire station, which sent a couple of dozen firefighters to extinguish the blaze. The cause was found to be the spontaneous combustion of rags saturated with linseed oil and turpentine. Roxanne had told employees to put the rags in a covered container, not realizing the risk of fire. Thankfully the

*No documents on the matter are in commission files because of the age of the cases. However, then-director of the commission Pat Ryan, in an e-mail of February 23, 2011, confirmed that the cases had been filed and dismissed.

damage wasn't extensive.

To keep buyers abreast of Burt's Bees' expanding product line, a new promotional catalog was published in 1992. Based on the company's earth-friendly philosophy, it presented the two dozen products in a more aesthetic setting with better lighting, new props, and tasteful design accents. The 34-page catalog featured green oak and maple leaves on a heathery beige background with the Burt's Bees name in three-quarter-inch letters in the center of the cover. On the inside welcoming page, six rows of Burt's Bees products were framed by an arched wooden cupboard bracketed by Doric pillars, giving the products an upscale look.

Roxanne's warmly worded introduction reaffirmed the company's inspiration:

> "[B]y the generosity, economy and balance found in Mother Nature ... by yielding to Her guidance we can aspire to fulfill ourselves as positive, productive elements in Her overall plan. It is toward that end that we dedicate ourselves and our work. May She be complimented by our humble efforts."

Burt's Bees was now making more than 30 items in several sub-line brands. Featured at the front of the catalog were the fast-selling products in the Baby Bee sub-line—children's soap, powder and skin crème, unisize kimono-style baby shirt, stretch knit cap, and herb-filled baby pillow. These products were targeted at the growing number of parents who wanted healthier choices for their children.

Other sub-line brands included Burt's Desserts bird food (suet cakes, fruit/seed/suet muffins, and a seed/suet/peanut butter mix to spread into crevices of tree bark); Burt's Bones (dog biscuits of whole grains and vegetables); all-vegetable oat straw pet soap; and Burt's Furry Feline Nettles, Parsley Cookies, and wheat grass seeds. The Bay Rum sub-line, the first line for men, included a soap and a fragrance of herbs, spices, and essential oils in brown bottles that looked like beer bottles. Incidental Burt's Bees items included unbleached cotton tee-shirts, linen kitchen towels, and aprons with vegetable woodcut graphics. Non-toxic soy ink was used in the printmaking for the first time.

The original beeswax products—including fruit- and vegetable-shaped hand-painted candles, honeycomb candles, lip balm, moisturizing crème, hand salve, gardener's soap, fruited honey, and Maine honey—were artfully packaged and beautifully photographed. Roxanne wrote that the beeswax stick candles were "veritable trompe l'oeil works of art," reproducing the color and texture of real bark. Each scented square candle carried a hang tag describing the symbolism of its herb ingredient; lavender, for example, was a symbol of devotion.

Besides displaying an increasing number of products, the second catalog was notable for its first mention of "sustainability" and "organic." For example, it called attention to farmers who practiced "sustainable agriculture by growing organically grown cotton" for Baby Bee kimono shirts and caps.

Roxanne also used the 1992 catalog to establish the company's commitment to recycling and reuse. This was not just a trendy move on her part; it was a personal principle. She had "walked the walk" as a homesteader—reusing water and clothes, composting food, recycling bottles and cans—and now she intended to serve as an example for the skin-care products industry.

The bright-yellow lip balm tin with the white-winged bee stood out cheerfully, and Roxanne didn't tamper with that surging little product. She did, however, make both the lip balm and the moisturizing crème available, alternatively, in terra cotta pots made in Haiti, which could be sent back to Burt's Bees for refills. The moisturizing crème, soap, and royal jelly eye crème containers were shipped in recycled cardboard boxes that could be returned empty for refilling. Non-pesticide-treated garden seeds were packaged in recycled paper envelopes.

Enough consumers complained about the terra cotta pots to force Roxanne to discard that container and look for another way to reduce waste. She had long wanted to sell lip balm in a recycled plastic tube but hadn't been able to find a plastics manufacturer willing to retool for the job. She kept after the manufacturers, however, and finally she wore one of them down. The supplier (whose name she couldn't recall years later) agreed to produce a 25 percent post-consumer plastic tube, eventually increasing the percentage to 100.* It was another pioneering move for the skin-care products industry.

The end page of the catalog gave credit to Burt, Alan LaVallee, and Roxanne's staff for making Burt's Bees "possible." It also mentioned Roxanne's deceased mother, Rebecca Willens Quimby, calling her "an angel."

Months after the catalog was mailed, LaVallee was watching a national

---

*The manufacturer benefited beyond Burt's Bees business; it had the distinction of becoming the only U.S. manufacturer to make recycled consumer plastic at the time and attracted other sustainability-minded companies.

news story on boutiques selling environmentally friendly products. "The reporter was talking to a store owner on Rodeo Drive in Hollywood and showing a salesperson folding Burt's tee-shirts for a well-dressed customer," said LaVallee. "I almost dropped my drink when I saw those shirts printed with [Tony Kulik's] engravings [of fruits and vegetables]. She had made it that big."

Burt's Bees caught the attention of *Inc.* magazine as one of the up-and-coming "bootstrappers" who were short on capital but long on imagination to grow their enterprises. Roxanne told writer Robert Mamis that moving from retail to wholesale distribution in 1989 had opened the door to new markets. The article featured a photo of 42-year-old Roxanne in a strong pose exuding self-confidence.

Millionaire

By 1993, Burt's Bees was looking like a lot more than a flash in the pan. Sales had increased from $87,000 in 1987 to $138,000 in 1988, $180,000 in 1989, $500,000 in 1990, $1.5 million in 1991, and $2.5 million in 1992. Thanks to Roxanne's rigorous customer terms, only $2,500 of bad debt was written off in 1992, and Burt's Bees had $800,000 in the bank. On paper, at least, Roxanne was a millionaire. She had allowed herself a salary of $36,000 since the move to Guilford, but in 1993 she doubled it, paying Bert and herself $72,000 each. No matter how many millions of dollars Burt's Bees might earn in the coming years, letting go of hard-earned cash, even to pay herself, wasn't easy for Roxanne, and it would be years before she could bring herself to indulge in such luxuries as high-priced homes and expensive spas.

Burt's Bees' list of accounts was impressive by 1993. Wholesale buyers numbered 4,000, including stores that were "the very pinnacles of good taste and selectivity: Henri Bendel's (Fifth Avenue, Manhattan), Zona (Soho District, Manhattan), and Neiman Marcus (Dallas)," wrote Roxanne in a letter to the American Craft Council. Among other customers were L.L. Bean, Bergdorf Goodman, Smith and Hawken, Gardener's Eden, Dean & DeLuca, The North Face, and Harrods, the famous luxury department store in Knightsbridge, London.

L.L. Bean, the big Maine outdoor retailer, had agreed in 1992 to carry Burt's Bees Lip Balm and Farmer's Friend hand salve at its main retail store in Freeport as well as in its mail-order catalog. First, though, Roxanne was required to take a tour of L.L. Bean's shipping facility so she could understand the company's strict packaging requirements. Shipping was automated, so L.L.

Bean required product boxes to be between 15 and 17 inches wide, and nonconforming or badly damaged boxes ended up in the "misfit" section, which delayed delivery to the customer.

Roxanne liked doing business with L.L. Bean because the company paid its bills on time and adhered to fair trade practices. Nordstrom and Macy's, on the other hand, were irritants because, as she remembered, "they would abuse [small] companies like Burt's." In the end, L.L. Bean removed the Burt's Bees products from its catalog (because the margin on the low-cost items wasn't high enough to pay for catalog space and shipping costs) but continued to sell the products in its stores.

Burt's Bees' first employee manual was a long time coming. The five-page document, written by Roxanne around 1992, emphasized in bold capital letters that safety was "of the utmost importance." Employees were required to receive fire-safety training and to report hazards to their supervisor "immediately without exceptions." The manual called attention to the dangers of working with hot beeswax, hot plates, and open flames. Given such hazards and to comply with state food and cosmetic workplace regulations, employees were forbidden to wear loose clothing, and those with long hair had to tie it back or gather it under a hat so it wouldn't accidentally get burned or caught in a blender.

Employees were told to enter through the rear door of the Edes building. Burt's Bees ran two shifts of eight hours each by this time, and each worker signed a time card when her shift started—and no earlier. An unpaid half-hour lunch or dinner break and two paid 10-minute breaks were allowed.

No personal telephone calls were allowed, and no alcohol could be consumed on the premises. New hires began on a five-week probationary period during which they received no benefits. After that, the benefits package for eligible employees included paid holidays, paid vacation, and paid sick days and personal days.* Job absences were allowed for sickness, injury, or family emergencies, but "[e]xcessive absenteeism will be dealt with strongly," the manual warned. All workers had to sign a confidentiality agreement to protect Burt's Bees formulations and designs.

---

*There were eight paid holidays for eligible employees (those who had worked at least three months). Employees who worked 20 or fewer hours received no benefits, but part-time benefits—including a half-day's pay for an official holiday—were available to those who worked 20 to 35 hours. Workers who were on the job 35 hours or more per week received full-time benefits. Two sick days and one personal day were available for anyone who had worked at least three months; those numbers increased to five sick days and two personal days at six months of service. Vacation time increased from one week after one year of service to two weeks after two years and three weeks after five years.

Despite the rules and Roxanne's expectations, there was fun to be had across the street at the Red Maple, a local hangout. One evening a group of night-shift employees left the job for a drink there with Burt, then returned to work. The next morning Roxanne fired them all. "I had no tolerance for drinking, stealing, and lying," she said.

One of the most important changes in staffing at Burt's Bees in 1993 was the hiring of Renee Quimby, Roxanne's sister, as the company's sales and marketing director. Renee had years of experience in sales, marketing, and finance. A graduate of Syracuse University, she had earned a master's degree in business from the University of South Florida. Renee had worked for American Express from 1982 to 1987 and then shifted to INVEST Financial Corporation, a subsidiary of Kemper Financial Services.

Renee went on the payroll on April 15, 1993. A formal letter from Roxanne a couple of weeks earlier welcomed her to the company at an annual salary of $55,000 plus $5,000 for benefits until the company could offer a formal benefits plan. Renee could also earn an annual performance bonus of up to $10,000.

Roxanne trusted Renee more than anyone else and was confident that her sister could handle big assignments. Renee was a skilled trainer and patient with people. Part of her job was to train sales representatives to market Burt's Bees products more effectively. Her addition to the Burt's Bees leadership team was game-changing.

Another strategic move was registering company trademarks. Roxanne had never found time to do it and possibly, in the early years of the company, did not even know it was necessary.* In an April 1993 letter to Burt, an attorney with Bangor-based law firm Eaton Peabody assured him that "the registration process should proceed smoothly." Applications were sent to Washington to register the mark BURT'S in four classes of goods: skin cream, face soap, and lip balm; candles; tea towels; and one that encompassed vegetable seeds, bird food, and dog biscuits. Since the cosmetics line was being expanded, the attorney suggested obtaining additional trademarks, noting that another company, Beach Bum Bert's, already had trademark approval for suntan skin preparations.

---

*The benefits of registration included the right to recover profits, damages, and costs in a trademark infringement action in federal court (and the possibility of treble damages and attorney's fees); a limitation on the grounds for attacking a registration that was five years old; and the right to deposit the registration with customs officials in order to stop the importation of goods bearing an infringing mark.

The Move to North Carolina

Burt's Bees was moving rapidly beyond the toddler stage, and Roxanne knew she couldn't manage her growing child without more professional help. Moving out of rural Guilford in order to attract top-quality managers seemed likely, although she didn't want to relocate her entire life. The closest metropolitan area was Bangor, Maine's third largest city, 50 miles east.

Burt called the Maine Department of Economic and Community Development office in Bangor to inquire about small business assistance programs but was told the official who could help him was on vacation. Time dragged by without a return call, and Roxanne soon grew impatient. "No one seemed to care that we employed about 50 people in a town that didn't have two nickels to rub together," she said. It reinforced her opinion that Maine was inhospitable to business, especially to small companies like Burt's Bees.

She still resented having had to defend her company from state regulators repeatedly over the previous two or three years. Particularly galling was a worker's compensation case in which the employee claiming an on-the-job injury had already received settlements from two previous employers for the same injury and was known to have been physically active while supposedly incapacitated by the injury at Burt's Bees. Roxanne was outraged by the "low standard of review" applied to the case by the Maine Workers' Compensation Board. Suspecting that the plaintiff would soon be driving around town in a new vehicle bought with the settlement, she was disgusted but not surprised to witness that very thing a few months later. The outcome, she felt, sent a message to the community that "you could make a good living beating the system and abusing employers."

Roxanne viewed Maine as shortsighted. Burt's Bees was a small "green" business on the rise, and it seemed ironic that such a good place to live and start a small business could be such an awful place in which to grow one.

Aware that Roxanne was contemplating a move, Guilford town manager Bob Littlefield tried to keep Burt's Bees in town by promising her larger quarters at the old middle school near the Edes building. But the new school was still on the drawing board, and the old one might not have been able to meet Burt's Bees manufacturing needs even with a costly refit.

Distance to markets, poor roads, and Maine's harsh winters also conspired against Burt's Bees staying in the state. In a *Maine Times* article, Burt speculated that Burt's Bees could become "a world class business" in a state that treated them right. "Any problem we had was like rocket science in central Maine," he said. "To get the tools and employees we needed, we had to go somewhere people understand production and government understands business."

After doing some research, Burt was keen on North Carolina as Burt's Bees' next home. The Research Triangle Park in Raleigh-Durham was one of the most successful business parks in the world and a sprawling center of innovation. The Tar Heel State offered lower corporate taxes and transportation costs; easier access to markets; plenty of non-union workers; and highly educated and skilled managers. The economic development team at North Carolina's well-oiled Department of Commerce, headquartered in the capital city of Raleigh, laid out a red carpet for potential new businesses, providing research and guided site visits.

The department's Business-Industry Division also had business expert Bill Teague, a sharp, likable, persevering booster with 25 years at the agency under his belt. Teague didn't care if a business employed five or 500 workers. "We were happy to have them all," he said.

As it happened, Burt's initial call to the Department of Commerce was put through to Teague. Burt described Burt's Bees as "a small cottage industry," according to Teague, "and he told a fascinating story of his and Roxanne's backgrounds." Teague could tell immediately that he was dealing with unusual folks.

Teague invited Burt and Roxanne to visit, and he met them at the airport. Years later he remembered Roxanne getting off the plane in a long coat with a beret over her page-boy haircut. While Burt did most of the talking, Teague knew within a half hour that "Roxanne ran the show. The brains of the business? It was Roxanne."

Teague was most impressed that Burt's Bees was debt-free. "Roxanne was tough," he said. "She was doing business like you were supposed to—doing it right." He hosted Roxanne and Burt for several days, driving them around the Raleigh area and looking at more than a half-dozen facilities in fourteen communities within a 50-mile radius. Burt's attention was diverted by rundown train stations that he expressed interest in seeing restored.

Teague laid out the case for North Carolina. If Burt's Bees relocated to the Tar Heel State, its workers' compensation costs would be cut in half and its unemployment costs would be lower. (North Carolina gave companies 100 days to decide whether to rehire a laid-off employee before penalizing a firm's unemployment rate, whereas Maine allowed only 25 days.) The state would also pay Burt's Bees for six weeks of employment training for workers hired off the unemployment or welfare rolls. And the company would be closer to raw materials such as beeswax, which was being shipped from Florida.

Roxanne liked North Carolina's "aggressive" business incentives and the fact that Bill Teague treated her and Burt as if they were special. "You were a rock star ... a hero ... if you brought your business to North Carolina, and they were happy to support you in whatever way they could," she said.

A Maine Department of Economic and Community Development business specialist did respond to Roxanne and Burt after a few weeks and visited them in Guilford to talk about keeping Burt's Bees in the state. Afterward, Roxanne met in Augusta with MDECD commissioner Michael Aube, who remembered that she was interested in state financing for a new building. He told her there were no grant programs for that purpose, only loan programs, and Roxanne didn't want to borrow money.

He believed that Roxanne had more or less made a decision to go to North Carolina by the time they talked. "Give me a reason not to go," he recalled her saying. North Carolina's incentives and tax policies were "hard to overcome," Aube said. "What Maine was fighting against with Roxanne was practical financial considerations and Roxanne's desire for a quicker return on her investment."

After the meeting with Aube, Roxanne delivered the good news to Bill Teague that Burt's Bees was heading to North Carolina. To cement the deal, he sent her a fat package of materials with tax and other business information by overnight express, making Roxanne feel welcomed with an exclamation point.

Roxanne didn't wait for the physical move to begin hiring new staff. Her first priorities were a plant manager and a graphic designer. She advertised both positions in the Raleigh *News & Observer* using a blind ad that didn't mention Burt's Bees by name, then started interviewing in August 1993 at Crabtree Valley Mall in Raleigh.

Andy Bougay, a former plant manager for Revlon, was employed to oversee Burt's Bees operations in its new location, and Mark Smith, fresh out of Pennsylvania State University's graduate school, snared the graphic designer position. While at Penn State he had worked as a freelance designer for Central Pennsylvania Festival of the Arts, one of the largest such events on the East Coast. Living in Raleigh, he was looking for a chance to break into the business world when he saw the ad seeking someone who could create product packaging and design catalogs and brochures. When Roxanne informed him during their first phone conversation that the job would be with Burt's Bees, he had never heard of the company.

At his later interview, Smith could see that Roxanne and Burt were rare birds. Roxanne's hair was disheveled, and she wore her everyday hippie dress and Birkenstocks. Burt was in jeans with suspenders, twirled his beard, and hardly spoke a word. When Roxanne showed Smith the range of Burt's Bees products, he found them appealing and wanted to be part of the venture. "Roxanne came across as very creative and the driving force of the business," he noted.

Andy Bougay's first task was to choose the most appropriate site for Burt's Bees. He recommended a 32,000-square-foot facility in Creedmoor, 25 miles north of Raleigh on the northern fringe of the Research Triangle, and Roxanne agreed. Creedmoor was close by interstate highways 85 and 40 and tapped an ample supply of local low-wage labor. The lease was $2 per square foot, just $64,000 per year. And it was rural enough to suit Burt, who didn't want to feel closed in by a city environment.

The empty metal building at 308 Hillsboro Street in Creedmoor was roughly five times the size of the Edes building in Maine, and to Roxanne's relief, it had a loading dock. The structure had last been used as a textile cutting and sewing operation for Carolina Sportswear, a maker of golf shirts and tee-shirts. The owners, three local women, offered Burt's Bees a reasonably priced two-year lease.

Creedmoor, with a population of 1,583, was nothing to write home about. It was "just another down-and-out town like Guilford," Roxanne remembered. Built on tobacco and cotton, it boasted a couple of eateries, including a diner with sassy waitresses, as well as a branch bank and a gas station. The only other manufacturing operation in town was a Kayser-Roth plant that made No Nonsense hosiery.

A few months after Roxanne and Burt's first trip to North Carolina, Renee Quimby accompanied them on a second visit. Teague was impressed with Renee's marketing skills and could tell she was a key player in the Burt's Bees enterprise.

Roxanne wanted to look at retail spaces for a possible Burt's Bees outlet, and Teague showed the trio a variety of locations from shopping centers to stand-alone buildings. Roxanne was most interested in the Carr

Mill Mall in nearby Carrboro, a small liberal city next door to Chapel Hill and the University of North Carolina. Progressive college towns could be counted on for populations of eco-conscious students interested in natural products.

Roxanne and Burt signed the lease for the Creedmoor building on December 13, 1993. The event was a swan song of sorts for Teague, who retired shortly afterward. He was so enthralled with the prospects of the little company that he told colleagues he wanted to be remembered most for luring Burt's Bees to North Carolina.

After Roxanne contacted the MDECD with the news that Burt's Bees was leaving Guilford, Governor John McKernan called the office to see if he could dissuade her. But neither Roxanne nor Burt was in the office at the time, and when Burt returned the call, McKernan wasn't available.

In the Press and On the Move

As she was pulling up stakes, Roxanne learned that *Forbes* magazine wanted to interview Burt and her for a feature, the third national story about Burt's Bees. Titled "Dear Dad," the two-page article by Dana Wechsler Linden was published on December 6, 1993, and constituted the most complete accounting to date of Burt's Bees' improbable origins. In it, Linden surmised that John Quimby had "forced [Roxanne] to worry about money at an early age, then disowned her."

Roxanne related how she wound up in the Maine woods washing diapers on a woodstove and launched a tiny business producing honey and beeswax products. She also talked energetically about her goal of growing Burt's Bees sales to $6 million within two years after operations restarted in North Carolina. The accompanying photos included a smiling Roxanne and an almost grinning Burt in their usual outfits of beret, cap, jacket, vest, and jeans; a smiling Renee in a sweatshirt, carrying an armload of Baby Bee powder boxes; and a table display of Burt's Bees products.

After the *Forbes* article ran, the *National Enquirer* contacted photographer Richard Schultz with a request to purchase the unpublished photos taken at Burt's Bees, and *Forbes* agreed. But when Roxanne got wind of it, she directed her attorney Gordon Scott to let *Forbes* executive editor William Baldwin know that she would sue the magazine if the photos appeared in any other publication. The photos never appeared in the *Enquirer*.

The *Forbes* article was a "wow" moment for 15-year-old Hannah Quimby, a sophomore at Gould Academy. It was black-and-white proof of the increasing national recognition her mother's company was receiving.

The same week the article was published, new graphic designer Mark Smith flew to Maine to see the Guilford operation before the move. Remembering that visit later, he described himself as young and "very impressionable and wide open—liberal." If he had been more "corporate," he might have been shocked at the state of affairs at Burt's Bees.

The Edes building was "cool," he reflected, its every nook and cranny stuffed with goods. Roxanne's second-floor office was extremely disorganized, with papers piled upon papers. "She had to fish around for one thing or another," he said. At the Oak Street facility, there was enough beeswax on the floor to cause Smith to think "the place was ready to go up in flames."

In fact, Burt's Bees operations at Oak Street had caught the attention of an Occupational Safety and Health Administration (OSHA) inspector worker not long before Smith arrived on the scene. The inspector looked around and rubbed his forehead as if he felt a bad headache coming on, Roxanne remembered. Before he could say anything, she asked, "'Would it help to tell you we'll be out of here in three months?' He said, 'If you can promise me you'll move, I won't write you up. But you do need to take the extension cords from under the carpet. Better people trip than start a fire.'"

Mark Smith concluded that Roxanne ran a lean company and that employment was not about a job title but about "filling a need." Despite his title as graphic designer, he was immediately given a spot on the production line to learn how to make the fruit- and vegetable-shaped molded beeswax candles so he could train new employees to do that job in North Carolina. Roxanne also assigned Smith to work at the Cambridge factory making dog biscuits, where he discovered what a sticky, messy job it was.

The Maine accents of some night-shift workers were so thick that Smith had a hard time understanding what was being said, and his eyebrows were raised by the conversations about prison terms served by some workers. "I was [in Guilford] to soak up everything, to get the flavor of Burt's Bees," Smith mused. Doing tasks that had nothing to do with his art skills would be the norm for him for a long time. His initiation was likely a test, he said. "You had to be very flexible to work for Roxanne."

Smith would be the only long-term employee of Burt's Bees who worked at the Maine factory buildings, stayed at Roxanne and Burt's Parkman property, and remained on the company's payroll as long as Roxanne owned the company. Colleagues came to consider him the company historian.

During Smith's visit to Parkman in late 1993, he slept at Burt's house—the one built with the state's eminent domain money. He loved the country, especially the pitch-dark of the night sky, the brightness of the stars, and the clarity of the Milky Way. When invited into Roxanne's cabin, Smith assumed from its modest exterior appearance that the interior would be spartan. Instead, like photographer Allan LaVallee in 1992, he was struck by the home's artful decor. "It had tons of character," Smith said. "Her creativity was on display."

Before the company's move, *Lear's*, a women's magazine, sent a reporter to Maine to see what the news media attraction to Burt's Bees was all about.* The writer, Martha Thomas, noted Roxanne's purple batik dress and lavender Birkenstocks. The photograph showed a slim, long-haired Roxanne outdoors in a field, holding a Burt's Bees sign.

The article traced the history of the business, focusing on the things that made it fun, funky, and unusual. Thomas concluded that Burt's Bees was successfully marketing "a kind of rural fantasy." While there was a variety of products, Thomas noticed a "theme" to it all. "There's a sort of benevolence to the products, a friendliness," Roxanne was quoted as saying.

Thomas closed by mentioning the pending relocation to North Carolina, and she was the first to write that Roxanne was thinking of selling the business at some point. Roxanne theorized that Burt's Bees would have to gross about $25 million before it became an attractive target for acquisition. "We're clean, honest, and straightforward," Roxanne said. "We have a good reputation, and we'd make [a new owner] look good."

When Roxanne informed her Maine employees that Burt's Bees was moving, she offered a bonus to those who stayed to help with packing up. Seven of her top workers were offered employment in North Carolina. None chose to leave Maine permanently, but four of them went with her for a short time to help her over the relocation hump.

Roxanne described the move as badly planned and poorly organized. New company manager Andy Bougay hired nine trucks to make the thousand-mile drive from Guilford to Creedmoor. As the trucks backed up to the doors of the Edes building, Burt's Bees employees "threw everything in there," Roxanne said. "They thought we would just sort everything out in North Carolina."

Lear's would cease publication in early 1994.

The Southern drivers, unaccustomed to cold winter temperatures, made the mistake of setting their vehicles' emergency brakes; the brakes froze, and the drivers' complaints added to the stress of the day, a stress that was only slightly relieved by townspeople stopping by to offer good wishes.

Leaving Guilford was physically exhausting, but she assumed she would "go to North Carolina and find another group of really dedicated, motivated women who are going to make candles again and do exactly the same thing but not have the Department of Labor as an enemy. [North Carolina was] going to be our friend, and we were not going to have a Worker's Comp Board that punishes you for success. We were not going to be paying eight percent to an unemployment board because [so many are] unemployed. So I was just really going down there to do the exact same thing [as in Maine] but not be paying the state through the nose every time I turned around. It never occurred to me we'd automate."

But the relocation would be a reckoning. She would be on a new playing field in North Carolina, and if Burt's Bees sank, the bottom would feel a lot deeper than in a remote country town in Maine. 🐝

Pulpwood piled next to the Penobscot River at Great Northern's East Millinocket mill in the 1960s.

Goodbye Maine, Hello North Carolina: 1994

Roxanne was too traumatized by the relocation to retain any memory of driving to North Carolina in her white Honda sedan. The ensuing days and weeks were a blur. The little star-lit company found itself in a desperate fight for its life.

Burt's Bees was producing 75 items when it left Maine, but until operations could be reestablished, there would be no manufacturing and no income. The financial clock started ticking on the last day of production in Guilford.

Chaos greeted Roxanne in Creedmoor. The truckers had dumped all the company's boxes and equipment in one big pile in the middle of the cavernous building. Upon opening the front door to begin Burt's Bees' new chapter, she collapsed weeping on the floor amid the jumbled boxes of lip balm, candles, catnip, and hand crèmes. Sapped of energy and afraid that leaving Maine might have been a huge mistake, she saw "not a ray of sunshine."

In those first weeks, other aspects of North Carolina loomed large. "It was overwhelming on a sensory level to have so much stimulation of commerce and society, people, cars, stores," she remembered. She recoiled from the strip malls and subdivisions, litter, billboards, and confusing highways. "All that red clay made the earth look like it had gashes all over it," she said. "One day you'd drive by these beautiful trees and two days later, the trees would be in a burning pile and the land torn open. The red [clay] made it seem the land was bleeding."

She yearned for Maine's wild beauty, clean air, verdant woods, and the small cabin where she could be alone, quiet, and feel her "free spirit." Maine was the only place that had ever felt like home, and the pain of missing it was so real that she began planning to take the company back there. But the return-to-Maine fantasy was short-lived, because retreating was ultimately more terrifying than staying. She reconciled herself to the fact that her company was acutely in need of the resources available in North Carolina. Staying was the only way to uncork the sales growth she believed was possible.

Although the business would stay put, Roxanne came up with an "out" for herself. She would commute between Maine and North Carolina, spending Tuesday to Friday in Creedmoor and long weekends in Maine. When she was in Maine, she would communicate with her staff using the phone, fax, e-mail, and FedEx. Such a plan was the only way she felt she could survive. Temporarily, she rented a hotel room at Springhill Suites near Raleigh's Crabtree Valley Mall, about 20 minutes from Creedmoor.

The Burt's Bees facility—a big, nondescript box with a flat metal roof—was identified only by a small sign over the front door. The small lot on which it stood was bordered by woods on one side and a down-and-out, bullet-ridden trailer park (where it was rumored drugs were sold) on another. Occasionally a pack of wild dogs gathered on a barren knoll overlooking the building or prowled the perimeter, sniffing for food. At other times, vagrants loitered outside.

Roxanne found the location unattractive but not troublesome; she had lived in similar rural settings in Maine. More to the point, it was an affordable place to reboot Burt's Bees. She figured she wouldn't keep the business in Creedmoor long. Four tasks topped her to-do list: hiring a workforce; getting enough materials and ingredients on the premises to create products; making sure the right equipment and machinery were on hand; and choosing and retaining the least expensive transportation carrier.

Before leaving Guilford, Roxanne had increased the production of selected products in order to build inventory reserves for the operational downtime in North Carolina. Unfortunately, she had miscalculated which products buyers would want. Orders poured in at Creedmoor for products that were in short supply or unavailable. With a substantial order backlog building up, Roxanne was rattled by more than her concern for lost or delayed income. Burt's Bees' reputation and survival were at risk.

"We just went into this paralysis for weeks and weeks," Roxanne recalled. Nor had she foreseen the problems they encountered setting up a new computer system. Burt's Bees' accounting software in Maine had been basic. Newer, faster technology and programs were needed in Creedmoor, but operational glitches plagued the upgraded system.

Roxanne found herself under assault on multiple fronts. Retailers were angry because product shipments were late. Sales representatives were upset when their commission checks fell six weeks behind due to computer glitches, and without new products to sell, they couldn't line up sales calls. And there were mold problems in the creams. "When I hit that hot climate, I realized all the things I used for preservatives [in Maine] would not work in [North Carolina]," Roxanne remembered.

Insomnia and anxiety dogged her. She thought Burt's Bees was beginning to implode. "I was so afraid I had blown it," she said years later. "I remember thinking, 'Oh, my God. This is as close to failure as I can possibly get without tanking this whole company.'"

Even the four supervisors from Maine feared that the company would not survive. "They said to me, 'God, what have you done, Roxanne?'" she recollected. To help her through the worst times, she relied on meditation, a practice she had taken up years earlier. Before beginning her workday, she closed the curtains in her hotel room and sat silently in the darkness for twenty minutes. Quieting her mind helped balance her emotions and cement her resolve to persevere.

She felt she was engaged in an evolutionary process, personally and professionally. "I never really knew where I was going with the business in those days," she said. "I would go one way and bump into an obstacle and then try another way. It was a pretty primitive way of doing things, fixing one bottleneck after another." She was afraid that she had lost her literal sense of direction too. She regularly got lost while driving to and from work, adding to her sense of being out of place. Another manifestation of emotional stress was losing her car and room keys. She had never needed keys in Maine, as she had never locked the door to her cabin or her vehicle. In North Carolina, "I had to lock the doors to the building, the car, and really pay attention to keys for the first time in my life," she said.

She knew her lapses reflected an awareness that she was in a much more dangerous world. In the Maine woods, the biggest threats were wet or green firewood or finding the spring frozen. Life was more complex in Creedmoor.

"I had stepped out of the protected, safe world of Maine and into this scary mainstream world where people stole, and you had to lock things up or you would lose them," she recollected.

Despite her anxieties—and because of her insomnia—she worked at the Burt's Bees plant at all hours of the night, mostly alone, and she liked it that way. Burt's Bees was all hers in those hours, and she enjoyed wandering about, taking it all in. "I'd open up boxes at midnight and blindly, randomly check for quality," she recalled. "I knew how everything should look and checked smell and consistency and to see if the labels were on correctly. Those were my babies. I knew exactly what I wanted."

In the factory section, she looked under the carpets for safety hazards. In the warehouse area, she gazed at and considered all her products lining the tall shelving racks, amused that she couldn't "pick" them to fill orders because she didn't know how to use a forklift. This was a long way from Parkman and Guilford, where ingredients, products, and packaging materials had been easy to reach.

If she got hungry at night, she searched employees' desk drawers for a candy bar or other goodies. Once she found a porn magazine.

A Left-Brain Organization

In Maine, Roxanne had run Burt's Bees as a "right brain" organization, with decisions driven by her intuition and creativity. Now she had to shift to a "left brain," logical approach, and for that she would need help. She would have to hire well-trained professionals with skills beyond her expertise, and she would have to grant them some decision-making authority.

Roxanne wasn't keen on letting other chefs into the kitchen, but she couldn't run a big, modern factory by herself. "I didn't have all the answers anymore, so I needed people who were tops in their fields," she said. "There were so many questions: Can we make this product? How many per day? Can we sell it? Can we package it? Can our customers pronounce the name of the ingredients? What kind of shelf life does it have?"

She concluded that Andy Bougay's skill set was better suited to a stable corporate environment than to the unpredictable challenges of a fast-growing entrepreneurial business, and she let him go immediately after the move. By March 1994, Frank Baldwin was the new plant manager.

Baldwin, an industrial engineer, had fifteen years of corporate experience at Mobil Chemical and Baxter Pharmaceuticals and had been a member of the top management team at Baxter, running a $40 million manufacturing division with 400 employees. By 1994 he was ready for a novel job experience and, like many others, could see the company's exciting potential. "There was something there," he recalled. Roxanne viewed him as having a "fabulous attitude ... willing to be a small company guy and do whatever it took."

Like Mark Smith, Baldwin could see immediately that Roxanne and Burt were unconventional—"eccentric and quirky"—and surmised that his new job might be an electric ride. Walking into the Creedmoor building for the first time, he was surprised that "everything was [still] in a gigantic, disorganized pile ... including wheat germ seeds for cat grass, kitty crackers, dog biscuits, fruit cakes, tee-shirts, and candles. It was really crazy. I didn't realize things were so bad." Some workstation tables were set up but not in use. The shipping area wasn't yet ready to go. There were no shelves or conveyor system for materials and products. Supplies and inventory were in disarray. The printing equipment wasn't working. The oven for baking dog biscuits was inoperable. When the boiler and air exchangers started up, dust spewed out and lint wafted down to the floor.

Roxanne gave Baldwin tough marching orders: stabilize Burt's Bees and start generating income within three months or resign. The company was losing $100,000 a month and had $500,000 in back orders. Baldwin told his wife, "'I left a $100,000 job [at Baxter] for this? How could I be so stupid?'"

He first revived shipping so that the finished goods on hand could be wrapped, weighed, and sent on their way. Then he organized the raw materials, established production lines, and had the bakery oven repaired. Within several weeks, he started to relax a little. The new computer system was running well, and the sales reports were positive. Roxanne also breathed a sigh of relief. The reports provided tangible evidence that the company was getting back on its feet.

Roxanne had hired every employee herself in Maine, but in North Carolina her new entry-level workers were sent by the state development office, with their first six weeks of work to be paid by the state. About forty people who had been on welfare or unemployment became the first Tar Heel cadre to make candles and other Burt's Bees products. Frank Baldwin viewed some of them as "clearly dysfunctional," and Roxanne agreed. "They didn't know a thing—how to make anything or ship anything," she said. "I'd tell them, 'You've got to do this,' and they'd say, 'Oh no, we can't do it that way.'"

The Maine supervisors did most of production-line training, but Mark Smith was also dragged in to show new employees the painstaking process of making molded fruit and vegetable candles and baking dog biscuits. After just a few months, the Maine supervisors returned home to their families. When the women left, Roxanne was truly alone and totally responsible. "The way we did things was completely lodged in the minds of just a few people—me, [the Maine supervisor] Wendy Rolfe, and her team," she recounted. "We didn't have an SOP [Standard Operating Procedures] manual." The knowledge of how to concoct Burt's Bees products had been passed from one woman to another through demonstration. Now Roxanne faced the prospect of devoting a good portion of her workdays to teaching new entry-level employees the ropes—a tedious job that she tired of quickly.

It was only now that Roxanne appreciated the capabilities of her Guilford workers. "I could not believe the difference in what I'd left in Maine," she said. It would take five years of culling her workforce time after time to reach the "same level of contribution as the people of Piscataquis County [Maine]." While her Guilford women had started at the minimum hourly wage—which had risen from $3.75 in 1989 to $4.25 when Burt's Bees left Maine—her production workers in North Carolina cost twice as much. Amazingly, neither she nor the state development officials had factored in the higher cost of labor when considering the benefits of the relocation package. It took Roxanne awhile to realize that Burt's Bees was now competing for workers in the Research Triangle area, and she would have to take more interest in competitive wage and benefit packages to keep her workers from going next door to Nortel, the big telephone corporation, or other large companies nearby.

While Roxanne was coping with an overly full plate, Burt spent his days puttering around, with limited involvement in the business. He was most valuable to Roxanne for emotional support when she was exhausted, depressed, or at her wit's end. She recalled one time when she was weeping and almost ready to give up and he told her in a firm voice, "Get a handle on it!"

With Roxanne's emotions on a razor's edge, her patience with workers was thin. As in Maine, she fired many newcomers within days of their hiring. "If you didn't cut it, you were gone," said Mark Smith. When Frank Baldwin arrived, he could see that people were "pissed off" at Roxanne's "very direct" management style and at Burt, too, for being "just in the way … a total eccentric." Baldwin did his best to separate the workers from the owners.

Initially there was no health insurance for entry-level employees, and

Roxanne pushed child care as a better option. When plans for an on-site child center were thwarted by regulations, she grudgingly instituted modest health coverage, though not for herself.

Like Mark Smith, Frank Baldwin found that many of the jobs and issues assigned to him were outside his job description. "You name it, I did it, from A to Z," Baldwin said. Surprise tasks were stimulating, but they came with headaches too. He expected to develop management-practice guidelines, write a new employee manual, and deal with hiring and unemployment hearings. What he didn't count on were things like managing Burt and shopping for product ingredients at the local grocery store.

Baldwin laughed at the memory of buying flour at a local Piggly Wiggly store for making kitty crackers. "I had gone from the corporate world—with a very professional approach to operations and sales, and where I wore starched shirts and ties—to dressing in cut-off shorts and boots. You just shook your head and went on." Baldwin weathered the situation because he believed he was helping Burt's Bees "go to the moon," he said. "I about worked myself to death."

Two other top jobs to fill were engineer and cosmetics chemist. Roxanne gave Baldwin the authority to hire for these positions, and his choices were excellent. The two new employees were perfect for the times and stayed with the company almost until Roxanne's ownership ended.

Roxanne was especially pleased with Bob Kingery, an energetic young mechanical engineer from North Carolina State University who was hired in June 1994. Before knowing Kingery, Roxanne believed that engineers were "deadly dull and boring." She was delighted to find that Kingery was an unstoppable force of energy, invention, optimism, and humor. He and his wife, Maria, were former members of the same church as Roxanne—the temple of hippies. They had followed their favorite rock stars around the country in a VW van, selling jewelry to make ends meet.

Like others before him, Kingery was smitten with the growth potential he saw at Burt's Bees. He anticipated there would be "plenty of challenges" and figured it could be a roller-coaster experience. He loved that Roxanne was "so mission-driven to succeed [and] do it the right way."

With almost no funding, Kingery set about to automate production of lip balm, moisturizing crèmes, and other products that didn't require hand-crafting. He was brilliant at inventing processes and machine parts to produce and assemble products. The pressure was always to speed up production, especially of the best-selling items, and to get the kinks out of the jerry-rigged, low-cost systems that were part and parcel of the Burt's Bees operation during the early years in North Carolina.

Lip balm, for example, was still being heated in a teapot on a hotplate and poured by hand into the tiny tin containers. It was quaint but time-consuming and highly inefficient. Kingery rigged up a used peristaltic pump, putting one end of its tube in the lip balm fluid and using the other end as a spout. He also devised a rotary wheel that crimped the tube when the tin was filled, and he rigged a buzzer to alert the operator. According to Kingery, the process increased capacity at least sixfold and cured the problem of liquid overflow and the ensuing wax-and-oil mess. It also reassured line workers that they had poured into each container the exact 0.15 ounce promised on the label.

Kingery invented dozens of other cost-saving production methods. After observing a worker placing tins on the table by hand, he came up with a mechanical way to drop tins into a hopper and align them with a burst of air. He figured out how to automate screwing the caps on products with just the right torque so that consumers wouldn't have a hard time loosening them. Innovation was also needed for labels. Hand gluing sometimes resulted in labels that were skewed or had air pockets under them. Kingery came up with a mechanical solution to stick the label on straight. "It was like a modern miracle ... magic ... that he could invent these things that made the manufacturing process go so much better," said Roxanne. "He took great pride in his work, and when a new invention worked, he would come to me and say, 'you gotta see this.'"

But with only one engineer on board and capital in short supply, Burt's Bees continued to rely on many labor-intensive, costly production methods. Employees used watering cans to fill tins of hand salve. They made crèmes in one-gallon blenders, transferred the mixtures to pastry bags, and then squeezed them into jars, making the "soft cone top" Roxanne wanted. Bath salts were mixed with a wooden spoon and bowl, and when production had to be ramped up to ten gallons at a time, workers put the ingredients in a plastic garbage can and mixed them with canoe paddles.

With a fleet of blenders operating at full capacity, breakdowns were frequent. Because Smith passed a small appliance store on his way to and from work, he was saddled with hauling the broken blenders to be fixed.

The least automated production was making candles. Workers had to manually open the vegetable and fruit molds and stick the wicks inside, which limited the average worker to only 200 candles a day. Beeswax purchased from a Florida company arrived in 10-pound blocks, and Baldwin was shocked one day to see blocks being cut with an ax, a dangerous expedient that he promptly put a stop to.

During the upheaval of 1994 and 1995, Burt's Bees had no annual budget and no financial forecasting. Roxanne chose what to fund based on how much cash was available and how quickly she thought the investment would bring the needed return. Baldwin coped with such unconventional practices by periodically submitting expenditure requests to Roxanne, with raw materials for making products topping the list.

Roxanne kept inventory as low as possible to avoid tying up money on the shelf, but that made life difficult for Bob Kingery because he didn't know from one day to the next what quantities of ingredients were needed to make products. Not surprisingly, the talented Kingery was good at guessing. "You had to take risks," Kingery said. "You had to give 110 percent at your job, or you were not in her boat."

"I really think that sometimes the lip balm carried the company through its struggles, because we struggled all the time," Roxanne remembered. "We were always struggling. I never could get over that initial sense that you have to struggle. I always called it the 'immigrant mentality' ... from my grandparents' struggles."

The grinding, relentless work and penny pinching paid off. The company broke even at the end of 1994 on revenues of $3 million, matching the sales of the previous year. Given the year's hardships, Roxanne and Baldwin considered this a rousing success.

Not long after Baldwin came on board, he noticed returns of moldy and rancid lip balm in the tins and moldy Royal Jelly, Baby Bee, Green Goddess, and Burt's Moisturizing crèmes. According to Roxanne, neither mold nor rancidity had been an issue in Maine, where the weather had been cooler, inventory buildup minimal, and storage times short. Baldwin now concluded that North Carolina's warm, humid climate would pose new challenges.

Roxanne's original cream formulations contained benzoin, a natural preservative extract from the *Styrax benzoin* tree that grows in Southeast Asia. The search for additional natural preservatives to prolong product shelf life would require a specialized skill set. Baldwin told Roxanne that she would need to hire a cosmetics chemist as soon as possible, and by late summer he had found one who was familiar with natural products. Chuck Friedman had 25 years of experience in cosmetics companies Lanvin-Charles of the Ritz, Almay, Estée Lauder, and Revlon, and had worked on natural products at Almay.

Studying the Burt's Bees catalog after being approached by Baldwin, Friedman found himself "salivating" at the prospect of making natural concoctions again. He was 48 years old and saw the job opportunity at Burt's Bees as his "last chance" at formulating natural products. Philosophically, he was "in total alignment" with Burt's Bees' mission and products, and he thought the fledgling operation "was in desperate need of someone with my background ... to bring it into the twentieth century." He believed Burt's Bees could rise to the top of the heap and that he could help the company get there. Leaving his old job meant a ten percent salary cut (from $77,000 to $70,000) and a loss of benefits such as profit-sharing. But he had "an epiphany" while sitting with Roxanne, Frank, Mark, and Bob on a picnic bench outside the Creedmoor factory as she displayed Burt's Bees products. "I was looking at [their] products that were 100 percent or 98 percent natural," Friedman remembered, and he suddenly recollected how effectively Proctor & Gamble had advertised its Ivory Soap as "99 44/100% pure"—a melodic slogan that even children knew. "I told Roxanne she ought to shout out the percentage of 'natural' on the front of Burt's Bees packages." She told him to figure out how to do it, giving Friedman the sense that he could "do [his] own thing, and that was a good thing."

Roxanne's alpha character was immediately evident to him. He viewed her as "a mustang [and] a bit of a loose cannon." Like other senior team members, he thought the journey with her would be exciting.

Hired as a consultant in September 1994, Friedman stayed on at Revlon for a time but set up his own lab for after-hours work on his immediate Burt's Bees task: arresting the mold in the crèmes. He soon concluded that he faced a heap of other daunting tasks as well. The product lineup, in his opinion, harbored "a veritable hornet's nest of non-compliance [regulatory issues] in desperate need of technical expertise." Burt's Bees had never had a quality assurance manager, and Friedman believed that he would have to shoulder that role, too, if the company was to avoid problems with regulators and customers.*

Spoilage of crèmes was a challenge for all skin-care product companies

*It was perhaps inevitable that Friedman—who was predisposed by training and experience to protect his employer from compliance issues above all else—would see things differently from Roxanne, who was trying to grow a business. Years later Roxanne said that occurrences of mold and product rancidity were rare. The two continued to differ on such issues for the duration of Friedman's tenure at Burt's Bees.

that avoided synthetic preservatives. Mold spores are in the air and settle into products as they are made, filled into containers, or when consumers open the jars or bottles. Bacterial contamination is inoculated into a product when consumers stick their fingers into the mixture. Mold tends to be more visible than bacteria and is harder to kill. Eliminating the visible mold made it likely that bacteria, which are more dangerous to consumers, were also eradicated.

The industry additives used most successfully to prevent mold were parabens—esters of hydroxybenzoic acid—but these were inappropriate for Burt's Bees' natural products. From the few natural preservatives available at the time, Friedman settled on glycerin, a sweet, edible liquid. Odorless and colorless, glycerin in sufficient concentration would bind the water in a mixture, rendering it unavailable for microbial growth. In addition, Friedman added natural borax to crèmes to improve the emulsions.*

He also introduced a matrix of other natural preservatives to Burt's Bees products to prevent spoilage during shipping, on retailers' shelves, and in consumers' bathroom cabinets. Microbiological labs were contracted to test the preservatives.

Friedman's checks of product color, form, taste and odor had to be subjective because the quality assurance program was rudimentary at best. For instance, he simply stuck his finger in the vegetable oils to taste them for rancidity.

Roxanne insisted on approving every proposed new ingredient before Friedman used it in "her" products, but she was relieved to have him on board. "Chuck understood the world you can't see," she said. Mold and bacteria would remain challenges as long as Roxanne owned Burt's Bees because of her determination to keep the products as free from synthetics as possible and her refusal to irradiate the herbal ingredients used to create infusions.† "It was adding insult to injury to bring non-irradiated herbs into the building," according to Friedman. The powdered rosebuds "had an enormous microbial burden."

The FDA (the U.S. Food and Drug Administration) not only had no definitions of "natural" and "organic" (and still doesn't), it also did not quantify the number of allowable non-pathogenic microorganisms.* The Federal Food,

---

*An emulsion is a mixture of two or more liquids that are usually unblendable. Mayonnaise, for example, is an emulsion of oil, egg yolks, and vinegar or lemon juice.

†An infusion is a liquid created by extracting the natural goodness of plants, such as antioxidants and essential oils, into an oil or other solvent in which the plants are immersed.

Drug and Cosmetic Act (the agency's primary underlying enforcement authority) decreed only that "personal care products should not contain kinds and numbers of microorganisms that could putrefy the product or cause harm to the user." Companies producing natural and organic products had to develop their own microorganism standards and hope they were sufficiently protective to avoid contaminations high enough to spark a product recall or worse.

Prior to Friedman's arrival, Baldwin had contacted the North Carolina Department of Agriculture for advice in dealing with mold. "They [the state] wanted to help," Roxanne remembered. "There was an atmosphere of support, even though they were regulators."

While the FDA never made an official inspection, representatives from the federal government's Occupational Safety and Health Administration (OSHA) paid several visits to the factory and handed out warnings. Baldwin attributed their visits to complaints from disgruntled employees who were hoping to get the company into trouble. "Things got pretty sporty at times," he recalled. His strategy was to "buddy up" to inspectors, hoping they might be more inclined to work with the company rather than slap it with fines. He pointed out how hard he was working to get the facility cleaned up, a "Good Manufacturing Practices" manual written, and working conditions improved. He also called in the Creedmoor municipal fire department to do compliance inspections. Roxanne liked his proactive approach and the positive response of North Carolina regulators. It deepened her belief that Maine officials had been punitive toward Burt's Bees and, in general, wanted to catch businesses doing bad things in order to fine them.†

While Baldwin, Kingery, and Friedman attended to management, manufacturing, and product development responsibilities, respectively, Mark Smith was working on product presentation. He began with Burt's Bees' already distinctive packaging, which conferred gift status on the company's down-to-earth products. Roxanne believed ever more strongly as time went by that packaging won customers. "Get them to buy and then use the product, and

---

*The U.S. Department of Agriculture (USDA) publishes standards for "organic" personal care products as well as organic foods, but regulation of personal care products falls to the FDA, which does not enforce USDA standards. This interagency confusion means that while the definition of "organic" food is clear (since a single agency established and enforces the standards), the definition of "organic" cosmetics is not.

†Roxanne would repeat this assertion numerous times over the years, and it would affect her negotiations with Maine state officials when she was acquiring land for a proposed national park.

you get the customer for life" was her theme song.

Still, Smith was confident he could further improve the allure of the packaging. He gave the typography a more sophisticated look, improved product photographs, and elevated the warmth of the greens, browns, and tans already in use. For a new line called Ocean Potion, Smith expanded the company's color range, using dark royal-blue graphics on a creamy-white background. The Ocean Potion brochure introduced the lassotherapy products, items that could enhance "health and beauty through the use of Mother Ocean's beneficial ingredients." The line featured seaweed soap, Dead Sea salts, dusting powder from kelp, sea clay, marine silts and essential oils, a detox dulse bath, and a sea clay mud pack.

Roxanne supported more color—but not too much. Before Smith was hired, cheerful, sunny yellow had been used sparingly on lip balm and Baby Bee product containers and boxes. The apple, pear, avocado, peach, orange, pepper, and corn candles were produced in their natural colors, as were some of the other fruit- and vegetable-based items. Bright enough to get consumers' attention was fine, but Roxanne did not endorse bold "in your face, look at me" tones. She wanted colors that were comforting and imparted a subtle look that would make customers feel they were "discovering" her products and thus become loyal to the brand.

Like Friedman, Smith was a one-man department for years. Knowing how important recycling was to Roxanne and to the company's philosophy, he sought out recyclable and recycled materials for use in packaging, and he instituted in-house recycling in the mid-1990s using a Raleigh recycling company, Phoenix Resources. He placed recycling bins on the floor into which employees were to throw their bottles, cans, paper, and other recyclable waste, and he collected the bins weekly to dump into larger containers for Phoenix Resources' monthly pickup. "I got into the habit of putting improperly recycled materials right in the middle of the offending person's desk," he said. "It was kind of like a scarlet letter for all to see. So we very quickly had the most extensive recycling program that Phoenix Resources handled." As operations and the number of employees grew, the volume of in-house recycling became so large that Smith handed over the effort to an outside waste service.

Renee Quimby continued to be part of the core team while operating from her home in Tampa. Her primary responsibilities were managing key accounts, overseeing trade show arrangements, and figuring out how to expand distribution channels. A workaholic like Roxanne, Renee spent most of her time on the road, dropping in at the Creedmoor headquarters when necessary and later joining the research and development group meetings to add her intelligence and talent.

Burt's Bees employees thought the world of Renee, describing her as smart, savvy, even-tempered, and fair. She interacted graciously, sat calmly through mind-numbing meetings, and dealt unemotionally with the "dirty work" of the business. She was "delicate and effective" with Roxanne.

Some described her as Roxanne's halfback, so dedicated to Burt's Bees that she would "take a bullet" for the company. Danielle Smith Bruce (formerly Bouthot), who knew both sisters well, recalled that Renee was not competitive with Roxanne and was willing to grant her older sister all the glory of the company's success. Roxanne remained the queen bee, but she later acknowledged that she couldn't have pulled Burt's Bees together in North Carolina without Frank, Bob, Chuck, Renee, and Mark. Rounding out the first-string Creedmoor crew was accountant Gordon Brown, hired by Baldwin in 1994.

As in Maine, people hired for minimum-wage factory jobs came and went. Frank Baldwin estimated that he fired 100 people while he was in charge of operations. Despite this turnover and restricted capital spending, he was able to institute a number of essential operational and administrative practices. Many ideas for modernizing and speeding up production had to linger on the backburner until profits increased, however. Delays in computer hardware and software purchases meant that financial data still had to be kept by hand and written in a ledger; product orders were also taken by hand and filed in boxes.

When she was in Creedmoor, Roxanne's first priority was meeting with her R&D team to discuss new products, though the sessions were not called R&D during the Guilford-to-Creedmoor transition. They were casual forums in which the team would knock around ideas. Everyone was free to voice an opinion about Roxanne's proposals, but no one argued against them. Her history of success was irrefutable.

The staff learned quickly that Roxanne was resistant to their own new product ideas. Her instincts had carried the company to this point, and no one knew more about Burt's Bees than she did. Still, sometimes one of the staff scored, such as Frank Baldwin with his lip-gloss-in-a-little-jar idea. Mark Smith was impressed that she would ditch without regret a product or process of her own devising if it wasn't working as well as she'd hoped.

In addition to the new product meetings, staff sessions were held weekly to discuss every slipup and mistake, assign a dollar cost, and find a solution.

Retail Sales

Even while reinventing the company in North Carolina in 1994, Roxanne plunged into a new direction: retail outlets. Wanting some of the action on that emerging front led by companies such as The Body Shop and Bath & Body Works, she hired Bob Kingery's wife, Maria, to scout appropriate East Coast locations for Burt's Bees' products.

The first outlet was in the Carr Mill shopping mall in Carrboro, 32 miles south of Creedmoor. The mill was an old brick building with hardwood floors and large glass windows. Roxanne decorated the leased space with Oriental rugs and custom wood display cabinets. The result was a classy, apartment-like area brimming with quality goods.

The grand opening on September 12, 1994, was announced by a brochure featuring Tony Kulik's image of Burt and noting that Burt's Bees had expanded its product line to "over one hundred fine products for the home, garden and bath and body." The enticing "free cappuccino and dessert bar" party attracted a good turnout. Roxanne hired a local performer, Dulcimer Dan, to provide live music. Burt dressed up for the occasion in a stylish cream linen suit.

Two more outlets were soon opened in the college towns of Ithaca, New York, and Burlington, Vermont. Now and then Roxanne, Burt, or both of them worked at the stores. She loved the hands-on sales, which reminded her of her flea and craft market days, and the personal interaction with customers was satisfying and informative. But the outlet experiment was short-lived. Expensive from the start, the stores were hard to keep staffed and hard to manage from a distance. Roxanne ordered the outlets closed by 1997, as their leases came up for renewal, and reckoned in hindsight that 1994 had been too early in the company's evolution for retail outlets to succeed.

Frank Baldwin thought Roxanne should have given the outlets more time to catch on, but she thought she could see less resource-intensive ways to build sales. During this time, she began working with distributors in Japan and Canada, thus making Burt's Bees international.

She next tried a Christmas mail-order catalog as an alternative way to boost retail sales, but scrapped that after one trial. She couldn't reconcile herself to printing hundreds of thousands of retail catalogs that would claim the lives of an untold number of trees, only to end up in community landfills.

Once again her instincts were well grounded. Retail catalog sales declined steeply in the mid to late 1990s as Internet traffic increased, and the mail-order companies that survived the transition more or less unscathed (L.L. Bean, for example) were those that built synergies between their Web portals and their catalogs. Burt's Bees dabbled with the Internet for a while before embracing the Web whole hog, and Internet sales quickly became an important source of income and proved a valuable way to connect with customers. E-mail feedback from customers was organized into a monthly report that gave senior managers a valuable read on consumer opinions.

Burt's Bees' homespun virtues were based on Roxanne's beliefs. From the earliest catalogs, brochures, and newspaper articles, the values of peace, love, and environmental protection were guiding principles. In Creedmoor, Roxanne went a step further by advocating openly that her customers become environmental, animal rights, and world peace activists.

To that end, Mark Smith produced brochures with information on vegetarian lifestyles, animal testing, the fur trade, and spaying and neutering pets. Illustrated with Tony Kulik woodcuts, most of the pamphlets defined a problem and offered a solution. Burt's Bees' solution for factory farming, for example, was to "support legislation that abolishes battery cages, veal crates and intensive confinement systems. However, the best way to save animals from the misery of the factory farm is to stop buying and eating meat, milk, and eggs." These printed materials were distributed at trade shows and included in retail store orders for Burt's Bees tee-shirts and writing journals. "They helped justify selling stuff," Roxanne said. She likened the activism-promoting brochures to "voting with your dollar. I was giving people information about their choices—how to make a better choice."

The Creedmoor Workplace

Anything could and did happen in Creedmoor. There was a knife fight in the bakery between two women employees, and an employee walked into Baldwin's office and threatened him. The warehouse manager failed to show up one day and was found murdered beside the road, the victim of a drug deal gone bad according to local rumor.

Even pets made things interesting in the workplace. Emily, the office cat, began as a stray who adopted Burt's Bees. When the staff went home on Fridays, they left Emily in the office area. One Monday morning, she was missing. Eventually she was discovered in the sewing area of the manufacturing section, where she was not allowed. Apparently smelling the catnip sachets being made there, Emily had wormed her way out of the office and pounced into a giant box of catnip. When finally located, she was passed out, perhaps in an overdose of pure pleasure.

When Burt was on site, his dog, Rufus, had the run of the plant. Accountant Gordon Brown brought two greyhounds to work. And three months into his new job, Burt came upon a stray dog on a road and left him in Frank Baldwin's office. Baldwin wasn't pleased when he found the dog standing on his desk chewing papers, but Burt talked him into taking the mutt home. The dog had mange and gave it to Baldwin and his wife and daughter. The resultant vet bills cost Baldwin $2,000.

Animals were banned from the Burt's Bees workplace once the state agriculture department found out they were present. Baldwin later guessed that a fired employee had initiated the agency's action.

Although doing its best to become professional in its own way, Burt's Bees remained a campy culture. The dress code was a matter of personal discretion, and so were job titles. Roxanne didn't care what title people gave themselves as long as they did their job and said yes to what she said needed doing. Working for Burt's Bees was about "filling a need, not job titles," recalled Mark Smith. People who were too "corporate" to get their hands dirty were short-timers at Burt's Bees.

If a staff member thought it would be advantageous when talking to a vendor to say that he or she was director of this or that, giving the impression that Burt's Bees was larger than it was, Roxanne would readily agree. Workers could be "managers," too, even if they had no one to manage.

Mark Smith enjoyed the titles caper immensely. In 1993–94, there was a company called Emperor of Tea with "some funny titles on their packaging, such as Emperor of this or that," he said. "Some of us took that as a cue to come up with these preposterous inflated titles and use them on business cards." Smith was Grand Master of Graphic Design for a while, and another staffer was Sultan of Sales. Smith made name plaques for staffers' offices, each one featuring the person's title and a relevant Tony Kulik woodcut. Gordon Brown chose an engraving of Rufus because of his love of dogs. Smith chose a half-peeled banana to be provocative.

The operative mode for job salaries was also atypical and caused conflict between Frank Baldwin and Roxanne. In Baldwin's experience, an employer provided an annual review of an employee's job performance to determine whether he or she was due a raise. Roxanne wasn't interested in annual reviews, however. If any of her staff wanted a raise, they had to ask, sometimes more than once or twice. "I had to force the issue [for myself and others]," said Baldwin. "You would think you were doing a great job if she gave you a $1,000-per-year raise."

Looking back later, Roxanne was amused by some of the absurdities at Creedmoor. An inventive method for making massage oils, one of Burt's Bees' short-lived products, was a case in point. With plenty of sun hitting the factory's metal roof, she wanted to take advantage of the heat to make herbal infusions. Workers hauled five-gallon buckets of oils and dried herbs up a ladder to the rooftop. The 100- to 120-degree-Fahrenheit temperatures up there heated the oils necessary for the herbs to gradually release their "goodness and scent," just as Roxanne had hoped. Staffers thought the practice was crazy, however, given the potential for an employee to fall off the ladder, and Roxanne eventually agreed that it was safer to cook the herbs indoors.

Hourly employees found the goings-on at Burt's Bees funny in some instances, confusing in others. Many had no idea what the company was about, and even some top staff were unfamiliar with the herbs being used. Roxanne was amused by Frank Baldwin's drawly pronunciation of calendula oil. "It came out as kal-in-du-lah oil," she said.

Residents of Creedmoor were largely oblivious to Burt's Bees. The company had no storefront to introduce the local populace to the "natural" way, although the local Baptist Church ran an outlet called Angel Gifts that sold a small number of Burt's Bees products. As a goodwill gesture and to underscore Burt's Bees presence in town, Roxanne sent samples of new products to employees of the city hall and the police station.

Roxanne Adapts

In 1995, after a year of hotel living, Roxanne was ready to buy a house. She purchased a new passive solar home on Kent Street in Durham with mature trees on the lot. Then one day Duke Power Company showed up to trim branches around the power lines. Roxanne stood at her window, weeping. "They were beheading them violently," she said. "It was so disturbing that I went out to talk with the guys doing it. They told me I wouldn't complain if the next hurricane caused branches to fall on the line and knock out my electricity. It was really devastating to me and seemed inhuman ... after George and I were so careful with every tiny birch tree we wanted to grow in our yard at the cabin [in Guilford]."

She lacked the energy and interest to pursue a social life or a hobby in North Carolina. She didn't make friends or go to the movies. "People would say, 'Let's go to the park or beach,' and I'd say no," she said. "My life in North Carolina was all about work."

When back in Maine for long weekends, she focused on creative projects such as developing new product ideas and promotional brochures, as well as strategic marketing plans. The isolation she could find there was essential for the creative process.

Burt had minimal involvement in the business in Creedmoor, and the staff didn't want him around. "He couldn't manage his way out of a paper bag," said Baldwin. "He was constantly pissing everyone off." Burt was clearly a fish out of water there. He yearned for Maine and never did buy a house in North Carolina. The Department of Agriculture's ban on pets in the workplace was the last straw. By the beginning of 1995, Burt and Rufus were back in Parkman, returning to North Carolina now and then for short periods. He would continue to own a third of Burt's Bees for another four years, and would make promotional appearances as the "face" of the brand.*

It hadn't occurred to Roxanne that she would have to struggle so hard to get the company up and running after the move to North Carolina or that she would have to radically change what she was manufacturing. She later admitted that she'd been naïve to assume she could just transplant operations to Creedmoor and be free to expand indefinitely.

By Christmas 1994, she accepted that handcrafting was just too labor-intensive to continue. What was driving the company's growth were the skincare products, especially the lip balm and crèmes—the very items that could be and needed to be automated. "We couldn't sit there and paint peach candles with a little spray gun anymore," she said. Frank Baldwin supported the idea of jettisoning the handcrafted products. "I felt lip balm could carry us

---

*"He was put in a tough spot in a lot of ways," Roxanne's son, Lucas, said years later in an interview for the documentary *Burt's Buzz*. "He was ... living in a little shack, just doing his thing, and then he was thrust into this business with this super-intense woman and these two little kids, and all of a sudden his life is not at all how he planned. In a lot of ways he was always trying to get back to that."

along" during the transition, he said.

Roxanne could smell the rich opportunity in personal skin-care products, a sector in which consumer interest in all things safe and environmentally friendly was increasing by leaps and bounds. She knew the health store and gift markets like the back of her hand; moving beyond them was a sign of confidence in her own increasing business acumen and in Burt's Bees' trajectory. She knew that goop, as pure as she could make it, was their ticket to future growth.

When Roxanne informed her staff of her decision, they were horrified. She was abandoning products that had *made* Burt's Bees and still accounted for half ($1.5 million) of its annual sales. Employees saw their jobs being placed at risk—and given that the workforce seems to have declined during the Creedmoor years, they were probably right. "Although it was cutting things really close to the bone, it was an excellent exercise in coming to an understanding of what [was] really essential and what was important," Roxanne reflected later. "And those decisions were based on life and death."

So in early 1995, Burt's Bees sold its candle lines to other businesses. Next to go were the honey, the organic cotton shirts, the kitchen towels, the novelty items, and the bird, kitty, and seed products. After the dog biscuit bakery shut down, the business gave away the tee-shirt inventory and sold the Haitian-made clay containers at trade shows. Burt's Bees soaps continued to be made by other manufacturers, such as Twin Craft in Winooski, Vermont, and were packaged by so-called sheltered workshops employing people with disabilities.

"If I hadn't made the right decision about what [products] to keep and what to jettison, the company definitely would have died," Roxanne reflected. "It was a wonderful discipline in understanding what were the most important things I had to do to lead the company and that nothing else was as important, even if it was louder and crying harder for my attention." She came out of that process with a goal of making products that would bring in at least $1 million a year each.*

As part of the product revamping, Roxanne asked employees to suggest ideas for a company slogan. The winner was Mark Smith's *earth-friendly natural personal care*. Of course, "earth-friendly" was a phrase Roxanne had used for

---

*At about this time, Roxanne helped four former Maine employees get a bank loan to purchase the Edes building in Guilford for Mothers of Maine, a new business making cookies, jams, and preserves that she felt had a chance of success in the national market. Roxanne recalled one "beautifully decorated cookie" in the shape of a pansy that the White House ordered for an event hosted by President Bill Clinton, bringing Mothers recognition in national magazines. Mothers of Maine failed financially in 1998.

years, but by connecting it to "personal care," Smith created a lilting "handle" to describe the Burt's Bees brand. The slogan began appearing quietly on packaging but was more noticeable on catalog covers, sell sheets, stationary, business cards, and special promotions. Newspaper stories about Burt's Bees used the slogan to describe the company's personality and philosophy.

To develop the personal care line, chemist Chuck Friedman began working full time at Burt's Bees in March 1995. Bob Kingery set him up with a funky lab, essentially a "rickety 2 x 4 bench" encrusted with old batter from the dog biscuit operation. Chuckling at the memory of his "irregular quarters," Friedman said, "I wondered if I was there to formulate lipsticks or bake biscuits." Dust and tufts of lint continued to float down from the rafters, landing on his lab bench. Previously he had worked in a modern, clean lab with professional workbenches costing thousands of dollars. Now he had to make do, with little money for the "do" part.*

Since most new products needed his seal of approval before moving into manufacturing, Friedman had an endless list of problems to address besides finding the right combination of natural preservatives with which to combat mold in the crèmes. He added antioxidants to the vegetable oils used in most Burt's Bees products to delay the onset of rancidity in them. To cure a softening problem with lemon butter cuticle crème, one of Burt's Bees' most popular items, he stiffened the mixture by reducing the lanolin and increasing the beeswax.†

Another task was to reformulate Burt's Bees products to allow the production of larger batches while maintaining the correct proportions and consistency of ingredients. Roxanne had created the concoctions using volumetric formulas—gallons, quarts, pints, scoops—doing much of it off the top of her head. For example, she could judge just the right amount of vitamin E or lavender to mix into a crème. She formulated new products in quart pots so that if she guessed wrong, she could toss out the batch and start over with virtually no cost to the business. She used the analogy of a cook making spaghetti sauce from scratch. "You add a little of this, a little of that, and you have a great sauce but probably aren't sure how you got there, whether it was more celery

*Thus far, the testing of body products had been "very informal," according to Frank Baldwin. As crèmes and lotions were developed, the staff would take them home to try. He recalled a time when Burt, Lucas, and he tested the Burt's Bees bug repellent lotion on a camping trip.

†Roxanne's recipe for lemon butter cuticle crème included almond oil, cocoa butter, yellow beeswax, vitamin E, lemon oil, and lanolin in proportions that remain proprietary.

or more garlic," she said.

Because she had taught her method to the Maine supervisors, they too had been good at making volumetric formulas her way and knowing how long to whip a crème or what the temperature of a batch needed to be. If in doubt, they could always run to her for a second opinion. In North Carolina, however, recipes had to be converted from volumetric to standardized weight formulas so that anyone could make batches of any size, scaling them up or down in response to product demand. To ensure uniformity, Friedman created "batch cards" on which were recorded the precise amounts of each ingredient and how and when to add it. Later he computerized the batch formulas.

Roxanne had developed many of the recipes with ingredients she had used since the company's beginning, regardless of their shelf life. For example, she loved sweet almond oil even though it turned rancid quickly. Friedman developed a sweet almond and sunflower hybrid oil that provided a three-year shelf life. Roxanne collaborated with Friedman on new products such as a sea clay mud pack for the Ocean Potion line, and in time allowed him to create new products on his own.

Another of Friedman's jobs was to institute a protocol of keeping retains, or samples, of product runs and coding them for tracking purposes in case a recall was ordered by the Food and Drug Administration. In effect, as he'd foreseen, he became the company's first quality assurance manager as well as its chemist.

Roxanne was reluctant to change her volumetric recipes and apply rigorous quality control; she was nervous about relying on Friedman when her ways and intuition had served her so well. "I could tell these [managers] were not particularly intuitive people ... but they were people who were able to push us through the boundaries of my [knowledge and] intuition," she said. She accepted Friedman's proposals only after being assured that the "naturalness" of the revised ingredients would not be compromised.

As a new era of personal care products took hold, Roxanne wanted it to be clear that Burt's Bees products served both genders and all ages and were not just "girlie" products that used a lot of flowers or pastel colors. "I wanted lines that would have wide appeal, products about the body, no matter what gender the skin happened to be in," she said.

She also held back from directly identifying Burt's Bees' products as "green." Giving customers "cues rather than making statements about it" was the best way to allude to but not commit to being "green," she believed, because the public had no real way of evaluating whether "green" pronounce-ments were true or not. Communicating the company's environmental com-mitment through the "earth-friendly" tag felt much more comfortable to her, and consumers could confirm the cues by reading the product ingredients.

As *natural* and *organic* products vied increasingly for consumer atten-tion, the staff discussed whether Burt's Bees should shift its identity from the former to the latter. Roxanne decided that "organic" was "too problematic and impractical," Mark Smith recalled, and that she didn't have to adopt that des-ignation to grow the company. "Organic" was new in the personal care sector, he said, and certified organic ingredients were difficult to source.

With new product lines, Roxanne became ever more driven to expand into bigger markets. Candles and honey were things of the past, and she was thinking now about the cosmetics sector. She wanted to create products that could compete with cosmetics giants Revlon, Estée Lauder, and L'Oréal, or even blast past them.

Her steaming ambitions fueled a wild faith in her staff that Burt's Bees was going to take off. Chuck Friedman recalled that his "heart and head swelled" because he had a stake in the company. The staff worked harder than ever, and it paid off. After being stuck at $3 million in 1993 and 1994, sales jumped to $4.5 million in 1995. In that year, lip balm, the jewel in the Burt's Bees crown, glowed most brilliantly. 🐝

Haskell Rock Pitch on the East Branch of the Penobscot. (Bill Duffy photo)

Burt's Bees Reincarnated

By late 1995, with the transformation of Burt's Bees from a hand-crafts producer to a personal care products company virtually complete and a lease renewal for the Creedmoor facility rapidly approaching, Roxanne wanted a better workplace. It wasn't a matter of needing more space. She had never liked Creedmoor and wanted to get out of a facility she found depressing. Senior staffers were commuting from Raleigh, a 50-mile roundtrip, and relocating Burt's Bees to the capital city area would save them time, energy, and expense. Moreover, the capital district was home to the Research Triangle, a hub of the U.S. cosmetics and personal care industry. The activity and energy there would be exciting, and they'd be eyeball to eyeball with the big competitors that Roxanne's soaring ambitions were pitting them against.

Frank Baldwin found an 18,000-square foot building in northwest Raleigh's Brownleigh Business Park. Fortunately, this relocation was easier than the last. The factory was only a half-hour drive from Creedmoor, allowing the move to be staged. Various parts of the business shifted from the old plant to the new one over a few weeks, and production continued almost uninterrupted. The phones at the Creedmoor plant were turned off on December 29, 1995. On January 2, 1996, operations resumed in Raleigh.

The contemporary textured-cement facility abutted William B. Umstead State Park, which meant that Roxanne could occasionally escape into the woods to breathe fresh air and wrap her arms around a big pine. They were also closer to the Raleigh-Durham airport, so she could make a fast getaway to Maine, and they were closer to FedEx and UPS depots and to universities with their pools of engineers and other professionals to help Burt's Bees grow.

"Creedmoor and Brownleigh Drive were like night and day," recalled Frank Baldwin. "Creedmoor had been a joke. Now we had a much better, newer building with nice offices and clean surfaces. The cosmetics lab wasn't pharmaceutical quality, but it was Good Management Practices worthy."

Roxanne's first-floor office overlooked the state park through the building's largest windows. The décor was plain—a coffee table between two couches and a desk off to the side. Eschewing overhead fluorescent lights because they hurt her eyes, Roxanne preferred natural light augmented with task lighting. Also on the first floor were a half-dozen cubicles for staff, a small walled-in area for production, and a vast open space for warehousing and shipping. There were more offices on the windowless second floor surrounding a central open space with cubicles.

Despite its new proximity to major personal care product companies, up-and-coming Burt's Bees was not yet on its competitors' radar. "They thought we were a bunch of kooks," remembered Baldwin, repeating what he had heard at the time from former industry colleagues.

Not long after moving to Raleigh, Roxanne put a sign on her office wall that read, "What is popular is not always right, and what is right is not always popular." The message was directed at employees who occasionally mistook her willingness to listen to an idea for assent to enacting it. Unless she gave explicit affirmation, the sign was saying, no one should assume that she was agreeing with or authorizing a proposal. The message was similar to one her great grandfather, Carroll Quimby, had displayed on his desk in Sheboygan. It said: "Please remember that because I listen to you with courtesy, I do not necessarily agree with what you say."

What mattered to Roxanne was the pursuit of what was right or true. She wasn't bothered by employees being upset because she disagreed with them or lacked tact and consideration. She wanted to be known as "someone who pursued her truth and persevered" even when doing so made her appear "not nice, ladylike." She wasn't going to compromise what she believed in to get along with people. "The truth should be enough," she said. "It should be valuable and honored."

Due to the transformation of the product line, Burt's Bees' workforce decreased from 50 to 60 in Creedmoor to perhaps 40 or fewer in Raleigh.* Worker turnover continued to plague the company. Temporary workers who weren't offered full-time jobs after three or four months usually left to seek better opportunities elsewhere.

There had always been plenty of applicants for minimum-wage jobs in Maine and in Creedmoor, but the majority of the available labor pool in Raleigh was comprised of unskilled Latino immigrants, raising the specter of documentation issues. Roxanne hired workers through a temp agency but wouldn't pay the firm's placement fee. When the agency wanted to place one of its agents on the factory floor to oversee the immigrants, she balked at that too. The temp firm was responsible for ensuring that the immigrants were properly documented, but Burt's Bees' staff came to suspect over time that some entry-level workers were illegal. No complaints were ever filed.

Burt's Bees would remain in Raleigh 4½ years, from January 1996 to June 2000, developing products and expanding output. Continued growth required more automation, more and better blending and filling equipment, improved budgeting, closer attention to product quality assurance and regulatory compliance, and attracting additional staff. It also required an evolution of the company's anti-commercial, unconventional image. Burt's Bees would have to gravitate toward the mainstream while trying to maintain its image of friendly quirkiness.

In a September 1992 article called "The Secrets of Bootstrapping," an *Inc.* magazine writer had observed that the recessionary period of the late 1980s had been "an utter wasteland" for companies without "basic access" to money. Yet bootstrap businesses had created ways around their lack of capital, substituting imagination for money and pouring in sweat equity. Citing Burt's Bees as an example, *Inc.* described Roxanne's move from retail into wholesale and plugging into new markets as smart moves.

But the resurgence of the national economy during Bill Clinton's presidency (1993–2001) can't be discounted in the Burt's Bees story. Many market sectors heated up, and skin care was one of them. Consumers had more disposable income and were more willing than ever to pay higher prices for

---

*Roxanne remembered 40–50 workers in Raleigh, while Baldwin thought there were fewer than 20. An April 20, 1996, article in the *News & Observer* reported that there were "about 20 full-time employees in Raleigh and another dozen" at the three retail outlets in Carrboro, NC, Ithaca, NY, and Burlington, VT. Given the rising volume of production at the time, however, 40 is a reasonable estimate.

natural and organic products. Having laid the foundations of Burt's Bees with imagination and drive during the recession, Roxanne had positioned the company for expansion just as the economy was expanding. Her timing, as it turned out, couldn't have been better.

Change Is the Only Constant

Frank Baldwin played a critical role in guiding Burt's Bees through the wrenching upheavals of the relocation to North Carolina, the transformation to a personal care products company, and the move from Creedmoor to Raleigh. Several months after the move to Raleigh, however, Baldwin left the company. Years later Baldwin said he "basically quit" over an issue of pay for a temp worker; Roxanne disputed this but could not remember what the real reason for his departure might have been. Perhaps with sales growth stalled since 1994 while expenses increased due to management hires and capital investments, she felt a need to shed a big salary. Perhaps she saw a critical need for more women on the management team to guide them in a woman-centric industry. At any rate, Frank Baldwin was gone.

He left with a lingering gripe over not getting the stock options he said Roxanne had promised him. "She told me she would make me a millionaire, and I'd never have to work ... that if I turned around the company she would give me five percent [of the business]." (Roxanne disputed this as well.) After he left, he formed his own company, Baldwin Marketing.

Roxanne turned over operations management to Bob Kingery, a job he would shoulder in addition to his engineering work until mid-1999. Like Baldwin, Kingery had been critical during Burt's Bees transformative period in North Carolina. Always operating on a shoestring, he was the ultimate bargain shopper as well as an ingenious inventor. Roxanne relied on and trusted him.

Development of the managerial staff moved forward in 1996 and 1997 with the hiring of two women who became essential to Burt's Bees. Sunne Justice had worked as a communications executive at Gryphon, the company that launched Bath & Body Works and the Victoria's Secret bath shop. In the mid-1990s, she had become a vegetarian, sold her full-length sable coat, moved from New York to North Carolina, and become a loyal customer of Burt's Bees. Her purse was full of lip balm, she fed Burt's Bees suet to her birds, and she burned Burt's Bees candles. Justice was so enthusiastic about Burt's

Bees that she wanted to work for the company. A friend was able to get her Roxanne's personal phone number, and Justice left such a convincing message on Roxanne's answering machine about what she could offer the company that Roxanne returned the call within 15 minutes, inviting Justice to Raleigh for lunch and a talk.

That 1995 lunch led to a visit at Roxanne's Maine cabin. The pair connected personally, since each had survived a failed marriage and was raising kids without a live-in partner. "Roxanne was a good witch," Justice gleefully recalled. "She got me very drunk and lectured me on how I had to change my ways."

Roxanne offered Justice a sales job at a salary well below what she had earned at Gryphon. Even though the position would require Justice to work twice as many hours and travel most of her work week, she signed on. She was primed for a life change and an unconventional job, and it was clear to her that Roxanne was a one-of-a-kind rule breaker who wouldn't let anyone push her around.

Roxanne soon saw that Justice was a dynamic, effective personality who had much to offer Burt's Bees beyond sales. "She was a movie star, and she needed an audience," Roxanne said. Trade shows provided a handy stage, and Justice was put in charge of Burt's Bees' product demonstrations. Buyers flocked to her demo sessions. She became a great hit and an important public spokesperson for Burt's Bees. Justice dubbed herself the company's "chief pollinator," and Roxanne agreed.

In 1997, Donna Hollenbach joined Burt's Bees to buy accessory packaging. Previously the company had relied on outside buyers to source bottles and other containers for company-branded products. These buyers had been men who took a practical approach to packaging—preferring, for example, what worked best on the production line. Now Roxanne wanted to expand the lineup of Burt's Bees accessories into such gift and novelty items as a shaving mug with Burt's face, sponges in animal shapes, flax-seed eye rest pillows, and Beanie Bee toys. She also wanted to offer more product sample kits, and she wanted a woman's aesthetic in the packaging because, as Hollenbach recognized, "Roxanne was all about aesthetics."

Hollenbach had worked at Northern Telecommunications for four years, first as a buyer and purchasing agent and then as a material control specialist. She then joined The Body Shop as a senior buyer and brand manager for accessories, but a long commute required her to be away from home twelve

hours a day. She left after two years when her first child was born and her husband finished graduate school. Soon, her friend Bob Kingery interested her in
working for Burt's Bees.

Hollenbach knocked on Roxanne's door in August 1997 hoping to arrange
part-time work from home. The interview was different from anything she
had ever experienced. Roxanne ignored her résumé, preferring instead to talk
about Hollenbach's work at NorTel and The Body Shop and to inquire about
the baby. "We talked more like friends. Roxanne wanted to know who I was as
a person," she said. "It was all so laid-back, and I left the interview not knowing if she liked me."

Roxanne agreed to let Hollenbach work part-time, with two days in the
office and one at home. After Hollenbach's second child arrived, she accepted
an offer of full-time employment, knowing by then that Roxanne "liked my
eye for things."

When Hollenbach was hired, much at Burt's Bees was as "irregular" to her
as it had been to Baldwin, Friedman, and Justice. Accustomed to a corporate
environment, she was struck by Burt's Bees' low budget, minimal automation,
and antiquated equipment and by the employees' jeans-and-sandals attire.
The workplace looked so much like a start-up business that Hollenbach felt
she was starting over.

In such a lean operation, Roxanne could tell which supervisors were working diligently and who wasn't. She could spot failings not just in machinery
glitches or missed production quotas but also in personal lapses. She remembered "strolling around, looking at their posture, whether they were gabbing
on the phone, if their desk was littered with sodas and junk, or if they were
really working." She wanted supervisors who could work as hard as she did,
and she wanted them to be honest and fearless and to require those under
them to be as good. Roxanne figured that if her top staff were like her, it was
"as good as having [myself] on the premises or even better."

Donna Hollenbach attended research and development meetings with
Bob, Mark, Chuck, and Renee. "It was all very loose," she remembered. The
management team would say whether they thought they could make the
products proposed by Roxanne, Chuck, and others and what packaging would
be necessary, but there was "no sense of organization or a timeline related to
the discussions," Hollenbach recollected. "No one kept up with anything."

A self-described organization freak, Hollenbach started taking meeting
notes and typing them up for the others to make sure things got done. The

next thing she knew, "I was expected to take notes, lead the meetings, and do real project tracking." Later she became the new-projects manager.

Roxanne would "come and go to the office with a vengeance," said Hollenbach. "She would have a strategy in mind and work in that direction for a while, and then disappear [out of town]. There were so many times we worked on a product for three months, and suddenly she would say we're not going to do it. No one had authority to make decisions [about new products] other than Roxanne."

Fortunately, Hollenbach liked the unpredictability. "It was feast or famine, exciting and fun." Others on the staff saw Roxanne as "erratic," Hollenbach said, and felt frustrated with the CEO's vacillating style, but she and Roxanne got along well. What mattered to Hollenbach was her belief that their natural products were "the real deal" and that Burt's Bees customers were devoted.

During this period, Chuck Friedman presented to Roxanne a memo listing the 21 products (of the 74 Burt's Bees was then selling) that he believed could potentially harbor "significant numbers and types of microorganisms." He kept trying to get her to focus more attention on potential contamination issues. She was not ready to hire a quality assurance manager, however, and left that responsibility with him.

Friedman's haranguing irritated Roxanne. "There could never be enough testing for him," she later remembered. "We haggled a lot." She viewed him as "conservative and negative" and believed those traits sometimes "dampened creativity" at the company. "His jargon ... would [sometimes] drive us crazy," she said. Still, she valued his contributions enough to give him stock options "for keeping me out of some problems."

Forgoing a personal assistant, Roxanne arranged her hectic life with the help of a weekly planner that doubled as a personal journal. In her black-, gray-, or red-covered planners, she tracked appointments, phone numbers, addresses, flights, birthdays, and business issues. Her notes had a fat-lettered, legible style, whether in print or cursive. More journal-like entries reflected the interplay of her creative and spiritual worlds. At the beginning of each book she drew astrological symbols applicable to the coming year. She included inspirational quotes from notable poets and encouraging notes to herself. The daily calendars reflected periods of flagging spirits, low energy, self-doubts, and questions around parenting and relationships.

On July 11, 1996, her forty-sixth birthday, she entered in her planner book an astrological description of her Cancer sign: "You are intuitive, unorthodox, sensual, loyal, often permit yourself to be taken advantage of by unscrupulous individuals. Time to be creatively selfish—have enough self-esteem to protect interests. Leo plays a role." She would later say that the description fit her except in one respect: She was not susceptible to being taken advantage of.

In any given year, Roxanne crisscrossed the country to attend the trade shows that consumed 25 percent of her work life. She regularly visited New York, Philadelphia, Baltimore, Atlanta, San Diego, Los Angeles, San Francisco, and Seattle. Her sister Renee and Sunne Justice usually accompanied her. Occasionally Mark Smith and other staff participated.

Given the proliferation of trade shows, a small company had to decide which ones were most important for its product lines and markets. Renee developed an annual timeline to ensure the company didn't miss any important events, each of which required an advance application and a payment to the show organizer of up to several thousand dollars to cover booth rental, cleanup, and drayage (hauling boxes to and from the booth location, usually with a unionized workforce). Each show was a big commitment requiring signed contracts; arrangements for electricity, Internet service, and communications in the booth; the design and construction of displays; a supply of promotional literature and product samples for attendees; and personal travel arrangements for staff.

No matter how much experience the Burt's Bees team gained on the trade show circuit, there were glitches. Catalogs would fail to arrive, or a box of products would get lost in transit. "It was always something with a trade show," Roxanne remembered. But the sales generated from a show usually more than compensated for the irritations and fatigue.

When Roxanne, Renee, and Sunne worked a show together, they shared a room. Accustomed to staying in first-class hotels such as the Four Seasons when she worked for Vogue and L'Oréal, Justice discovered that the Burt's Bees travel budget dictated humbler arrangements. "It was a take-the-bus-there-and-stay-at-the-Red-Roof-Inn approach," Justice laughed. Nevertheless, she, Roxanne, and Renee looked forward to "girl time" in the off-hours because they had so much fun together, talking about their personal lives and learning interesting things about one another.

Justice was surprised at how light Roxanne traveled. On a trip to San Diego, for example, Roxanne took only the outfit she wore, extra underwear, a tube of Tom's of Maine toothpaste, and a comb. Justice lugged two big bags with a change of clothes for each of the five days. "I was Ms. Vogue, and

Roxanne was Ms. Homeless," Justice said. "We were at [opposite] ends of the fashion spectrum."

She was one of the few people whom Roxanne allowed to influence her when it came to personal matters. Sunne bought Roxanne an underwire bra and mentored her on facial products. "I had used freezing cold water from the stream by the cabin and a moldy towel to keep myself clean, so I had no clue," Roxanne said later. "I had missed a whole lot of stuff, hanging around with women, knowing what the right kinds of shoes and clothes were—the kind of things you [learn] in your twenties and thirties. I didn't have a mirror, so I didn't think about hair or [makeup] or these little amenities."

At the time, Burt's Bees was producing single products for the face. Justice opened Roxanne's eyes to the necessity of adopting the "suite" system that millions of women had been trained to use by the big cosmetics companies. Convinced that they needed complementary products to cleanse, exfoliate, tone, and moisturize their faces, women liked a one-stop shopping approach. "So, OK, I figured I'd hitch my star to that wagon because it could be an important avenue for products and sales for the company," Roxanne said.

Trade shows had value beyond sales. Each one gave Roxanne a chance to study dozens of competitors' new products and get feedback from buyers. "Reading the [trade show] culture and responses people gave in an unedited way allowed me to understand what [the market] wanted," Roxanne said. It harked back to her early days at flea markets and craft shows, except that now she was observing buyers, not consumers, which made the stakes higher.

She provided chairs for the buyers and other participants to encourage them to sit down and stay awhile. She was especially interested in conversing with the "heavy hitters from corporate buying offices" who showed up at the booth. These impromptu chats often provided insider information and sometimes eliminated the need for a formal appointment with a leading buyer—meetings that could be difficult to schedule.

Roxanne also took the opportunity to study other companies' booths, calculating their square footage as one gauge of strength and pondering how she could out-compete them. Her research efforts were unscientific but cheap and effective, and she didn't have to justify her way of doing things to anyone.

Employees who worked a Burt's Bees booth needed stamina for the six- to eight-hour shifts. The chairs Roxanne put out were reserved for customers; staff members were on their feet the entire day. Lunch breaks were difficult to schedule in the busy booth. Sometimes even getting to the restroom was hard.

Sunne Justice's product marketing sessions were lively and engaging. A willowy, attractive woman, blonde-haired Justice bubbled over with enthusiasm for the company's mission and products. Feminine, body-conscious, and a big user of the products herself, she was a highly effective spokesperson.

She would open her three-hour training events by articulating the Burt's Bees mission, especially emphasizing its environmental consciousness. She would drive home that Burt's Bees used non-toxic ingredients and was committed to recycling and reuse, noting what a "huge polluter" the personal care industry was in general.

Justice promised her audiences that the products were made "with the best ingredients found in nature, including herbs, flowers, beeswax, clay, and essential and botanical oils. We use them in their simplest and least processed forms. They are the healthiest and most natural products on the market today." She reiterated what Roxanne had been saying publicly for years: that Burt's Bees products were so safe they could be eaten, and that they were, in effect, "food" for the body. She described the skin as the largest organ of the body and emphasized that crèmes, lotions, lip balm, and other substances put on the skin were ingested into the bloodstream. She asserted that this absorption factor made it essential for women to use toxin-free products.

Dabbing a bit of orange essence cleansing cream on her arm or putting a taste of lotion in her mouth, she would invite trainees to do the same. Participants followed her lead, gingerly. "You can always feel safe and confident about recommending Burt's Bees products to your customers because they are safe enough to eat," she would then reiterate. "We make FOOD FOR YOUR SKIN!!" She urged the women to check the ingredients in their personal care products at home and to throw out anything that couldn't be eaten.

Justice carefully explained the Burt's Bees product lines and suites. Emphasizing that facial care could be more confusing than body care, she recommended that retailers who sold Burt's Bees products be able to demystify the process.

Upon reviewing Justice's training script, chemist Chuck Friedman urged her to tone down some of her product-efficacy claims, thinking they couldn't be substantiated scientifically and might potentially lead to liability suits. But Roxanne knew that Friedman was predisposed to err on the side of caution. She considered Justice's claims to be fair, and Friedman could never convince her otherwise. "He took a more scientific and doctrinaire position in his use of words, and [Sunne] was at the other extreme in her use of words—loose, using laymen's terms. I'd listen to both sides," said Roxanne. "I just wanted to keep us out of trouble. I didn't think Sunne would get us in trouble, and she never did."

Many product samples were given out at training seminars, just as recommended by Burt's Bees' former broker Sol Solomon. At 25 to 50 cents apiece, they were an expense Roxanne would have preferred to avoid, but she saw the advertising value of giveaways. Free samples won new customers.

New Home, New Catalog

Roxanne sold her house in Durham after the tree-cutting incident in 1996 and bought a new place 250 miles away in Arden, a suburb of Asheville in western North Carolina. Rather than flying back to Maine for the weekends, she could drive to Arden in the same amount of time. She did not mind driving, and the passive solar home on Shady Lane Drive offered beautiful views of the Pisgah National Forest and the Great Smoky Mountains. It didn't feel like "my stomping ground," Roxanne said, but it served as a nice getaway. Asheville was arguably the most progressive city in North Carolina.

Burt's Bees' shift to personal care products led to a new catalog in 1996, the first since the move to North Carolina. Roxanne purposely did not include a date on the catalog, hoping to get multiyear use from it. "That was definitely unorthodox, but we were pretty small ... back then and could get away with it," said Mark Smith.

This 25-page gray catalog featuring Tony Kulik's signature woodcut of Burt and the company mantra, "earth friendly natural personal care products," would become a collector's item for those interested in Burt's Bees memorabilia. Like the previous two, it was meant for distribution at trade shows and similar venues, such as Sunne Justice's training sessions; it was not designed for direct-to-consumer sales.

The 1996 catalog was a milestone for two reasons, the first being that the company defined for the first time what it meant by "natural" while disclosing the percentage of natural ingredients in each of its 46 products. A natural product, according to the catalog, was "any substance that is harvested from nature and then isolated and purified by a variety of environmentally sound techniques including filtration, fermentation, distillation, expressing and other like processes." Chuck Friedman wrote the definition loosely, he said, because there might have been other processes of which he was unaware that could produce "natural" products.

In disclosing the percentage of natural ingredients in all its showcased products, Burt's Bees set the bar for the entire personal care products industry. Because there was no government standard, companies could and did use the word "natural" on products that contained only one natural ingredient, and consumers had to read labels to understand just how natural a product might be.

It had been Friedman's job to calculate the percentages of natural ingredients in each Burt's Bees product, and his results appeared in the catalog's last three pages. The lowest percentage of "naturalness" was 94.45 (for pollen night crème), and 17 products were reported as 100 percent natural (including Farmer's Friend Insect Lotion and Green Goddess Moisturizing Cream). The small percentages of artificial ingredients were not identified in the list.

Formulating all-natural or mostly natural products was a challenge for any company, because natural preservatives provided only limited shelf life. Synthetic preservatives were the Mack trucks of the mainstream personal care industry—cheap, reliable, and long-lasting—but toxicity was (and still is) the dark side of synthetics. Aromatic petroleum-derived fragrance ingredients comprised the lion's share of the synthetics, according to Friedman. A fragrance could "easily have 25 to 200 ingredients," he said. "That is why the legal term 'fragrance' is employed to encompass the many aromatic ingredients."

One or more synthetics lurked in any product that was less than 100 percent natural. Burt's Bees used synthetics not only in fragrances but also in emulsifiers and chelators. Emulsions were difficult to concoct or hold together without synthetics; synthetic chelators prevented precipitation of soaps in hard water; and denatured alcohol was mandated by the FDA to be used in some personal care products so they wouldn't be consumed orally.

When Friedman joined the company, there were synthetic fragrances in the seven products in the Burt's Beeswax line; eight products in the Baby Bee line; and in the Coconut foot crème, avocado hair treatment, tomato toner, lettuce toner, carrot soap, and tomato soap. The company's Milk and Honey lotion contained synthetics both in its fragrance and its emulsifier. The FDA permitted the synthetics in fragrances to remain proprietary, but other synthetic ingredients had to be identified in product labels.

Roxanne was often quoted as saying that "if it's not at least 92 percent natural, it's not a Burt's Bees product." Listing the percentage of natural content in each product created an aura of honesty around Burt's Bees that built loyalty among buyers and consumers.

The second milestone inclusion in the 1996 catalog was a definitive mission statement written by Roxanne that explained "who we are, what we believe, what's in it, [and] what's not in it," as well as how Burt's Bees reduced, recycled, and reused containers. Roxanne wrote that Burt's Bees was a "manufacturer of all-natural, Earth-friendly personal care products including: herbal soaps, aromatherapy bath oils, powders, bath salts, salves, and balms" that were sold through more than 3,000 stores, including the company-owned outlets in Carrboro, Ithaca, and Burlington.

"We believe that work is a creative, sustaining and fulfilling expression of the Inner Being," the statement read, and then continued:

> We believe that what is right is not always popular and what is popular is not always right. We believe that no one can do everything but everyone can do something. We believe that the most complicated and difficult problems we face as a civilization have the simplest solutions. We believe that Mother Nature has the answers and She teaches by example. We believe that by imitating Her economy, emulating Her generosity and appreciating Her graciousness, we will realize our rightful legacy on our magnificent Planet Earth.

Product ingredients, the statement continued, were "the best that Mother Nature has to offer: herbs, flowers, botanical oils, beeswax, essential oils and clay. We leave out the petroleum-synthesized fillers like mineral oil and propylene glycol, and artificial preservatives such as methyl paraben or diazolidinyl urea. Take a closer look and read the label."*

While acknowledging that Burt's Bees products were packaged in "bottles, jars, tubes, caps, closures, bags, dispensers, containers, and 'convenient' throwaway plastic," Roxanne promised that the company was working to reduce its use of plastic and "exploring the use of simple, safe, effective and time-tested materials made of cotton, paper, metal and glass." The company reused many containers and encouraged customers to do the same. It also offered to take back empties, either to reuse at the factory or to recycle.

---

*As of 2014 there was still no official definition of "natural," but after Roxanne left Burt's Bees, there would be pushback on the question of whether a natural ingredient was always better than a synthetic one. According to a February 6, 2008, article on the website Retail-Wire, for example, the Personal Care Products Council "thinks Burt's Bees ads are misleading by suggesting natural ingredients are somehow safer or more effective than synthetics."

The disclosures and the mission statement resulted in more dedicated devotees for Burt's Bees products. The forthrightness of disclosing the percentage of "natural" front and center on the label earned consumers' respect. While Roxanne ran Burt's Bees, there were no public interest groups investigating and publicizing the health effects of synthetic ingredients in skin-care products.

Roxanne understood that there was amazing power in the company's biography—and especially in its rural Maine years—and she sought to exploit that. Encouraged by Mark Smith, she wrote the most memorable of her Burt's Bees essays for the 1996 catalog and called it "Minding Our Beeswax." This warm-hearted introduction to Burt's Bees was illustrated with two photographs: a fuzzy color shot of the decrepit schoolhouse factory in Parkman with Hannah, Lucas, and Roxanne's Honda out front; and a photo of Burt sitting on his 1961 motorcycle, with his kinky beard and frizzy globs of hair poking out from beneath his cap.

The story had an easy tongue-in-cheek style that made readers shake their heads and chuckle. "I guess you could say it all started because there weren't many jobs up there north of Bangor," Roxanne wrote, telling the tale of meeting Burt, messing with beeswax products to start a new career for herself, and turning the old schoolhouse into a crude production factory. "Well, how we got started making lip balm and ended up in North Carolina is another story, and a long one at that, so I'll save it for some other time," she wrote.

The catalog's 46 products were divided into "bedazzling" sub-brands— Baby Bee, Burt's Beeswax, Farmer's Friend, Farmer's Market, Green Goddess (with gold foil stamping on the package), and Ocean Potion. The stand-out product was lip balm in the new, partly plastic tube that Roxanne had worked so hard to obtain. Within three months of sending out cases of lip balm in the new tube to buyers, however, the company was getting scattered returns due to rancidity. Chuck Friedman identified the problem ingredient as sweet almond oil, which was unstable, and replaced it with sunflower seed oil. Since the 1996 catalog was the first to give the "percentages of natural" in each product, wholesale buyers could see that the lip balm was 95.29 percent natural. It contained synthetic vitamin E to help stabilize the product. (The percentages were also on product labels.) The Farmer's Market line used an old idea of Roxanne's in a new way. She had been the first to make novelty candles in the shapes of fruits and vegetables back in Maine. Now she introduced ten skincare products with fruit and vegetable ingredients, including apple, grape, orange, coconut, lemon, avocado, and carrot. The line's riskiest product was carrot nutritive crème, which could cause reddening of the skin, discolor the neck of a white shirt, and smell bad. Her R&D team tried to convince her not to go ahead with it, but Roxanne prevailed. The product sold very well because carrot seed drew blood to the skin's surface, helping heal skin damage and giving skin a radiant look.*

A half-dozen new products were offered in experimental lines called Rebound and Wise Woman. Rebound bath and body items targeted "the active individual" like Lance, a fictional "young warrior" in a marketing tale called "Deliverance." The story told how his sore muscles received healing relief from Rebound products. The Wise Woman products were aimed at women seeking a little herbal comfort in a salve or massage oil. In keeping with Burt's Bees' quirky style, the items were illustrated with a photograph of a U.S. Route 1 highway sign pointing the way to Wise, a township in the Virginia mountains.

The Ocean Potion line, using powered kelp, dulse, sea clay, marine silts, and sea salts, was highlighted by a vignette entitled "Strange Laundry," which described Roxanne and Burt's visit to Larch Hanson's seaweed camp in coastal Steuben, Maine, in July 1994. Always casting around for novel ideas, Roxanne had seen a notice for the unusual camp in the Maine Organic Farmers and Gardeners Association newspaper. Hanson, the owner of Maine Seaweed Company, ran a camp for adults every June after finishing his commercial harvest.

Wanting to learn about the potential uses for seaweed in Burt's Bees products, Roxanne decided to attend the camp, and Burt joined her, taking along an old Army canvas tent for them to sleep in for the week. Hanson rowed his clients out to sea for a tutorial on seaweeds, to watch seals, and to relax and have fun. He cooked them his favorite seaweed dishes for dinner.

When Mark Smith suggested that Roxanne write an article about her experience for the new catalog, she liked the idea, figuring people would be interested in learning how Hanson harvested kelp, dulse, and Irish moss from the cold Atlantic, lugged it back to the mainland in homemade wooden dories, and pinned up the seaweed on a clothesline to dry.

The catalog also offered advice about babies and how to plant by moon phases; told a whimsical story of Green Goddess ingredients, such as flower devas and violet signs; and reprinted a poem about a wheat harvest by Alice

---

*All of the carrot products contained carrot seed oil. Tons of seeds had to be pressed to obtain the oil. It was an expensive process, and the cost was the reason most companies wouldn't use carrot seed oil as an ingredient.

C. Henderson. Last, Burt's Bees suggested "good medicine" for life: "fasting, meditation, sunlight, deep breathing, clean air, clean water, right livelihood, green vegetables, hard work, sound sleep. And the wind in your hair. And the stars in your eyes. And love in your heart."

At this point in Burt's Bees' evolution, most of its products were identified by lines, such as Farmer's Friend Gardener's soap, Green Goddess foot powder, and Farmer's Market Avocado Butter. Consumers had to look on the back or bottom of a package to find the Burt's Bees name, and Burt's face and the Burt's Beeswax branding remained on the fronts of only a few products. Three product supplements followed the 1996 catalog with fresh items and humorous and nonsensical text. The first of these, again with Burt's face on the cover, featured an expanded Bay Rum sub-line of cologne, shaving and exfoliating soaps, and accessories that included a shaving brush, mug, razor, and gift tote. Roxanne's "Stepping Out" sidebar commentary said that Burt's "favorite fragrance is the aroma of his thrice reheated beans smoldering on the wood stove," but that he sometimes washed up and stepped out "wearing Burt's Bees Bay Rum Cologne, which he adroitly combs through his beard while congratulating himself upon past and future conquests. The self-assurance, success and sublime subtlety this carefully crafted scent bestows upon the wearer cannot be exaggerated," she wrote. "This is unbridled animal magnetism at its most powerful."

Speaking of animal magnetism, the supplement's expanded Furry Friends pages depicted a woodcut of "Mr. Wonderful," Rufus. "Let's not overlook the ecstatic unity of unconditional love found in the unfathomable depths of a pair of brown eyes," Roxanne wrote. Among the nine Furry Friends items were oat straw pet soap, tea tree pest powder, and calendula flower hot-spot ointment to soothe pet skin. This seven-page supplement also introduced the short-duration Kitchen Cupboard collection of hand and nail products.

The other two supplements were slim mail-order promotions. Their covers displayed photographs of backwoods Burt. One showed a bespectacled, relaxed Burt reading on the front porch of a country store, with Rufus sitting in an old wooden chair. An Ex-Lax ("The Chocolate Laxative") advertising tin thermometer was nailed to a porch beam, and another tin sign advertised Dr. Lynas Hair Grower and Toilet Cream. There were no articles in the supplement, just a variety of skin-care products and novelties. In the photograph for the second supplement, Burt was standing in the doorway of a log cabin—the picture-perfect image of a scraggly recluse—with Rufus at his feet.

On August 1, 1997, weeks away from receiving his first social security check at age 62, Burt resigned as vice president of the company. He continued to own a third of the company and would continue to represent Burt's Bees in promotional events at health food stores, fairs, and college campuses. He was a celebrity who attracted droves of people wanting to meet the one and only Burt and get a free Burt-autographed tee-shirt.

Roxanne had continued to live on the property in Parkman with Burt, but now she wanted to move away from him and fulfill her longtime dream of living on the Maine coast. Her search for a waterside location led her to Winter Harbor, a small fishing village with a year-round population of about 900 near the entrance to the Schoodic Peninsula section of Acadia National Park.

She was wealthy enough by this time to purchase an impressive summer "cottage" in Winter Harbor's Grindstone Neck enclave, but instead she signed purchase papers on October 1, 1998, for a modest house built by a Fairfield, Connecticut, family on Jordan Pond Road. While not an impressive address, the property offered extraordinary views across Frenchman's Bay to the hills and cliffs of Mt. Desert Island.

Roxanne's new home was known locally as "the mushroom house" because the two stories of living space sat like a wide cap atop a stem. Modern in design, the building was a mere 1,200 square feet and was accessed by an outside metal spiral staircase; another space-saving spiral staircase led to the upper floor. In the guest bedroom on the main floor, Roxanne hung the decorative Burt's Bees wooden signs she had painted for the Edes building. The house gave her heat and lights at the flick of a switch, a modern kitchen and bathroom, and a postcard view of Acadia National Park. Still, she fostered her memories of her years in the cabin on Salmon Stream—formative years that created "a wealth of strength I could tap into all the time."

"Hoards of Buyers"

Burt's Bees made its debut at the National Association of Chain Drug Stores trade show in San Diego in June 1997. A public relations wire story reported that "hoards of buyers" flocked to the booth to see the hand salves, lip balms, and soaps. According to the article, comments such as "this is just what the trade needs" and "we're really interested in this line ... rang in the ears of Roxanne Quimby." Two big new national accounts—Long's Drug

Stores and Fred Meyer grocery stores—placed orders for Burt's Bees products at the show. Roxanne's willingness to sell to these chains was a calculated step in the direction of mass marketing.

New Age Journal and Business North Carolina each caught up with Roxanne in 1997 and retold the Burt's Bees story with the usual poverty-to-wealth angle, but media coverage remained thin. While sticking to her determination not to spend precious financial resources on expensive advertising, Roxanne knew she had to be proactive on the publicity front to fuel consumers' appetite for Burt's Bees products.

On February 26, 1998, Nancy Behrman of Manhattan-based Behrman Communications called Roxanne, and the two met several times to plan a public relations campaign. This turned out to be another timely idea. Through the Internet's PR Newswire service, Behrman had an easy feed into newspapers and beauty, fashion, and lifestyle magazines. Within five months, she landed Burt's Bees in People magazine with celebrities such as Brooke Shields and Kirstie Alley lauding the benefits of Burt's Bees lip balm and Baby Bee products. A Forbes article followed a few months later, focusing on Roxanne and Burt as successful "bootstrappers," just as Inc. magazine had done in September 1992. Then came articles in Fortune Small Business, Entrepreneur, Vanity Fair, Family Circle, and Business Journal and spots on CNN Cable News, National Public Radio, and the Today Show, putting Burt's Bees in front of millions of consumers' eyes.

Behrman would later claim that the "Burt's Bees' brand was really built on PR," and Roxanne agreed that Behrman Communications was instrumental to the company's success. By the time Roxanne sold Burt's Bees, the publicity firm had placed 900 articles and product highlights as well as some ads in the print media. The publicity was worth millions of dollars.

The company's success called for a new catalog with a fresh look—a marked stylistic departure from the crunchy granola past. The 1998 publication featured a bright white background and replaced Tony Kulik's signature woodcut with a photograph of Burt oozing a "dude" attitude instead of a "harmless old geezer" air. Sporting oversized black sunglasses under a gray wool cap, Burt wore a black leather jacket over a black fleece vest and a red plaid shirt. His hands were stuffed into his worn jeans. His beard and mustache remained characteristically wispy and untrimmed. His no-apologies stance made him appear tough enough to ride with any motorcycle clan.

The saucy name "The Buccaneer of Buzz" was printed across the bottom of the cover under Burt's photo. The iconic yellow and red tin of lip balm was featured too, with the tag "The World's Best Lip Balm."

The "Buccaneer" catalog added to the company folklore. This time Roxanne's introduction was titled "Lucky in Love," illustrated by a full-page photo of Rufus licking Burt's face as man and dog sat in the back of a dark-green pickup with a bumper sticker for the famous Benson, North Carolina, Mule Days parade. Roxanne's story described how Burt and Rufus had met, finding each other by happenstance. Roxanne had been looking for a successor to her own beloved dog Sid, and Burt had gone along for the ride. But as soon as Burt and Rufus laid eyes on each other, they had an "in love" experience, Roxanne recounted—though Burt wouldn't let Rufus move in with him until the little golden retriever was housebroken. "It's hard to believe Burt would be so fussy about a few puppy accidents," wrote Roxanne, "'cause I could tell you stories about his housekeeping that would make your toes curl, but I guess his own brand of 'inferior decorating,' as he calls it, looks a lot better to him than it does to me."

In the catalog, she related one of her favorite tales about the pair. While waiting for her in the lobby of an upscale hotel with a 'no pets' policy, Burt and Rufus sat together on a satin brocade divan while the hotel staff looked on in "dumbfounded horror." Likely, Roxanne said, man and dog were able to wrangle a room because they were so unusual.

While the narrative built on the same "unusual" story of Burt's Bees, the 1998 catalog fired up Burt's image. The catalog sidebar for Bay Rum products showed Burt without his shades and smiling. "Animal Magnetism in a Bottle," read the headline, implying that Burt was more appealing than his looks might suggest. The Bay Rum line was beefed up with four products for men, such as shaving soap and a shaving mug and brush accessories. Burt was also featured with the Rebound products as "Bahama Burt" playing golf and dressed in red-and-orange shorts and shirt with white socks, shoes, and visor. "He was cooler than a cucumber as he addressed the ball," the catalog explained.

Burt appeared again in three poses on the catalog's back cover. In all three he was without his leather jacket, and in two he was smiling and without sunglasses. "We Deliver What Others Only Promise!" proclaimed the headline. Burt's Bees commitment to recycling was highlighted by a statement in small print indicating that the catalog was printed with soy-based inks on 50 percent recycled paper, half of it post-consumer waste.

The sub-lines in the1998 catalog included 78 products, of which 28 were new, from jasmine décolleté crème to Lifeguard's Choice Weatherproofing Lip Balm and Fruitsicle soaps. Available in three flavors, Fruitsicle was a popsicle-shaped soap made by an outside contractor. Later it was referred to in a *Consumer Reports* article as "a dumb idea," and Roxanne quickly eliminated it. She also took Burt's image off the face-care products after the 1996 catalog because women customers complained about the image of a bearded, aging man on their facial products.

Sales increased to $6 million in 1997 and $8.225 million in 1998. The company's portfolio of products grew to 100 that year, yet Roxanne remained habitually frugal. She limited capital expenditures to $75,000 in 1998, equal to the salary she paid herself that year. Burt's salary was $25,000. 🐝

Katahdin, from Lunksoos Camps. (Bill Duffy photo)

The Tiger Roars

I n 1999, Roxanne took another major gamble with a new line of lipsticks called Wings of Love, which introduced glamour into the Burt's Bees brand and constituted a marked departure from the hippie, granola image of lip balm, soaps, skin crèmes, and lotions. For the first time, photographs of women were used on packaging and in magazine ads.

Cosmetics were unfamiliar territory for Burt's Bees. "Color cosmetics was a different animal from skin care and sold on a different premise," Roxanne said. Burt's Bees was launching itself into a dog-eat-dog market sector in which the company had no clout and was unknown to the customers it would try to reach.

"There were $50 million companies that sold just lipstick," Roxanne explained. "So we had to figure out how to differentiate ourselves from them and become more compelling than the other ones to win their customers and attract new ones." She couldn't depend on Burt's Bees' success with lip balm or lemon cuticle cream to give them any credibility in color cosmetics.

Expanding into cosmetics was a hard choice for Roxanne personally as well. She thought the standard cosmetics marketing message equated a woman's self-worth with beauty and exaggerated the beauty image. As a feminist, she saw makeup as a façade, a mask. She herself never wore lipstick. She didn't

186

want to send messages that would make her "sisters" believe they needed to look prettier or younger, and she certainly didn't want to use an Estée Lauder–type model for the products.

On the other hand, marketplace realities had pressured her to rethink her stand against color cosmetics. Based on the fabulously profitable lip balm, she knew natural lipstick had the potential to become a major profit center. Lipstick would cost more to manufacture than lip balm, but she could charge five times more for it because it was a beauty product.

One of Roxanne's fond childhood memories was seeing her mother put on bright-red lipstick to transform herself for a night out with John Quimby. Roxanne would watch her mother's reflection in the mirror. "I was about five or six, and the feeling was, 'wow, my mom is so beautiful.'" It didn't happen often—Rebecca Quimby usually wore a housedress with or without an apron, because she was continuously cleaning the house and washing dishes—but when it did happen, it was memorable.

"It was magical for me to see Mom with her lipstick on," Roxanne recalled, "and I thought I could capture that magic" of enhancing women's good feelings about themselves. "So I thought, okay, you can do lipstick … a very healthy lipstick, not anything with Red Dye No. 2." She wanted a lipstick line that would emphasize health and equate it with beauty.

Yet even after getting "right" with herself about entering the color cosmetics arena, Roxanne couldn't get a lipstick line into the market right away. She had trouble finding a manufacturer that could make a completely recyclable lipstick tube to meet Burt's Bees' recycling requirement. "It wasn't our right to create trash," she explained.

Conventional lipsticks came in a plastic casing welded to a metal swivel unit, allowing it to be turned up and down. After looking for an alternative for three years, Roxanne found a small company in Italy that still had machinery from the 1950s that made push-up lipstick tubes. The push-up unit was 100 percent recyclable aluminum and was raised with a recyclable plastic lever. This achievement enabled Burt's Bees to proudly say that most of its packaging was made from aluminum, recycled cardboard, or glass.

The Wings of Love lipstick line was a landmark for Burt's Bees in that humans other than Burt were used for the first time as models. This change, too, required Roxanne to shift her personal politics. She had always disliked professional models' "arrogant and cold-looking" poses on packaging, as well as the advertising that suggested "they had something you don't but you would if you aspired to the model's level of beauty and bought the products [they advertised]." Instead of professional models, Roxanne used women she knew: her daughter Hannah, twin nieces Megan and Morgan Quimby, Lucas's girlfriend Jennifer Amara, yoga and astrology friends, and a waitress and owner of a restaurant in Asheville.

As always, the product had to express Roxanne's commitment to natural ingredients, human health, environmental protection, and Burt's Bees' personality. The initial lipstick was promoted as "all natural," with beeswax, natural pigmentations, essential oils, and herbal extracts, though it also contained the same synthetic vitamin E that was used as a stabilizer in the lip balm.

The cover of the advertising brochure featured Hannah Quimby holding a dog, and the inside copy referred to the lipstick as "true, *living* color; free of the drying chemicals and metallic residues found in synthetic dyes." It also called attention to the new "retro push-up aluminum lipstick case" that minimized packaging "so you can easily recycle it with your soda or beer cans."

Wings of Love lipstick came in seven "heavenly hues," from pearl to brownish-red. Roxanne thought these natural pigments were much more complementary to a woman's face than synthetic shades. She playfully named the colors after Angel card names—honesty, strength, willingness, play, adventure, grace, and spontaneity. The lipsticks could be purchased in full-sized containers or in a sample kit containing all seven hues in smaller containers, a strategy Roxanne had employed successfully to introduce consumers to other product lines. Along with the lipsticks, three all-natural powdered facial tissues of rice paper and cornstarch were introduced.

The Wings ad copy used sensual language, and the models struck enticing poses. The word "love" was used generously, along with "kiss of color," "deliciously kissable collection," and "supple kissability."

The colors were limited to seven because the pigments had to come from nature rather than a chemist's lab—and Roxanne felt that seven was plenty. She believed that women would love a natural lipstick choice because they would prefer not to ingest the plastic and silicone used in conventional brands.

To launch Wings of Love with a splash, Behrman Communications arranged a luncheon at the Library Hotel in New York City for the top editors of the beauty magazines. "Since our lipsticks were made of all vegetable ingredients and were much safer than the commercial lipsticks available at the time, we decided to make a graphic demonstration on the safety," Roxanne recalled. "It is a fact that women who wear lipstick basically 'eat' four pounds of lipstick over the course of their lives, because, of course, the lipstick they apply to their mouths is eventually ingested." Chuck Friedman went along, hand carrying four pounds of lipstick in a bag. At the hotel, he asked for a platter and was given the largest one in the kitchen.

Friedman donned an apron and chef's hat, cut up the mounds of lipstick, and placed them on the platter to show the editors the amount of lipstick consumed by a typical woman over a lifetime. "He went up to one of the beauty editors with the big load of lipstick and pretended to serve it to her," Roxanne recollected. But while Friedman was attempting to spray whipped cream on the lipstick, the nozzle malfunctioned and sprayed the beauty editor. Roxanne thought it was pretty funny, but the beauty editor didn't laugh, and neither did Friedman. He thought it might be his "last supper."

Donna Hollenbach was the only member of the R&D team who was not "super excited" about Burt's Bees lipsticks. A Bobbi Brown cosmetics customer, she was skeptical that the new lipsticks would fare well in the highly competitive lipstick sector. Charged with sourcing the lipstick containers from Italy, she bought 3,000 of them initially. They were sold out in three months, and it was six months before Burt's Bees could get a resupply, which meant shipping orders were delayed.

It would be another two to three years before Burt's Bees launched other components of the natural makeup line—tinted moisturizer, blushing and concealing crèmes, facial powder, eye shadow, eyeliner, and eyebrow pencils. It took a great deal of time to test the market for natural color cosmetics, build consumer demand, and develop those products with beauty-enhancing and unusually "clean" ingredients.

Burt's Bees didn't produce any anti-aging products while Roxanne owned the company. She was busy enough without trying to develop products to erode the "old" stereotypes of beauty. She hoped that any woman, whether 22 or 85 years old, would buy Burt's Bees products because using them would be fun and would enhance natural beauty and health. "There are more important things to be than pretty," she believed.

Body lotions were another matter, however, and Roxanne knew the company had to offer these if it wanted to become a household name. There were two problems: the lotion had to meet her definition of "natural," and it couldn't be packaged in unrecycled plastic. Finding a way to preserve lotions naturally became another challenge for Chuck Friedman. His solution was to use a milk and sugar enzyme preservative that was revolutionary at the time, enabling Burt's Bees to become the first company to market a 98.67 percent natural Milk and Honey lotion.

Glass bottles weren't feasible, being too heavy and expensive to ship. Roxanne was willing to package the lotions in recycled plastic bottles if she could find a manufacturer that would make bottles for such a small business. Finally Burt's Bees was able to team up with the much larger personal care company Aveda and convince a vendor to take an order. "We really had to pull [the deal] out of the vendor to [make] post-consumer plastic," Roxanne said. The three body lotions produced by Burt's Bees made a significant contribution to 1999 sales.

All told in 1999, Burt's Bees introduced 22 new products, more than it had ever introduced in a single year. What kept motivating her to grow the company was not money, although she wouldn't deny she loved the feel of cash in her hand. "I'm in it for the challenge," she told an *Inc.* magazine writer. "It's about the game. The money is just kind of the score. I'm still very curious about how far I can push this."

The Company Takes Off

One of the key changes Roxanne made in 1999 to strengthen the Burt's Bees brand was to eliminate the sub-brands established three years earlier. She had thought that sub-lines such as Ocean Potion and Green Goddess would make their respective suites of products more distinctive in the marketplace, but it was hard enough to build the Burt's Bees brand without trying to build twelve sub-brands at the same time.* Sub-lines diffused the company's marketing energy and confused retailers and consumers, who didn't automatically connect a sub-line product to its parent company. When a company sales rep complimented a store manager on a Burt's Bees Green Goddess display, for example, the manager might respond that the store didn't carry Burt's Bees. Many thought Green Goddess was a stand-alone company.

Roxanne's solution was to put all the sub-lines in yellow packaging by the end of 2000, with the Burt's Bees name and beehive logo prominently displayed above the product name. Older lines with annual sales of less than $1 million wholesale were eliminated.

---

*The gold foil stamping on the Green Goddess packaging had been eliminated by this time because it was costly and not environmentally friendly.

Knowing that Burt's Bees' competitors used flashy colors to get attention, Roxanne and Mark Smith redesigned the packaging for all products with lively colors, including more yellow as backdrop for hearty red lettering. Roxanne correctly predicted that the conspicuous yellow and red would unify the branding and make a statement on retail shelves.

Another nervy step forward in 1999 was the opening of the first Burt's Bees showroom and sales office for vendors at the Jacob Javits Center in Manhattan. The idea was to more closely connect the company with marketing centers and provide a venue to create buzz for Burt's Bees products. One of the immediate benefits of the showroom was a deal with Starbucks. While walking through the gift center, the company's buyers happened to see the Burt's Bees showroom and were attracted to the lip balm. Starbucks signed a deal with Burt's Bees to carry the product in the Seattle-based company's stores during the Christmas season and to include it among the coffee items in their Christmas gift baskets. Roxanne was elated with the trial run; the Starbucks deal was a great example of the alternative distribution channels she wanted in the Burt's Bees sales mix.

Behrman Communications convinced Roxanne to try commercial advertising in national magazines to see if it would boost sales appreciably. An advertisement for Baby Bee skin-care products was placed in *Woman's Day* magazine, which was read by baby boomer women. Roxanne was shocked when it generated more than 10,000 calls to Burt's Bees' toll-free number. An ad in *The New Yorker* pulled in only 1,500 responses.

The cumulative impact of these changes was dramatic. Sales jumped to $13.40 million in 1999—an amazing 63 percent increase over 1998 and almost $3 million beyond Roxanne's target for the year—and then kept on climbing. Another 67.7 percent increase in 2000 catapulted sales to $22.46 million. Roxanne was elated that her intuition of 1989 that she had a tiger by the tail had been confirmed by the marketplace. She had grown Burt's Bees almost to the magic $25 million she thought was needed to attract investor or acquisition interest.

The U.S. market for natural personal care products was valued at $5.2 billion in 2000 and was forecast to exceed $12 billion by the end of the decade. In eight years, Burt's Bees had moved to the forefront of the natural-products business sector and was nationally recognized as a leader in the personal care products industry. Some even said Burt's Bees was the leader. But with less than a 1 percent share of a rapidly growing market, the company had boundless room to grow.

One casualty of superheated growth was the company breakfasts. For a number of years, the Burt's Bees staff had been treated to a celebratory on-site breakfast each time the sales jumped another $1 million—a practice dating back to Guilford days. That ended when the company hit $20 million in sales between 1999 and 2000. After that, sales achievements were celebrated with a catered meal. Roxanne would circulate a printed menu from Salsa Fresh in Raleigh and would order in whatever her staff wanted.

Burt's Bees' success was good for other small natural products companies too. Bill Whyte, who had founded Badger Balm in Keene, New Hampshire, almost 10 years after Burt's Bees began, saw his tiny enterprise grow quickly, thanks partly to the "larger and larger presence" of Burt's Bees in the market-place. "We came behind that curve and with a similar line, but Roxanne had already set the tone ... and acceptance for [natural products]," he reflected.

Whyte's business did $125,000 in sales in its first full year of operation in 1996, then hit $600,000 in 1997 and $1 million in 1998 as he added more products. His approach differed from Roxanne in that 98 percent of Badger Balm products were anhydrous—"simple, no water, the minimalist approach," he said—and he followed the customary practice of paying retailers' charge-backs—penalties levied on suppliers for early or late shipments, violations of a retailer's shipping requirements, defective or missing labels, and so on. Roxanne had always refused to pay chargebacks, and Whyte was impressed by her "my way" business style.

Whyte noticed that Roxanne gained a leg up on competitors with her product displays. Having observed that customers would purchase multiple items if her products were clustered, she wrangled deals with stores to group Burt's Bees products rather than dispersing them to multiple category sections with competitors' items. She also provided stand-alone "hive" displays made of wood, wire, or other materials for end-cap displays. The racks stood out, maximizing visibility, and the more visible a product was, the better it sold.

Customers couldn't walk into a gift or natural foods store without find-ing Burt's Bees products in front of them. "Back then, when I asked any store buyer why they gave so much space to Burt's Bees, they said Burt's sells like crazy," Whyte said. Typically a supplier could only suggest or offer incen-tives to a store owner to gain better shelf placement, but Burt's Bees was the exception. The display arrangement with Henri Bendel stores years before had taught Roxanne a lesson she never forgot: The closer to a store's front door the products were, the better the sales.

Whyte and other entrepreneurs were aware that Roxanne ran Burt's Bees, but they didn't know her well or at all. Darrin Duber-Smith of Green Marketing, Inc., a Colorado-based strategic planning firm, observed that Roxanne kept a "low profile" among marketing consultants and others outside the manufacturing side of the personal care products sector. She didn't take a leadership role in the industry, he said, nor did she speak at conferences or other industry events. Despite the fact that Burt had only a one-third share in Burt's Bees until 1999, "people assumed Burt owned the company," Duber-Smith said.

Burt turned over his share in the company to Roxanne in 1999 for $130,000, making her the 99.9 percent owner.* Neither of them explained this turn of events at the time or for years after, but Burt broke his silence in an 88-minute documentary, *Burt's Buzz*, by Canadian filmmaker Jody Shapiro that debuted at the Toronto Film Festival in September 2013. It was the first time Burt, then 79 years old, had spoken so openly to the media.

In the film, Burt recounted the beginnings of Burt's Bees in Maine and seemed to take a generous share of credit for its rise to phenomenal success, yet he referred to Roxanne as wanting only "money and power, and I was just a pillar on the way to that success." He told Shapiro that he had slept with other women, and when Roxanne found out, "she went crazy. She accused me of sexual harassment and went completely berserk.† She consulted a lawyer," he went on, "and put [a termination] paper on the desk and said, 'There. Take it or leave it.'" The paper he signed forfeited his share of the company. He said he hoped never to see her again.

Roxanne declined to appear in *Burt's Buzz* or to be interviewed for the documentary. When the *Associated Press* asked her to respond, she did so in an e-mail saying simply, "Everyone associated with the company was treated fairly, and in some cases very generously, upon the sale of the company and my departure as CEO. And that, of course, includes Burt."‡

For this book, Roxanne disputed the circumstances but not the reasons for Burt's departure. She said his termination was not forced on him; rather,

---

*The remaining tenth of a percent of the company's stock was set aside as options to be dispensed to senior staff.

†Lucas said in an interview for the film that Burt had "started a relationship of some sort with one of the college kids" working in one of the company-owned stores.

‡When Roxanne sold a majority interest in Burt's Bees to AEA Investors in 2003, she gave Burt $4 million in consideration of his past contributions to the company's success. The payment was voluntary, not contractually obligated.

he signed the agreement because he understood that it was in the best interests of the company. Their prior personal relationship was not a contributing factor, she said. His actions had placed the company at risk.

After surrendering his share of the company, Burt continued to receive income for the use of his image and name and to represent Burt's Bees on promotional tours.* In August 1999, the company started "Burt Tours" to college campuses, health food stores, and bookstores. The objective was to test the appeal of Burt's Bees products to young adults, especially women students. The idea of college campuses as a new distribution channel fell into Roxanne's lap when a company intern studied the 18- to 25-year-old demographic in an MBA project and gave Roxanne the results and a business plan. Roxanne hired a college bookstore sales specialist to manage these sales.

Burt ranged to the West Coast and beyond (the documentary shows him in Taiwan), handing out free samples of products, posters, and Burt tee-shirts at colleges and malls and receiving "rock star" attention from Burt's Bees devotees, who lined up for his autograph. The events personalized the company's relationship with customers, enhanced customer loyalty, and often drew standing-room-only crowds. The tours showed that Burt was a real person to whom people could relate, just as Roxanne had hoped back in 1986.

Knockoffs and New Hires

Roxanne frequently scouted retail stores in various cities to see what the competition was selling and how it was displayed. One such foray in late 1999 turned up an unpleasant surprise: A Manhattan drug store was carrying the real Burt's Bees lettuce, carrot, and tomato soaps but also sold a knockoff of the three soaps made by a French company. The following week, Roxanne found more knockoffs made by yet another company. She concluded that someone connected with Burt's Bees had sold her out, despite the confidentiality agreement she required employees to sign.

Knockoffs of small private-label products were hardly new, and suing was an expensive remedy that Roxanne didn't want to pursue. She told *Inc.*

*Burt appeared in a documentary called *Bee Movie* in 2007 that called attention to Colony Collapse Disorder, a growing threat to honey bees. He spoke about the important pollination role bees have in agriculture and noted that Burt's Bees was helping to fund research seeking a solution to CCD.

magazine that the best way to "bullet-proof your brand" was to make sure consumers knew who originated the product and how natural it was.

To enhance the Burt's Bees brand among Manhattanites, Roxanne hired an actor dressed in a bee costume to walk the streets handing out free lip balm, Burt-signed posters, and tee-shirts. She loved thinking up such unconventional promotions. "It would have been seen as ridiculous for Revlon or Clinique to have done things like we did," Roxanne said, but she knew her company with its countercultural image could get away with such antics.

For three years, Bob Kingery had performed an extraordinary job filling in as Burt's Bees' plant manager while also overseeing manufacturing. By mid-1999, Roxanne felt it was time to hire a new operations manager. She picked Larry Groseclose, a former Revlon executive recommended by chemist Chuck Friedman. Retired at the time, Groseclose was a seasoned executive with a background in management, financing, and budgeting. Friedman believed his former colleague's skills would be the right fit for Burt's Bees' transition from a small and quirky operation to a modern, mid-size manufacturing company.

Wanting to take some extended time off in Maine, Roxanne made the significant decision to relinquish oversight of the company's day-to-day operations to Groseclose, someone she didn't know well and hadn't worked with long. Uncharacteristically, she allowed her new overseer to work on the premises only three days a week—Tuesdays through Thursdays. Relying on his strong credentials and experience to lead the company in the way she wanted, Roxanne departed for Maine in the summer of 2000 for an eight-month sabbatical.

Groseclose's title was director of finance and operations. "Larry was a rah-rah guy who got the team going," remembered Mark Smith. "He'd fire people up, whip them up to a frenzy—do this, do that." He was "incredibly successful" at moving the company forward financially, Smith said. Burt's Bees sales went from about $13 million to $30 million under Groseclose. Consumer demand outstripped the company's capacity during his tenure. "It was unbelievable growth," he said.

Years later, Groseclose remembered Roxanne as aggressive, focused, single-minded, smart, talented—and intimidating at times. She was unusually creative, penurious to a fault, and attuned to her customers "to a T." Her weaknesses, he said, were her lack of training or knowledge in the leading-edge technology and manufacturing processes that Burt's Bees increasingly needed in order to make innovative products.

Groseclose knew that mass merchandisers were beginning to push out of business the smaller stores that carried Burt's Bees products. The "big boxes" were determined to get a piece of the action in natural skin-care products, and Roxanne was going to have to come to terms with that, he believed. She might not want to do business with Walmart, Target, or other huge operations, but the mass merchandisers "were not going to let her alone."

During Groseclose's first weeks on the job, he was struck by how "tough" the Burt's Bees employee culture was and how continuous was the coming and going of entry-level production workers. Employee training never stopped, he said, since replacement numbers were so high. By 1999, there were about fifty salaried and hourly employees.

Before Groseclose was hired, Burt's Bees leased a second facility near the Brownleigh Drive plant to handle the fattened administrative and manufacturing operations. Yet even that additional space wasn't enough to accommodate the company's rapid growth. Roxanne directed Groseclose to start looking for a new manufacturing site that would house all operations under one roof, possibly outside Raleigh to keep costs down.

Just after Groseclose joined the company, Sheila Clark was hired as Burt's Bees' accounts receivable manager. The words that came to her mind when thinking about her first months on the job were "excitement," "thrilling," and "stress." Although the company was almost 15 years old, Clark viewed production and the workforce culture as "not corporate at all yet." She was surprised that some processes remained antiquated. The flow of paperwork and orders was still messy, and there was still no database to track orders. It was a situation conducive to mistakes and dissatisfied customers.

It took Clark awhile to figure out the working environment but not long to realize that almost everyone, including Groseclose, wanted to shield Roxanne from problems. And the sales numbers were so good that a lot could be hidden under the rug. (Groseclose later recalled that he was just doing his job as he saw it, which was to handle operations and "not delegate those issues upward" to Roxanne.)

At the dawn of the new century, Roxanne viewed her team as top-notch. "I thought we could do almost anything," she remembered. Renee was cranking sales, Sunne Justice was scoring big training seminar successes, and her on-site staff was full of talent and commitment. But her financial officer, Gordon Brown, quit without warning one night because, according to Roxanne, he disagreed with her management style and politics and was fed up by his run-ins with her. Roxanne immediately called her sister Rachelle, an MBA. "You gotta come," Roxanne told her.

Rachelle flew from her home in California to Raleigh and stayed a year to sort out Burt's Bees money matters. An environmentalist and a vegan, she further "greened" the Burt's Bees culture, according to Mark Smith. Some of the long-time staff remembered that she was impressively energetic, exercised religiously, and ate bunches of bananas and oranges at work. She was also highly professional, and the staff minded their p's and q's around her.

When Rachelle returned home in 2000, she took several key accounts to manage long distance. She remained with the company until 2002.

Chuck Friedman worked overtime developing and testing natural preservatives for the new product lines, but he also remained vigilant about the company's claims of product purity and safety. Public concern about health and safety was increasing, as were lawsuits against companies in response to product contamination and failures that resulted in recalls. He was a formulating chemist, not a microbiologist, and he believed that Burt's Bees should commit the necessary funds for a rigorous testing program. Failure to institute such testing could place the company in violation of the Food, Drug, and Cosmetic Act, he said in a proposal for microbiological compliance written in the late 1990s.

His four-page plan pointed out that the act required a commitment from all manufacturers to establish and maintain a total quality program covering raw materials (those of "natural origin") and those that were water based. He listed 53 Burt's Bees products (such as the lip balm and Farmer's Market Carrot Crème) that had self-preserving characteristics and could be deemed safe without testing. Eight other products (including Burt's Bees Crème and Kitchen Cupboard Crème) required a preservative system, and 13 others, such as the Green Goddess Clay Mask and Baby Bee Buttermilk Bath, could harbor microorganisms. "It would be prudent of us," Friedman wrote, to hire an outside lab to test those 21 products, which were possibly unsafe for consumers and in violation of federal law. He projected the annual cost at $11,500.

"The short-term program is a band-aid approach designed to evaluate our current liability and minimize our risk," Friedman wrote. "Complete microbiological compliance that will both satisfy the regulatory agency, and adequately protect our products and the consumers that use them, is something that is beyond my scope to create and administrate."*

*Roxanne said in 2015 that she was unaware of any instance in which a consumer was harmed by a Burt's Bees product.

Groseclose took Friedman's report seriously and, with Roxanne's approval, hired an outside lab, Loricon, to take on the testing job. With Friedman's urging, Roxanne also allowed Groseclose to employ Burt's Bees' first quality assurance manager.

As natural and organic products found increasing acceptance with consumers, they fueled the rapid growth of health food stores. Whole Foods, which had become the largest organic foods chain in the U.S., had been an important Burt's Bees outlet for years. The many natural personal care product companies competing for shelf space there included Tom's of Maine, Kiss My Face, Nature's Gate, JASON Natural Products, and Avalon Natural Products, but only some of them competed with Burt's Bees across product lines with comparable prices. Prowling the aisles of Whole Foods, Roxanne concluded that the competing brands were not effectively educating the public about their products and natural ingredients. Even the older companies with the best name recognition—Aubrey Organics, Dr. Hauschka, and Dr. Bronner—"didn't hit the consumer between the eyes" with their packaging or messaging.

Burt's Bees' packaging made the products stand out on retailers' shelves. The yellow and red "told you to STOP," she said, snapping her fingers, "like the Tide detergent bull's eye." Eighty percent of consumers walking down store aisles would give a brand one to three seconds of attention. "They have a million things on their minds, and you had to have a really simple, clear message that would hit people between the eyes." The company's relatively low pricing and unisex products made it a leader in lip care and a strong competitor in skin care, color, and other areas. Roxanne pointed to Dr. Hauschka's $25-an-ounce rose day cream "that no guy or child used and only women who cared enough about skin care to [spend that amount] bought." In contrast, she said, "dads, kids, sisters, grandmothers—everyone—carried the little $2 containers of lip balm in their pockets. Aggressive pricing helped Burt's Bees get a foot in the door to woo consumers away from Estée Lauder and other glitzy, more expensive personal care products.

By the late 1990s, mainstream grocery stores and pharmacies began to take serious notice of natural and organic brands as potential new sources of revenue. Because her eventual goal was to move into the largest retail leagues, Roxanne started roaming the aisles of Walgreens pharmacies and other national chain stores to assess their strengths and weaknesses. She looked at the displays of lipsticks, lotions, and face powders, learning which brands were given eye-level shelf space, which were on the bottom shelves, how much shelf space each brand received, how the products were packaged—and, most important, what message they sent to consumers.

By the time a brand showed up in Walgreens, Roxanne reasoned, it was already established with consumers. If Burt's Bees could compete in the chains, it could compete anywhere, and she was encouraged by what she saw. "What I took from my national chain market study was that I'd have no trouble reaching the top there because those brands [already doing business in the big stores] weren't really thinking about the right things," she said.

Sweet Sixteen

By 2000, when Burt's Bees turned sixteen, the company bore little resemblance to its 1984 beginnings, yet the "Beemachine" still brimmed with the energy and promise of a hormone-driven teenager. At 50, Roxanne herself was no longer the fireball she had once been, but the most pronounced change was in her looks. The many photos of her in media coverage over the years showed a progression of hairdos from pigtails to very short hair, then long, then short again. Her shape changed from sturdy to trim to skinny and back around again. She typically wore no makeup, though she and her daughter, Hannah, wore eye and face makeup (and Roxanne adopted a page-boy hair style) for an article in the May 2000 issue of *Family Circle* magazine. Her casual clothes (usually slacks and loose-fitting tops, often with a scarf around her neck) spoke to her past and her politics. Although she didn't try to look glamorous with her own company's cosmetics, she could impart her stylish artistic flair to whatever she wore. The main constant through the years, almost regardless of the occasion, was her sandals.

Burt's Bees' sales growth of 67.7 percent in 2000 set an all-time record for the company. The gross revenues of $22.46 million that year put the company well on its way to the $50 million in sales that Roxanne optimistically predicted would be reached in 2002.

By 2000, market trials in new chain outlets were bringing in heartening revenues from Bath & Body Works, Hannaford supermarkets in New England, and Publix Super Markets and Winn-Dixie grocery stores in the South. Burt's Bees' supercharged growth overwhelmed the workforce. "The company couldn't catch its breath," said Mark Smith. A lot of people burned out, from the top ranks to the bottom. He recalled the situation as "edgy. There was a perverse entertainment aspect to it." Burt's Bees ranked #2 that year on *Triangle Business Journal*'s list of the 50 fastest-growing companies in the Research Triangle.

Such stellar growth as Burt's Bees experienced in the late 1990s and early 2000s forced Roxanne to reinvent the company time after time. About every 18 months, she could tell which managers could not adapt to the "weight and pressure" of increasing responsibilities. An annual sales growth of more than 30 percent flushed out who needed to be let go, she said.

The gangbuster product fueling Burt's Bees' growth in 2000 was lip shimmers—lip balm with a touch of color. Lip shimmers were Roxanne's creative response to the slow sales of the Wings of Love lipsticks. "Lipstick wasn't a bad seller," she mused, but her target buyers—women accustomed to conventional lipsticks—didn't rush to embrace her natural option. "My crunchy granola Whole Foods crowd didn't care too much about lipstick," she said.

Lip shimmers, however, caught the attention of young girls awakening to the lure of cosmetics, an untapped market for Burt's Bees. In 1973, Bonne Bell, the family company founded in 1927, created Lip Smackers, a flavored lip gloss for preteens, and commandeered the bulk of that product sector. Roxanne reasoned that she could take away some of Bonne Bell's customers "who were open to experimentation," hold on to them, and depend on their brand faithfulness to grow her color cosmetics line. "By the time the girl consumers were using color cosmetics for real, I would have established a position with them, and they would continue to use [the lipsticks]—just like the MAC [Cosmetics] or Estée Lauder customers wouldn't think of changing their lipstick in their thirties or forties."

To make sure parents would be amenable to their tweens or teenagers wearing lip shimmers, Roxanne promoted it as a "harmless" lip moisturizer—like lip balm—rather than a lipstick. Roxanne packaged the product in a slim wind-up recyclable plastic tube, a classy lady-like product for the younger set. The price was cheap—under $5—in easy reach of many girls' pocketbooks. Shimmers came in more than a half dozen colors such as champagne and coffee.

With lip shimmers in the lineup, Burt's Bees hit $33.49 million in sales in 2001, up 49 percent from the previous year. Roxanne calculated that shimmers were outperforming the reliable lip balm and constituted "the home run" she had hoped the lipsticks would be. Starter kits added considerable profits too. Burt's Bees was one of the only skin-care companies that offered kits as a regular part of its product lineup. Sales of the assortments of seven to twelve trial-sized samples in a reusable, resealable package grew at a compounded rate of 100.7 percent between 1997 and 2002 while also boosting the stand-alone sales of the kit's component items.

Roxanne's thinking by 2002 was that "every product [should] be a gem that could be taken out of its little family, sit on the shelf and radiate out a message all by itself. I wanted jewels rather than a lot of costume jewelry." Her five best jewels were lip shimmers, lip balm, lemon butter cuticle cream, Farmer's Friend hand salve, and coconut foot cream, and she was their creator.

The organizational chart at Burt's Bees still showed glaring absences for a company growing so rapidly. Between 2000 and 2003, Roxanne hired managers and other staff right and left. Good people management, she had learned, was critical to business success. Many people "want to be managed ... feel best when you are setting goals, helping them achieve ... and grow in their ability to take on responsibility," she observed. "There are some who don't ... and are totally unmanageable." She liked to work with both kinds. "I've had very, very productive work relationships with people who are totally unmanageable ... [I]t [was] usually very short, like a laser beam project, sometimes just a day because they are usually the more brilliant ones. The others may not burn as intensely but are totally dependable in getting things done, and you need a good proportion of those" to run a business.

Several of Larry Groseclose's former Revlon colleagues followed him to Burt's Bees, including Tom McGraw in customer service and Margie McDaniel in purchasing and planning. John Hoyle and Mel Stevens joined the team to oversee packaging, order fulfillment, and shipping. Later, other Revlon executives replaced those who were fired or resigned, such as Ken Troshinsky, who replaced John Fragomeni as chief financial officer. Groseclose also brought in some lower-level former Revlon employees, among them supervisors and mechanics. Gossipers at the office water cooler called the newcomers "Groseclose's gang."

Mike Abramson, who joined the staff in 2000 as Burt's Bees fifty-fourth employee, had been director of human resources at Productivity Point International and Family Health International for a total of eight years. His task at Burt's Bees was to engage and manage temporary workers, oversee staffing, and devise management strategies for the growing workforce. He was expected to create a productive and happy work culture by using effective "employee branding," hiring a personality type that best represented the company values.

That "type" for territory sales reps, he recollected, was hard-working women in their late thirties with a natural look: little makeup; nice complexion; and low-heeled shoes. His other responsibilities included developing employee salary increase recommendations for Roxanne.

"I most certainly had to prove myself to Roxanne," Abramson recalled. "All her senior managers had to work very hard and continually prove themselves to her. She valued honesty and diligence, and managers had to be on top of their game. Everyone warned me about Roxanne's moods. I warned others."

Abramson evolved into "Roxanne's henchman." He compared himself to the Anne Hathaway character, Andy, in the movie *The Devil Wears Prada*. "I was Andy to Miranda Priestly [the powerful editor-in-chief of a fashion magazine who scared all her underlings in the movie]," he said. She confirmed that he was her "soulmate. I'm sure we've been around the world together in other lifetimes. [I] could just hear [my] soul and feel totally trusting [of him]."

Abramson kept Roxanne abreast of gossip so she would know what was going on behind the scenes. He provided documentation of warnings to employees, and those who received two or three warnings "were out." In *The Devil Wears Prada*, anyone who wanted to see Miranda Priestly had to go through her assistants. Similarly, people had to go through Abramson to get an appointment with Roxanne, and he was offered a lot of free hockey and basketball game tickets by vendors and journalists. But Abramson only reported to Roxanne who wanted to see her; she made her own appointments.

Roxanne thought Abramson was "the most wonderful HR guy ... a real humane person and very smart. He kept the workforce reasonably happy and kept me happy." Donna Hollenbach recollected that a lot of employees felt threatened by his close relationship with Roxanne. Roxanne was aware that Abramson was "not that well-liked ... [because] he was so close to me ... my eyes and ears. People didn't like that, so they didn't like him that much. But he was invaluable."

One of Abramson's primary jobs was hiring. Roxanne had learned long before how disappointed she was when new hires didn't live up to their résumés. "People could look so great on paper ... so I learned not to trust résumés," she recalled. Learning how much stock Roxanne put in the occult, Abramson asked job applicants (though not production workers) for their astrological signs and noted this information at the bottom of each résumé.

"I'd look at the sign and know what this person could achieve if they aligned themselves with their highest purpose," Roxanne said.

Abramson also developed a salary range for each job—the first time such scales had been established at sixteen-year-old Burt's Bees. The company paid "the market rate in the lower percentile" at the time. Roxanne repeatedly told Abramson, "I want to always be seen as fair, but not generous." She made it clear that women were to be paid on par with their male counterparts and cared not only about the salaries but also the job progressions of women and minorities. Abramson said she went out of her way to hire older workers.

Burt's Bees paid more for certain factory jobs—$12 per hour for a "batcher" who mixed ingredients into volumes of product, for example. "A good one cost $16.50 an hour," Abramson remembered, and the result of hiring a less skilled worker was spilled liquids, "a continuing issue." The "fair but not generous" stance applied to benefits, too.

Abramson was in charge of salary determinations up to the managerial ranks—always subject to review by Roxanne. She alone decided what to offer top-tier hires. The two of them also established an annual system of merit pay increases for tenured employees. As Roxanne later remembered it, there would be no ad hoc raises because someone did something "to save my life" on a certain day.

Abramson believed that Roxanne trusted him. "She would let you die on the vine if she wanted to get rid of you," he said. "The message [from getting the brush-off] was get another job." He attributed his longevity to never being disagreeable with her and never initiating a project on his own.

Morale ebbed and flowed. "Anytime someone with a senior position was fired, it scared people down the line," Abramson said. "Just her style freaked out some people. It could be very exciting but also stressful."

During Roxanne's eight-month sabbatical, from the summer of 2000 to spring 2001, she visited the office unexpectedly on occasion, and her arrivals always caused a stir. Abramson would spread the word to staff, who made sure they looked busy. Sheila Clark observed that "Roxanne never liked slackers." They all knew that her arrival might signal trouble—perhaps a reprimand or a firing.

To boost staff morale, Roxanne continued to provide free product samples, service awards for tenure, and catered Thanksgiving lunches to employees. Workers were encouraged by managers to have a cookie-club exchange at Christmas and bake cakes in the shape of Burt's Bees products. Abramson tried to create a positive attitude by making sure everyone knew the Burt's

Bees story—how far the company had come from its origins and how important the employees were in that success.

In 2001, company financials told Roxanne that she could hire her own
sales reps for less money than she was paying in commissions to independent reps. She also felt she could count on an in-house sales force to be more
enthusiastic and knowledgeable about Burt's Bees products than salespeople
who were representing multiple companies. The only products in her reps'
sample cases would belong to Burt's Bees, and their income would depend on
her lines alone.

The first in-house rep, Andrew Schlindler, had worked for the vitamin
company Natrol. Upon being interviewed by Roxanne at a Starbuck's outlet,
he found her "very professional. She had definite ideas and a clear direction."
He understood that he was the test case to prove or disprove Roxanne's theory
that in-house field reps would be more effective. Schlindler wasn't personally
enthusiastic about Burt's Bees products—he thought too many of them were
for women—but he was excited about their success and the opportunity to
align himself professionally with an interesting, unique company that was
going places. He was assigned to sell to 400 accounts from Virginia to Pennsylvania, and his 2001 sales confirmed for Roxanne that an in-house sales
force was the way to go.

Sunne Justice trained Schlindler as well as the twelve other company reps
who eventually made up the field sales force. All were required to become
skilled public speakers. Schlindler visited five to seven stores a day to promote
Burt's Bees, gave product demonstrations several times a week, and handed
out samples at every opportunity. He recalled sitting down in the middle of a
room full of women retailers who wanted to touch and smell the products and
examine the packaging. "They talked about loving Burt's Bees," he said. Hearing buyers express emotional and intimate feelings for personal care products
was a first for him.

Buyers and customers rarely asked questions about the non-natural ingredients in the less- than-100-percent-natural products. Nevertheless, Schlindler
coached buyers to "always have an explanation ready for what the remaining
percentages of ingredients were. We always made the point that being natural
was voluntary and pointed to other brands that didn't quantify their product
ingredients."

While traveling 45,000 miles a year to make sales, Schlindler found that
his biggest challenge was addressing Roxanne's unwillingness to give special

discounts or incentives to buyers. "It was an even playing field for anyone [at Burt's Bees]," he noted. "Roxanne was going against the grain of the industry in that respect."

Renee Quimby became supervisor of the sales force after 2001. She demanded honest feedback and was analytical, yet balanced her rational approach with humor and wit, according to Schlindler. Roxanne also had a good sense of humor, but her strongest trait was creativity. "Her branding vision was masterful," he said.

The Last Catalog and Other Changes

When writing copy for ads and brochures, Roxanne used the twelve words identified in a Yale University study as having the greatest power to increase business profits. She wrote the words in her 2000 daily planner: you, love, easy, money, results, safety, proven, new, discover, health, save, and guarantee. Underneath "The Yale 12," she added her personal guidance words and phrases: meditate, live purely, bee quiet. Do your work with mastery. Like the moon, come out from behind the Clouds. Shine! Buddha!

Knowing that the continued growth of Burt's Bees depended on the continued improvement of its branding, Roxanne published another promotional catalog and brochure in mid-2000. Titled "Bad Company," this catalog introduced the lines, "We put the beauty in the product, folks. We have to." It was a not-so-oblique reference to Burt's looks. Burt's face was on more products than ever, from Therapeutic Bath Crystals to lemongrass Insect Lotion.

As "hard-favored" as Burt might appear to some, he looked decidedly virile in the "Bad Company" photographs, a remake of his crusty image to appeal to younger consumers. Even the catalog introduction and product descriptions had a suggestive edge, a major departure from the homespun marketing of the past. The pitch for therapeutic bath crystals, with Burt's still-hairy woodcut face on the tin, asked "Feeling kinky?" The copy for Doctor Burt's comfrey ointment inquired, "Feeling funky?" The catalog's cover shot showed Burt astride his BMW motorcycle, wearing a black leather jacket, jeans, and blue-striped railroad cap and giving a thumbs-up. Inside the catalog and on the cover of the accompanying brochure, Burt and four manly pals posed in front of the Parkman Auto Body Shop on North Dexter Road. Two of his buddies were shirtless, revealing muscled chests; another was drinking a Budweiser, and a fourth was smoking a cigarette.

Roxanne adopted an irreverent tone in the brochure's text, noting that "testosterone runs deep among the men of Parkman." There was "always lots of business" at the body shop (a state inspection station) but "not many paying customers," so the "boys" had plenty of time for Burt when he stopped by, she wrote. Burt had found the motorcycle covered "with rust and dust" in an old garage in nearby Monson and had it fixed up, according to her account. His jacket, she noted, was a "splurge" that Burt had found at the thrift shop in the basement of the Methodist Church. It had carried a $200 price tag that Burt dickered down to $3. "It drank up about a gallon of his special homemade beeswax leather dressing before he could get it to bend at the elbows, and, of course its only moving part, the zipper, was broke."

Burt "wasn't much of an organization man," Roxanne wrote, but that didn't prevent him from becoming a member of the United Bikers of Maine Motorcycle Riding Club. After touching on motorcycle-related politics in Augusta and the sidecar Burt had bought for Rufus at the North Dexter Grange flea market, Roxanne segued into Burt's upcoming tour of college campuses. Offering a harbinger of Roxanne's post–Burt's Bees pursuits, the back cover of the catalog pitched a proposed Maine Woods National Park and Preserve, asking consumers to contact RESTORE: The North Woods to find out how they could help. The catalog's last page showed Burt from behind, riding his motorcycle down a tree-lined road. Beneath the photo was the tag line, "We deliver what others only promise!" and an announcement that the catalog was printed on 100 percent recycled paper, saving 111 trees.

"Bad Company" was part of the guerilla marketing strategy that, through the years, had helped define the unique character of Burt's Bees, a point that was underscored by a photograph of Burt with his arm around a man wearing a guerilla mask. Roxanne explained that guerilla marketing—including product sampling and Burt and Rufus's college tours—was an inexpensive, unconventional, experimental alternative to the saturation advertising of the big corporations. "[W]e're not sure yet if it works or not, but it's the best shot we've got," she wrote, deliberately understating the company's market prowess.

Burt's Bees printed 70,000 "Bad Company" catalogs and 110,000 brochures. The photo of Burt and his four pals in front of the auto body shop was reproduced on 4,400 tee-shirts and 5,000 posters.

In 2001, the owner of Parkman Auto Body sued Burt's Bees, Roxanne, Burt, and the catalog's photographer for $300,000, charging them with defamation, invasion of privacy, trade name infringement, and infliction of emotional distress, among other allegations. In an affidavit, he objected to the catalog because it gave "the impression that Burt and I are friends and hang out together, which is not at all true." He said one photo suggested, inaccurately, that the man shown in the photo worked at the shop and drank beer on the job. Furthermore, he took exception to the catalog page that encouraged people to support the proposed Maine Woods National Park and Preserve, an idea he opposed.

The federal district court ruled in favor of the plaintiff on the trademark infringement allegation, awarding him $25,000 from Burt's Bees. The other allegations were remanded to the state court, where the case lingered for two years. The final papers in the three-inch-thick court file confirmed that the case was dismissed without costs in August 2003.*

The lawsuit caused Roxanne to stop publishing catalogs. The suit took the fun out of doing catalogs and creating humorous stories. A catalog was not worth exposing the company to legal and financial challenges, she said, especially because catalogs weren't critical to the future of Burt's Bees.

When Sheila Clark moved from accounting to customer service, it was her job to solve problems in that department—order-entry mistakes, shipping delays, and phone system problems. Clark went through customer complaints once a week to identify problem areas. She was well aware that Roxanne didn't like mistakes anywhere in the operation because they could cost money and undermine customer trust. Even a mistake as seemingly insignificant as an incorrect ingredients label "scared the heck out of" Clark because of the potential liability.

One of the most irritating issues was call waiting. Customers were often forced to wait several minutes to give an order due to a cranky phone system; Clark worked to reduce the wait time to four seconds. That improvement particularly pleased Clark's supervisor Renee Quimby, for whom call waiting had been a pet peeve. In Clark's opinion, Renee was tougher than Roxanne when it came to cutting waste and saving money. "Renee pinched pennies harder. She lived and died by Burt's Bees," Clark thought.

Meanwhile, plant manager Larry Groseclose found a larger home for Burt's Bees in Durham, a hop and a skip west of Raleigh. The home of Duke University, Durham was a less expensive location from which to operate than Raleigh. It also retained a bit of the old manufacturing ethos and infrastructure

*Such a docket notation typically indicates an out-of-court settlement.

from its halcyon tobacco days, so large spaces with loading docks and parking lots were in ample supply.

The company moved to the 105,000-square-foot building at Keystone Office Park in 2000. Compared with Burt's Bees' previous facilities, the space was gigantic. About 25,000 square feet of the building (more than half the size of a football field) was dedicated to fourteen production lines that could churn out 32 million packages annually.

In Durham, Chuck Friedman's lab was state-of-the-art. Roxanne didn't require anything fancy. Her office footprint was minimal. She worked at a table alongside other staff in the art studio, a big open space, and used a conference room down the hall when she needed privacy. Roxanne didn't like cubicles—"I didn't want anyone putting me in a box," she said. Neither did the graphic designers want cubicles; instead they wanted an open and airy space with lots of "cross pollination," according to Mark Smith "It was the other folks—the accountants, human resources, customer service—who wanted to be in cubicles or the 'Dilbert Zone' as I affectionately referred to it."

Not long after moving to Durham, the company leased another 32,000 square feet of adjoining space. The number of hourly and salaried employees increased in Durham, as did the full-time contract consultants. Most of the employees worked in manufacturing and purchasing. The company had a better-than-ever package of benefits, including discounts for alternative medical treatments and vitamins and supplements. In its 401(k) retirement plan, Burt's Bees matched up to 50 percent of the first six percent of a full-time employee's salary after a year of service.

Roxanne was uncomfortable in the cavernous new facility. "There were all these cubicles, assembly lines, and aisles," she said. "I thought, 'I can't work here.' I freaked out when I saw the accounting department and the cafeteria." It all ran counter to her sense of being a free-spirited artist, someone who wanted to follow her bliss. She treasured spontaneity but had become more and more hemmed in by the business's unending demands. She had more than enough money for herself and the twins. Why stick around, she wondered, when the staggering creative energy it had taken to build Burt's Bees was over?

For a time, Burt's Bees ran smoothly enough with Groseclose in charge of operations and Roxanne in Maine handling marketing. She traveled to trade shows when needed and periodically stopped in at headquarters to confer with Groseclose or handle other on-site business. But this dynamic didn't work for long. Roxanne felt she had to constantly enforce the management practices and philosophy she wanted him to follow. "He was a hierarchical guy," she explained. "I remember trying to make a point about inclusion by drawing concentric circles on the wall. I thought it was very important to listen to everyone, not just the people who wanted to please you. I wanted him to 'get' that."

Instead, in her estimation, Groseclose ran the company as he had run things at Revlon. He changed Burt's Bees into a more conventional corporate operation with greater emphasis on setting and meeting goals, tracking production, and improved recordkeeping. He even wanted the staff to dress less casually to give the workplace a more businesslike atmosphere. Staffers who had favored tee-shirts, shorts, or stained pants found themselves buying new slacks and buttoned-down shirts for work.

According to some staff, Roxanne's creativity was sorely missed when she wasn't on site. There was a lull in new products on the drawing board. Groseclose challenged senior employees to generate ideas, but they told him "no, that's not the way it's done here," Sheila Clark remembered. Roxanne was the creative genius of the company, and "the only reason the rest of us were there was to support what Roxanne wanted," Clark said. "Anyone who came in [to manufacturing] and thought they could change things was out of their mind."

In time, Roxanne's loyalists agreed that Groseclose was leading the company down the wrong track and product quality was slipping. Behind closed doors, they questioned his decisions and directives and talked about reporting their feelings and fears to Roxanne, whom they knew to be obsessed with product quality. Withholding bad news from the boss is a time-honored practice in business, but Roxanne never wanted problems hidden from her. (In Groseclose's view, operations was his bailiwick and marketing was hers, and he worked on "quality" matters as best he could. "Did we resolve all issues? No, because there was a constant stream [of them] to be addressed," he remembered.)

Sheila Clark and Alison Smith decided to go over the heads of their supervisors to Roxanne. Smith, then a part-time customer service employee, was a "crusader for excellence," said Clark, "and she had no fear of going directly to Roxanne and criticizing the second-highest ranking person in the company. I used to call her Paul Revere." Their message to Roxanne, said Clark, was "you'd better get down here." Asked about this incident later, Groseclose called it "strictly a power play. I never misled Roxanne."

Roxanne later praised Clark for her honesty. There were "very few people who were honest enough and rigorous enough with maintaining [company] standards to come forward with something like this," she said. "Sheila was someone who would. It was more important to her to fix something than be right or look good. I always had a problem with people who wanted to look good. You should want to be good, not look good."

When she hired him in 1999, Groseclose had told Roxanne to let him know when she wanted him to leave, and he would bow out gracefully. Now she told him that the company's rapid growth and his central role in its manufacturing operations required him to be in Durham five days rather than three days per week as originally planned. Not wanting to work onsite full time, Groseclose returned to his family's ancestral estate in the Virginia mountains in June 2001.

A few days before his departure, Groseclose confided to Margie McDaniel that his days were short. She didn't ask him to explain. "The less you asked, the better off you were," according to McDaniel. Years later, Groseclose remembered how much fun he had working at Burt's Bees. He was satisfied with his contribution to the company and bore no grudge against Roxanne.

Looking back on the "revolving door" of her operations managers, Roxanne acknowledged that meeting her demands had been an almost impossible job. "Their job was to make an enormous amount of money, which meant they had to have the most efficient, well-run operation that could be imagined," she said. Roxanne's definition of efficient and well-run was extreme: "no wasted moments, no wasted motions, no wasted materials, no safety hazards, no disorder of any kind, and every employee had to have their nose to the grindstone." She realized that kind of job description "gets rid of most people."

For years, the pressure of holding her workforce to such a high standard had been "a terrible weight to bear," she said. Besides that, there were unending problems with manufacturing, accounting, and information technology. "There were always little places where one thing was a little behind, which would keep the business stalled" and unable to meet sales demand, she said. "Manufacturing was always a problem. If it wasn't manufacturing, it was IT, and if it wasn't IT, it was accounting. The things that I didn't do well [were] genetically flawed in the whole business. I was not an accountant and had no interest in it; I had no interest or skill at IT or manufacturing. They became the weakest parts of the business. What I was really interested in as an artist was graphic design, which was a strong part of the business, and marketing and sales. Sales outpaced our ability to fulfill. Sales dragged us along."

But Roxanne realized she "couldn't keep that manufacturing, accounting, and IT thing going. I wasn't interested in it; I couldn't relate to the kind of people who did those things well, and they couldn't relate to me. They would be like, 'Who is this chick, I can't believe she's my boss.' Here I am, and they would come to work with their ties on, and they were just so straight. I knew they had to be because you don't get hippie accountants and hippie IT guys, really. It was a big culture gap."

Roxanne had begun to contemplate selling the company in the late 1990s, and by 2000 she was talking about it openly. She wasn't ready to actively seek a buyer, but she was candid with some of her staff about feeling tired and no longer interested in being in charge of a runaway enterprise year after year. "I was not meant to be in a factory," she said. "The whole thing about factories is that you do the same thing in the same way all the time, and you want people who will do the same thing all the time. I like to do things different every time. I like to create chaos and see how it all comes together and use serendipity to inspire the next thing ... and be really fluid and unpredictable." She wanted to turn to other projects that would stimulate her creativity once again. 🐝

The East Branch of the Penobscot near Whetstone Bridge. (Bill Duffy photo)

Leaving
Burt's Bees

While contemplating her exit from Burt's Bees, Roxanne was faced with hiring a replacement for Larry Groseclose, and she chose Charles Alley. Alley had been director of domestic manufacturing for a personal care company and head of operations for an Internet start-up, and he was already working as a consultant for Burt's Bees, evaluating planning software and assessing financial accounting. When his six-month consultancy contract expired in April 2001, he took over as interim vice president of manufacturing.

His first day on the scene stuck in his mind for years. A barrel of product had sat in a hot truck over the weekend, and the bacteria in it had bloomed, causing the barrel to burst. Chuck Friedman used the episode "to really drive home a message that we needed to tighten up our processes in adherence to FDA good manufacturing practices," and Alley agreed. Burt's Bees didn't have a "sealed environment" for maximum protection from microorganisms, Alley noted, "because we were in a growth stage."

Alley viewed Burt's Bees as a company that was expanding too fast for its own good. Key buyers were complaining about shipping delays. The company's inventory of finished goods was too large and "sucking up cash." Some of the equipment purchased to augment batch volume wasn't generating enough

212

savings to pay for itself. And the company's forecasting wasn't as effective as Alley thought it should be.

Capital investment was another drain on cash. In 1999, Burt's Bees had spent $297,000 on expansion. That figure had skyrocketed to $957,000 in 2000 and fell back to $638,000 in 2001. Another $860,000 of capital investment was scheduled for 2002.

Alley and Friedman experimented with ways to augment preservation. Because the milk powder harbored a natural flora of bacteria, they suggested that it be irradiated, but Roxanne nixed the idea on the grounds that it would be inconsistent with the brand and the company's principles. So they tried other approaches, one of which was a memorable disaster. While trying to sterilize milk powder in a three-minute test, Alley blew up Friedman's lab microwave. "The stench was there for months," he said. The simple process that finally solved the preservation problem was mixing the powder with very hot water, which, in effect, pasteurized it.

Alley said that mold in "end-use products was not a major issue. It would show up on occasion in a [store tester] jar that had been opened and left out for awhile. But we would backtrack the product each time we heard of the matter to ensure there was no general product failure. And we never found one."

While Alley was overseeing manufacturing, the company got an additional fill line and another large mixing kettle, which provided Burt's Bees with most of the automation capacity it needed on-site. "We were on a four-day, 10-hour schedule in the plant and had contingency plans to expand the schedule and add a weekend shift if needed to match demand," Alley recalled. "But we never had a shortage of filling capacity that required it."

The outsourcing of production varied over time. During Alley's tenure, he moved the filling of lotion and crème containers from the Burt's Bees plant to a Virginia firm that had a more sterile production environment. But that contractor didn't package the items to Burt's Bees' tight specifications, so Alley pulled the filling back in-house.

He also brought back in-house the filling of small glass sampler jars for crèmes. "It was generally significantly less expensive to fill in-house," he explained, adding that if he could give Roxanne "a good financial justification" for buying the equipment needed for filling, she was willing to spend the money.

While attending to the pressures of running Burt's Bees in 2001 and 2002, Alley also had the chance to experience some of the "old days" chaos. At one point the company ran out of sample kits when no hourly labor was on hand. "We had to pull all the salaried planning, quality care, human resources, and management people [including myself] onto the floor to man the assembly line until we had enough product to meet orders," he said. "Roxanne got a kick out of that."

Alley was commuting from Winston-Salem—a 1½-hour drive each way— and it was difficult for him and his family. After a year overseeing manufac- turing, he left in the summer of 2002. He counted his major contributions as reducing inventory to a more cost-effective level, improving forecasting, and increasing cash flow.

He was replaced in July 2002 by Jesus Osuna, an executive from Max Factor, whose marching orders were to augment business efficiencies in prepa- ration for a possible sale of Burt's Bees. Despite his brief time (less than a year) at the company, Osuna claimed successes in streamlining manufacturing pro- cedures, further automating the labor-intensive assembly lines, and boosting production.

Still, Roxanne cut him loose in May 2003. After Osuna she chose an in- house woman, Margie McDaniel, to hold the second-in-command post.

McDaniel had worked with Groseclose at Almay, starting on the assembly line and moving up through the organization over the years. She had followed Groseclose to Revlon, where she rose to become manager of the manufactur- ing process for the Oxford plant, and she was excited when Groseclose invited her to work with him at Burt's Bees. She was hired as a private contractor for Burt's Bees in 2000 and became a full-time manager for the company a year later. McDaniel oversaw materials planning and then took charge of manufac- turing, production, scheduling, distribution, and outside contractors.

Roxanne hoped that a collaborative leadership arrangement with another woman would be a better match for her and Burt's Bees, and she got her wish. She and McDaniel clicked as a team. McDaniel ran a tight ship and earned everyone's respect, Roxanne said.

Years later, Roxanne looked back on the firing of five plant managers and many others in the workforce without regrets. She regarded the ease with which she could "let go" of almost anything and anyone as a strength and a necessary attribute of a CEO. She was sure she had stumbled when hiring top managers. "I made tons and tons of mistakes." She had never done a seri- ous background check or contacted references, although Mike Abramson did take on that duty when he was hired as human resources manager in 2000.

When fired or forced out, more than one of Roxanne's top managers were uncertain why she had cut them loose. Sometimes it had to do with style, she said. There was trouble right away if a plant manager was overconfident, didn't always level with Roxanne about problems, didn't listen well to her, didn't understand or accept her way of doing things, or was inappropriate with employees. In her experience, anyone guilty of one or more of these sins would invariably start taking Burt's Bees in a direction Roxanne didn't want it to go.

Entrepreneur of the Year

In 2001, Burt's Bees launched other components of the Wings of Love makeup line—tinted facial moisturizer, concealing crème, facial powder, and blushing crème—and in doing so made the wrong kind of news. "Burt's Bees Fumbles, But Buzzes Back on Course" was the headline in the April 20, 2001, issue of *Women's Wear Daily*. The color chart on the tinted facial moisturizer packaging listed light, medium, dark, and ethnic options. "We totally made the wrong move," Roxanne told the newspaper, and the company received a lot of complaints from African-American women, some of whom were employees. The slight, while unintentional, touched a nerve. Roxanne ordered the word *ethnic* removed from future shipments.

In 2001 Burt's Bees also introduced a Baby Bee shampoo bar and a wild-lettuce toner in the Health Skin line and launched a new line, Natural Remedies, with a lavender mint toothpaste and a rosemary shampoo bar.

Health food stores remained Burt's Bees' biggest customer category, accounting for 40 percent of sales. The second and third strongest outlets were gift and specialty stores, respectively. Longs Drugs on the West Coast was a loyal customer, and Wegman's Pharmacy on the East Coast was a new account, but neither of these chains was close to the size of big-box chains Walmart and Target.

In 2001, Ernst & Young named Roxanne (and Burt's Bees) Entrepreneur of the Year in the Carolinas for achievement in manufacturing. The ensuing publicity highlighted the company's all-natural products. Roxanne told the *Charlotte Observer* that if the company had not kept its "all-natural threshold high ... I don't think we would have much."

In Maine, away from the day-to-day world of Burt's Bees, Roxanne was working on other investment and entrepreneurial ventures and throwing herself into land conservation in the north woods. Her philanthropic causes gave her life "more meaning," she said in the *Observer* article. "Many successful business people eventually come to the realization that there's more to living than making money—the Rockefellers, Bill Gates. I think all of us want to leave the earth a better place than we found it."

Her children were choosing business paths, too. Lucas had started a restaurant with his mother's help, and Hannah was getting her feet wet working for Burt's Bees.

During the summers of 2000 and 2001, Hannah and her college mate and boyfriend Brooks Juhring volunteered to promote Burt's Bees on the West Coast, where the company had no sales representation. The pair were attending Prescott College in Prescott, Arizona, and during summer breaks they drove to touristy places like Sedona and Monterey to hand out product samples and give talks at health food stores explaining the benefits of natural products. For the most part, their efforts were *pro bono*.

In 2001, Juhring ventured to concerts to promote products—another guerilla marketing tactic. With his van full of lip balm, body lotion, and teeshirts, he followed the summer music festival circuit to venues such as the first Bonnaroo Music and Arts Festival in Manchester, Tennessee, and Smilefest in North Carolina. He told event participants that they could trade in their lip balms of competing brands for a free Burt's Bees lip balm, and if they already had a Burt's Bees product, he offered them a free tee-shirt. Giving products away enabled him to avoid paying vendor fees, and he could set up a product table at a spot of his choosing.

After graduating from Prescott in May 2002, Hannah and Juhring signed on with Burt's Bees as the first sales reps in New England. Juhring's territory was Connecticut, Massachusetts, and Rhode Island; Hannah was assigned Vermont, New Hampshire, and Maine. Their accounts included independent health and gift stores and Hannaford grocery stores.

Hannah met with buyers for the health and beauty department at Hannaford, showing new products, doing the inventory of store products, helping with marketing, and giving out brochures and marketing sheets. She set up demonstrations, distributed samples, and provided consumer training to employees—a service she also provided at Whole Foods and other stores.

Between 2001 and 2004, Juhring traveled up and down the East Coast to gift shows and expositions as Burt's "handler." While company sales rep Andrew Schlindler sometimes viewed Burt as a scruffy prima donna,

Juhring saw him more as "a mascot" and developed a good deal of affection for him.

Juhring experienced Roxanne and Renee's workaholic natures firsthand. "They demanded the best you had to give," he recalled. "They wanted you to work, work, work." He said Renee "went out of her way to make sure we knew how to do the job."

Renee gave him a list of 500 stores in his territory that carried Burt's Bees products, charging him to meet all of the buyers and try to sell 120 products to them. Both he and Hannah worked five to seven days a week. In the first five years of his Burt's Bees career, Juhring slept in a hotel about 250 nights each year.

Hannah and Juhring each spent three days every six months with Sunne Justice, who went on the road with them to their best accounts. Juhring remembers the years 2002–04 as a prolonged blitzkrieg. "I think Burt's Bees got a lot stronger with company reps," he said. He eventually took over Hannah's states while Hannah moved into the job of rep trainer. For years he stationed himself at L.L. Bean's retail store in Freeport in the week before Christmas. People who bought $25 worth of Burt's Bees products received a free tee-shirt.

Renee kept up with the duo even on weekends. "She might call at 8 a.m. on Sunday and ask, 'Where are you?'" Juhring remembered. "Then she would say she was just giving you a hard time. But they wanted you to work your butt off." He considered Renee his mentor. "She pushed me to be as good as I could be," he recalled. "I gained her respect, and it was a huge relief that I was doing what she wanted." After Justice left in 2004, Renee became the sales manager. Later Juhring took over sales and oversaw the training of sales reps.

When he started as a rep, the refrain Juhring heard most often from consumers was, "I can't find you anywhere." But by 2004 and 2005, that had changed to "you're everywhere." He was thrilled to walk into a store and hear customers say how much they loved Burt's Bees. "Who says 'love' [when talking about] a brand?" he exclaimed.

Financial statements from 1998 through 2002 provide testimony to Burt's Bees' explosive growth. Sales skyrocketed from $8.2 million to $43.3 million during those five years, an average annual increase of 52 percent. One result of Roxanne's years of product development and her ruthless winnowing of those that failed to meet expectations was almost two dozen products that achieved her goal of $1 million in sales per item. In 2002, sales of the top 20 products averaged $1.3 million each. The bestsellers were Beeswax Lip Balm in the tin and tube, the Head to Toe Starter Kit, Facial in a Kit, Lemon Butter Cuticle Crème, Milk and Honey Body Lotion, Coconut Foot Crème, Hand Salve, Almond Milk Beeswax Hand Crème, and Baby Bee Buttermilk Lotion.

Having built Burt's Bees on candles and honey, Roxanne had transformed it in the mid-1990s into a personal skin-care business. By 2002 sales by the eight major sub-brands reflected the market power of the lip- and skin-care product lines, with Healthy Skin accounting for 26 percent of sales and Lips, 16 percent of sales. Starter kits represented 19 percent of sales.

Burt's Bees was supplying 131 products to more than 21,200 diverse accounts, ranging from Bath & Body Works to Books-A-Million. Specialty and health food stores represented 40 percent and 31 percent of the company's 2002 sales, respectively. Sales to chain pharmacies, grocery stores, and specialty stores had increased more than 107 percent since 2000. And these gains had been achieved despite Roxanne's refusal to grant trade allowances and other concessions to retailers.

According to Darrin Duber-Smith of Green Marketing, Inc., the mainstream personal care industry watched the flourishing natural product and health movement for a long time before believing it was strong enough to try to capitalize on. Once it was clear that consumer interest in natural and healthy alternatives wasn't going away, industry leaders began to plan how to take a slice of that pie.

During the development of Burt's Bees, the differences between natural and organic in personal care, body care, and cosmetics had been blurred in the absence of a government definition or standards. Burt's Bees, Tom's of Maine, and other natural-product manufacturers had written their own definitions and labeled their products accordingly. Consumers had become more interested than ever in what they put on their skin and what they ingested, but they embraced both "natural" and "organic" products.

The U.S. natural and organic personal care market hit $7.5 billion in 2005, with global sales soaring to $21 billion. Two years later, U.S. sales reached $9.23 billion with an annual growth rate of 23.3 percent, according to *Nutrition Business Journal*. The numbers were testimony to the spreading acceptance of the natural and organic messages about health and wellness, toxins and the environment. Women especially gravitated to "green" products, from baby products to anti-aging cosmetics.

The mass merchandisers knocked harder on Roxanne's door in 2002, and she agreed to meet with Target and Walgreen representatives. She had already opened the door to CVS Pharmacy, Longs Drugs, and other drugstore chains on the basis that they weren't stigmatized as big-box stores by her dedicated customers. Her talks that year with Target Corporation in Minneapolis and Walgreen Co. in Chicago came to naught, however, because they wanted her to change some of the ways she had always done business. Target wanted Burt's Bees products to be packaged with more cardboard, a suggestion Roxanne adamantly refused, believing that the company was "already drowning in waste." Later she would think that she and Target could have "picked our way through our differences," but she wasn't in a compromising frame of mind at the time.

She met Walgreens officials at their corporate office in Chicago in October. "It was the straightest company you can imagine," she remembered. There was a complete Walgreens store set up in the building so that executives could show potential clients like Roxanne where their products would be on the shelves. On a bulletin board she read an announcement to employees of upcoming "casual days" and saw that there were six during the year. "I thought 'these people put *this* on a calendar! In another eight weeks, you get to have a casual day and can wear chinos and denim shirts. OK, my God.'

"I sat down with the purchasing guy, the health and beauty guy, this guy and that guy," she recounted. "All guys, always. They wanted to discuss buying Burt's Bees, but they more really wanted to talk about Burt. I totally understood that in their lives, where they could have casual days on six days a year in the suburbs of Chicago, they wanted to be Burt, wanted to know all about him. They were in love with [Burt] because he represented freedom and a life they had little connection with." She didn't tell them everything about Burt—just enough so they could dream. "What they really were dreaming of was an escape from the life they had bought into, where they had to have too many fences. Men always said, 'If not for my wife and kids, that's the way I'd be living.'"

The first meetings with Target and Walmart generated enough distrust in Roxanne that she backed off from a move into the mass markets. She didn't think Burt's Bees could stay true to its values and the purity of its ingredients if it accepted the proffered deals, nor did she want to manage the exponential growth the company could face in that sector. She was sure by then that she was going to sell the company, and it made strategic sense to dangle the potential of mass markets to a new owner and let someone else deal with the issues of the next big leap forward.

Suitors Come Calling

Dozens of companies expressed an interest in buying or investing in Burt's Bees, but the most serious of these were buyout firms with expertise in dressing up an acquisition for resale. They "were salivating because they saw Burt's Bees' sales and growth and profit margins without ever having tapped into the big boxes or [many] international markets," Roxanne said. "They thought 'if we get our hands on this, we'll immediately ramp up and sell to Target and others [in mainstream markets].'"

Analysts tracking the health and beauty industry speculated that Roxanne could be a hard owner to deal with because of her public opposition to the predominant beauty ideal. "I like to think that women, who are coming into their own power and do not necessarily need confirmation from men to feel accepted, are willing to discard the conventional definitions of physical beauty and would rather develop spiritual beauty based on living in alignment with higher values," she told the *Grand Rapids Press* in March 2003. Her desire that any future owner of Burt's Bees remain committed to the company's high standard of product purity was also on record.

She began to meet with suitors in 2001, recalling later that she "ran into some of the most hysterical people you can imagine." She estimated she "went out with 100 guys over time. Some would fly their private jets into Raleigh-Durham Airport, and we'd meet in a private suite at the airport; sometimes [we'd meet] at a trade show and go to dinner; sometimes in [the] Burt's Bees conference room; sometimes in the lobbies of hotels."

The suitors were "very powerful men, very rich men, very well-connected men," Roxanne said. "They were far more sophisticated than me. But I had absolutely not one glimmer of self-doubt because I thought, 'Hey, you know what? I can split a cord of firewood. I know how to get myself warm. I know how to build a house. I know how to live on rice and beans. I can walk to the nearest town in a blizzard. You got nothing on me, because if the shit ever hits the fan, I'm the one who's going to be okay, not you guys.' I always carried that experience with me, and sometimes I consciously pulled that out when I needed to feel like I was the equal of anybody around me. Unconsciously, it created this wealth of strength I could tap into all the time. Even now, I touch back to that understanding of myself."

Executives from one cosmetics company she didn't wish to name "thought they knew everything. It was a very good drill to go through because by the time I actually did get serious about selling, I had already been through so many scenarios, and I was getting very good at reading people. In these intense negotiations, you could tell if [suitors] were nervous, like when they lit a cigarette, went to the bathroom, or shifted their weight. We were in a game like poker, and the stakes were pretty high, so it was in my best interest to understand what kind of cards they held and see how far they'd go. I was practicing on them," she said, "like I had done with the Maine suitors. They were on their best behavior while courting me, but what kind of partner would they be for the long haul?"

By the fall of 2002, Roxanne was ready to do business with a broker, and the perfect one appeared as if on cue. Roxanne would later say this was the universe guiding her.

Gail Zauder ran a fledgling boutique investment office, elixirAdvisors, in Manhattan. She was starting fresh after sixteen years at Credit Suisse in what she called the "clubby male world of private equity." Zauder telephoned Roxanne out of the blue one day after seeing a mention of Burt's Bees in *Women's Wear Daily*. "Everyone was talking about natural personal care products," she recalled, and she was investigating the possibility that Roxanne was at the point of wanting to sell and needed a broker's help.

Roxanne wasn't at the office, so Zauder went off on vacation to the south of France. Burt's Bees' chief financial officer John Fragomeni returned her call later, letting her know that Roxanne had been trying to reach her.

Roxanne liked Zauder immediately and hired her in October 2002, making Burt's Bees the first major account for Zauder's new firm. They agreed on an all-or-nothing deal; Zauder wouldn't get paid if the company wasn't sold. Roxanne believed this would ensure that Zauder would work hard to make a deal happen.

About that time, Roxanne received an unexpectedly high offer from a potential investor valuing Burt's Bees at $92 million, but Zauder convinced her that it was in her best interest to survey the market before accepting a deal. "We believed that she owed it to herself to take her time pursuing this 'once in a lifetime' event," Zauder said.

Chief financial officer John Fragomeni, graphic designer Mark Smith, and Zauder created "the playbook," a 70-page spiral-bound report that included Burt's Bees' financial data, sales numbers, and an analysis of markets and competition. Zauder sent it to dozens of companies that might be interested in buying Burt's Bees and had the resources to do so. "Almost all were interested because [the company] was so profitable and had room to grow," Zauder said.

When she had winnowed down the long list of prospects, Zauder sent the shortlist to Roxanne and Renee, and the fun began. Roxanne went on the road again to meet more prospective buyers with power and money. In an article posted on April 22, 2003, the mergers-and-acquisitions website TheDeal.com was the first to report that Roxanne was shopping for a buyer, speculating that she might get up to $150 million for the business.

Meetings took place over a five-month period into mid-2003. Accompanying Roxanne to the sessions were senior staff, who were there to explain their due-diligence protocols. Donna Hollenbach teamed up with Chuck Friedman to present information about the R&D process and remembered how "nerve-wracking" it was.

On the other side of the table, senior executives of one company after another told Roxanne about themselves, how they would grow the company, and how happy she would be if she sold it to them. Initially, Roxanne wanted to find an investor who would continue to grow Burt's Bees but allow her to retain an active role in the company. "I could tell a lot about them by their offices, how they dressed, how they talked," she said. "I eliminated tons of them because I was intuitive. I eliminated people I didn't like and knew I couldn't work with. Gail [Zauder] eliminated people who were marginal or couldn't get their financial-technical side together. We came up with a shortlist."

Zauder and Roxanne traveled to Columbus, Ohio, to meet Les Wexner, founder of The Limited apparel company (now owned by Sun Capital Partners). After talking turkey at his palatial home, Roxanne concluded that the fit wasn't good, and Zauder crossed The Limited off the list.

Next came a visit to Manhattan to meet with several other finalists from a number of equity investment firms, among them Apax Partners, Wasserstein & Co., North Castle Partners, Charterhouse Group, and AEA Investors. Roxanne dressed casually, as usual, while the interested parties were dressed to the corporate "nines." She could tell none of them had much knowledge of the personal care products business, and she quickly became bored with conducting the same kind of meeting and repeating the same company rap over and over.

Refreshments—cookies or a full lunch—might be served during the sessions. Although the suitors didn't know it, Roxanne was a foodie and, to her, food was an important element of the negotiations. She considered food an art form and was interested in its presentation as well as its taste. At the time, she preferred vegetables and desserts. Mediocre food disappointed her and caused her to pay less attention in a meeting.

Realizing that food might make or break a deal, Zauder called ahead to each potential buyer, asking them to serve unusual gourmet food. The prospect of a delicious meal helped Roxanne maintain her interest in a presentation and remember a company's personality.

She was looking for character in a buyer, and one way to judge character was to consult her Tarot cards. She chose a Tarot card for the head person at each firm, and the results seemed to mirror her intuition. The Devil card came up for one prospective buyer who wanted the company badly enough to tell her that money wasn't an issue. She distrusted him instinctively and rejected his offer. Sometimes she consulted her psychic about the sale.

Roxanne believed that it wasn't only the money that was important. "If there's no trust, then they'll find a way to screw you in the end," she told one reporter. "Money is an illusion because there's always ways they can make things go badly for you if they're not honorable."

Ninety-seven parties showed interest in Burt's Bees, and six made fully financed binding final offers. The firm that most interested Roxanne was AEA Investors, a private equity buyout firm started by the Rockefellers and Mellons. AEA specialized in dressing up companies for resale.

"I fell in love with the chairman [Vincent Mai]," she recalled. "I adored him. He was so gorgeous—six-foot-five, from South Africa. He had two sidekicks, and I loved them too. There was no sleaze factor with them. They meant what they said, unlike a lot of the others that were so sleazy that you knew the minute they had what they wanted you were toast."

Astrologically, Burt's Bees and AEA were "a fantastic match." Roxanne asked senior executives for their astrological signs to further inform her intuitive knowledge of whether she should sell to them. She drew Tarot cards that supported an affirmative decision and put the bid letter on her home altar.

After the standard due diligence meetings in which Burt's Bees provided inside information to AEA, a separate meeting was convened to cover the company's microbiological policies. Roxanne and Chuck Friedman attended the meeting with AEA officials, their lawyers, and their FDA consultant.

Friedman, on the hot seat, explained that the microorganism policy was written to accommodate the non-pathogenic bug levels in the natural raw materials Burt's Bees used. Greater tolerance was a necessary adjunct to using natural
"raws" and was acceptable for harmless non-pathogens, he told AEA.

AEA also wanted to know why a half-million dollars of crèmes and lotions
had recently been recalled due to mold. Friedman explained that the recall had
come from a single high-profile retailer, and he (Friedman) had identified the
culprit as the biovert enzyme and substrate that Burt's Bees had been using as
a natural anti-microbial preservative for about six years. The German supplier
of the preservative had shifted its manufacturing from Europe to the U.S. in
2000 and sold Burt's a defective batch from its American plant. The resultant
failure had been latent, allowing mold to grow weeks or months after the products had been made and distributed. The preservative supplier had eventually
compensated Burt's Bees for inventory and distribution costs.

Although the mold issue didn't sink the deal with AEA, it was the final straw
for Roxanne and Friedman's collaboration. The two had pushed natural preservative systems to the cutting edge of available technology, but the tension
between them—creative in the best of times—had taken its toll. Just prior to the
due-diligence meeting with AEA, Roxanne notified her chemist that she could
no longer work with him. "We are going to plan your exit strategy," she recalled
telling him on his fifty-sixth birthday. One of several long-term employees with
company stock options, Friedman received a favorable exit package.

Many of the senior staff were close to Friedman, and when word of his
departure became known, they were in shock. "Some wondered if Roxanne
was subconsciously trying to torpedo the AEA deal, since this very high-level
firing occurred precisely during AEA's due diligence," Mark Smith said.

"Chuck and I had the worst fights over risks," Roxanne remembered.
"He must have thought I was absolutely crazy. He probably thought I was
foolhardy." She recognized she had "a more rigorous and stabilized product
because of his conservative, scientific bent, and for that, I'm certainly grateful.
[But] after awhile, it was just too hard to deal with that level of conservative,
risk-averse, carry-it-too-far warnings."

Roxanne and AEA Investors came to an agreement in November 2003,
under terms of which AEA paid $185 million for 80 percent of Burt's Bees,
according to the elixirAdvisors website. Roxanne retained a 20 percent equity
share plus $15 million of cash that was on the Burt's Bees balance sheet at clos-
ing. (Roxanne disputed these figures but provided no alternate ones, saying the

actual amount was undisclosed.) The purchase price was twice what she had considered selling for when she began talking to prospective buyers, and she trusted the AEA principals. Having retained a big equity stake, she wanted to hand the company over to "people who wouldn't let me down ... who wouldn't turn around at the next sale and get their lawyers to find some fancy loophole" to void her payout. She didn't have "the background or experience on what to anticipate. I had to go on trust. I implicitly trusted AEA to do the right things, and they did everything they said they would do."

AEA didn't commit to retaining Roxanne's values or principles, and she didn't ask them to; she didn't want to hamstring the new owner. However, she was "very concerned," recalled Zauder, "with retaining people or giving them appropriate severance." The sale provoked criticism from consumers and some in the natural products industry who worried that the quality of Burt's Bees' products would be compromised. Specialty and health food stores—the foundations of Burt's Bees growth—feared that as more chains carried Burt's Bees' products, retail discounting would force them to drop the brand.

It's hard not to wonder what Burt Shavitz thought of the sale. The one-third share he had once owned would have been worth $77 million in 2003 if the elixirAdvisor figures are accurate. When Roxanne signed the deal with AEA, she paid Burt $4 million. She didn't think he was happy with that amount, but she thought it was "ample." (When asked for a closing remark during a Burt's Bees PR event in Taiwan years later, Burt told the audience, "It's important to separate your wants from your needs.")

Four years later, when AEA sold to Clorox for almost $1 billion, Roxanne received another handsome (but undisclosed) payout for her remaining equity.*

Transition

Roxanne agreed to continue to run Burt's Bees for a year during the transition to new ownership. Once AEA hired a new chief executive officer, she

*Other reported prices for the sale of Roxanne's 80 percent share to AEA Investors included $179 million (*Triangle Business Journal*, February 9, 2004); "around $155 million" (the *Deal Journal* blog of the *Wall Street Journal*, September 28, 2007); $141.6 million (*New York Times*, January 6, 2008); and $146 million (*Los Angeles Times*, May 17, 2009). *USA Today* reported online (June 8, 2014) that Roxanne reaped "more than $300 million" from her Burt's Bees ownership in total, including the sale of her remaining 20 percent share to Clorox in 2007; that same figure was used by the Associated Press on June 4, 2014. Celebritynetworth gave the figure as $350 million.

planned to move into the role of creative services director and serve on the board of directors. The sale was a huge relief to her. She could continue to work at what she felt she did best—create new products—and have time to concentrate on her budding land conservation efforts in Maine. During the transition, she planned to continue to work primarily from Maine.

Roxanne hired a young woman to replace Friedman, and the new cosmetics chemist was a stark contrast to her predecessor, coming across to senior staff as much more breezy and flamboyant. During her tenure, Friedman's volumes of compliance and formulation data and SOPs vanished. It wasn't long before she was let go.

Burt's Bees' sales topped $59.4 million in 2003, a 37 percent increase over 2002. By then the company was manufacturing more than 150 personal care products and selling them in 9,000 natural foods and specialty stores in the U.S. and Canada and on the company's website. Roxanne believed that AEA was capable of continuing Burt's Bees' unrelenting growth, and she was right. Her forecast for 2006—a dizzying $100 million—would be exceeded by $70 million, undeniable testimony that consumers were mad for Burt's Bees products.

But in 2004, Roxanne really didn't know whether AEA would still own Burt's Bees two years later. The buyout firm might well want to recoup its investment after opening the door to the big boxes and thereby making Burt's Bees all the more attractive to a mainstream company looking for a stake in the supercharged natural skin-care products market. She told the *News & Observer* on January 8, 2004, that she would lead Burt's Bees through a major expansion into mainstream outlets, although she didn't specifically mention big boxes. There were a host of new products on schedule for release, she reported, including a toothpaste for children.

Roxanne was especially excited about a new product line for girls that she thought would be as irresistible as lip shimmers. Her new idea was a compact made out of paper with a little pot on the inside that was filled with a color product. "It looked like a pot of eye shadow," she recalled. "It was a creamy blush with a little 24K gold dust and would be used on eyelids, shoulders, whatever you wanted to look glittery, like fairy dust." She saw it as the anchor product for a new line.

After the sale, Roxanne had to deal with a board of directors for the first time in her working life. John Replogle, a member of AEA's board at the time and general manager of Unilever's Skin Care North American operations, thought she was "very effective" with the directors. "There were quite a number of strong players" on the board, but none with strengths that Roxanne had, he said.

Replogle named three attributes that were unique to Roxanne: brains, brand, and Birkenstocks. She was "fiercely smart and street smart," he said. "She had an incredible read of people and consumers. Hers was a unique perspective" because she had created the company and the brand. "She was the keeper of the essence of Burt's Bees. It was not a touch that others had ... a sense of who we are, what we stand for. She kept the stewardship flame alive." As for her shoes, Replogle said, the Birkenstocks were a reminder of Burt's Bees' roots and a message to "let's not forget where we came from. Let's not be pretentious ... not get too buttoned-downed [but be] fun, light, and quirky."

Replogle said that Roxanne's "very strong voice" on Burt's Bees operations and her decades of being "the decider" caused her sometimes to "not fully consider" her words. Once, while discussing a packaging idea with him, she said simply, "It looks like shit," the sort of retort that could make a recipient defensive.

As 2004 wore on, Roxanne became impatient with the search for a new CEO. AEA's headhunters sent a number of candidates for interviews in which Roxanne participated. "None of them were really right," she said. By this time she was working on conservation projects in the Maine woods, and she didn't want the responsibility of the top job one day longer.

Frustrated with AEA, she finally decided to back Doug Meyer, 55, who had an impressive CEO résumé in consumer packaged goods. "He looked like a scrappy guy and not afraid to get his hands dirty," Roxanne said. "I kinda said hire him because I was leaving in November. So they did." Upon relinquishing the CEO position in early September, Roxanne moved, as planned, into the position of creative services director.

Meyer had begun his corporate career at Colgate-Palmolive in the early 1970s as a summer intern. His rise in the company followed the traditional route up to vice president and general manager of the firm's oral care division. He then became president of Sterling Drug, the maker of Bayer Aspirin, and went on to serve in the same position at Benckiser North America. After the merger of Benckiser NV with Reckitt & Coleman plc in late 1999, Meyer had worked as a consultant and then as an executive with Charterhouse Equity Partners before being tapped by AEA Investors to succeed Roxanne as CEO.

Burt's Bees had about 130 employees on the payroll when Meyer came on board, with up to 75 workers from temp agencies, and those numbers would double during his short tenure. The early years of a handful of women laboring in the cold, stripped-down trailers in Parkman making candles seemed almost fiction.

Two or three days after becoming CEO, Meyer circulated an organization chart showing who reported to whom, and the chart showed Roxanne reporting to him. When Mark Smith saw it, he knew sparks would fly. Roxanne was livid, he remembered. There was no way she was going to be subservient to Meyer. No one knew Burt's Bees better than she did.

After working with Meyer for almost a month, Roxanne was certain that his overbearing management style was ill-suited to the company she'd built,* and she asked AEA's chair Vincent Mai to fire the man because he wasn't right for the job. "I remember poor Vincent tried so hard to explain to me that [AEA was] leveraged to the hilt—tons of borrowed money and very little of their own [in Burt's Bees]," Roxanne said. "They were accountable to these banks and retirement funds," and Mai told her the banks would think AEA was "nuts" if they fired Meyer so soon; in the buyout world, a company didn't fire a new CEO after just a few weeks.

In Roxanne's world, however, a firing was done when it needed to be done, no matter how little or how much time the person in question had been on the job. "I remember saying [to Mai], 'Would you like to look bad or be bad?' They left [Meyer] in place, and I couldn't work with him," she said. "So I had to go."

She was bitter and angry but didn't want "to spread my negative energy around the company." The best resolution, she decided, was to leave Burt's Bees on a weekend when no one was around to ask "what are you doing" or "why are you leaving?" "I was not able to speak the truth because it was so destructive," she recalled, "and I was unwilling to lie and pretend everything was okay. So I just took my marbles and left."

Roxanne's last day was a Sunday. One of her "redneck friends" drove her to the Durham headquarters in a rental truck, pulling up at the door nearest her office. In the quiet of the empty building, she collected her belongings and materials and closed the door on more than 20 years of marriage to Burt's Bees.

*Smith agreed that Meyer came on too strong, "trying to prove he was capable."

Mark Smith had figured that Roxanne would not be able to tolerate working with Meyer, so he was not surprised that she was gone. Nevertheless, her empty desk in the middle of the art department raised a lot of eyebrows. Some employees wondered aloud where she was. It took several days for many of the staff to realize she had left for good without saying good-bye.

A little more than a year later, on January 19, 2006, Meyer was replaced by Unilever's John Replogle, who was named CEO and president of Burt's Bees. Roxanne thought he was "very good, very polished." His mission was to take Burt's Bees further into the mainstream markets. Roxanne had once said that she wanted Burt's Bees products to reach "everyone, everywhere," and Replogle believed in that goal too.

In Roxanne's wake, AEA turned its attention to building a new management team at Burt's Bees and strengthening the company's manufacturing capabilities. Replogle discovered that unconventional Roxanne had priced some products unconventionally. "Sometimes products were priced on a cost-plus basis, working backwards from the consumer price point," he explained. "For example, an item they wanted to price at $9 at retail was assigned a wholesale price of $4.50, regardless of production costs." Replogle hired a consulting firm to assist in developing new pricing, and he loosened Roxanne's rigid trade terms, which he found illogical and limiting.

Burt's Bees grew phenomenally during Replogle's two-year tenure, and he sold the company for $925 million to the Clorox Company in late 2007. One of the major reasons Clorox wanted Burt's Bees was that consumers considered it the leading natural brand in the U.S. Replogle said the sale to Clorox enabled Burt's Bees to expand into new markets "in a cost-efficient and effective way and made a dramatic [impact] on a major corporation. Little Burt's Bees taught an elephant to dance," he added, noting that issues of animal testing, sustainability, product safety, and human health received more attention as a result of Burt's Bees' operating principles and philosophy.

In 2011, Clorox chief executive Don Knauss acknowledged that the company had paid too much for Burt's Bees and wrote down the value of the company by $258 million. Replogle agreed that Clorox might have "overpaid" if the deal were judged purely on a financial basis. But he believed that Clorox also received unquantifiable values from purchasing Burt's Bees, including innovation, sustainability, and certain decision-making processes.

Replogle left Burt's Bees in early 2011 to take over Seventh Generation, Inc., a "green cleaning" enterprise that needed a makeover in order to prosper in an ever more competitive market. Reflecting on the natural versus organic paths, Replogle said that "Roxanne was pioneering a pathway. She had to put preservatives in [some of the products for them] to have shelf integrity. Otherwise, consumers could get home and have a bad experience. The science wasn't there for 100 percent pure organic. At the time, organic was only 70 to 80 percent, and the other percentages were crap." In his view, Roxanne took the "high road" by sticking with natural.

Looking Back

When Roxanne looked back on how far Burt's Bees had come, she could hardly take in its success or her own. The company had played a role in shaping the American natural personal products business and renewing the sense of meaning in consumption. When Roxanne left the company, she noted, Burt's Bees was positioned to move to "the forefront of the *mainstream* personal care sector."

She believed that the impact of Burt's Bees in the natural personal care sector was due to its amazing sales growth. "I think if the company had not been really profitable and its sales not been fast, and if it hadn't cashed out for so much money, it would have had far less impact," she theorized. Burt's Bees "was an ingredients story—a clean, green ingredients story. In that way, it shaped the market because everybody wanted to make a lot of money, so they see you making a lot of money with clean, green ingredients, and they'll try whatever it is that's creating that kind of success for you. Because we made a big deal about our ingredients story, they were apt to copy it, which improved the standards all around."

Burt's Bees didn't change American beauty standards for women, she said, adding, "It was not a big mission of ours." But the success of Burt's Bees made the public more aware of a natural standard of skin-care excellence that hadn't existed before. "It was powerful enough to birth a national brand on natural, green values and make enormous profits," she said. 🐝

Katahdin, from Lunksoos Mountain. (Bill Duffy photo)

Family Matters

Through the Burt's Bees years, Roxanne's nonstop work and travel had left her limited time with Hannah and Lucas as they grew up. Their mother's prolonged absences and their parents' contrasting personalities caused the twins to feel that their dad was more the mother in their family.

Hannah and Lucas recalled George St. Clair's steady presence and affection. Lucas appreciated that his father initiated conversations with him about the concerns of adolescent boys. "Sex, drugs, and rock and roll," said Lucas. "Dad was more hands-on with those matters."

Roxanne modeled a tenacious work ethic and, beginning when the twins were young, required them to help her with everything from craft fairs to Burt's Bees production operations in Maine and North Carolina.

Hannah learned about spending and saving from observing her parents' habits. "My dad always talked about his budget and seemed concerned about money," she remembered. "My mom didn't really talk about it." Despite Roxanne's increasing annual income in the early 1990s, Lucas said his mother didn't shower them with luxuries.

It was important to Roxanne for the twins to be acquainted with Judaism. In the summer of 1990, when they were 12, she sent them to a Jewish summer camp, Camp Yavneh, on Lucas Pond in Northwood, New Hampshire. She also made arrangements to give them bat and bar mitzvahs when they turned 13, rite-of-passage traditions that she believed appropriate to enact in memory of her relatives who had died for their faith during the Russian revolution.

Burt introduced Roxanne to Rabbi Moshe Wilansky of Portland, a member of the Jewish Orthodox Chabad Lubanvitch tradition, who agreed to prepare the twins and oversee the ceremonies. For several months, Roxanne drove Hannah and Lucas to the rabbi's Portland home on Sundays to study Hebrew. The rabbi described the twins as "definitely willing and good students."

Rabbi Wilansky conducted two joint ceremonies. The "official" one was in Portland at his home, where a tent served as a synagogue. Roxanne invited her immediate relatives to be witnesses. Rebecca Quimby had died three years before, but Thais Willens and her daughters Liliane and Jacqueline attended. An abbreviated and more casual event took place in Wellington, 18 miles south of Parkman, at the non-denominational Burdin Memorial Chapel. After the bat and bar mitzvahs, guests gathered on the lawn for a buffet lunch, with a bluegrass band providing live music.

Roxanne then took Hannah and Lucas to the West Coast, wanting them to see "the world beyond the little Maine villages with white churches and meeting houses." They drove from San Francisco along the Big Sur highway to Seattle, where, later, Lucas would live for several years. At SkyCity, the restaurant in the Space Needle, one of the Pacific Northwest's most notable landmarks, Roxanne looked over the pricey menu and deemed it far too expensive for the three of them. Instead she drove them to another notable restaurant, The Herbfarm, but she was too frugal to dine there either. She allowed herself $36,000 a year, which was $8,536 above Maine's median household income at the time, but every dollar mattered: She and George would soon be sending the twins to a first-rate boarding school for high school.

A year later the twins headed off to Gould Academy in Bethel, Maine. Roxanne wanted her children to attend a boarding school to obtain a more concentrated education and greater opportunities than the local high school in Dover-Foxcroft could provide. Also, she was going to be on the road at trade shows more frequently and would be less available to parent them. George didn't like the idea of prep school, according to Roxanne, because he would miss being part of their daily lives. Gould was considered pricey at the time, with annual per-student costs of $16,600 for room, board, and tuition, but the cost of a good education was an investment Roxanne was more than willing to make.

Hannah and Lucas had contrasting views on going to prep school. Lucas was gung-ho to leave Guilford. The *Bangor Daily News* in 1992 had published an article on Burt's Bees with a "Rags to Riches" headline and details about the money the company was making. A copy of the article was pinned to the school bulletin board and made Lucas feel awkward. "Everybody started to treat us a little differently," he said. "Kids suddenly wanted to hang out with us." Hannah didn't want to leave home and friends, but she agreed to go. Like everyone else in the family, she was tired of the constant shuttling back and forth from one parent's house to the other under the shared custody arrangement. At Gould, the twins could unpack their bags and stay put for four years.

Lucas jumped into soccer, downhill skiing, basketball, hiking, and even art classes. He liked the student diversity, liked living on his own, and even liked doing his own laundry. Hannah, too, became involved in sports and art classes and made new friends. She found the stability she wanted. Still, she felt somewhat like "a poor cousin" because her classmates' parents took them on exotic vacations, owned expensive condos at ski resorts, and drove new cars.

One of Gould's strong points was its outdoor programs. Hannah and Lucas went on multiple-day camping trips and participated in other outdoor programs that would strengthen their love of the natural world as adults.

Gould required parents to participate in some of their children's events, and Roxanne and George showed up to cheer on the twins. Parents had to attend every annual graduation ceremony while their kids were enrolled.

As the twins were entering prep school, their father, too, was charting a new path. When the kids were sophomores, George left Dover-Foxcroft to earn a master's degree in social work from the University of Southern Maine in Portland. He became a licensed clinical counselor in South Portland.

In the spring of 1997, Roxanne's mind was diverted from business by Lucas's first big solo quest, a nonstop "thru-hike" of the 2,181-mile Appalachian Trail (A.T.) from Georgia to Maine. The family was familiar with the nationally revered trail because its Maine route passed near their cabin in the woods outside Guilford. The A.T.'s famed Hundred-Mile Wilderness meandered through Elliotsville Township near Monson, and the twins had enjoyed outings along Big Wilson Stream in the trail corridor during their childhood. They had met their first thru-hiker in Baxter State Park with George when they were about 10 years old and thought it would be wonderful to do the entire trail themselves when they were older.

To support Lucas, his family drove him south to the start of the trail. George was nervous about Lucas's long hike. Roxanne wondered aloud if her son really wanted to put himself through such a grueling challenge. Hannah cried. Two women (one of them from Maine) had been murdered off the A.T. in May 1996 in western North Carolina, and their killer remained on the loose.

A.T. thru-hikers typically pick a trail name for themselves, and George came up with "Skyscraper" for Lucas, since his son had grown to six-feet-five inches. Off Lucas went, carrying a 60-pound-plus backpack and feeling confident he could sprint to Katahdin, the northern end of the path, in about four months.

Roxanne became a trail mom. She tacked up an A.T. trail map in her office and marked Lucas's northward progress with red pins. She sent him care packages with healthy foods and surprise treats and made sure she was available when he could find a phone to call her. She needed to hear his voice from time to time, just to know he was all right.

Her daily calendar for 1997 noted his march northward. After he reached Virginia, she met him several times in trail towns. By the first of July, Lucas had logged more than 1,500 miles from the start of the A.T. on Springer Mountain, Georgia, and was bearing down on New England.

He took time to send Roxanne a birthday card, thanking her for being his mother and being with him in spirit and telling her how energized he felt after their phone conversations. Roxanne could tell the weeks and months of quiet hiking and reflection were helping Lucas to become more open to her, and she loved how sweet and honest he was.

Lucas was in New Hampshire's White Mountains in late August when tragedy struck. A thru-hiking friend collapsed, and the wind was too strong for a helicopter to evacuate him to a hospital. The young man died of an aneurysm. Traumatized, Lucas and his buddies took time away from the A.T. to ponder whether to finish the hike. Within a week, however, they decided that their companion would have wanted them to reach their goal, so they all met back in the Whites and tramped onward to Maine.

On September 22, Lucas arrived at Katahdin Stream campground in Baxter State Park and feasted his eyes on the high, rocky Gateway section leading to Katahdin's Tableland and the last mile of the A.T. Roxanne drove to the park to meet him, joining other families of thru-hikers to celebrate. Roxanne didn't climb the mountain with the bedraggled hikers, but invited them home to Parkman for a feast and an overnight stay. The trail tribe was ravenous for the two roasted turkeys with all the fixings and blueberry cobblers prepared by Roxanne.

After completing the A.T., Lucas was ready for more outdoor experiences. In January 1998, he went to Patagonia, South America, with the National Outdoor Leadership School (NOLS) program, where he learned mountaineering and sea kayaking. Returning to Maine by April, he prepared to travel again, this time to follow the Northern Forest Canoe Trail, a 780-mile water trail through New York State, Vermont, Quebec, and Maine. Hannah joined him on the trip in the summer of 1998.

He then took a time-out in Roxanne's house in Arden, North Carolina. When he was ready to go to work, he talked his way into a job as a pastry cook at Sara Foster's gourmet restaurant in Durham. Lucas promised Foster that he could bake anything in the dessert cookbook *Martha Stewart's Pies & Tarts*, and she hired him. Lucas wasn't kidding about his capabilities. As a child, he had been intrigued by recipes and cooking. For inspiration, Roxanne had bought him *Pies & Tarts*, which he soon mastered.

Following the stint at Foster's restaurant, he went to Europe, spending the summer backpacking before settling down to a serious study of food and wine at the elite Le Cordon Bleu's London school. His interest in fine food had been stimulated by the NOLS experience.

There were other important family milestones as well. Roxanne had publicly labeled her father a "despot" during their estrangement, but after 1993, the relationship between father and daughter softened. As it turned out, her business success was the vehicle to the rapprochement. After almost 20 years, John Quimby was able to turn the page on his ancient disapproval of her radical lifestyle and politics, and he now begrudgingly admired his eldest daughter, as he did his other two daughters who had achieved MBAs and business careers.*

Roxanne's beloved grandmother, Thais Willens, died on May 12, 1998, at the age of 95, and was buried beside her husband in a West Roxbury, Massachusetts, cemetery. Baba had spent time with Roxanne in Maine after the

*In 2011, Roxanne purchased a home in Portland, Maine—across the street from her own home—for her father and the woman with whom he had been living in Florida, Helen Blanchard. However, John Arthur Quimby learned shortly after the move that he had cancer. He and Helen returned to Florida and then relocated to Germantown, Tennessee, where he died on June 23, 2013, just short of his ninetieth birthday.

death of Benjamin, but Maine didn't feel like a place she could call home. She had moved back to Massachusetts and lived in a nursing home in Newton Lower Falls until her passing.

Roxanne and Baba hadn't seen much of each other after Burt's Bees moved to North Carolina in early 1994, but Roxanne remembered receiving a sign from her grandmother the day she died. "I looked up [in the sky] and saw a perfect circle of contrail" from an airplane, she recalled, even though she didn't see the plane or any other contrails. "It was clearly not a cloud, just a perfect circle," said Roxanne. "I thought, oh, my grandmother is telling me life is a perfect circle. No beginning and no end. She wanted me to know that right away."

Hannah left Bennington College in Bennington, Vermont, after one semester in 1996, transferring to Lewis & Clark College in Portland, Oregon. After a year there, she decided Lewis & Clark wasn't right for her either. She elected to take time off from college and immerse herself in the outdoors.

Lucas's A.T. thru-hike inspired Hannah to plan to make the strenuous journey herself in 1999. Roxanne was concerned about Hannah's safety and signed her up for self-defense classes. For months, Hannah ran five miles a day, exercised in a gym, and lugged 40 pounds of free weights in her backpack for miles in the woods behind Roxanne's house in Arden, North Carolina, to get fit. She was eager to get on the trail, where she could "think about her life."

In March 1999, George St. Clair took a bus to North Carolina to meet Hannah and drive her to the start of the northbound A.T. (Lucas was traveling in Europe at the time.) Accompanying Hannah was her friend Hillary Harrison, who started calling Hannah "Songbird," from a Lou Harris tune. Hannah took it as her trail name. As she had during Lucas's hike, Roxanne put up the A.T. trail map on her wall to follow Hannah's progress with red pins. She knew the ropes—care packages, phone calls, travels to trailheads to meet her dirty, tired child, and encouragement that only a mom could give.

In an article published in *JUMP* magazine's April 2000 issue, Hannah described her trip. She detailed how hard it had been at first, getting accustomed to the hefty pack, the changing weather, a cranky stove, sore muscles, and shelters overrun with mice. Relief came in Roxanne's food packages with sprouted-seed bread, chocolate-covered pecans, dried fruit, peanut butter, and dehydrated tofu and vegetables.

When Hannah stopped at trail towns, she saw Burt's Bees products on store shelves. She was flooded with childhood memories of the earliest products made on Roxanne's kitchen woodstove and "my mom working so hard." Now she could see the end result of Roxanne's drive and success, and she felt a greater emotional connection between them.

By the time Hannah had trekked almost 500 miles to Virginia, her feet were swollen, making her boots too tight, and they had been wet for weeks. As a result, her toenails were turning black and falling off. She was in so much pain that she didn't know if she could continue the hike. Hannah's May 26, 1999, journal entry said: "OK, now I'm scared. My feet are killing me.... The other day I sat down on the side of the trail and cried from the pain."

Roxanne rushed to her daughter's aid, meeting her at a trailhead near Charlottesville, Virginia. She took Hannah to a hotel and administered first aid to her feet, including massages, soaks in hot water with tea tree oil, and rest. After a few days of TLC, Hannah was sufficiently recovered to continue her journey. Roxanne dropped her off where they had met, and Hannah trotted off in new boots—though she was solo now because her friend Hillary had returned to Maine.

When Hannah reached Vermont in July, her father joined her on the trail for three days. Hannah had been bitten by ticks and had developed Lyme disease–like symptoms. Fortunately, antibiotics prescribed by a doctor cleared up her fatigue and headaches.

Just before entering Maine's Hundred Mile Wilderness near her childhood home, Hannah left the trail for a few days. She thumbed to Parkman, borrowed Burt's truck, and shuttled several of her thru-hike pals to Roxanne's cabin for a blow-out food bash. She touched the Katahdin peak sign on September 26.

"As I made my way up, I cried and kept stopping," Hannah wrote in her journal. She was so happy to be completing her journey and elated that her own passion had pushed her through. "It was an all-consuming feeling of exhilaration—like no future challenge would ever be too great," she wrote. Roxanne and George were waiting at the bottom of the mountain to greet Hannah when she finished.

In the fall of 1999, Hannah entered Prescott College in Prescott, Arizona, where she studied human development and photography. After graduating in May 2002, she furthered her photographic studies in Maine for a time and then, uncertain what she wanted to do with her life, accepted the job in sales and marketing at Burt's Bees offered by Roxanne. She stayed at Burt's Bees for six years before spending two years working for her mother's post–Burt's Bees children's clothing venture. In 2009, she matriculated as a graduate student at the California Institute of Integral Studies (CIIS), where she earned a master's degree in integrative health.

Following graduation, she became certified as a fitness instructor and nutritionist and was hired by a women's fitness/nutritionist center in Mill Valley, California.

The twins' journeys and her own new knowledge of the A.T. and thru-hiking made Roxanne a major fan of "the university of the A.T." She saw that her children had matured from the experience, and this influenced Roxanne to become an enthusiastic, generous benefactor of the storied footpath.

At Home in Maine

Roxanne was a low-key summer resident of Winter Harbor for a couple of years after purchasing a house on the Jordan Pond Road in 1998. It took awhile before the possibility of transforming the town from a quaint but struggling fishing outpost to a vibrant mini–Bar Harbor seized her imagination. If Winter Harbor could become a much more integral part of tourists' experience of the Schoodic Peninsula, it could mean new business development and more jobs. Some 250,000 people passed through the village on their way to sea-swept Schoodic, the remote, mainland portion of Acadia National Park, a 20-minute ferry ride or an hour's drive from Bar Harbor.

Her son's desire for a restaurant of his own provided the immediate impetus for this vision. After attending Le Cordon Bleu cooking school in London, Lucas had worked in U.S. restaurants as a pastry chef and by 2000 was confident he could make a go of a seasonal bakery. Roxanne backed him, renting the Harbor Shop on the corner of Main and Newman streets in Winter Harbor and converting it from a gift shop to Mama's Boy Bakery. (Lucas had been affectionately called his "mama's boy" while growing up.)

Mama's Boy was a hit, and after a couple of summers, Lucas and his then-girlfriend, chef Jennifer Amara, were ready to experiment with a fine foods restaurant. Roxanne had purchased the Harbor Shop property with the idea of expanding the small bakery building into a restaurant, but after consulting with builder John Libby, they agreed that a new structure for the expansion was a better way to go. The bakery building was moved, and the 1860s house on the property, still known from the 1920s as "Doc Holt's place," was torn down.

In its place rose a three-story Victorian-style, timber-frame edifice that made an impressive architectural statement. The 4,500-square-foot structure featured multiple gables for the upstairs windows, cathedral ceilings, rows of windows on the first floor, and a side porch looking out to sea over Henry's Cove. Mama's Boy Bistro opened in 2002 with a menu focused on locally sourced organic vegetables, seafoods, and meats.

In the early 2000s, Roxanne bought several other old houses to renovate and resell. "I like to transform things like buildings," she said. "It's very satisfying and fun and a way of putting money here and there, hoping it could increase in value." In 2005, she created a real estate holding entity, Seaside Properties LLC, and expanded her property portfolio with a number of expensive houses and commercial properties in Portland and Palm Beach.

In 2004, long-time Winter Harbor benefactor Eugene "Fitz" Dixon asked Roxanne to purchase J.M. Gerrish, a Main Street ice cream parlor and eatery that had been a mainstay for almost a century. Dixon, a Philadelphia Main Line multimillionaire who summered in Winter Harbor's exclusive Grindstone Neck enclave, had two conditions for the sale: Roxanne had to agree to keep the name Gerrish's and continue selling ice cream cones. He wanted to ensure that this old-fashioned aspect of the town survived.

Roxanne bought the unprofitable Gerrish's as a community service, and Lucas and Jennifer Amara agreed to run it along with Mama's Boy Bistro. They gave it a new flair, adding "Provisions" to the name, renovating the building, and turning it into a slicker operation, with food and market stuffs that were scarce in such an out-of-the-way area as Winter Harbor. Wi-fi was an extra draw.

With family in the food business, Roxanne enrolled at Le Cordon Bleu's Paris-based school and began basic pastry classes in the fall of 2005, living in a hotel room within walking distance of the school. Mornings were devoted to lectures and demonstrations, and afternoons to cooking. Roxanne's Aunt Liliane Willens accompanied her as companion and translator (Liliane held a doctorate in French, while Roxanne's French was shaky), but the school would not let Liliane attend classes, so Roxanne was left to understand the lectures as best she could. "I felt, ok, my God, here I am failing," she remembered. Her final grade was a D, and she received a score of 50 on her final exam. Besides botching some recipes (she recollected baking a cake the texture of which so incensed the teaching chef that he whisked it into the garbage and made her start over), she guessed she might have been downgraded for refusing to wear the required white shoes and white hat.

Back in Winter Harbor, Roxanne enjoyed baking at Gerrish's and was thrilled with how well her pastries, croissants, tarts, and pies turned out. "I had lines [of people] out the door," she recalled. Things changed when Lucas and Amara split up in 2005. Lucas left Maine for Seattle, where he worked as a restaurant sommelier and then as a wine importer and distributor. The Bistro and Gerrish's were closed.

In 2006 Roxanne tried to open a cooking school, Havre d'Hiver Ecole de Cuisine (Winter Harbor School of Cooking), offering basic training in pastries and specialty foods. Because of the town's outstanding coastal location, she thought it could become a cuisine vacation destination.

To house students, she bought and refurbished an 1885 ten-room Grindstone Neck "cottage." Neighbors, however, were unhappy about one of the mansions on the Neck being converted into a dormitory. "They didn't want change," said Larry Smith Sr., a long-time Winter Harbor resident and caretaker, and Grindstone Neck's residential/recreational zoning allowed no business uses. That zoning restriction hadn't stopped Fitz Dixon from converting a cottage into a restaurant years before, but this time was different. What the zoning issue boiled down to, according to Smith, was that "Roxanne wasn't one of them." Lacking the necessary permit, she ditched the cooking school plan.

Meanwhile, in June 2006, she purchased a home at 55 Carroll Street in Portland's fashionable Western Promenade neighborhood for $1.39 million. The 1907 residence had been built by James Phinney Baxter Jr., brother of Percival P. Baxter, the creator of Baxter State Park. Roxanne saw a potential for creating an arts renaissance in Portland and giving the city a new cultural brand.

A name brand herself at this point, Roxanne made headlines with just about anything she did in Portland, and she was encouraged by the local support she received. Over the following six years, she acquired and renovated several properties in Portland's arts district and the Congress Street historic preservation district for art studio and gallery space, but her projects ran afoul of building code and zoning restrictions. She also found that owning apartment buildings and dealing with tenants was awful. Because she managed her properties herself, tenants called her when things didn't work. "[T]hese people are calling me because their dishwasher isn't working. It's like, 'What?'" She sold her Carroll Street home in 2012 and the apartment buildings thereafter, afterward residing in Winter Harbor and Gouldsboro when she was in Maine.

In 2012 the Bistro in Winter Harbor reopened for business, this time as an Internet café called Schoodic Peninsula Visitors Center. Along with Maine and Acadia maps, brochures, and books, it offered a light breakfast, lunch, espresso bar, cold drinks, live Sunday music, and other cultural events. As she had at Gerrish's in years past, Roxanne lent a hand in the kitchen cooking pastries.

Continuing to increase her Winter Harbor real estate portfolio, she bought and tore down the closed gas station at the corner of Main and Newman streets and purchased two other nearby buildings—empty Main Street storefronts with upper-floor apartments. By May 2013, she owned eighteen properties in Winter Harbor and had torn down six buildings on Main Street. She controlled so much of Main Street that "it has started to affect things," observed Larry Smith, Sr., who worked for Roxanne at times and counted her a friend.

Her real estate activities in Winter Harbor "upset a lot of people," observed Larry Smith Jr., a town selectman. The Winter Harbor planning board reacted to the number of her building demolitions (and permit requests for more) by proposing a moratorium on tearing down any buildings over 50 years old pending public comment. At a town meeting in June 2013, however, voters defeated the idea 25–9. In 2014—thinking the town should have a sheltered venue for its farmer's market—Roxanne erected an Amish-built barn on the old gas station site across the street from her Schoodic Visitor's Center.

Entrepreneurial Encores

Roxanne felt great relief upon leaving Burt's Bees in 2004. Suddenly she had time to enjoy arts and crafts, knitting, reading, and gardening. She quickly discovered, however, that she didn't want to retire. She was nervous with free time on her hands. Wanting to get back into the competitive game of business, she founded Happy Green Bee in 2006. The organic cotton clothing venture for babies and toddlers gave her another opportunity to enter a retail niche market and see if "lightning would strike twice." Having made her mark with Burt's Bees, she felt more relaxed and less anxious this time about proving herself or making money.

Roxanne picked children's clothes as her new enterprise because she thought they made "awesome gifts for others. People who are buying something for another, particularly as a gift, relax a bit with their spending," she said. The Happy Green Bee line was promoted as stylish and environmentally friendly kids' clothing. Her designs of dresses, sleepers, socks, hats, and leggings made a bold statement on store shelves with their vibrant green, yellow, red, and orange colors. One of the most popular items was a petal shirt dress. The clothes were stretchy knits that would "grow" with their wearers. When pitching the line, Roxanne talked about the benefits of organic cotton free of pesticides. "I feel my job [with Happy Green Bee] is to educate people about the benefits of organic agriculture and organic cotton, how that impacts our planet and our health," she told the media.

There was no domestic source for organic cotton, so Roxanne bought her fabric in India and had the clothes manufactured in a fair trade factory in China. The goods were sent to a warehouse in Garner, North Carolina, where they were packaged for shipment to stores or to individuals who ordered via the Internet. In addition to several employees at the Garner office, Roxanne hired a sales rep to sell her line across the country.

Roxanne's return to a start-up retail business meant returning to fairs and craft events as far away as Alaska. "It [was] really hard work when you didn't need the money to keep going," she remembered. Her sister, Rachelle, and Lucas's wife, Yemaya Maurer, handled part of the work. Roxanne enjoyed playing with prices. "Where is the price people can't resist?" was a question she asked over and over. Her favorite customer type was "the granola grammy [who has] a lot more time than moms who come in the booth with their strollers and kids ... running around crying or spilling something. The moms are on a budget ... whereas the grandmother has more disposable income, has more time, comes in without kids ... and is indulgent."

As a guerrilla tactic to gain customers' attention without expensive magazine ads, she offered free in-store photo shoots of children wearing Happy Green Bee clothes. The shoots (some of which were done by daughter Hannah) created a "very high touch, very lasting connection" with moms who signed up for them, recalled Roxanne. "They were great for sales because [the host] stores ordered tons of outfits in anticipation of the promotions."

Selling children's clothes was such a different challenge from Burt's Bees that Roxanne found herself "back at square one ... beating my head against the wall" to figure out what would sell where. Sales hinged on customers putting together outfits, and a lot of customers had to be shown how to match shirts with pants and create other combinations.

There were also geographic markets Happy Green Been couldn't seem to penetrate, such as California and Los Angeles in particular. "Nobody [bought] our stuff there," Roxanne recalled. The Northeast proved another hard nut to crack. The best regions for her infant/toddler/preschool items were the South and the Midwest, where sisters, aunts, and grandmothers lived in close proximity to children and knew their clothing sizes.

Seasonality was another problem. People bought Burt's Bees lip balm year-round, but that wasn't true for Happy Green Bee items. "You couldn't sell a tank top in November or a sweater in July no matter how hard you tried," Roxanne said. Her low opinion of the garment industry didn't help, either. The business was "cut throat," she said.

Roxanne moved the company in 2008 to a large barn on West Bay Road in Gouldsboro, Maine. For a while, operations were handled by a few employees there. But the business wasn't profitable, and it weighed on her. She found her energy for it lagging and slowly let Happy Green Bee sink. After a close-out sale in late 2012, she shut down the website in 2013.

Not one to be idle, she made new plans for a working farm on her 25-acre property in Gouldsboro, calling it Raven's Nest after a dramatic promontory on Schoodic Peninsula. The strong influence of her homesteading life on her children made Roxanne want to give her grandchildren the experience of raising animals and vegetables. She acquired a menagerie of Red Bourbon turkeys (a heritage breed), chickens, rabbits, and two Welsh ponies. Unlike her long-ago homestead in the woods, the Gouldsboro farm provided plenty of sunlit space for vegetables, herbs, and flowers.

To improve her cooking skills, Roxanne traveled to Italy in 2012, learning how to make pizza in Sorrento. She returned in 2013 to take a course on pasta in a small town near Genoa, following which she founded a handmade vegetable pasta enterprise also called Raven's Nest. In early January 2015, she took a course at the San Francisco Baking Institute on baking artisan breads.

Wearing a brimmed light-green rain hat, top layers, and light-red pants, Roxanne listened politely as one customer at Maine's Common Ground Fair in the fall of 2014 looked at the Raven's Nest product labels and said they reminded her of Burt's Bees. The woman rattled on with her version of how Burt's Bees began in Maine, not realizing she was talking to the founder. Her version was incorrect, but Roxanne just smiled and listened.

Despite her amazing success with Burt's Bees and her subsequent business endeavors, it was in land conservation that she most ardently yearned to prove herself—a desire that would make her the most controversial woman in Maine. 🐝.

Log drivers in a bateau on the West Branch of the Penobscot.

Imagining a National Park: 2000

T he rise of the pulp and paper industry in Maine between 1880 and 1920 was capitalism on an epic scale. Huge investments in paper mills, water rights, and timberlands flowed into Maine from out of state. The Great Northern pulp and paper mill on the upper Penobscot at Millinocket was the world's largest when it was built in 1898 by Italian immigrants. By 1950, GNP was producing nearly 1,000 tons of newsprint per day from its Millinocket mill and almost as much from a newer mill in East Millinocket. By 1970, GNP, International Paper, Georgia-Pacific, Oxford Paper, Fraser, S.D. Warren, and Scott owned nearly half of the state's commercial forestlands, ensuring an uninterrupted supply of wood to their mills. One-quarter of Maine's manufacturing workers were employed in paper mills, and paper companies accounted for nearly $3 of every $10 of Maine's economic output.

Then came the hostile takeover of Diamond International Corporation in late 1982 by Sir James Goldsmith. The British corporate raider sold off most of Diamond's mills over the following years, getting a return that was twice his investment, but he retained 1.7 million acres of timberland, including a million acres in the northern forest.

Large blocks of the northern forest had been changing hands for more than a century, but this time was different. Once a papermaker, Diamond

International had, in effect, become a real estate holding company. The distinction was critical but not immediately appreciated. In a 1987 analysis of economic forces in the northern forest, former American Forestry Association president Perry Hagenstein warned that "more changes are likely.... The large holdings, more than ever before, are viewed as profit centers by their owners and are expected to earn returns themselves that justify continued ownership." Citing thin soils, short growing seasons, and ever-increasing management costs, he concluded that the value of northern New England's forestlands was no longer for timber production. Increasingly it was as real estate to be developed for recreation, tourism, and vacation homes.

Hagenstein's report proved prophetic in early 1988 when Goldsmith and Diamond International CEO "Chainsaw" Al Dunlap renamed the company Diamond Occidental Forest and began auctioning land to speculators.* In the forest industry paradigm shift that followed, Maine timberlands became a "profit center," more valuable for development and as a real estate investment than for supplying fiber and logs to mills, just as Hagenstein had foreseen. Wall Street came to expect that timber holdings would be liquidated as paper companies consolidated. The promotion of forest company stocks by financial firms was contingent on that tactic.

The Diamond Occidental land divestiture involved 970,000 acres of land in Maine, New Hampshire, Vermont, and New York State, with the bulk of the

---

*Goldsmith installed Dunlap as CEO of papermaker Crown-Zellerbach in 1986. When Dunlap slashed the workforce by 22 percent and eliminated 18 of 22 distribution centers, costs plummeted and profits soared. Goldsmith then transferred Dunlap to Diamond International, where Dunlap again slashed costs and drove profits up. Goldsmith nicknamed him "Rambo in Pinstripes," but British naturalist John Aspinall came up with the name that stuck: "Chainsaw Al."

When Dunlap became CEO of Scott Paper Company in 1994, the company had $2 billion in debt and had lost $277 million the previous year. Dunlap cut 11,200 jobs—more than one-third of the workforce—and sold the S.D. Warren papermaking subsidiary for $1.6 billion. His visits to Scott's mills became known as the "Chainsaw Massacre Tour." He cut Scott's 1995 research-and-development budget in half and cancelled all plant and equipment upgrades. And he inflated revenues by offering limited-time 15 to 30 percent rebates to retailers, inducing them to order more inventory than needed. Scott booked the revenues immediately, whereas the rebates did not have to be paid until the products were sold to consumers—and Dunlap gambled that he could sell the company by then. He was right. In July 1995, Kimberly-Clark agreed to buy Scott for $9.4 billion, delivering a 20-month return to shareholders of 225% and a $100 million payout for Dunlap. Only after the sale was complete did Kimberly-Clark executives realize they'd paid far too much.

In July 1996, Dunlap was hired to turn around the Sunbeam Corporation, and there his tactics caught up with him. At Sunbeam, as at Scott, he used "bill and hold" tactics to pump sales to unsustainable levels, and when the scheme collapsed, he was fired in 1998. Sunbeam never recovered and declared bankruptcy in 2001.

property in Maine. Rushing to get in on the sell-off were investment groups, speculators, land developers, timber liquidators, logging contractors, state governments, land trusts, and "kingdom buyers" desiring personal forest retreats.

After generations of stable ownership, some nine million acres of Maine timberland—half of the state's entire commercial forestland—were sold and resold between 1988 and 1999. One new owner that struck particular terror into the hearts of environmentalists was Plum Creek Timber Company of Seattle, at the time the largest corporate landowner in the U.S. Six months after SAPPI (South African Pulp and Paper Industries) put its 905,000 acres of former Scott Paper Company lands on the market, Plum Creek bought all the Maine acreage. When the deal was announced on October 6, 1998, Plum Creek was already notorious in the Pacific Northwest and the Rockies for converting cutover forest into expensive subdivisions. The company reorganized itself as a real estate investment trust (REIT) in 1999, underscoring its intention to make money as much by cutting up the land as by cutting down the forest.

After denying for three years that it planned anything other than timber harvesting in Maine, Plum Creek unveiled its first development plan around First Roach Pond. The lots sold like hot cakes. At that time, it was the biggest subdivision in the history of Maine's wildlands, but it was soon to be dwarfed by Plum Creek's next venture, announced in 2004: 975 house lots, two resorts, a golf course, a marina, three RV parks with convenience stores, beauty salons, gas stations, and more than 100 rental cabins on Moosehead Lake. The announcement raised widespread alarm, especially among conservationists, not only about Plum Creek's plans but also about the intentions of other absentee investment groups that were buying up large swaths of Maine, many of whom hid their identities behind limited liability companies.

Between 1994 and 2005, the share of the Maine woods owned by traditional forest products companies such as Great Northern Paper fell from 59 percent to less than 16 percent, while ownership by financial investors rose from 3 to 33 percent.* The paper companies had depended on a sustainable harvest; not so these speculators. Managed by fiduciaries of private and public investments, the objective of the new entities—which included timber investment management organizations (TIMOs) as well as REITs—was to monetize the forest and recover the initial investment in 10 to 15 years by

*The remaining shares were owned by families and individuals, the public, conservation organizations, and Native American tribes.

cutting timber faster than ever, never mind that the woods couldn't regenerate that quickly. A companion strategy that quickly gained popularity was to sell development rights on forestlands the speculators intended to log but not subdivide. In effect, the speculators were paid not to develop land they had no intention of developing anyway—while selling off the lands that were most desirable for residential and commercial development. They separated the "plain vanilla" timberland from developable areas around forest-swathed lakes, ponds, and scenic areas, parcels they labeled the "highest and best use" lands. Often these high-value lands were ecologically valuable too, and protecting sizable portions of them was important to wildlife habitat integrity. These deals became known as "conservation easements," a term that had a protective ring to it. Public agencies and nonprofit land trusts got into the action. Instead of being used to buy park land, tens of millions of public and philanthropic dollars were paid to appease forest owners who threatened to develop their woodlands.

Thanks to the ongoing exodus of the pulp and paper companies from Maine to the southern U.S. and to other countries with fast-growing trees and few regulations, a century-old way of life was ending in Maine's woods and mill towns. The mills had provided secure jobs with good pay and benefits to generations of Mainers. Now those jobs were disappearing. Some people went on welfare; others moved away. Houses were abandoned. Property values shrank. Small businesses dried up from lack of patronage. Families disintegrated.

And if that wasn't bad enough, many feared that the tradition of virtually unrestricted public access to the paper companies' huge landholdings was unlikely to be honored by the new breed of landowners. Hunters, fishermen, snowmobilers, and ATVers were already encountering no-trespassing signs, gated roads on lands they had once roamed freely, and new fees to access private lands.

Such was the state of affairs in the north woods when Roxanne Quimby turned her attention there in 2000. But national park adversaries seemed uninterested in discussing what opportunities could emerge from a park. In fact, the opposition to any new national park in Maine had deepened and hardened.

RESTORE's Big Idea

Three years before the 2003 sale of Burt's Bees to AEA Investors, Roxanne had begun to immerse herself in the national park mission of RESTORE:

The North Woods. She had become aware of the ambitious plan at Maine's Common Ground Fair in 1997, and in 2000 she contacted Jym St. Pierre, the organization's Maine director, to let him know she was interested in helping.

By then, a half-dozen years had gone by since RESTORE had announced its campaign for a big national park and wilderness preserve surrounding Baxter State Park. The Maine Woods National Park and Preserve was to include 3.2 million acres, making it almost as large as Connecticut, larger than Yosemite and Yellowstone parks combined, and nearly 70 times the size of Acadia National Park. RESTORE proposed that hiking, cross-country skiing, camping, boating, fishing, and visitor facilities be permitted in the national park area, and that these activities, plus hunting and snowmobiling, be permitted in the national preserve area. The acreage in each area, however—and the final determination of permitted and prohibited uses—would be decided through a public planning process. Not allowed under RESTORE's proposal were logging, mining, dumping, jet skis, ATVs, herbicides, and private development (with the exception of existing camps, which would be grandfathered).

RESTORE had built significant grassroots support in the 1990s by collecting thousands of petition signatures, conducting presentations, doing mailings in Maine and beyond, and garnering extensive news media coverage. The organization invited businesses to become Maine Woods National Park Business Partners and allied itself with other nonprofits via the Maine Woods National Park Coalition.

St. Pierre called on pilot Rudy Engholm to fly Roxanne over the proposed park area for a three-dimensional view of the terrain. In the early 1990s, Engholm had founded Northern Wings, a volunteer aviation service that flew planes in the aid of environmental causes. He took Roxanne and Burt on a five-hour flight over a wide circle of the proposed park encompassing the north woods jewels of Baxter State Park and Moosehead, Allagash, Umsaskis, and Chesuncook lakes. "Roxanne was very interested in how to buy land for the [national park]," Engholm recalled. He was impressed by how serious she was about restoring wilderness in the north woods.

What RESTORE needed was money to finance an all-out campaign and a partner who could begin to acquire land for the proposed park. Roxanne believed she could be the catalyst to move the park idea forward because she had the wealth, the business acumen, and the passion. She was seized with excitement by RESTORE's vision. She had proven with Burt's Bees that she too thought big and was attracted to far-reaching visions that demanded daring and unwavering tenacity.

"She talked in very spiritual terms of how important it was to protect this earth," St. Pierre remembered, adding that Roxanne spoke of how she believed "she was put on this earth to do something big in terms of conservation."

Roxanne couldn't have appeared at a more opportune time for acquiring land. In the next few years she would negotiate with some of corporate America's most notable business owners for the sale of Burt's Bees, and she was savvy enough to know that landowners would play money games with her. But she also knew that a willing seller and a willing buyer can almost always reach an agreement in time. She knew that investor groups were motivated by profit, not emotions.

Her buying power became a heady topic of conversation. It was clear that she could pay prices beyond the standard timber value. Some forest industry landowners courted her. Some conservation groups with limited funds worried that her quest for land would jack up prices and shut them out of deals.*

She stood out among the new investors who were gobbling up the old paper company empire: Not only was she the only female, she was also one of a small handful of investors with *wilderness* objectives. For decades, wilderness had been a fighting word from northern Maine to the halls of the Maine Legislature in Augusta. To industry-friendly politicians and reactionary conservatives, "wilderness" was synonymous with putting a big lock on the north woods.

Roxanne's eventual purchases would be just a tiny fraction of Maine's industrial forest, much of which was divvied up among TIMOs and REITs. But she became a target of fear and hostility because she didn't obscure her identity behind an anonymous investment corporation, was interested in donating land to the federal government, and closed her properties to logging, hunting, snowmobiling, and ATVs, making no secret of the fact that she didn't want any activities on her land that wouldn't be allowed in a national wilderness area or a wilderness sanctuary within a national park.†

Roxanne was the park opposition's worst nightmare—RESTORE with money. She had the financial power to purchase land, influence Washington

*In reality, the new TIMOs and REITs were already bidding up prices by parceling the high-value lands in their ownership.

†Logging is prohibited in national parks but allowed in national forests. Hunting and off-road vehicles are prohibited in national parks and regulated in national forests. Regulated hunting is also permitted in national wildlife refuges, national preserves, and designated wilderness areas—but logging and motorized vehicles are generally prohibited in wilderness areas. RESTORE proposed that snowmobiling be permitted in the preserve area of its national park.

politicians, and make a national park a real possibility. A successful business-woman with a back-to-the-land background, preservationist attitudes, a vege-tarian lifestyle, and formidable wealth, she was the perfect new antagonist for anti-park activists to fight.

There were other factors at work, too. Roxanne, like RESTORE, was "from away"—from Massachusetts, to be precise. Roxanne had been born in Cam-bridge, and RESTORE was headquartered in Concord at the time. These out-of-staters had no business trying to dictate the best use of the woods or to put any areas off-limits to logging, hunting, and motorized use, park oppo-nents said. They ignored the fact that St. Pierre was a Maine native and life-long resident and that RESTORE had spent years soliciting support for the park. RESTORE's insistence that park lands be acquired only from donors or willing sellers didn't seem to matter either, nor did the fact that RESTORE's plan would benefit hunters, trappers, and snowmobilers. Many park oppo-nents assumed they had heritage "rights" to do what they wanted, when they wanted, where they wanted, even though most of the north woods was cor-porate-owned. Park advocates were portrayed as an existential threat to the northern Maine way of life.

The strongest reaction to Roxanne was blatant sexism. Some opponents even tried to goad her by making lewd remarks on the Internet about her per-sonal appearance and posting unflattering photographs from her hippie days.

Her advocacy for RESTORE's proposed national park with its wilder-ness sanctuary area was not just daring and admirable; it was historic, given that the idea for something akin to a national park or comparable preserve in northern Maine had been lingering in the air for more than 150 years. The idea had been conceived by Roxanne's hero, Henry David Thoreau, and had since been carried forward by others who understood the priceless value of it. An acclaimed writer of our time, Bill McKibben, loved the bigness of RESTORE's proposed park because it was large enough "for the wolf and the cougar and the caribou and the wolverine to rejoin the bear and broad-winged hawk, the loon and the beaver," but also because it was "big hope."

Roxanne Begins to Buy Land

Roxanne joined RESTORE's board of directors in October 2000 and began publicly promoting the organization's park plan through Burt's Bees. Her prominent role generated national publicity that told and retold her rags-to-riches personal story and how the profits from Burt's Bees were going to be used for land conservation for "the greater good."

At the same time she began working with two well-connected real estate agents, John Cochrane and Jim Trimble. Cochrane was often first to know what was for sale in the north woods because of his long-time association with forest landowners and logging contractors; Trimble had known Roxanne since the late 1980s, when he owned a real estate business in Sebec and a coffee shop in Dover-Foxcroft.

Cochrane drove and flew with Roxanne to various parcels. "We had a lot of fun," he said. "She was a fast learner. You just had to tell her something once. And she had a terrific work ethic." When word got around that Cochrane was working with her, people in the woods industry "would screech and holler about that Bee-lady buying land."

Also accompanying Roxanne on numerous early scouting trips was RESTORE's Jym St. Pierre, who acted as an unofficial advisor. In the spring of 2000, he went with her to look at property in Elliotsville Township, having "no idea of the money she was talking about spending." Burt Shavitz was there too, he recalled, "sort of like a ghost who floated in and out."*

Numerous people had contacted St. Pierre over the years to donate land for RESTORE's park, but they talked about "lot" size parcels—far too small for RESTORE's ambitions. "I had no idea at the time that [Roxanne] was willing to spend megabucks on large tracts" and could be "the angel" RESTORE had been dreaming about, he said.

August 4, 2000, was a red-letter day for Roxanne—the day she bought her first north woods property. The tract was 2,407 acres along Big Wilson Stream in Elliotsville Township, a dozen miles north of her old Guilford cabin. The parcel—which was within the boundary of RESTORE's proposed park—bordered the Appalachian Trail and was close to Borestone Mountain, where Roxanne had taken her children on their first hike. After high school, the twins had each hiked the entire 2,185-mile footpath from Georgia to Maine. The positive effect on both of them so impressed Roxanne that she resolved to buffer the federal trail corridor in the Elliotsville area with her conservation purchases.

To acquire the land, Roxanne had to do business with Herb Haynes of Winn, who had made his reputation and wealth by liquidation logging and subdividing

*Burt had given up his ownership share in Burt's Bees the year before but was still making promotional appearances for Burt's Bees. Apparently the break between them wasn't yet absolute.

the shorn land into house lots. She paid Haynes's development entity, Lakeville Shores, $575,000, or $239 an acre. It was the first of a number of deals she would make with the titan of Maine's growing contractor/ landowner sector.

On the same day, Roxanne also purchased from Haynes 5,800 acres some 70 miles north of the Big Wilson Stream parcel as the crow flies, in Township 8 Range 11 (T8R11 WELS)* in Penobscot County, for $1,630,000, or $267 an acre. The Bluffer tract (so named because of a ridge within it) bordered The Nature Conservancy's 4,850-acre Big Reed Forest Reserve, the largest remaining stand of old-growth forest in New England. Ten miles north of Baxter State Park's northwest corner, it too was within the bounds of RESTORE's proposed Maine Woods National Park. Roxanne rescued T8R11 just in time. Unknown to her, Haynes had contracted with another forest liquidator, Dick DeLaite, to cut the southern half of the township, which sheltered an unusual white cedar–forested wetland. As DeLaite's skidders had prepared to start cutting down the trees, nearby sporting camp owners Jack and Josie McPhee had steeled themselves to intervene and try to save the site. It was at that point that Haynes sold the entire piece to Roxanne.

When Roxanne stopped other landowners from using the old logging roads on her new Bluffer property, Seven Islands Land Company, owned by the Pingree heirs, built a bypass around her land to reach their timberlands. In time, Josie McPhee named the bypass "Queen Bee Bypass" after Roxanne.†

Roxanne loved a good value, and she viewed land as "something incredibly rare" and undervalued. "I couldn't believe paying [$230–$267] an acre," she reflected. "It was the most precious treasure and yet was less than an ounce of gold [per acre] … or the cost of a good meal [in a fine restaurant]."

By acquiring land the old-fashioned way—paying willing sellers the market rate—Roxanne had taken tangible action toward creating a national park in Maine's north woods. She explained that owning land in the north woods gave her a "voice" and "standing" in the national park effort.

Yet owning big tracts of land was counterintuitive to her. Since the 1960s, she had believed that private property was a large contributor to the demise of

*When Maine separated from Massachusetts in 1820, the uninhabited area was divided into square numbered "townships." A column of townships was called a "range." WELS means west of the easterly line of the state, a north-south line from Hamlin to Amity in Aroostook County.

†Maine wardens collected the names of new roads in the unorganized territory and passed them on to DeLorme Inc. to include in new editions of the *Maine Atlas and Gazetteer*. The "Queen Bee Bypass" ended up in DeLorme's 2009 edition.

the planet. "This whole idea of cutting it up into pieces and having individuals of means have this concept they own it in some way and could determine its fate created a lot of problems where the earth suffered," she said. In her opinion, a national park was every American's property. "So if an American goes into a park, they feel it's theirs, in a way, and are entitled to feel it's theirs, as well as everybody's and nobody's," she said. "It's a good way of expanding our understanding of land and the ethic that could create a sustainable relationship with the land. Short of everyone living in a commune where no one owned anything, the National Park Service kind of approximates that communistic idea within a democracy. People participate in it willingly ... without feeling they are radical. It's almost like a radical idea in conservative clothing, very benign apple pie."*

Hearing her views about communal ownership, some park opponents spread rumors that Roxanne was a communist and disdained the culture of private property that was at the heart of northern Maine's cultural values, while at the same time embracing capitalism for her personal gain. The right-wing element among the park opposition proclaimed that the end result of a national park would be a "rural cleansing" and the denial of public access to public land.

Park Opposition Gears Up

Roxanne's first acquisitions worried Jym St. Pierre. Although he was delighted that she was rescuing interesting properties, she had only a general familiarity with her new lands, and her plan of what and where to buy next wasn't clear to him.† He was concerned that the cutover woods, noncontiguous parcels, networks of logging roads, and leased camp lots on her properties would pose major management problems.

Land conservation is a complicated business. Although Roxanne had begun with a business approach, she had not thought about forming coalitions with north woods residents and recreational and environmental groups. St. Pierre hoped his advice would help her become savvier about land ownership and ameliorate the personal attacks he knew would intensify.

*Pulitzer Prize–winning novelist Wallace Stegner called national parks "the best idea we ever had. Absolutely American, absolutely democratic, they reflect us at our best rather than our worst."

†Roxanne said later that she sometimes kept her plans to herself in order to keep sellers from trying to capitalize on her intentions.

As Roxanne was starting to buy land for a national park, RESTORE's leaders continued their efforts to garner public support for a multimillion-acre park. During the summer of 2000, green-and-white lawn signs listing the driving distance to the proposed park appeared in front yards along the planned "Road to the Park."* Activists recruited nearly fifty new small-business partners to join the existing 300 pro-park enterprises. And Beth Wheatley, a RESTORE staffer, completed a "Pedal for the Park," biking 500 miles across the northern forest from the Adirondack Park in Upstate New York to the shore of Moosehead Lake to attract publicity for the park vision.

The vociferous opposition to a national park made it seem as if the majority of Mainers were in the "no" camp, but statewide opinion polls told another story. The first such poll,† in August 1997, showed that 63 percent of Mainers supported a national park. In July 2000, another opinion poll confirmed that RESTORE's vision for a national park was supported by nearly two-thirds of Mainers.‡

These pro-park poll results, the momentum of RESTORE's outreach efforts, and Roxanne's entry into the new mix of landowners created a sense of panic among opponents. Second District Congressional hopeful Dick Campbell sought to galvanize the opposition to gain votes for his 2000 campaign. In an op-ed article in the July 16, 2000, issue of the *Bangor Daily News*, he accused RESTORE of "audacity and arrogance" and charged that Roxanne had returned to Maine not to improve the business climate but to "eliminate the longest existing industry in Maine—forest products." Roxanne and "her Massachusetts-and-Washington–based environmental protectionist groups have little or no respect for Maine people who are working very hard each day to preserve and protect our respected environment...."

Amid all the uproar, the Greenville Economic Development Committee invited RESTORE leaders Michael Kellett and Jym St. Pierre to discuss the

---

*Approximately 1,000 signs were placed in yards across the state with the mileages "to the park" penned in.

†The poll was done by Abacus Associates. Some 500 registered Maine voters were questioned, with the Portland media market 67 percent favorable and the Bangor and Presque Isle markets 56 percent favorable.

‡Eleven other polls from September 2000 to October 2011 confirmed support ranging from 56 percent to 78 percent. A poll by the Sportsman's Alliance of Maine in May 2013 found that 55 percent of those asked favored a national wilderness area in northern Maine if hunting were allowed. It should be noted that the polls didn't ask if respondents would support a park they would have to pay a fee to enter. Whether there would be a gate fee in the park Roxanne is proposing was unknown as of this writing. Only 133 of the 405 existing national parks charge an entrance fee, and where a fee is charged, people 62 and over can get in free.

revenue issues posed to northern Maine towns by removal of park lands from property tax rolls. The subsequent discussion of federal payments in lieu of taxes led to an invitation to RESTORE to participate in a larger public session in Greenville on the park concept.

The gathering at the local high school on August 31, 2000, turned out to be an ambush for Kellett and St. Pierre. When they arrived, they were mobbed by protesters carrying placards and wearing stickers proclaiming "No Park Ever." The auditorium was jammed with park opponents, along with some supportive aging hippies, "good lifers," and environmentalists. Kellett and St. Pierre's opening statements about the potential benefits of a park and the most recent statewide opinion poll irritated the hostile majority. The duo got nowhere with their pitch for a feasibility study to provide everyone with trustworthy facts and eliminate misunderstandings about a park's potential effects. "It was a lynching, angry crowd," recalled St. Pierre. "People against the national park were screaming."

Private forester Mark Armstrong bluntly told St. Pierre, "So much of what you have to say is outright baloney." Two Republican state legislative candidates walked down the auditorium aisle to deliver a "gift" to St. Pierre. "This box of dirt ... from Aroostook County ... is all you are going to get," Steve Martin of Amity declared to a round of applause. Greenville town manager John Simko used the occasion to reiterate what he had said in newspaper op-eds published on the eve of the meeting—that he was declaring "war" against RESTORE and its park plan. At the same time, he proclaimed that he and other opponents were open to "commonsense approaches" to diversify the area's economy.

U.S. Congressman John Baldacci (who represented northern Maine and would be elected governor of Maine two years later) inserted himself into the event with a statement that made clear his opposition to a park. "As the saying goes, if it ain't broke, don't fix it," Baldacci said through a representative. "Maine's North Woods are not broken, and are certainly not in need of the 'fix' proposed by RESTORE."*

---

*Garrett Conover of Willimantic, a celebrated Maine wilderness guide, was in the crowd and had listened to local complaints about RESTORE's national park idea for years. He was troubled by opponents' lack of interest in a feasibility study to document the pros and cons of a park. He and his partner at the time, Alexandra, worked for a decade in the area promoting the positive experiences of existing park gateway towns near the Adirondack Park in New York State and the Boundary Waters Canoe Area in Minnesota. But the Conovers got nowhere with small-town politicos and businesspeople, who didn't want to hear about positive park experiences in other states. He concluded that Mainers in the industrial timber country had lived in a "corporate serfdom" for so long they didn't want a choice of a more diverse economy. "They felt more comfortable with the familiar jailer of their prison," he believed.

After the Greenville meeting, Jym St. Pierre cancelled a couple of park presentations due to threats of disruption, heckling, and possible violence. Thinking that if Greenville did not want to be the principal gateway community to the future park, Millinocket might, he met in early September with Millinocket's town manager, Eugene Conlogue. Although St. Pierre thought they had a friendly exchange, Conlogue was, in fact, planning a trap. He followed up their meeting by notifying St. Pierre that a public forum in Millinocket had been scheduled for presentations by national park proponents and opponents. When St. Pierre replied that he had a long-standing commitment to be out of Maine on the designated date, Conlogue said they would hold the session anyway. On October 3, 2000, park opponents gathered in the local high school to shout at an empty chair on the stage.

Both Simko and Conlogue remained intractable park adversaries. Playing off RESTORE's name and tag line, Conlogue posted a sign in Millinocket announcing that the town was "National Headquarters of RESTORE: Boston, America's Next Great National Park and Preserve." Next came a bumper sticker, "RESTORE: BOSTON," which sent a message to the Massachusetts-based organization to focus on advocating for parks in Paul Revere state's capital, not Maine. The rebuff to park advocates was clever enough to generate smiles even among park advocates. Anti-conservationists rallied around the slogan, and soon the "RESTORE: BOSTON" message was traveling south on cars and pickups.

Undaunted by the tactics of park opponents, Roxanne's imagination went to work after her Big Wilson Stream acquisition. Soon she was thinking about a visitors' center on Big Wilson—in the trees. Treehouses would be connected to one another by rope bridges so that visitors could get a new perspective of the forest and hopefully be more inclined to save the woods from "development and ruthless harvesting," she explained.

Speaking about her idea to the *Maine Times*, she envisioned that each treehouse would focus on a certain aspect of the north woods—its history, starting with Native American life and culture, the logging and paper industry, the flora and fauna of the region, and recreational uses of the woods. "I thought a camp kitchen would be a great working exhibit for the history of the logging era, complete with iron cookstove, flapjacks, and boiled coffee," she said. Since the center would be near the A.T., she wanted to provide showers and other amenities to thru-hikers.

But the treehouses went on the backburner in the summer of 2001 as Roxanne got involved in her third land purchase, this one on famed Mt. Kineo.

The Greenville-based weekly *Moosehead Messenger* broke the news of the purchase on June 20 with a front-page headline: "Kineo land sold to RESTORE supporter." A second article the next week was headlined, "Quimby outlines plans for Kineo." Although it was just 77 acres, the tract purchased by Roxanne was the largest undeveloped parcel on the 1,150-acre Kineo peninsula, an iconic Maine landmark jutting into Moosehead Lake that had been attracting tourists for a century and a half. Roxanne's acquisition abutted the Mt. Kineo Golf Course and state park property protecting the famed 800-foot-high Kineo cliffs.*

Chip Foster, owner of the Kineo Freight Company of Rockwood, had a state permit for twelve house lots on the 77 acres. When Roxanne took Jym St. Pierre for a look at the parcel, state and private conservation entities had already tried without success to buy the land from Foster. Realtor Jim Trimble, acting for Roxanne, then talked to Foster, and they worked out a sale. On June 15, 2001, Roxanne paid Foster $350,000, later telling Trimble that the parcel cost her "275,000 lip balms."

Roxanne was interested in Kineo because it was available, "totally underpriced," and threatened by development. "I had been there, it was really pretty and would have been really ugly with houses on it," she said. "So many people told me later, 'I just can't imagine seeing lights on that slope, and people living there.'"

What made the purchase especially satisfying to Roxanne was the fact that Henry David Thoreau had walked across the land to climb Kineo on July 24, 1857, and young Teddy Roosevelt had visited there in 1870. "It was a neon piece of real estate," said St. Pierre. "We even thought about a kiosk at Kineo saying 'Welcome to the future Maine Woods National Park.'"

During Trimble's discussions with Roxanne about Kineo, he tried to talk her out of buying land for a national park. "I told her, 'You are way smarter and nimbler than the federal government. The feds have no money and can't take care of a national park.' She got pissed," he recalled.

Roxanne's Kineo acquisition put anti-park activists on high alert. Conservative Mary Adams must have been reading St. Pierre's mind, as she blogged on her website "The *Adams Report*" on July 7, 2001, that "Roxanne may have just bought the gateway to the proposed park." The *Bangor Daily News*, the most widely read newspaper in northern Maine, quoted Roxanne in its July

*Moosehead Lake, at 74,890 acres, is the largest water body in New England.

10, 2001, editorial as saying that 3.2 million acres "should be big enough to accommodate" everyone's recreational needs—wilderness, snowmobiling, and hunting.

Letters to the editor followed, most of them condemning Roxanne's land-buying activities. Greenville town manager John Simko was incredulous that the *Bangor Daily News* had described Roxanne "as a modern-day Percival Baxter.... Shame on you for giving the inference that RESTORE (Quimby) is akin to Gov. Baxter." A letter from Millinocket town manager Eugene Conlogue appeared a week later, saying "it is arrogant to buy land for a purpose not supported by those who would be most affected." His message to Roxanne: "Leave us and our way of life alone." Other letters followed in a similar vein, most expressing disdain for outsiders whom the correspondents saw as trying to muscle in on the north woods way of life.

Roxanne had thought everyone would be glad to see Kineo's talus slope saved from a subdivision. The criticism "was just totally ridiculous," she retorted, adding that the Maine Department of Conservation likely was pleased because her conservation purchase abutted its 800-acre state park. With so many opponents sounding off, writer Robert Kimber wrote a pro-park essay in the July 2001 issue of *Down East* magazine saying that the need for a large protected block was driven by the "malady" of industrial logging as the major use of the forest. The north woods, he wrote, had gradually been converted from a majestic multi-use forest to "an industrial fiber farm" scarred by "human manipulation." Mainers were "so accustomed to an impoverished forest that we don't know what we're missing."

To further the cause, Roxanne, as CEO of Burt's Bees (a title she would retain until September 2004), agreed to be featured in a RESTORE-produced video promoting the park. "My company's mission is to return the productivity that we have realized back into saving as much of the north Maine woods as possible through acquisition and setting an example to others who might be interested in doing that too," Roxanne told viewers. She said the land in the north Maine woods "is basically up for grabs. All they want for it is money. It seems like an incredible bargain to me. They're making money all the time, but they're not making any more land. If we are going to be able to do something as ambitious as putting more than three million acres in conservation, it has to be through the concept of a national park."

Neither she nor RESTORE talked about what percentage of the proposed park might be designated as a preserve and thus available for hunting and snowmobiling. That was something to be decided later, when the lands were identified and in the hands of the National Park Service. Nor did opponents make an issue of that question, likely because they didn't want a park of any size and didn't believe the campaign would get to first base with Maine's Congressional delegation. While there was no legal requirement that Maine's delegation be in favor of a park, their support was considered politically necessary in order to get a bill through Congress creating the park or even authorizing a feasibility study. First District Representative Tom Allen, a Democrat, had announced in 2000 that he was considering introducing legislation for a park study, but he backed off after learning of the raucous public meeting in Greenville with RESTORE.*

Roxanne and The Nature Conservancy

In September 1998, two years before Roxanne began acquiring land, International Paper (IP) had put up for sale 185,000 acres along the upper reaches of the famed St. John River in far northern Maine. A bid from The Nature Conservancy (TNC) and a private partner was initially unsuccessful, but when the two higher bidders failed to finalize the deal, IP offered the land to TNC.

By that time, however, the conservancy's private partner was no longer interested, leaving TNC to come up with $35.1 million if it wanted the St. John property. It was the organization's largest conservation land project in the northeastern U.S. and represented the largest investment to date of TNC resources. TNC's Maine director, Kent Wommack, was so enthusiastic about the project that he committed to raise $10 million in pledges and borrow the remaining funds from the conservancy's national land preservation fund. Wommack had never led a capital campaign to raise more than $5 million; now he faced the challenge of convincing philanthropic patrons that the St. John deal was a once-in-a-lifetime opportunity.

In the meantime, Roxanne had quietly made it known to Bud Fackleman, executive director of the new North Woods Wilderness Trust, that she was ready to invest $5 million through that group toward RESTORE's goal of acquiring 3.2 million acres for a park. Fackleman had bought Burt's honey and had what he recalled as pleasant conversations with Roxanne and Burt

*Tom Allen left Congress and wouldn't be a factor in the north woods debate after 2009.

about investing in conservation lands. The North Woods Wilderness Trust had been formed in 1997–98 by RESTORE to purchase land for a national park. Fackleman had been a member of RESTORE's board of directors and had agreed to run the trust.

In Fackleman's opinion, "there was only one project that had a chance of flying" at the time, and that was TNC's St. John project. "I contacted TNC and told them of Roxanne's intention," he recollected, and Roxanne signed a pledge of $2 million from Burt's Bees to TNC. The pledge was Roxanne's first step into the conservation philanthropy limelight, and the $2 million figure was widely publicized in stories about Roxanne's investment in the north woods. Fackleman, however, did not inform RESTORE that he was pledging $2 million to the TNC acquisition in the name of Roxanne, Burt, and Burt's Bees.

Roxanne mistakenly believed that TNC's St. John property was within the proposed boundaries of RESTORE's park and would help the plan become a reality. Burt's Bees issued a press release in July 1999 about the $2 million pledge with the headline, "BURT'S BEES Bee-LIEVES IN GIVING BACK TO MOTHER NATURE." In the release, Roxanne effused about contributing "to such a beautiful stretch of land that everyone can enjoy. Our philosophy at Burt's Bees has always been to protect, utilize, and enjoy the finest ingredients found within nature, and that's why we're so happy to be associated with this project."

The St. John donation crystallized for Roxanne her true philanthropic mission: "Once you have enough money, what do you do with the rest of it? Give it away in some form that's meaningful to you and your family," she said. "So I felt I was fulfilling this basic business need of turning money into something that will grow in value. That's why I chose not to give it to the Red Cross or some other such organization. I didn't have the same feeling of growing the value that I saw in the land."

The St. John project stopped all development while allowing public access. Of the 185,000 acres acquired by The Nature Conservancy, 45,000 acres were set aside as eco-reserves and wilderness, and the rest was to be managed for sustainable timber harvesting. TNC's Kent Wommack obtained his goal of $10 million in pledges from wealthy donors and then went to work paying off the loan in the promised five years.

Meanwhile, RESTORE's leaders were taken aback by Roxanne's pledge. Marion "Mimi" McConnell, a special projects consultant for RESTORE, was sent to Palm Beach, where Roxanne was staying at the time,* to inform her that the 185,000 acres were not within RESTORE's proposed park area but north of the boundary. "She was not happy to hear that," said Jym St. Pierre. "If she had used those funds to buy land within [the proposed park area] … it would have given a huge boost to the momentum of our campaign…. [It would have] demonstrated to other potential donors that the vision we articulated for America's next great national park could become reality."

The pledge was to be fulfilled at the rate of $250,000 per quarter starting in late 2000, but Burt's Bees was sold after five payments had been made, and the new owners declined to carry on with the pledge, which had never been legally binding. At a meeting on December 18, 2002, Roxanne offered TNC her 5,800-acre Bluffer parcel in T8R11 WELS, contiguous with TNC's Big Reed Preserve, as a way to discharge the remainder of her pledge. But TNC declined the land, which their scientist described as damaged and devalued by heavy logging prior to Roxanne's ownership, she said.†

Roxanne decided at that point not to pursue further collaborations with The Nature Conservancy—a decision that affected another TNC campaign as well. In February 2001, Kent Wommack had met with her to seek money for a $15 million Machias River project in eastern Maine. This was another once-in-a-lifetime conservation opportunity outside RESTORE's proposed park boundaries, one that would protect an entire watershed of 28,000 acres and 213 miles of shorefront. Roxanne had been supportive, pledging $1 million for the project, but when the St. John collaboration ended, so did this one.‡ She did not communicate again with Wommack or others from TNC and did not return their phone calls. TNC raised money elsewhere to cover the shortfalls.

---

*In 2004, Roxanne would purchase a 3,000-square-foot three-bedroom house with a pool in Palm Beach for $1.8 million, one indication that she was allowing herself luxuries she once would have rejected as upper-class waste. She would also invest in other Palm Beach–area properties to renovate, rent, and resell, and she found that she enjoyed relaxing at the exclusive Canyon Ranch resort spas in Tucson, Arizona, and Lenox, Massachusetts. She also would begin taking her family on trips to faraway places such as Africa, Antarctica, and Hawaii.

†Roxanne said later that The Nature Conservancy could have accepted the property and sold it to raise cash if its conservation value was deemed insufficient to justify continued ownership. Roxanne later sold the parcel in question for $3 million—well more than the balance of her pledge to TNC—because it was far from the borders of the national park she ultimately proposed.

‡Like the St. John pledge, Roxanne's signed pledge for the Machias River project was not legally binding.

Navigating the North Woods

In the late 1990s and early 2000s, Roxanne was the only individual forest landowner who was making a name as a wildlands philanthropist in Maine. Although Liberty Media mogul and billionaire John Malone would eventually own nine times more Maine acreage than Roxanne, he expressed no interest in preservation or land philanthropy for his Pine Tree State properties. There were, however, many new nonprofits rushing in to protect high-value lands.

Conservation easements became a popular alternative to outright purchases, as they were a cheaper way to protect large acreages. Easements often kept the land open to the public for multiple recreational uses and thus were less controversial than outright purchases. Easements also allowed landowners to continue to log their timberlands. Property owners selling no-development conservation easements on selected acreages had typically not been intending to use the land for development anyway.

On the heels of The Nature Conservancy's St. John River project, the New England Forestry Foundation announced in March 1999 a $30 million campaign to buy an easement covering 754,673 acres owned by the Pingree heirs. While this was touted as the largest conservation easement in America, it did not guarantee public access to the scattered and often remote townships involved. Also in March 1999, the State of Maine acquired 65 miles of shoreline on Moosehead and Flagstaff lakes and the Kennebec River in a $5.26 million land swap and fee purchase that blocked development and preserved public access. In June 2000, the Forest Society of Maine and the State of Maine began acquiring 329,006 acres along the West Branch of the Penobscot River, 282,000 acres of which were covered by a conservation easement that allowed continued logging and public access but prohibited most types of development. More than $14 million was raised from private and public sources for purchase of the easement. The remaining 47,000 acres were sold in fee simple to the State of Maine for $20.7 million financed by taxpayers through the U.S. Forest Legacy Program and $1 million from the Land for Maine's Future fund.

Once Roxanne awoke to the importance of concentrating her conservation efforts, she started buying blocks of lands in Elliotsville Township that would increase protection along the Appalachian Trail corridor in the area. Shortly after her Kineo purchase, she bought two tracts adjacent to the Big Wilson Stream parcel. On July 2, 2001, she paid Champion International Company $375,000 for 285 acres around Little Greenwood Pond, and three months later she acquired 198 acres along Peppermint Brook from Herb Haynes's timber company, Lakeville Shores, for $45,000.

During the latter negotiations, Haynes, the state's largest logging contractor, presented himself as a country boy from Wytopitlock who still did daily chores at his farm in Winn. "I liked Herbie," Roxanne said. "I had no problem with him." For Haynes, Roxanne would prove to be good business. He had plenty of cutover land to sell year after year, and she didn't shy away from parcels that had been heavily logged, as she knew the forest would grow wild in time.

Around this time, Roxanne also met with Maine Governor Angus King, an Independent. To give credence to its statements that a national park could improve the economic health of the north woods, RESTORE had commissioned a study of the economic impacts of the proposed national park by an economic expert. Dr. Thomas Power unveiled his report in September 2001, providing dollar figures and job numbers for RESTORE's vision. The study concluded that a national park could generate between $109 million and $435 million in annual retail sales and support 5,000 to 20,000 new jobs. Opponents dismissed the study as biased because it was paid for by RESTORE, yet it was the most authoritative work on the topic to date and was cited in subsequent scholarly reports and articles.

Roxanne knew that Governor King was opposed to shifting commercial timberland to a national park but wanted to see if she could change his mind. Accompanied by Dr. Power and RESTORE's special-projects staffer Mimi McConnell, Roxanne met with King in his State House office in August on an inauspicious date—September 11, 2001. It was their first face-to- face session. On his way to the office, King had heard about a plane hitting the World Trade Center in New York City. Like other Americans, he assumed at first that it was an accident.

As Roxanne and King were getting into a discussion about a new national park, they were interrupted repeatedly by phone calls. After about twenty minutes, a member of King's staff walked in and told him about the second and third planes crashes. "I knew we had a [national] problem then," King recalled. Not knowing if the terrorists were planning to attack state office complexes, he ordered an evacuation of the state building. Still unaware of the national emergency, Roxanne and her delegation were mystified.

King and Roxanne walked downstairs out of the capitol building and through the connecting tunnel to the State Office Building. When Roxanne saw people in the employees' cafeteria gathered around a television, she thought maybe they were watching a football game, but it was the second World Trade Center tower falling. King was whisked away across town to a protected underground facility at Camp Keyes, headquarters of the Maine Army and Air National Guard. After the meeting, King reiterated that he would not support a federal park in the north woods; rather, he saw a need for more small state parks in populous southern Maine. Earlier in his administration, King had said that "any governor who turned one-third of the state over to the feds should be impeached," inaccurately characterizing RESTORE's 3.2-million-acre park proposal, which would encompass less than half that area. "I wouldn't lock up northern Maine and send the key to Washington," he declared.

King attributed his opposition to an earlier bad experience with the U.S. Department of the Interior. RESTORE had petitioned in 1992 to list the imperiled Atlantic salmon as endangered. The five-year recovery plan for wild salmon—hammered out in 1997 between the federal government and the state—included an agreement to hold off on the endangered species listing, which King claimed could "well spell the end of [salmon] aquaculture in Maine." But in late 2000, Interior Secretary Bruce Babbitt, pressured by Trout Unlimited and other conservation groups, determined that the state was moving too slowly on salmon restoration and ordered the endangered species listing. King was still burning about that when Roxanne tried to change his mind about a north woods national park.

During the summer and fall of 2001, national media coverage of Roxanne's park quest moved from the *Boston Globe* to the *New York Times,* the *Christian Science Monitor,* and *People* magazine. *People* titled its story "Green Acre."

"The rank and file of Maine's struggling forestry industry, millworkers, lumberers and sportsmen—all … want Quimby to mind her beeswax," *People* wrote. Greenville's town manager, John Simko, and his counterpart in Millinocket, Eugene Conlogue, were quoted as trivializing the economic benefits that would flow from a national park. "We're not interested in trading [mill] jobs that pay $20 an hour for trinket-selling jobs at $6 an hour," said Conlogue. A national park, he asserted, "would be the death of the wood products industry"—postulating an either/or choice while ignoring the "some of each" third option. Roxanne stated again for the record that she wasn't planning to buy all the land RESTORE wanted for a park and couldn't afford it even if so inclined. She hoped to buy enough to give the national park effort momentum. While acknowledging her surprise at the vehemence of the pushback, she said she wasn't discouraged: "My father used to say, 'Whoever yells the loudest is probably wrong.'"

To compete with Roxanne's star power, the opposition began organizing to expand their base and make alliances with Maine government officials. A new group called the Maine Woods Coalition, led by Simko and Conlogue, gained momentum. Millinocket, with its downsized mills, had plenty of laid-off workers and retirees in their sixties and seventies with time on their hands to fight a national park that might jeopardize their fishing and hunting privileges on Great Northern Paper Company lands. They had years of experience resisting limitations on activities, such as hunting and snowmobiling in Baxter State Park. In the fall of 2001, the towns of Greenville and Millinocket passed resolutions opposing a national park in northern Maine, and so did the Bangor City Council and the Piscataquis County commissioners. Fifty state legislators sent an anti-park resolution to Congress.

As the attacks against Roxanne grew stronger, the silence of mainstream national and Maine environmental groups became more obvious. The Wilderness Society, The Nature Conservancy, the Natural Resources Council of Maine, and Maine Audubon Society all chose to stay out of the national park debate. The Sierra Club had an on-and-off history with RESTORE's proposed north woods national park. These and other groups refused to back the campaign because they had not initiated it, were too busy with other issues, or saw no clear road to success. Brownie Carson, NRCM's executive director at the time, told the *New York Times* that "you can't pour energy into protection of a single area, even though it's large and hugely important, without risking losses, big losses, in other really important areas of Maine's north woods forest." At the time, NRCM was battling Plum Creek's controversial Moosehead Lake resort development plan.

Despite the Sierra Club's lack of official support for RESTORE's park campaign, the Maine chapter's north woods staffer, Karen Woodsum, publicly appealed for a rational, fair debate over the project. "Polarization and inflammatory reactions are the road to nowhere," she wrote in a July 28–29, 2001, *Bangor Daily News* op-ed. Woodsum argued that "there is room for well-managed timber-producing forests and fully protected natural wild forests.... [E]ither/or is counterproductive. We need to shift our focus from attacking individual philanthropists and deal instead with the real threat to the northern lifestyle: the rapidly changing face of the paper industry, from Maine-based companies invested in the people and the land, to multinational investment and paper conglomerates that move to the beat of global economic forces."

But reasoned consideration of the issues wasn't forthcoming. There were too many political, geographic, class, and cultural divides at the heart of the conflict. National parks might be venerated American institutions, but to generational conservatives and many hard-line Republicans and Libertarians, Roxanne represented liberal Democrats, or worse, radical Greens and eco-freaks. The fight highlighted the divide between the "two Maines," with people in the southern, more populous and progressive areas generally supportive of environmental protections, and the northern, rural, conservative counties more aligned with the powerful forest industry and its business allies.

A fiery issue that faced Roxanne after she began purchasing land was dealing with lessees who maintained seasonal camps on her properties. Here she was treading on hallowed ground. Great Northern, International Paper, Scott Paper, and other large timberland companies, had been leasing land on a year-to-year basis to individuals and businesses for family cabins and sporting camps for a century or more. Many of the lessees were mill and woods workers. Camps, typically on lakes and rivers, had become part of Maine's north woods culture. Lessees built structures ranging from meager shelters to houses that could be lived in year-round. Sporting camps were big investments that catered to hunters, anglers, snowmobilers, and other recreationists. From the 1950s to the 1970s, lessees had paid as little as $25 to $100 a month for a camp lot. Demand for the leases increased dramatically when log drives on the rivers ended in the mid-1970s and road access into Maine's north woods greatly expanded. The timber companies retained ownership and control of the land.

When TIMOs, REITs, and other new landowners made purchases in the north woods, some cancelled camp leases, raised annual rental fees, or gave camp owners an ultimatum to buy their lots at market prices or leave. Camp owners raised a ruckus, and the Maine Leaseholders Association fought the changes.

There had been earlier legislative efforts to address this issue, but it was not until Roxanne asserted her private-property rights, informing camp owners that they would have to move out with or without their buildings before the expiration of a final one-year lease renewal, that a special legislative panel was formed. The committee struggled with how to balance the conflicting rights and interests of owners and lessees, but private property rights prevailed in the end, and lessees were left with few legal protections.*

*RESTORE staffers pleaded with Roxanne to tread carefully with lessees and to make changes slowly, but she forged ahead to raise fees and terminate leases. Stories began to spread. One apocryphal tale—which Roxanne later described as unfounded rumor—involved a man in his mid-sixties who had one lung. When she gated her Little Wilson property (and before she cancelled his lease) in Elliotsville Township, she allowed him to use an ATV to supply his camp only once a year, according to the story. True or not, such tales made enemies.

Differing with RESTORE

The five properties that Roxanne bought in 2000 and 2001 as a starting point for RESTORE's proposed national park comprised 8,667 acres. Title was held in her personal estate for the time being.* Buoyed by her position as a game-changer, she then purchased another eight tracts totaling 6,212 acres, most of them bordering the Appalachian Trail's Hundred Mile Wilderness in Elliotsville, Monson, and Willimantic. Those purchases confirmed that safeguarding the trail was going to be a central conservation focus for her. "I remember my kids and others saying the A.T. was just a 'beauty strip,' and you could hear chainsaws," said Roxanne. "So I had made up my mind that when land on the trail [in that area] became available, it would be a good place to start to conserve a buffer [along the path]."†

The new parcels protected the viewshed of Borestone Mountain, an Audubon sanctuary with a rich assortment of upland, wetland, and aquatic habitats. The streams sheltered native brook trout, and the landscape showed signs of Canada lynx, a threatened species of special interest to Roxanne, for whom animals were messengers. "I have little books that tell you what it means when a certain animal shows himself to you as he flies by or peeks out of the woods," she related. "What does it mean? How can it reflect on you for your soul's growth? I really like that way of looking at animals—an ancient way."‡

After Bud Fackleman steered the North Woods Wilderness Trust away from the vision of a national park, RESTORE laid the groundwork for a new land trust, Maine Woods Trust. This time the trust would be a subsidiary of RESTORE so that it would not spin out of control. Roxanne acquired one of

*Knowing that Roxanne was a rich buyer for north woods tracts, real estate agents knocked on her door with many parcels to consider. "I sit here drooling," she told the *Maine Times* in January 2002.

†Some of these purchases were outside RESTORE's proposed park boundaries, according to Jym St. Pierre.

‡When Roxanne learned that she had bought land that was good for lynx "and they chose to be there, I thought 'Okay, well, they've sort of made themselves known to me.' I'd never heard of a Canada lynx, and when I saw them, I thought, 'Oh, my God, these giant paws.' I'd never really liked cats that much to live around or have one. But the lynx is a pretty cool animal, and if I can provide some hospitality, I'd like to. I like the fact that they're very secretive and seldom seen. I think in the little book I've read on animals that when a lynx appears to you, it's like looking at the unseen." Accustomed to being surrounded by lots of people at Burt's Bees, she mused that she didn't have "enough of that lynx spirit—drawn back and quiet. I need to develop those [lynx] qualities."

her newest properties in Elliotsville Township, dubbed "Seven Ponds," with the understanding—according to RESTORE leaders—that she would turn it over to RESTORE when its land trust was up and running. She closed on the 5,820-acre property on June 25, 2002, paying $2.4 million, or $412 an acre, to Hancock Timber Resources Group, an arm of the Hancock Life Insurance Company, which had gotten into the forestland speculation business when the old-line paper corporations began dumping millions of acres.

RESTORE completed the paperwork to create its new land trust and secured a lead pledge of $1 million toward the purchase of Seven Ponds, only to learn that Roxanne intended to keep the Seven Ponds land in her own control. According to RESTORE, she offered instead to buy another, smaller property in Elliotsville and resell it to the trust. When she changed her mind on that too, RESTORE took stock of its options. (Roxanne disputed this version of events, saying that it was never her intent to buy land for RESTORE. Her intent, always, was to donate land directly to the National Park Service.)

By then the State of Maine and a number of conservation nonprofits had begun acquiring land in response to the fire sale by the timber companies. A decade after RESTORE and other environmental groups had focused attention on the threats and opportunities in the Katahdin-Moosehead-Allagash region, a million acres had gained additional protection thanks to a slew of deals by an array of conservation buyers. RESTORE decided to refocus on outreach and advocacy and leave land buying to the rich players. The organization put its Maine Woods Trust on ice, eventually letting it fade away.

Roxanne's Elliotsville acquisitions initiated an important transition for her. She began to shift away from RESTORE, albeit slowly. RESTORE had provided important support and advice to her for years. Now, without seeking RESTORE's counsel, she created a landholding entity of her own, naming it Elliotsville Plantation Inc. (EPI) after the location of her first purchases. "She became concerned that her identity with RESTORE and the national park could slow her down in advancing her goals," said Jym St. Pierre. "It was a big speed bump in our plans." RESTORE was losing its wealthiest supporter.

Another problem for RESTORE was Roxanne's vision for a park, which was more restrictive than the organization's proposal. Hunting and snowmobiling were to be permitted in the preserve portion of RESTORE's park, but Roxanne wanted her lands to be managed as wilderness in an absolute sense, with no logging, hunting, trapping, or motorized uses and with minimal road access—an ecological refuge and haven for quiet recreation by foot and canoe.

Something else was at work, too. As in her dealings with The Nature Conservancy, Roxanne's instincts and independent nature often led her to reverse direction and discard former alliances. She believed that her business skills and instincts, wealth, and property rights would overcome future difficulties, and that collateral casualties along the way were an unfortunate cost of achieving her life's true mission.

The next time Millinocket town manager Eugene Conlogue slammed Roxanne, she responded in a letter published in the *Bangor Daily News* on August 12, 2002—one of only two times she wrote letters to newspapers. She expressed surprise that Conlogue "clings to his 'No Park' slogan with such fervor," given that another 200 jobs were being cut at Great Northern Paper's Millinocket and East Millinocket mills. "It is well known … that the recreational enticements of Baxter State Park are providing the only ray of light in the otherwise bleak financial prospects of the Katahdin region." She went on to say that "an expansion of our beloved Baxter State Park to include more of the northern forest is the will of the citizens of Maine and can do more to attract the dollars of the new economy than the last gasps of a dying giant. It is the fiduciary responsibility of Mr. Conlogue to provide a vision for a sustainable economic future for his constituency. 'More park' is a solution to the current woes of this community."

Three days later, Greenville town manager John Simko fired back in a letter to the *Bangor Daily News* that Great Northern Paper Company's "average wage for a full-time employee … is more than $50,000 a year. One would have to sell a lot of lip balm to earn a similar wage at the corner store."

Accustomed to acting on inspiration, Roxanne now came up with a new idea for a park visitors' center. Rather than treehouses on Big Wilson Stream in Elliotsville, she envisioned a welcome center and mini-museum in a log cabin in nearby downtown Monson. She quickly purchased several properties in the center of Monson village and had the houses torn down.

Monson was already a noted Appalachian Trail town. Shaw's boarding house was a well-known rest stop for A.T. thru-hikers, and the Pie Lady turned out mouth-watering desserts. A visitors' center in town, Roxanne reasoned, would enhance the community's position as a gateway and bring more dollars to the local economy. Monson could become another Asheville, North Carolina, the bustling progressive town near the A.T. and Great Smoky Mountains National Park where Roxanne had lived for a time. She envisioned tiny Monson with an Internet café, good restaurants, a north woods museum, and a welcome center. John Tatko, owner of a slate business in town, agreed that a visitors' center was just what was needed because "Monson had gotten worse economically—lost jobs, no industry."

Although the welcome center was not proposed for Greenville—six miles north of Monson—that town's selectmen signed a resolution against it on October 2, 2002, at the urging of their town manager John Simko and local anti-park activists, contending that it would give visitors the false impression that the region favored the creation of a national park. Monson officials, however, were open to discussing the idea. Roxanne met with town leaders on February 5, 2003. "I, for one, believe we should welcome her initiative with good will and see the potential of what she can bring to Monson," downtown improvement committee member Darryl Witmer told the *Bangor Daily News*. But the national park controversy eroded the community's interest and increased local distrust. Roxanne eventually dropped her plans for Monson.

She had no lack of other ideas to explore, such as running for governor. She let that cat out of the bag in an interview with the *Portland Phoenix* on December 13, 2002. She ruminated that "being governor is sort of like running a business in a way. They have a budget, they've got a certain amount of dollars, and they have to make stuff happen with it." She went on to say, "I think I have experience running a business, creating something from nothing. I'm very economical. I'm very frugal … The first thing I would do as governor is a complete audit of the cash flow situation—what money is coming in and how are we spending it. I can't stand waste."

Her campaign slogan, she added, would be "make parks, not war!" The idea would have to percolate before she was ready to make a formal announcement. 🐝

A log boom under tow on Chesuncook Lake, sometime before the opening of the Golden Road in 1972. The logs would have been sluiced over the Ripogenus Dam at the south end of the lake, then floated down the West Branch of the Penobscot to the Great Northern mills in Millinocket and East Millinocket.

A New Vision: 2004

R oxanne resigned from RESTORE's board of directors in March 2003. "I was getting enough flak on my own without being on the board of RESTORE," she said. In her two years as a board member, she had attended meetings infrequently. By her own admission she was "terrible on boards" and felt that anyone who wanted her on one would regret it; she showed up for few meetings, rarely answered board-related e-mails, and sometimes disrupted a meeting that struck her as boring or overlong.

"She didn't like the decision-making process with others," Jym St. Pierre recalled. "She preferred to make decisions by herself or with a very small number of people, and board meetings can be messy." St. Pierre was struck by how she could let go of things she didn't like with "no emotional investment. But her credibility was hurt when she pulled out in a sudden way. It was jolting to people in her personal and professional life."

Although off the board, Roxanne wasn't ready to cut her ties with RESTORE completely. She helped launch a RESTORE subsidiary called Americans for a Maine Woods National Park ("Americans"), which was staffed by RESTORE. Two other RESTORE offshoots, the Maine Woods National Park Coalition and the Maine Woods National Park Business Partners, had remained mostly dormant, but "Americans" seemed to have a better chance to thrive. Special projects director Mimi McConnell recruited Robert Redford, Harrison Ford, Leonardo DiCaprio, Jane Goodall, Peter Matthiessen, Wendell Berry, E. O. Wilson, former U.S. Secretary of the Interior Stewart Udall, and other high-profile supporters to stimulate new, broader interest in a north woods national park.*

As the effort unfolded, it became clear that co-chairs were needed. Roxanne agreed to serve, as did Will LaPage, a professor of tourism at the University of Maine and a previous head of New Hampshire's Division of Parks and Recreation. The team conferred frequently, working on strategies and approaches for "Americans" with the understanding that, at the right time, RESTORE might spin off the group, in part to free it of the animosity directed toward RESTORE in northern Maine.

Before introducing "Americans" publicly, Roxanne, LaPage, and McConnell traveled to Washington to court Maine's congressional delegation. Roxanne later remembered Republican Senator Susan Collins informing her that "what I needed to do to get her support" was to convince residents of the proposed park region to back the idea. Second District Representative Mike Michaud of East Millinocket wrote to Roxanne and LaPage assuring them that he saw "no reason that a successful forest products industry, recreational access, and conservation cannot be advanced simultaneously," but he did not endorse the national park proposal.

Roxanne and her cohorts also met with Gilbert Grosvenor, chair of the National Geographic Society, on March 31, 2003. "Our discussion with you yesterday was one of the most important of our lives," Roxanne wrote to Grosvenor in a follow-up letter. "Your generosity of spirit and your love for this planet will continue to inspire us as we march on toward creation of the [park]." Grosvenor responded that he felt "energized by your example and particularly your spirit. I hope we can realize, together, a broadening of the way people envision their place on this planet and their interdependence with one another." He suggested that Roxanne's personal story appear in the *National Geographic* magazine "to provide a light that others might follow."†

*Adversaries mocked the approach, noting that many of the "Americans" were outsiders who knew little about northern Maine.

†An article about the park proposal ran in *National Geographic* online on February 2, 2004, but Roxanne was not mentioned.

Promoting the park outside Maine was uplifting to Roxanne because she encountered so much support south of Kittery. People who lived in the major East Coast urban areas knew well, it seemed, that Maine was the least developed, least densely populated state on the Atlantic coast, a place where they might still find respite in wild nature.

With enough VIPs signed up to make a splash, "Americans" was rolled out to the media in May 2003. The May 12 issue of the *Bangor Daily News* published an op-ed column by Roxanne and LaPage concentrating on the economics of a national park. "It could be a classic counter-cyclical move for Maine's economy," they wrote. "It's a way to truly diversify the economy rather than simply adding more industry. What the opponents never mention is that no industry comes close to tourism in its opportunities for small business investments."

"National parks are inevitably born in controversy—often fierce and emotional controversy having little, if anything, to do with the park idea," they noted. "Seemingly wild and often unsubstantiated claims from both sides tend to get the spotlight. This confrontational stage seems to be a necessary prelude for getting beyond the rhetoric and moving on to a more reasoned debate on the merits of the idea itself."

Because a lot of skepticism about the park plan revolved around the proposed size and type of park designation, Roxanne and LaPage underscored the importance of a federal feasibility study that could not only look at the pros and cons of a north woods national park but also examine different sizes and designations that could be more palatable to local residents.* "Surely we can collectively create one more, one that is best for Maine," wrote Roxanne and LaPage. But the question of whether opponents would trust any feasibility study done by big government was left for later discussion.

A lot was riding on making "Americans" a galvanizing force for the national park proposal, but tensions and disagreements between RESTORE and "Americans" were not long in developing. Mimi McConnell, a long-time staff member, resigned from RESTORE on December 16, 2003, the day the *Lewiston Sun Journal* published a story about the national park campaign that contained comments from Jym St. Pierre she deemed "disastrous" to the park cause. The article, in McConnell's opinion, jeopardized the "careful, behind-the-scenes work" that she and "Americans" had done in 2003 to cultivate support from the Maine congressional delegation. She believed St. Pierre's

*There were 21 different classifications of units in the national park system in 2003.

comments put Representative Michaud on the spot regarding the feasibility study, cast unnecessary aspersions on Governor Baldacci's land protection efforts,* implied that all land conservation by other groups in the park area would eventually be part of the proposed park, and "connected 'Americans' directly with RESTORE—again—despite the agreed-upon need for independence."

In the ensuing fallout, Roxanne proposed that McConnell work for "Americans" using EPI's office in Portland; she offered to pay McConnell's expenses and a possible stipend. Roxanne continued to assume that "Americans" would become an independent organization. The national park vision would not be realized, she felt, until the perception that RESTORE "owned" the idea was overcome.

No Deal

At about the time RESTORE was rolling out Americans for a Maine Woods National Park, Roxanne was lobbied by Sam Hodder, Maine director of the national nonprofit Trust for Public Land (TPL), and Ralph Knoll of the Maine Department of Conservation's Bureau of Parks and Lands about buying 43,000 acres of land that Canadian-based Irving Woodlands LLC had listed for sale in the Allagash Wilderness Waterway area. They met her in Ellsworth, near her Winter Harbor home, to assess her interest. Roxanne appeared to Knoll not to understand or care about the politics of owning large tracts. "I was trying to understand what made her tick, how to get some of her money, how to achieve our objectives and hers," he said. "It was very difficult to do."

Roxanne agreed to travel to the Allagash to look at the Irving tract, and Department of Conservation commissioner Pat McGowan, a pilot, flew her, Knoll, and Jym St. Pierre to the waterway on June 30, 2003. They stayed overnight at Nugent's Camps on Chamberlain Lake and talked over beers about conservation prospects. "She was mostly a listener ... a good listener," said Knoll. "She was cordial, never flew off the handle." No headway was made with her on the Allagash land, however. She was by then focusing her money and interest on lands in proximity to Baxter State Park or along the Appalachian Trail.

---

*Opposed to any national park initiative, Governor Baldacci had unveiled his own north woods conservation plan in November 2003. His plan, called the Maine Woods Legacy, was designed to maintain the industrial working forest and protect large land parcels through easements that helped to ensure continued commercial logging and traditional public access to private lands..

Real estate broker John Cochrane had notified Roxanne that Fraser Papers was in financial trouble and might want to sell its strip of land abutting Baxter State Park and the Penobscot East Branch. She gave him the go-ahead to explore a deal. Cochrane remembered that the price discussed with Fraser was $340 an acre, but when company officials learned that Roxanne Quimby was the interested buyer, there was no deal.

Roxanne also lost out on acquiring a large tract in close proximity to the historic Katahdin Iron Works and not far from Roxanne's Elliotsville purchases. It was a gem of a parcel, with the main attraction being the viewshed of a significant stretch of the Appalachian Trail. Hancock Timber Resource Group conducted a blind bid on the 32,180-acre tract, with Roxanne, the Appalachian Mountain Club, and Carrier Timberlands (a Canadian company) submitting bids. Hancock sold the property to Carrier for $10.56 million, or $330 an acre. Floating around in the conservation community was a rumor that Roxanne had bid more than Carrier, but Hancock chose to sell to a company in the forest industry rather than Roxanne.

The Katahdin Lake Saga

Irving Woodlands owned all the land abutting the eastern boundary of Baxter State Park except a few minor in-holdings. Ironically (given the subsequent drama over this land), Irving had acquired its 84,521 acres on both sides of the East Branch of the Penobscot River in 1999 as an afterthought in a purchase of 1.1 million acres of the former Great Northern Paper Company's holdings. GNP's prime timberlands in the Ashland and Oakfield districts of Aroostook County had been the prize Irving was after in that purchase, but those holdings had failed to achieve the negotiated acreage total, so the land east of Baxter—a region 40 percent the size of Baxter State Park and adjacent to the park's eastern edge—had been thrown in for good measure. Irving's newly acquired East Branch lands were remote from its mills and unimportant to its operational plans—little more than a rounding factor in a million-acre purchase—and in 2003 the company decided to sell the lands.

The holdings spanned four townships and included 71,978 one-of-a-kind acres on the west side of the East Branch. Besides abutting 26 miles of Baxter State Park, the land contained portions of four major river and stream systems—Wassataquoik Stream, Sandy Stream, and the Seboeis River in addition to the East Branch, which drains the remote northern and northeastern slopes of Katahdin via the Wassataquoik. The East Branch boasts beautiful waterfalls, spine-tingling pitches, and cataracts that make paddling it a first-class canoe trip. Thoreau himself paddled the East Branch in July 1857 and camped two nights there.

None of the East Branch townships contain a high-profile mountain feature like Katahdin or the Traveler range, but they included valuable, not-to-be-sniffed-at ecological and scenic resources. They afforded views of Baxter State Park and formed a big part of the viewshed from the park's peaks, and they provided diverse year-round outdoor recreation opportunities. The forest included the easterly slopes of Baxter's Traveler, North and South Turner, Bald, and Billfish mountains.

Katahdin Lake is the only water body of any size in the quartet of townships. Near the lake shores—where Thoreau, Teddy Roosevelt, and Percival Baxter had once camped—were a thousand acres of old-growth trees up to 300 years old. The diversity of habitat and biota was extraordinary—from Marble Fen, a peatland with rare flowering plants and mosses, to rare floodplain forests of silver maples, exemplary blueberry lichen and spruce-heath barrens, rare purple clematis, fragrant fern, and dragonflies and butterflies. A 1982 study of Maine rivers by state and federal agencies* had noted the potential for restoration of ocean-run Atlantic salmon and a high-quality native brook trout fishery. The township in which Katahdin Lake is located (T3R8 WELS) stood out as the only one that had escaped Percival Baxter in his quest to establish his park. The views from the lake westward to the mountain's jagged Knife Edge are as dramatic as any Maine has to offer. Katahdin Lake had long been a magnet for notable painters such as Frederic Church, James Fitzgerald, and Marsden Hartley, who produced some of their most striking canvasses from the lake's sandy beaches. Teddy Roosevelt visited the Katahdin Lake area in 1878 while a junior at Harvard College; he had great luck there catching square-tail trout.

To the region's residents, the East Branch townships were important for hunting, fishing, and snowmobiling. Vintage summer camps and a popular sporting camp dotted the riverbanks. There on the eastern flank of Mt. Katahdin—in land that had been a footnote in a timber company transaction—a dramatic fight for the heart and soul of the north woods was about to begin.

---

*The U.S. Department of Interior, the Mid-Atlantic Council of the National Park Service, and the Maine Department of Conservation.

The development potential in the four townships was obvious. Subdivision lots along the townships' network of logging roads would provide mountain and forest views rivaled in Maine only by Acadia National Park on the coast. Irving hoped to pocket at least $50 million from the land.

Given its strong history of working with the government in New Brunswick, Irving first offered the East Branch lands to the State of Maine. Irving's land manager, Chuck Gadzik, who had served previously on the Baxter State Park Authority, spent a year in discussions with the state, initially with Baxter Park officials. However, the park had no money for land acquisition, even for such an extraordinary opportunity.

Gadzik next gave the Maine Department of Conservation a chance to bid. Commissioner Pat McGowan was eager to achieve an important conservation legacy and believed the state could offer $470 an acre, but Irving wasn't interested, and the state couldn't afford to pay more—or didn't think it could at the time.

At that point wilderness advocate and businessman Charles FitzGerald contacted Gadzik with a zeal to buy all of the Baxter-abutting townships. In early 2003, he had purchased—sight unseen—the Katahdin Lake Wilderness Camps right in the middle of T3R8. He didn't own the land under his camps— he was an Irving lessee—but he had a stake in the outcome of Irving's East Branch sale.

FitzGerald was a dreamer. There was nothing he wouldn't sacrifice for the north woods, and he had a rich history of do-or-die conservation efforts. Founder of the now-defunct Board & Bowl chain of wood products stores,* FitzGerald had lost a $1 million deposit when Diamond Occidental Forest declined to briefly extend a deadline for him to purchase 61,000 acres of high-value Maine forestlands in the late 1980s. With the help of the Northeast Wilderness Trust, he had managed to protect thousands of acres in the Atkinson area, where he had once had a farmstead, but that effort, too, had resulted in financial losses. FitzGerald fell back on his New York City real estate as collateral for his conservation endeavors, yet by the 2000s his credibility as someone who could pull off an expensive purchase was shaky.

FitzGerald's talks with Chuck Gadzik came to naught. "Irving wanted ready cash," said FitzGerald, and Gadzik concluded that Fitzgerald couldn't come up with it. It was then that Roxanne became involved. She and FitzGerald

*FitzGerald retained the store in Bar Harbor, Maine, changing its name to In The Woods.

were acquaintances from her homesteading days, when he lived several miles from her in Atkinson, near Dover-Foxcroft. They often talked on the phone. He knew the north woods, and she had the cash and the conservation interest. When he contacted her about the East Branch lands, she was eager to approach Irving to see if she could work out a deal for the four Baxter-bordering townships.

Gadzik met extensively with Roxanne and was "impressed with her self-confidence. She was an accomplished woman." But Roxanne always had a price beyond which she would not go. There were exceptions, of course, but she deemed Irving's price too high even for such an extraordinary opportunity.

With Baxter State Park, the state, FitzGerald, and Roxanne unable or unwilling to purchase the townships at Irving's price, a piecemeal sale ensued. Roxanne negotiated for the most northerly of the East Branch lands, T5R8.*

When word spread that Irving was working with a mystery buyer—most likely Roxanne—for some or all of its East Branch lands, opponents and locals gathered on August 28, 2003, at Shin Pond Village outside the northern entrance to Baxter State Park to discuss north woods ownership shifts and potential new restrictions on recreational uses and camp lessees on the East Branch. David Soucy, the new director of the Maine Bureau of Parks and Lands, attended the Shin Pond meeting, which he described as "crazy mad." A lot of the fevered discussion was about Roxanne and what the state had or hadn't done—given Irving's possible sale to her—to protect the continuation of multiple-use recreation, long known in Maine as "traditional recreation." Participants at the meeting were sure that Roxanne was going to use T5R8 as the anchor for "her" national park. A key question was whether she would shut off the major north-south snowmobile trail, ITS85, which brought needed winter revenue to sporting camps and other nearby businesses.

Roxanne closed the deal for T5R8 on November 24, 2003, paying $12,041,500 for 24,083 acres. The $500-per-acre price caused her to wince, "but that's what real estate value is all about ... unique location," she said. "Baxter Park is a strong persuader and compelling neighbor. Hopefully we can muster the will and funds to get all those townships into protection."

---

*Gadzik was surprised that Roxanne didn't try to purchase the Katahdin Lake township, T3R8. It was at the top of the list of Maine land conservation priorities, and it was the one that "got away" from Percival Baxter. Roxanne was aware how "rapturous" people were about Katahdin Lake, and she seriously considered negotiating for it, but Irving wanted $2,000 to $3,000 an acre for that most heart-tugging township, and she turned away because of its price tag.

She intended that T5R8 would be a wilderness sanctuary to complement that of Baxter State Park. "I'm interested in creating wilderness to allow natural processes to evolve," she said, keeping human impacts as minimal as possible. Gadzik urged her to be cautious in her national park advocacy, but she "was not interested" in his opinion, he said. "She had built something [Burt's Bees] and was proud of it. She had some blind spots on ownership and the surrounding communities. But she wasn't interested in taking anyone's advice."

Roxanne quickly confirmed local people's fears by blocking roads and banning timber harvesting and hunting in T5R8. Motorized access, such as snowmobiling, would be allowed but limited, she said, until she decided what to do about the ten leased lots on the property, including Bowlin Camps, a popular destination for sportsmen and snowmobilers. What to do about T5R8's logging roads was another thorny question for her. There were two significant gravel roads to leased camps and one major haul road that was the closest artery to access wood markets to the north. Industrial landowners traditionally traded road access, but Roxanne wasn't in that club. Her neighbor to the south, Fraser Papers, had reason to worry that she would shut off the haul road permanently. Roxanne said her purchase "change[d] the paradigm. I don't want what they have to trade ... because I'm not in the logging business and don't need roads for access." For awhile she entertained the idea of a possible compromise that would allow access to Bowlin Camps. A gate went up to close the road while she pondered the matter.

A new player buying an entire Maine township receives statewide attention, and Roxanne's purchase of T5R8 was no exception.* A township, generally six miles wide by six miles long, or approximately 23,000 acres, is a lot of land. "People were calling me, angry that we sold to her," Gadzik recalled. Roxanne received threatening letters and e-mails. She felt that "the stinging [personal] criticism I was subjected to ... was discouraging and unfair." Roxanne's holdings in T5R8 and south in the Hundred Mile Wilderness at this point totaled 40,000 acres worth $20 million. She was now the second largest private non-corporate landowner in Maine, after John Malone, who had acquired the 53,524-acre "Frontier Forest" on the western Maine border with Quebec for $14 million in May 2002, increasing his Maine holdings to 68,924 acres—all of it outside the boundaries of RESTORE's proposed Maine Woods National Park and Preserve.

---

*Sales of Maine townships were usually publicized in the *Maine Times* and local newspapers.

Following Roxanne's purchase, Irving consummated the sale of the remaining East Branch lands to prominent logging contractors/land speculators Herb Haynes and William T. Gardner. Gardner plunked down $25 million for 25,546 acres, including the northern half of T3R8 (with Katahdin Lake) and the southern part of T4R8. Haynes bought the south half of T3R8 and Irving's partial ownership in T2R8—a total of 22,309 acres—for $9.2 million. Haynes also bought 12,500 acres in T5R7 and T4R7 on the east side of the East Branch for $6 million.

Conservationists believed that Gardner intended to strip the forest, including the old-growth stands, and then subdivide the land into lots for vacation homes. A quarter-mile-wide strip around Katahdin Lake was weakly protected by protective zoning, but even that could be changed with enough political pressure. Charles FitzGerald put his sporting camps on the national historic register in the hope of blocking any future owner of the lands on which they stood from altering them.

The speed with which the lands left Irving's hands had been stunning. Nine months after putting the property on the market, Irving had raked in $52,241,500 from Roxanne, Gardner, and Haynes. It was about a quarter of the amount the company had paid Great Northern for its entire million-acre purchase back in 1999, and Irving had logged an untold amount of timber off the lands during its brief ownership.*

About 150 people in the Millinocket area worked for Gardner's contracting and other forest-related businesses. He quickly started cutting trees in T3R8 and extended a gravel haul road to within a mile of the east shore of Katahdin Lake. Like many others, FitzGerald was worried sick that Gardner would move into the stands of old-growth forest before he could be bought out or otherwise stopped.

A Confrontation in Brewer

The year 2003 had been pivotal for Roxanne. Besides purchasing her first entire Maine woods township, she spoke publicly at two events—one that brought her face-to-face with supporters, and one that brought her face-to-face with adversaries.

---

*Burt's Bees would gross $59.4 million in sales in 2003. H. C. Haynes Inc.'s Dun and Bradstreet profile, as of June 2003, listed his company as a $101 million enterprise.

The Maine Green Party, excited about Roxanne's interest in running for governor, invited her to speak at their June convention, and what she said sparked more publicity around her potential candidacy. She told the convention attendees that if she ran for governor, it would be as an independent, not under the banner of the Greens or any other established political party. Maine voters had proven they would support Independents for governor, as they had done in 1974 with James Longley and in 1994 and 1998 with Angus King.

Fast Company magazine added to the publicity about her political aspirations in a December 2003 Web feature headlined "Roxanne Quimby for Governor." The article pinpointed the moment that Roxanne had thought about running for political office as January 2003, while she was in Winter Harbor listening to newly elected Governor John Baldacci's first public radio address. When asked about his position on the national park proposal, he said it was "a nonstarter."

She told the reporter she thought she would have a good chance of winning, since she had the funds to finance a statewide campaign. She also thought that Maine, which had never had a woman governor, might like such a change, especially if the new governor were a successful businesswoman.

Oddly, Roxanne's interest in the governorship received little media attention in Maine. What did get news coverage was when she finally confronted her opponents in late 2003, accepting an invitation to speak on December 4 at the monthly Industrial Forest Forum in Brewer. The city is just across the Penobscot River from Bangor, which had been called the lumber capital of the world in its nineteenth-century heyday. The invitation to the forum said, "Perhaps no other person in Maine's forestry circles inspires a similar mixture of suspicion, frustration, intrigue and respect than Roxanne Quimby. Whether you agree with her strategy or not, Ms. Quimby is practicing a personal land ethic like no one else since former Maine Governor Percival Baxter, who spent years … acquiring tracts as a prelude to a state park."

A small group of demonstrators from the Maine Woods Coalition greeted Roxanne as she arrived at the forum. A police cruiser patrolled the parking lot in case things got out of hand. One demonstrator wore a cartoonish wolf mask with a Little Red Riding Hood cape to make the point that Roxanne was a predator masquerading as an innocent in the conservation debate.

Roxanne had been warned to be prepared for a hostile audience. Dressed like the rest of the crowd in jeans and a plaid shirt, she spoke calmly, without prepared remarks. She showed slides of her proposed park and popped questions to the group about national parks. To those who gave correct answers, she handed out Burt's Bees gift packs.

She said she was pleased that people were showing interest in the park issue instead of being indifferent. Her hope was that all involved could find "common ground." Her desire was "to leave the world a better place than I found it," she said. "The park idea is a tremendous opportunity and an example that one person [can] make a difference." She didn't consider herself "Queen of T5R8," she said, getting a laugh. She admitted she was "a lightning rod, a symbol people can project their fear of change on."

She mentioned her personal background as a back-to-the-lander, her ancestral connections with the Abbot-Sebec area, and her sense of having a higher calling. "There is something I'm meant to do [here]," she explained. Returning profits to the land was closing the circle of using resources, she said, not just spending it aimlessly. "It's the thing I could do ... my service work ... something with a moral imperative and weight to it," she told the group. The reason she preferred the national park model was "wide recognition" among the public that these lands are "awesome places ... [where] people can get in touch with themselves and inspire peace." Also, she emphasized how Americans love national parks.

Her first visit to a national park, she recounted, had brought her "in connection with something bigger than myself. It was a humbling experience. We need to feel that humility and that graciousness at being on this planet.... I think that's what makes a human being aspire to goodness and peace."

For the first time she emphasized the issue of "branding." No one could doubt that Roxanne was finely attuned to brands, given the success of Burt's Bees, and she reasoned that the national park "brand" would bring a new recognition of northern Maine beyond its history as a region of timber and papermaking, drawing enough tourists to invigorate the teetering local economy. In her opinion, Penobscot and especially Piscataquis counties had "too few people to create" sustainable, diverse communities in the face of the forest industry decline.

As she rambled from one topic to another, some in the crowd started fidgeting. One attendee tried to derail her talk, but others called out, "Let her speak!" When pressed to give answers to their urgent concerns, such as camp leases and recreational options, Roxanne didn't mince words. Lessees shouldn't plan on bequeathing their lots to their kids and grandkids, she responded. She was considering road access for neighboring landowners, such as Fraser Papers, to haul their wood to market—but for a fee. She acknowledged that the conflict between her goals and the old arrangement with Fraser presented "a bad situation." She promised "to work as graciously" as she could to resolve the problems.

Roxanne didn't have a management plan yet for T5R8, she explained, so she couldn't say exactly what restrictions she would impose on recreational uses. She noted, however, that she didn't want logging, hunting, bear-baiting, or motorized vehicles on her land. "I want quiet enjoyment" of the property, she said.

Some people in the audience criticized her for moving Burt's Bees out of Maine to North Carolina. They said the loss of 44 jobs in Guilford showed that she didn't really care about the community. She answered that it had been a "heartbreaking decision" to relocate the company, but the Guilford area didn't have enough available workers with "skill sets" she needed to grow the company as fast as the market was demanding. She mentioned having to employ a teenage accountant from the local high school. "I was hamstrung in Maine," she said. "The company wouldn't have survived in Piscataquis County."

The contingent of mill and woods workers grumbled at her comments. Some said they were insulted that she thought there weren't enough smart, talented, educated people in Piscataquis County for Burt's Bees.

Then two questions tripped her up. Someone asked why she didn't want to give the land to the U.S. Forest Service and let it be managed as a national forest instead of a national park—an option that would allow traditional logging, hunting, and multiple recreation uses to continue. She hesitated, then replied that she really didn't know the difference between a national park and a national forest except that logging wasn't allowed in national parks. A gasp rippled through the audience.

Then, when asked if she identified herself as a conservationist or a preservationist,* she admitted to "feeling really ignorant" on the differences between the two. Her weak responses caused a palpable discomfort among her supporters. How could she advocate a national park and not know that it would be managed by a different federal agency under different laws with different mandates from a national forest? The moderator jumped in, saying, "Let's move right along."

---

*A preservationist seeks to maintain or return land to its natural, wild condition. A conservationist advocates active use and stewardship of natural resources. A preservationist would permit no roads, off-road vehicles, hunting, or logging in a forest; a conservationist would permit such uses when they are compatible with habitat and species stewardship.

When Roxanne was asked if her lands were included in the state's Tree Growth Tax program, which gave a tax break to owners of tracts over 10 acres, she told the crowd that she had withdrawn the lands from the program because she would have had to file timber management plans. Instead, she put her properties in the state's Open Space program, which also allowed a tax break but didn't require a forest management plan.

Roxanne reminded the audience that she was a believer in "free-market economics" and private landowner rights, and she had paid negotiated prices for the land she had bought. "I'm not forcing anyone to sell to me. People are happy to sell to me. In most cases, lands are being offered to me. I also happen to be a philanthropist and intend to donate it to America."

She was then asked why she wouldn't give her East Branch land to Baxter State Park, a question that would come up repeatedly over the years. "It would be an obvious solution," she said. "I love Baxter and the way it's managed. I'd be honored to give it to them. But I like the national park better. It has more name-brand recognition; it's a bigger idea." If she wasn't successful in establishing a national park, she said, she would be "honored to extend [Percival Baxter's] park to the East Branch."

By the end of the meeting, RESTORE's Jym St. Pierre was in a state of shock. He wondered if Roxanne had said she didn't know the difference between a national park and a national forest simply to avoid the issue while being confronted by "scared and angry forest industry guys," or if she really did not understand the distinction. From the audience's reactions, he "knew instantly something had changed, and it wasn't good. She had made herself the leading voice of the national park campaign to advance the grand idea, and suddenly her credibility was in question." In the aftermath, Roxanne told St. Pierre she thought the meeting had been a success, but later, upon reflection, she realized she had not performed as well as she wanted. It was not to be the last time Roxanne stumbled when talking off the cuff.*

A *Bangor Daily News* editorial four days later, entitled "A Bee of a Different Stripe," said that the Brewer meeting proved that "Roxanne Quimby ... is not a radical. She is a shrewd businesswoman. Except for the fact that she advocates for a national park, she is not much different from the investment

---

*Millinocket town manager Eugene Conlogue told the *Boston Globe* after the meeting that a national park in the area "would be less welcome than finding Saddam Hussein hiding in a hole." Roxanne's supporters, however, gave her a lot of credit for her willingness to stand up and speak her piece in such a forum.

companies that now own millions of acres in the Maine woods. They have limited public access to their land [and have] terminated some leases ... with minimal public complaint. If Ms. Quimby wore a suit and hired Canadian loggers to cut trees on her land, there would be much less controversy over her purchases." The editorial concluded, "If those who live, work, and recreate in the north woods are concerned about access to the land, they should be much more concerned about purchases by developers than by a conservationist."

A Grand Design

On December 10, 2003, six days after her appearance before the forestry group, Roxanne participated in a meeting in which a "grand design" for buying out the owners of unprotected East Branch lands was laid out. Others at the meeting included the state's Department of Conservation commissioner Pat McGowan; his deputy, Karin Tilberg; Parks and Lands director David Soucy; Maine Forest Service director Alec Giffen; RESTORE's Jym St. Pierre; Katahdin Lake Wilderness Camps owner Charles FitzGerald; and Jim Page, president of James W. Sewall Company, a land survey firm based in Old Town.

In a small room in the Sheraton Hotel at Bangor International Airport, Jim Page laid out a map of the north woods ownership to help guide the group's discussion. St. Pierre presented a slideshow depicting the conservation values of the lands, and FitzGerald excitedly proposed a "grand plan" to save them, which would mean buying back the tracts that were in the hands of Gardner and Haynes.

FitzGerald was ready to remortgage or sell his New York City real estate—again—to raise several million dollars toward the land purchases. He viewed Gardner's holdings in T3R8 and T4R8 as a place where a wilderness Eden could evolve, and an all-out effort was necessary to acquire it before the old-growth stands of timber were cut. Roxanne didn't say much but indicated that she would consider trading some of her land on the east side of the East Branch to private interests as a way to purchase more acres on the west side of the river. Department of Conservation officials said they were tentatively willing to trade then-unidentified public lands or commit funds, and their priority was acquiring land around Katahdin Lake, in T3R8.

The parties left the meeting without a concrete blueprint but with renewed eagerness that they might pull a rabbit out of the hat if they all worked hard enough. The Department of Conservation team met with William Gardner that same day in Lincoln to discuss a buyout. McGowan and Tilberg reported to the others that the meeting had been positive. FitzGerald and Roxanne kept talking. He felt comfortable confiding with her on East Branch opportunities, "calling her constantly along the way" with the message of how important it was to protect this assemblage of townships adjoining Baxter Park. He viewed Roxanne as "an empire builder." While he let his emotions get in the way of business negotiations, he saw Roxanne as "utterly unflappable" and able to "stand her ground. Money is temptation to sellers," FitzGerald said, and the fact Roxanne had so much made her a formidable figure in the East Branch drama. "She had in her mind a long vision"

While FitzGerald and state officials worked on "grand plan" strategies, Roxanne soldiered on, buying more land in the targeted area. In February 2004, she purchased 9,896 acres in T3R7 from Hancock Timber Resources Group for $4 million.* The property, which she named Three Rivers, contained most of the northern third of the township—including portions of the East Branch, the Seboeis River, and Wassataquoik Stream—and abutted the state's 2,430-acre public preserve on Wassataquoik. The combination of Roxanne's acquisition and the state land preserved more than 13,000 acres along the waterways. Besides the riverfront, the tract included 1,950-foot Deasey Mountain (site of a historic state fire tower) and large stands of timber untouched for a half century.

Meanwhile the effort to convince the Maine congressional delegation of the benefits of a national park continued. Roxanne, Mimi McConnell, and Rebecca Rundquist traveled to Washington in late May 2004. Will LaPage was unable to go but sent letters to Maine's two congressmen, Tom Allen and Michael Michaud. "To lose this golden opportunity, at a time when Maine needs every economic answer it deserves, would be unconscionable," LaPage wrote. A "new park designation can ... capture an enormous economic windfall" for Maine. If the congressmen were unwilling to support the large national park RESTORE proposed, what about giving protection "to the most critical sites" in the north woods, he asked. "And then let the park prove itself—and grow along with the inevitable growth in public support. Those critical sites would remove zero acres from timber production, and yield the very same dollar benefits of a much larger park." He challenged the congressmen to use

---

*"No one said boo about that purchase," Roxanne noted.

"statesmanship" to work out an agreement "before the 'Maine Woods' become synonymous with private estates. Somewhere in that option array is an answer that fits—a truly Maine-created solution."

Eviction Notices and Property Rights

Although Roxanne's land acquisition pace slowed in 2004, the attacks on her continued. The summer camp lessees she had inherited by purchasing T5R8 created a stir that summer. Roxanne had notified them, as well as those on her properties in the Elliotsville Township area, that there would be changes in leases, fees, and restrictions. They figured, correctly, that their bargaining power was nil and their days numbered, and they faced the loss of something they valued deeply.

RESTORE's Jym St. Pierre had urged Roxanne not to inflame the simmering antagonisms against the national park idea by canceling leases or sharply jacking up rents. Charles FitzGerald sent her similar advice but "never got a response." Roxanne tripled the rents to what she considered fair market values, and the increase was enough to cause Al Ellis, who operated the Patten IGA grocery store, to leave his camp. Ellis said he felt "betrayed," and that losing his camp broke his heart. Eighty-nine-year-old Muriel Fortier, known locally as "Mother Nature," garnered newspaper headlines by declaring that she would fight to keep her camp. She had summered on the west bank of the East Branch since 1969 and had expected to hand down her place to her family.

Roxanne did not, however, force the lessees out of T5R8 quickly, choosing instead to cancel the leases gradually. Five lessees who had owned their camps for an average of 25 years held on for another five years, Muriel Fortier among them. She would be 94 years old when she left her camp for the last time, telling the media that Roxanne was to be commended for her Burt's Bees success but had stepped on toes in the north woods.*

Leaseholders took out what personal items they could before they vacated their camps for good. Fortier's camp was burned down along with eight other camps in T5R8, but a few were left for land management staff. Three more camps in T4R8 were burned after Roxanne purchased them, according to Loren Goode, a former Baxter Park ranger who helped burn down the camps.

*All of Roxanne's lessees in T5R8 were gone by June 1, 2009.

The owners of the historic Bowlin Camps stood to lose the most from Roxanne's policies. Mike Stroff, a retired marine, and a dozen other investors had invested $2 million in the business, having bought the camps (built in 1895) and 13 acres in 1999 and leased another 17 acres. Bowlin Camps relied on income from people who paid big money to hunt bear and other game, as well as winter traffic from snowmobiles traveling the stretch of ITS85 that ran about 12 miles north-south through the East Branch townships.

Seven of the ten Bowlin cabins and part of the access road to the camps were on Roxanne's new land. Stroff and his partners wanted to continue to run the camps and work out "a happy ending" to the situation. Roxanne saw Bowlin as a special case and didn't want to disrupt the business. FitzGerald went to the camps on his own to talk with the owners, trying to smooth the waters. Later, after meeting with the owners, Roxanne didn't raise their rent by much (as she had done with camp lessees) and gave Bowlin a five-year lease. Her plan to close ITS85 was a critical issue for the Bowlin owners, however. They offered to sell her the camps or, conversely, to buy some of the leased land, but Roxanne refused. She didn't want to own a sporting camp, and their sale price of $700,000 was more than she wanted to pay. The ensuing stalemate would fester until 2005, when the grand game of land acquisition in the north woods shifted the landscape once again.

Meanwhile, in October 2004, respecting the concerns of snowmobilers who wanted to use the ITS85 snowmobile trail in T5R8 that winter, Roxanne told the Matagamon Snowmobile Club that she would keep it open for one season and would then pay $50,000 to relocate it to the east side of the East Branch. The club countered by asking her for two seasons, and the negotiations fell apart.

She reiterated to *The Washington Post* on November 28, 2004, that the north woods were large enough for everyone to coexist. Her private property rights, she said, gave her the power to "control its fate while I own it." Her detractors again called her dogmatic, but she was only doing what Great Northern and all other timberland owners did—asserting her goals for her private property.*

*The clashes between Roxanne and her East Branch lessees prompted Governor Baldacci to form a task force on traditional uses and public access in Maine. Appointed by Baldacci to the group, Roxanne said at the first meeting on October 20, 2004, at Shin Pond village, that she was looking forward to learning what the participants had in common. Not liking to sit for hours at meetings, however, she designated her land-holding nonprofit's executive director, Rebecca Rundquist, to participate in her stead. Like the legislative panel looking at similar issues in 2001, nothing tangible came of the meetings.

Divorcing RESTORE

While purchasing T5R8 adjacent to Baxter State Park, Roxanne had continued the work of establishing Americans for a Maine Woods National Park, which remained under the control of RESTORE. Mimi McConnell had numerous ideas for the "Americans" team—a book project, a portable photo exhibit to show the "majesty and beauty of the future park," and plans to organize a speakers' bureau "to win the hearts and minds of Mainers and increase visibility and effectiveness."

However, ongoing difficulties between RESTORE and "Americans" made moving forward difficult. RESTORE's executive director Michael Kellett felt that "Americans" was being hijacked from the parent organization by McConnell with the consent of Roxanne and LaPage. Eventually it all came to a head—but under the public radar.

On April 4, 2004, an e-mail from Roxanne and LaPage to Kellett stated that "'Americans' feel a far greater urgency to get this park established than has been evidenced by RESTORE. We might like to prolong the niceties of a negotiated divorce, but that is not going to happen. The separation is irreversible and in the best interests of all parties and the park mission."

Kellett was taken aback. RESTORE had established Americans for a Maine Woods National Park and had invested a great deal of money and effort in creating the committee, building its membership, and planning for its future. RESTORE had paid for McConnell's work on "Americans." And this attempted takeover of "Americans" had appeared without warning or any attempt to consult with RESTORE.

Kellett was convinced that Roxanne was truly committed to a national park, but he believed that McConnell and LaPage had never shown such a commitment and would settle for a less protective land designation than a national park. Kellett felt that RESTORE's oversight of "Americans" was critical to the park goal. Concerned about the infighting, board member Rudy Engholm wrote a memo to Kellett on April 10, 2004, saying that Roxanne was, "more than any person I know … probably in the best position to single-handedly create the nucleus of the park if she chooses to." Engholm ventured that fund-raising would be "very difficult" if word got out about a power struggle. He did not believe that RESTORE would win a war over ownership of "Americans," and "it would be a war that would have many expensive and sad casualties." He suggested giving RESTORE's blessing to an independent

"Americans," focusing on RESTORE's strengths, and preserving RESTORE's fund-raising capacity.

A negotiated peace, however, couldn't be reached. Roxanne and LaPage resigned as co-chairs of "Americans" on April 30, 2004. RESTORE's board agreed with Kellett's recommendations and voted in June 2004 to keep Americans for a Maine Woods National Park in-house and retain ownership of the name. Roxanne's relationship with RESTORE was officially over, although her adversaries would assert incorrectly for years to come that she hadn't broken ties with the organization and still supported the goal of a 3.2-million-acre national park around Baxter Park.

Next, Roxanne and McConnell started an independent initiative called Maine Woods Forever to win support for a feasibility study of conservation options for northern Maine. Roxanne envisioned several-times-a-year roundtables of state leaders and activists in areas of conservation, business, and recreation. To get the organization started, McConnell put up the $100,000 she had donated to RESTORE and taken back, expecting Roxanne to reimburse her. Failure to secure permanent protection for at least the portion of the Maine woods that inspired Thoreau's famous observation, "In wildness is the preservation of the world," could not be permitted, Roxanne said.

Roxanne was the major draw in the first Maine Woods Forever session on September 17, 2004, in Unity. Dozens of people showed up. It was her only appearance at the group's meetings. Maine Woods Forever operated in a low-key manner, made no big headlines, and generated no criticism from park opponents, but neither did it accomplish much, although the roundtables continued into 2015.

Despite their contentious parting of the ways, RESTORE felt that Roxanne had given an important boost to its national park campaign with her leadership, inspiration, and ability to attract public attention. Even her refusal to convey land to RESTORE for its proposed park had ultimately been helpful, according to Jym St. Pierre. Establishing a land trust would have distracted from RESTORE's park advocacy work, and joining the competition for philanthropic dollars would have been increasingly difficult, as by then new land-buying conservation nonprofits were flooding the scene.

But shifting the face of RESTORE's park campaign to a rich woman "from away" had generated tremendous opposition from the deeply conservative, male-dominated northern Maine establishment. And her later efforts to separate her 150,000-acre national park and recreation area proposal from

RESTORE's 3.2-million-acre vision sounded like stinging public criticisms to RESTORE.

Roxanne's seven-year association with RESTORE had been vital in fixing her bearings for the long fight ahead. Though she had not always followed his advice, she had benefited from St. Pierre's extensive guidance. She credited him with being a treasure trove of information and data about the north woods that greatly aided her efforts in the early 2000s.*

RESTORE and Roxanne agreed on the goal of saving and restoring a piece of the Maine woods for all Americans for all time. Both were prepared to challenge the status quo, and both were terrific at generating news. Indeed, the public debate they generated underscored the value of wilderness and national parks; some observers considered this a golden contribution to the environmental cause.

High Stakes in the East Branch

Just as conservationists had expected, up in the East Branch lands, logging contractor/land speculator William T. Gardner was cutting hard in the Katahdin Lake township, T3R8, by 2004. His crews were logging in the Wassataquoik Valley and building logging roads that led uphill to sweeping views of Baxter State Park. So far they had stayed away from the old-growth forest between Baxter State Park and the lake, but it seemed just a matter of time before Gardner would order his crews to fell that area too.

Charles FitzGerald had a face-to-face meeting with Gardner, offering him a $3 million nonrefundable down payment on the 24,083 acres that Gardner had purchased from Irving in 2003. The offer was contingent upon Gardner accepting a phased acquisition by FitzGerald over a one-year period, during which FitzGerald would raise the funds. In the meantime, Gardner would sit on the land. If FitzGerald came up with $25 million to $30 million to buy out Gardner, they would close the deal; if things didn't work out, Gardner would still have $3 million free and clear. Gardner didn't go for it.

---

*Roxanne felt no obligation to become deeply educated about land protection and ecology. "I never studied any science," she pointed out. "Anyone who ever took one science class knows more about habitat and ecosystems than I do." She continued to feel comfortable relying on her intuition about purchases; she was "not confused by education." Her intuition and personal views allowed her "to be opinionated about what my opinions are and a lot of my opinions are driven by beauty," she explained. "I'm an artist, really, at the end of the day. I find the natural world ... the epitome of beauty. I can't imagine anything created more beautiful than an untouched natural landscape, so anything that interferes with that is offensive, and I'd like to preserve nature in its god-given form."

True to his character, FitzGerald didn't stop trying. There were more meetings, and at one point FitzGerald made "a colossal [unsuccessful] offer of $20 million" just for the Wassataquoik Valley, which featured mature hardwood stands. Gardner turned down that deal as well.

With the window of opportunity to save the old-growth forest closing, Governor Baldacci directed Department of Conservation Commissioner Patrick McGowan to reopen talks to acquire the township encompassing Katahdin Lake. McGowan brought in the Trust for Public Land's Sam Hodder to rejoin the state's team.

So began three years of torturous high-stakes negotiations that one participant called "a bad dream." Charles FitzGerald re-entered the scene and convinced Roxanne to re-engage too.

There was no time to waste. Gardner's loggers had moved into the area between Baxter State Park and Katahdin Lake and were preparing to cut the old-growth forest near FitzGerald's sporting camps on the southeast shore. "It's war now," FitzGerald declared. If the old-growth forest stands were cut, neither FitzGerald nor Roxanne would be interested in a deal with Gardner. The more meetings Sam Hodder attended with Roxanne, the more he saw what "a ... one-of-a-kind individual" she was. "She assumed she was on her own ... there was none of that sense with others of a mutuality of goals," he said. "Her conservation agenda was her own, and she wasn't looking for help or to help others." But he also understood that she believed in compromise— being flexible—when absolutely necessary.

There were so many twists, turns, and suspicions that it seemed the project would fall on its head. The state officials didn't trust Gardner, whom some called "a pirate." He had the upper hand and could set a record price for the township (at one point increasing his asking price by 50 percent on the spot), or at least the Katahdin Lake area. FitzGerald believed that state officials wanted to marginalize him because they doubted his financial capacity and wanted to rid the area of his lease if the state became the owner. Roxanne, for her part, retained a distrust of the state going back to the early 1990s, when, in her opinion, the state had made life difficult for Burt's Bees and had shown no interest in keeping the company in Maine.

One negotiator for the state said that working with Roxanne "was like pushing string" and made deal-making more difficult. Another was frustrated by Roxanne's condemnation of "traditional" recreational uses, such as hunting, and by her constant advocacy for wilderness despite her personal wealth of "creature comforts."

Rebecca Rundquist, the executive director of Elliotsville Plantation, was candid about the "hate and distrust" expressed toward Roxanne "mostly when she wasn't present [at meetings]. I listened to that part and was the buffer [to Roxanne]," Rundquist reflected. "Often, they had a right to be angry and deserved to be heard. I listened to a lot of anger. Often it crossed boundaries into threats. I was at one lunch meeting in Portland and realized I had been followed. Someone I didn't know was noticeably eavesdropping, and when he realized he was noticed, he left suddenly."

"There were abrupt changes in traditional [recreation] uses in a lot of situations due to the purchases," Rundquist said. "Anger came from state officials, nonprofits, and the Fin and Feather [club members]. It was not isolated to any certain group. The [Native American] tribes were never disrespectful about her or me or to her directly, no matter how they felt. Those meetings with people, such as Barry Dana and John Banks of the Penobscot tribe, be it alone with just me or with Roxanne were always respectful." Rundquist "often got past the angry conversations" at meetings and was able to work to find solutions. "This is often when Roxanne came into the conversation, and she really did try to negotiate solutions within the limits of what her plans were for the property [at issue]. When she was present at large meetings with stakeholders, the behavior was different," Rundquist said. "When she wasn't there, talk was a lot more aggressive. Bart DeWolf [Roxanne's science director] did his part, as did Roxanne's land manager, to communicate as effectively as possible.... We did eventually have productive conversations with many people, even though we didn't necessarily agree. These were usually confidential and not witnessed by the public. These people couldn't be known to have meetings with us. Those are the parts of the work that were the most rewarding. If nothing else, there is greater understanding when time is spent in a room together hashing it out respectfully. I really can't remember [Roxanne] getting angry at anyone in a meeting. I remember her getting really angry at me once, but not anyone willing to come to the table."

In Pat McGowan's enthusiasm to build up the Baldacci administration's conservation legacy, he made spontaneous, unrealistic promises to Gardner, making it difficult for his department's negotiators to work out a financially defensible agreement based on third-party appraisals of the land to be purchased. Tentative deals were made, changed almost on an hourly basis, then abandoned. Gardner's team complicated the situation by issuing ultimatums.

McGowan accepted that Roxanne was critical to the outcome of the East Branch lands protection, but he didn't feel comfortable with her. She was "very smart," he said, but also "very coy." He saw early on that she was going to do things her way, and if a deal wasn't "Roxanne's deal, Roxanne's way," she wouldn't play. He had a name for her strategy: "exclusionary conservation."

When the negotiating progress stalled, the state stepped aside to see if Roxanne or FitzGerald could buy directly from Gardner. She brought in Jim Page, president of James W. Sewall Company (who would be appointed chancellor of the University of Maine System in 2012) to be the go-between. Both Roxanne and Gardner trusted Page, who was known as an effective communicator.

Roxanne considered an exchange of lands with Gardner—her 5,800-acre Bluffer parcel in T8R11 west of The Nature Conservancy's Big Reed Preserve and 12,000 acres of her T5R8 holding on the east side of the East Branch, including the Bowlin sporting camps and the ITS85 snowmobile trail, plus $3 million, in exchange for his 10,400 acres in T4R8. Getting to an agreement was an uphill battle, however. Roxanne wanted to keep a 500-foot buffer along the east side of the East Branch, but Gardner refused. Also, Roxanne didn't like having to pony up $3 million along with the traded land. As Roxanne put it, "there were many misunderstandings and miscommunications" because of "too many parties involved, including state lawmakers, adding too much complexity and confusion." One of the players recalled that FitzGerald would "go off in flights of fancy … [such as] having a marine sanctuary designation for Katahdin Lake," making it more difficult to reach a resolution with Gardner.

On January 26, 2005, Gardner rejected Roxanne and FitzGerald's best offer: 19,000 acres of her timberland and $10 million from the two of them to protect the Katahdin Lake/Wassataquoik area. They made no additional offers. Roxanne felt she had done all she could. "I don't feel it's my duty to save the state" by writing a big check, she said. She took a time-out from involvement.

Shortly thereafter, the state made a smaller proposal to Gardner. The proposed acquisition was divided into three parts—6,019 acres around Katahdin Lake, 1,975 acres in the northwest corner of the township, and 8,910 acres in the Wassataquoik Valley, east of the lake. Tied to the proposal was a demand that logging stop in the Katahdin Lake area while negotiations and an appraisal were in progress. After so much public and private pressure over protecting the township, Gardner was in a more receptive frame of mind.

Unaware of this latest initiative by the state, Roxanne also was oblivious to the rumor circulating in the spring of 2005 that Gardner was planning to apply to the state for a permit to build a bridge across Wassataquoik Stream to truck out timber from his land in T4R8. In the fall, the rumor came true when Gardner applied to the Land Use Regulation Commission, the agency responsible for permitting in Maine's unorganized townships, to locate a span across Wassataquoik's Orin Falls. In late September, RESTORE sounded the alarm, issuing an action alert about Gardner's bridge application, but he was unmoved by the public pressure against it. Gardner contacted Roxanne about using the primary haul road in her T5R8 township to take his timber to markets to the north. She didn't reply.

The threat of a bridge, however, caused Roxanne to agree to take an up-close look at Orin Falls. Her guides to the falls were Dick Anderson and Don Hudson, leaders of the International Appalachian Trail, who wanted her to see the pristine Wassataquoik Stream for herself. Anderson told Roxanne that she was the only individual on the planet who could stop the bridge and preserve the stream, described by Appalachian Trail icon Myron Avery as "a brawling mountain torrent of the clearest water, tumbling along a bed choked with enormous pink granite boulders."

Listening to Anderson's plea on the bank of the Wassataquoik, Roxanne made the decision he and Hudson were praying for. She would try to buy the heavily cut Wassataquoik Valley land and restore it to wilderness. Charles FitzGerald was also in the running as a purchaser.

Gardner's harvesting activities in T3R5 also provoked an ad hoc group calling themselves The Katahdin Lake Forest Defenders to send out an e-mail warning that they had spiked several hundred trees on the west side of Katahdin Lake to stop "the destructive logging practices perpetrated" by the contractor-landowner company. "We have placed large metal and ceramic spikes into the largest and most 'marketable' trees within the 6,000-acre parcel of land between Baxter State Park and Katahdin Lake," the Defenders said. They didn't want to hurt loggers but aimed to "create a large enough impact in Gardner's profits to ensure that this area be left intact as wildlife habitat."

It took only a few months for Jim Page to negotiate a deal between Roxanne and Gardner. They agreed to trade land—14,426 acres of Roxanne's land on the east side of T5R8 for 10,400 acres of Gardner's land in T4R8.* The exchange was consummated in October 2005.

*The difference in acreage reflected the higher market value of wood on Gardner's tract.

Besides stopping the proposed bridge, the agreement protected about eight miles on the north side of Wassataquoik Stream, leaving a 3.5-square-mile roadless area from Big Robar Pond to Baxter State Park's eastern border. The deal also left intact the significant old-growth forest stand. With Gardner the new owner of the east side of T5R8, snowmobilers and hunters breathed a sigh of relief, knowing they could count on continuing traditional recreation uses. Bowlin Camps was free to operate without the restrictions that Roxanne would have imposed and which would have jeopardized their business, especially by ending income from their winter snowmobiling clientele.

Additional intense negotiations ensued between Gardner and the state, in which Gardner agreed to swap 21,400 acres in T3R8 encompassing Katahdin Lake for lands of equal value that the state owned or would purchase. Thirteen million dollars had to be raised to buy the land Gardner wanted; The Trust for Public Land and the Department of Conservation had eight months to come up with that amount plus $1 million to pay for the fundraising campaign. It was the most ambitious and, at $2,111 per acre, the most expensive per-acre purchase of any Maine woods conservation project ever. Some 1,050 people, including schoolchildren, contributed to the $14 million campaign. Tom's of Maine, Poland Springs, Nestlé Water, and L.L. Bean, Inc. each chipped in up to $1 million or more. More than 60 percent of the donations came from Maine residents.

Despite the agreement with Gardner, hurdles remained for the Katahdin Lake deal into 2006. The entire land transaction had to be approved by a two-thirds majority of the Maine Legislature. The Sportsman's Alliance of Maine, the Maine Snowmobile Association, and the Maine Forest Products Council joined forces to oppose it. A heated conflict ensued during 100 hours of debate. One thorny question was whether the land being added to Baxter State Park would be designated a nature sanctuary (as was 81 percent of the park) or whether hunting would be allowed, as had been permitted in two small areas of the park after pressure from hunters. The ideological debate over hunting was emotional and angry, despite Department of Inland Fisheries and Wildlife statistics indicating that the hunting for deer and other game was mediocre at best in T3R8. Chris Drew, former long-time chief ranger for Baxter State Park and a hunter himself, penned a column in *The Maine Sportsman* pointing out that the hunting in T3R8 wasn't good when Teddy Roosevelt climbed Katahdin via Katahdin Lake. "The fishing was good ... the hunting was not.... [L]ittle has changed in 128 years," he wrote. Drew noted that moose attracted 10,000 people a year to Sandy Stream Pond in Baxter State Park. Katahdin Lake was less than 2.5 miles away, so he concluded that "the value to both the public and local economy of a living moose" in Katahdin Lake "is of greater value than the carcass of a moose."

The politics got even messier on May 16, 2004, when the Maine Republican Party met and adopted a platform that included a plank opposing a national park in the north woods.

There were many sleepless nights for Department of Conservation negotiators and supporters of the Katahdin Lake deal. Commissioner Pat McGowan remembered how the agency's acquisition members were "berated" by anti-park lawmakers. "But any struggle like that benefits the cause," he recalled. "It's like canoeing the St. John at low water—a really slow, long paddle, cold, and people get irritable. But at the takeout, it's a great trip, a great river."

In the end, the legislature ratified the acquisition bill, and the paperwork was completed in 2007. The Baxter State Park Authority agreed to accept 4,119 acres around Katahdin Lake as a sanctuary, raising the park's total acreage to 208,452 acres. The grandeur and beauty of Katahdin Lake had been rescued.

Lawmakers stuck a provision in the bill that allowed hunting and snowmobiling in the state's new 1,975-acre multiple-use recreation parcel outside the park. On paper, it looked like a win for hunters and snowmobilers, but snowmobile association executive director Bob Meyers complained that, in reality, the hunting and motor groups had lost. The concession was "a bone tossed to us ... [T]hat land was never really worth a bucket of spit to anyone. It is for all practical purposes inaccessible [and] too steep to support any meaningful wildlife habitat."

Despite the various land deals with William Gardner, the much-sought-after Wassataquoik Valley remained in his hands. But the Department of Conservation managed to obtain an option from him to buy it within a few years. Should things not work out between Gardner and the state, Roxanne remained an interested party. The Wassataquoik Valley moved to the conservationists' backburner for the time being.

Bridges between Adversaries

Now began a new game of chess as Roxanne the business strategist made a series of moves to add to her T5R8 township and to secure the acreage for a national park between the east side of Baxter State Park and the Penobscot

East Branch. On September 1, 2006, she acquired 24,574 acres below Katahdin Lake in southern T3R8 and northern T2R8—the southernmost lands bordering Baxter State Park—paying $10 million, or $435 an acre, to landowners/ contractors Herb Haynes and R. A. Crawford.

Snowmobilers and hunters immediately raised an alarm, anticipating a loss of access to another big chunk of forest, this time in the township closest to Millinocket. Exclusion from Roxanne's latest purchase would disrupt the approaches to their favorite deer hunting areas and their links to ITS85 and other important snowmobiling trails.

Maine Environmental News reported that the deal with Haynes and Crawford had been on the backburner for six months to give the state time to finish its Katahdin Lake acquisition without provoking another controversy. George Smith of the Sportsman's Alliance of Maine and Bob Meyers of the Maine Snowmobile Association had been unaware of the deal, and both organizations now joined anti-park advocates in the Millinocket area pressuring legislators to reopen the Katahdin Lake purchase. Smith and Meyers argued that the funds for Katahdin Lake should be withdrawn and instead used to buy land accessible to the Millinocket area for hunting, snowmobiling, and ATVing.

Department of Conservation commissioner Pat McGowan had received clear encouragement from state lawmakers during the Katahdin Lake hearings to purchase the Haynes-Crawford land, but now he too learned that Haynes already had a buyer lined up with more money than the state could offer. It was too late. The state's Katahdin Lake deal was not revisited. However, Roxanne surprised everyone by giving the state a two-year option to purchase the 5,061-acre portion of T2R8 that was closest to Millinocket, plus a "working forest" easement on 6,647 acres of land on the east side of the East Branch in T3R7. The easement included guaranteed public access to benefit hunters, snowmobilers, and ATVers, and permanently protected the existing ITS85 snowmobile trail.

Next came another surprise that perplexed even the politically astute George Smith. Roxanne phoned him on a Sunday in October 2006. "Oh sure. Who is this really?" he asked the caller. They talked for a half hour about personal topics, and to Smith's surprise, he enjoyed the conversation with a woman he'd been demonizing for years. "Was it possible I might like this woman?" he asked himself.

Roxanne also contacted other staunch adversaries at this time, inviting them to meet so they could all get to know one another better and perhaps work out a compromise. She had learned at Burt's Bees to abandon products that failed to sell well in favor of those that did; now she was abandoning a failed approach to conservation in favor of a more collaborative one.

Roxanne, George Smith, Bob Meyers, and Millinocket town manager Eugene Conlogue formed what they dubbed "a working group," and over the course of the next five-and-a-half years—sometimes joined by the Trust for Public Land's Sam Hodder, Millinocket-area state legislators, and snowmobile club officials—this group met once a month in search of common ground. Jim Page facilitated most of the meetings, and the participants agreed on rules of order to prevent discussions from devolving into angry exchanges. George Smith remembered that no one at the table was a fan of Roxanne or inclined, early on, to accommodate her goals.

Smith's impression of Roxanne was that she was "quite obviously very smart, witty, and smart enough not to put everything out there on the table." She was "very firm about what she wanted—an unsullied nature preserve without hunting and trapping and motor-propelled vehicles. The more we learned of what she wanted, the better chance I thought we had to explore alternatives other than the national park."*

He recalled they had to meet several times before he "was confident we were getting to the heart of some of the issues. She was cautious, very cautious … she was sitting with people very critical of her. But as we went along, we became more open about our various goals and interests." Smith considered her "very open to suggestions we made."

At the group's second session on October 18, 2006, she told the members she would allow hunting, ATV riding, and snowmobiling for at least a year on the tract she had purchased a month earlier (in T3R8 and T2R8) from Haynes and Crawford.

Sam Hodder sensed "a respect and understanding" evolving among the working group parties as the months went by. A "compelling moment" for him was when Roxanne talked openly about what was driving her to establish a national park. She gave a short family history about the violence and

---

*It was clear by this time that Roxanne's wilderness designs were focused on the lands between Baxter State Park and the East Branch. Their high scenic and habitat value and their proximity to the state park made these tracts obvious acquisition targets. More than four years would pass before she would publicly announce her proposal for a 70,000-acre national park in this area—just 2% of the acreage in RESTORE's proposed park—and in the intervening years she pondered what kind of federal designation she would ultimately seek from the National Park Service.

poverty that drove her Russian ancestors to America. "America was a beacon for them and maybe saved their lives," she said. National parks symbolized "American opportunity" for her family, Hodder related. "It was an ice-breaking moment for me to hear such a personal story." He also recalled that during meetings Roxanne alluded "to spiritual stuff. But you could never tell how serious she was about it."

After conversing with Roxanne for a while, Eugene Conlogue had something positive to say about her. "Roxanne deserves a great deal of credit for bringing together groups with a very different vision than her own and getting all of us to roll up our sleeves and develop a solution that works," he said. Bob Meyers thought that Roxanne's effort showed she had developed an understanding about how her park plans would affect the lives, recreation, and businesses of ordinary Mainers. Neither Conlogue nor Meyers changed their opposition to her national park goals, however.

An eyebrow-raising article in the *New York Times* in November 2006 suggested that Roxanne might be softening her "ban" attitude and considering alternatives to a national park, including a national forest, which would allow logging and other mixed uses of the land. But confirmation of such a thaw remained elusive, partly because of Roxanne's own media statements. A December 2006 *Wall Street Journal* article on the growing popularity of off-road parks for ATVs mentioned Roxanne's efforts to keep ATVs and snowmobiles off her land in Maine. "It's bad news for them when I buy a piece of property," she said. She confirmed that she had erected gates, taken out bridges and culverts, and dumped boulders across access roads to stop motorized use.

Showing that bygones could be bygones, RESTORE gave Roxanne a second leadership award on December 7, 2006, at their annual meeting in Freeport. Jym St. Pierre praised her for "tremendously accelerat[ing] the long-standing vision of protecting all the lands between Baxter Park and the East Branch of the Penobscot." In early 2007, Roxanne made the Dallas-based *Land Report* list for the first time as one of the 100 largest landowners in the U.S. She was number 100, thanks to the more than 66,000 acres she had acquired in the previous six years for $40 million—55,552 acres in the East Branch area, 10,180 acres in the Elliotsville Township area, and 379 acres in Acadia National Park.* Roxanne also turned up in *Vanity Fair* magazine's second

---

The Land Report listed Roxanne as owning 21 acres fewer in Acadia than Roxanne's own figures reported at that time. She kept her Acadia purchases quiet because she was afraid her involvement would stir up more controversy about her proposed national park campaign.

annual Green Issue in May 2007 as "The Purist." In it she was quoted as saying of her adversaries, "They're trying to preserve their way of life; they're preservationists as well."

On April 24, 2007, Roxanne bought 2,683 acres in T4R7, on the east side of the East Branch, from Herb Haynes for $2,550,000. Soon after that she acquired another 659 acres in T4R8 in the Wassataquoik Valley from Charles FitzGerald for $809,030,* and on August 6 she bought 4,918 acres in T3R7 (including Deasey Ponds and the historic lumbering-era Hunt Farm) from Haynes's Lakeville Shores Inc. for $2,459,000. An ardent supporter of the relatively new International Appalachian Trail (IAT), she approved development of a new section of the footpath through her land in T3R7 and T3R8, part of an extension of the trail from its northern terminus on Katahdin to the northern end of the Appalachian Mountains at Belle Isle, Newfoundland, and Labrador, Canada.†

Herb Haynes's death on September 11, 2007, did nothing to slow Roxanne's dealings with his company and others.‡ All timberland sellers were aware of her by this time and knew that if they owned land in areas of interest to her, they could cut as hard as the law allowed and still have a good chance to sell to her. Cutover land was a bargain to Roxanne—cheaper to buy and guaranteed to evolve back into wilderness if left alone.

After the Katahdin Lake purchase, the state concluded that it lacked the money to exercise its purchase option on the 8,911-acre Wassataquoik Valley. The valley was a key piece of the puzzle for Roxanne's national park bordering the East Branch, and she struck a deal with Gardner for $6.1 million, or nearly $700 an acre. Roxanne said that the tract would be managed for wilderness, like her other lands adjoining Baxter State Park.

At this point she owned almost all the land bordering Baxter State Park's east flank that was not otherwise protected. The sole exception was the piano key–shaped parcel in T4R8 that Fraser Papers had declined to sell to her in 2003 and had sold instead to Heartwood Forestland Fund V Limited Partnership, a North Carolina TIMO.

---

*FitzGerald had purchased 877 acres from William Gardner and Prentiss & Carlisle in 2006.

†The IAT was not legally associated with Elliotsville Plantation, Inc., the holder of Roxanne's lands.

‡Haynes's children had been involved in his business for years and took the helm when he died.

The outward thaw between Roxanne and her critics continued into 2008. George Smith, perhaps her most politically powerful opponent, declared a truce with her in his May 21 column in the *Kennebec Journal.* "Roxanne Quimby used to be my enemy," he wrote. "And when she reached out to me to find common ground, I did not want to like her. Getting to know foes as people helps us understand each other." Smith invited Roxanne to speak at the Sportsman's Alliance of Maine's first Conservation and Recreation Forum in Augusta, where "she correctly described us as friends," he wrote.

Smith concluded that it "amazes me that we were able to move so far beyond the bitterness and disappointment of our earlier relationship to a place where I look forward to our conversations and meetings. My 'Ban Roxanne' bumper sticker is off the Jeep," he told readers.*

As Roxanne, Smith, and others in the working group continued to seek common ground, larger forces were at work that would further devastate the region's economy and increase residents' anxieties. In September 2008, the Great Northern paper mill in Millinocket closed, laying off the last 150 workers on its payroll there, and the national economy skidded into a frightening recession. Great Northern's East Millinocket mill was still running, but workers' fears that it too could be shuttered would soon be realized. Roxanne's proposed park was left as the only significant economic prospect in the region at the time.

Against this economically worrisome backdrop, and despite media interest in what she was acquiring next for her park, Roxanne was able to buy and sell parcels in 2009 without attracting notice. On February 13 she paid Charles FitzGerald $294,014 for 419 acres southwest of Wassataquoik Stream in T4R8. (FitzGerald retained an adjacent 508 acres that were embedded within the state's 1,975-acre parcel in the northwest corner of T4R8.)

Six days later, on February 18, she sold her 5,800-acre Bluffer tract in T8R11, next to Big Reed Preserve, for $3,060,000, turning a handsome profit on the parcel she had bought for $1,630,000 in 2000. She had offered this parcel to The Nature Conservancy more than six years earlier to fulfill her St. John River conservation pledge, but TNC had refused it. Now she sold the entire piece without conservation restrictions to a consortium of forestry businesses. The sale gave her a fresh influx of capital to reinvest in future land purchases.

---

*Roxanne would become a sponsor of Smith's online blog after he left the Sportsman's Alliance of Maine.

A Feasibility Study

By 2009, Roxanne owned most of the land she wanted to preserve, but she was no closer to receiving support from Maine's Congressional delegation or even the major environmental organizations. Seeking a way forward, she hired the Pew Environmental Group to assess the most "feasible approaches" toward a park or "some other formal public designation" that would "showcase the land, confer permanent protection, and brand it as a national tourist destination." Pew was also charged with recommending the key components of a public education and advocacy campaign to increase support for her project.

When the report was presented to her on September 15, 2010, one of the top priorities it identified was winning the backing of Maine's prominent environmental groups. "For any statewide conservation campaign to succeed, it is essential that the environmental community provide active support," the report said. Environmental endorsements would "help legitimize the effort and provide a ready-made constituency to advocate on behalf of [Roxanne's] project." The Natural Resources Council of Maine, The Nature Conservancy, and the Appalachian Mountain Club were identified as organizations that "could play key roles in furthering this effort." Pew suggested keeping away from RESTORE and other unnamed groups that "would not be as beneficial or may serve as a hindrance to the campaign."

The report recommended that Roxanne develop "a clear and compelling narrative for this vision that resonates with Maine residents and relevant constituent groups." Her goals, Pew said, remained "largely misunderstood, even among the most interested parties." As an example, Pew mentioned the "general confusion" as to whether Roxanne was still working for RESTORE's proposed 3.2-million-acre park. Her position on logging was also unclear, the report said.

Acting on the report's recommendations, Roxanne commissioned an economic study of the proposed national park and began meeting with conservation and environmental groups. The night before she spoke to a gathering of environmental and business leaders assembled by Maine Conservation Voters (MCV), the Millinocket town council approved a resolution against her proposed national park. "These kinds of resolutions are very damaging ... [and] create obstacles," she told the gathering, adding that they were "rife with misinformation and propaganda."

In the MCV meeting and other gatherings, Roxanne asked conservationists to take action to support her park mission, emphasizing that a small group of her opponents was dominating the debate "because they are so well organized, joined at the hip with [the forest] industry." Conservationists needed to get similarly well organized to put pressure on the Congressional delegation for a feasibility study, she said. If her park effort collapsed, Mainers would be "the victims of change, not the managers of change."

To the argument that the East Branch lands lacked the outstanding qualities of a national park, Roxanne told the gathering, "I think [opponents] are not seeing the forest for the trees. I think there's amazing territory, mountains, forests." Her science director, Dr. Bart DeWolf, had spent years on her East Branch and Elliotsville properties documenting their natural, cultural, and wildlife values and proposing long-term conservation and restoration goals. He wrote reports on each East Branch parcel as Roxanne purchased them, and in 2014 combined all of the findings into a single 212-page volume made available on the Internet.

At the Maine Conservation Voters meeting and a subsequent Maine Audubon board meeting, Roxanne was questioned by conservationist Sherry Huber, whose family company, the J.M. Huber Corporation, had large timberland holdings in Maine.* The head of the pro-industry Maine Tree Foundation, Huber wanted to know why Roxanne was so determined to create a national park rather than simply giving the land to Baxter State Park. As she had in the past, Roxanne replied that Baxter State Park lacked "the drawing power" of a national park, and enlarging it would thus not be as effective for attracting tourism dollars to the region.† In her visit with the Maine Audubon board of directors, she "took us to task in a diplomatic way" for not getting behind her project, said Ted Koffman, executive director of the society. After the meeting, Maine Audubon joined the proponents of a study of Roxanne's lands for a national park and offered to help behind

---

*Huber Resources was the tenth-largest private landowner in the U.S.—with 600,000 acres of land across the country, including 357,000 acres of Maine timberland—prior to selling its Maine holdings to Conservation Forestry, LLC, of New Hampshire, between 2009 and 2011. The J.M Huber Corporation also owned oil and gas properties in several western states as of 2011.

†Huber, a member of Maine Audubon's board for years and an advisory member at the time of this writing, declined to go on record explaining her conflict with Roxanne's plans. Huber had once entertained gubernatorial aspirations, having lost in the Republican primary in 1982 and as an Independent candidate for governor in 1986. In 2013, Huber Resources donated a 142-acre parcel with extensive frontage on Katahdin Lake to Baxter State Park.

the scenes; in return, Roxanne made a donation to the organization to fund an assessment of the ecological values of the proposed park and recreation area and how to enhance them.

As conservationists braced for the state's approval of Plum Creek's development plan for the Moosehead Lake region, writer Bob Kimber again appealed to the public to support federal ownership of "some large, road-free wilderness areas closed to logging and all motorized vehicles ... where biodiversity, scenic beauty, clean waterways, and flourishing fisheries and wildlife would be maintained." With Plum Creek's project pushing Maine into a new era, "we've crossed a divide," he wrote in *Down East* magazine in June 2009. "If we hadn't understood before, we surely must understand now that leaving free-market forces in control [of the north woods] is a sure path to the fragmentation and loss of the last large stronghold of relatively wild land left in the Northeast. If the public is going to continue to have guaranteed access to the Maine woods and have access to woods that are worth having access to, the public has to own those woods.... [I]t's a ten-million-acre miracle, one with plenty of nicks, scrapes, and deep wounds in it, but a miracle nonetheless, one we can rescue if we can just summon the will. We've got to work together."

Elliotsville Purchases, 2010–11

In 2010, Roxanne began a three-stage acquisition of 28,984 acres near Elliotsville from logging contractors Haynes and Crawford, which completed her ownership around Big Benson Pond. The parcels covered land in Barnard, Katahdin Iron Works, Williamsburg, and Elliotsville townships. Most of the new acreage was contiguous with her other lands and adjacent to the Appalachian Trail. Another parcel abutted the Appalachian Mountain Club's "Katahdin Forest" tract.

Roxanne didn't require lessees to vacate, but most were informed that their annual leases would increase from $600 to $1,500 after one year—similar to rates elsewhere in Maine—and that hunting, trapping, and the use of motorized vehicles would be prohibited. Most camp owners chose not to renew their leases after the initial year, and their vacated buildings were burned. One lessee, Michael Weymouth of Boston, was allowed to stay on, perhaps as her eyes and ears in the area. An artist, photographer, and poet, Weymouth was sympatico with Roxanne as a lover of the natural world. He offered to let other writers, photographers, and artists use the camp when he wasn't there.*

She added more holdings in the Elliotsville Township area in 2011, purchasing 965 acres of Little and Big Wilson streams that adjoined and connected her two existing sanctuary lands—Little Greenwood and her 10,000 acres adjacent to the A.T. that extended seven miles along the Hundred Mile Wilderness.

To show her desire to give back to the community near the site of her homestead years earlier, Roxanne announced her intention to transfer, at some unspecified time, 30,000 acres in the Sebec-Brownville region to Maine's Penobscot tribe and give 839 acres to the state to augment Peaks-Kenny State Park outside Dover-Foxcroft. Her wish for the Peaks-Kenny addition was that it be used as a backcountry area to complement multiple uses of the existing park.

East Branch Dealings, 2011

In January 2011, following land appraisals, the 2007 deal Roxanne had struck with the state (through the Trust for Public Lands) to benefit Katahdin region sportsmen was completed. Roxanne received $2,160,528 for 5,061 acres in T2R8 that would be dubbed "the Millinocket town forest." She also received $617,760 from the state for the conservation easement she granted on 2,849 acres of her Hunt Farm tract in T3R8. The easement extinguished development rights and conveyed the ITS85 snowmobile trail corridor to the state. Roxanne remained the title holder of the land, retaining all other rights of private ownership. Funding sources included the federal Forest Legacy Program, funds authorized by the North American Wetlands Conservation Act, and the Land for Maine's Future Program.

---

*In 2010, camp owners around Big Greenwood Pond leaked information that Roxanne was planning to log and subdivide the 142 acres of her land there into fifteen lots. The camp owners told the media that she had promised to protect her land with a conservation easement, and her agent had written to them in 2004 encouraging them to join in a "cooperative conservation effort ... to protect the area and ensure that it remains unspoiled." They said they were shocked and dismayed that she hadn't followed through. Roxanne said later that the plan had been to offer affordable camp lots to displaced lessees and other buyers, thereby increasing the taxable basis for the 142 acres and countering the criticism that her conservation purchases were taking land from the tax base. Camp lots were in short supply in the Maine woods with so much acreage locked up by large owners, she said, and since this land was outside the proposed national park boundaries, it seemed a good parcel to subdivide. The proposal was scheduled to go before the Willimantic Planning Board in December 2010, but the uproar and negative publicity caused Roxanne to drop her plans.

Finalization of another easement covering 3,567 acres on Roxanne's Three Rivers tract in T3R7 on the east side of the Penobscot East Branch was delayed due to conflicting appraisals affecting the market value. That proposal involved the state acquiring a working forest easement and snowmobile trail rights. While negotiations continued, Roxanne allowed the use and maintenance of an old snowmobile trail on the parcel, an alternative trail to the main ITS85.

The fee sale and easements seemed to be a win for all parties, with Roxanne selling off cutover land that didn't abut Baxter Park and receiving another cash influx to spend on land that would be more strategic to her purposes. Roxanne also considered it a conciliatory gesture toward the Millinocket anti-park contingent and the snowmobile and hunting lobbies, letting them know she was sympathetic to their wishes for continued multiple-use recreation. The anti-park forces, however, continued to work as aggressively as ever to derail her park plan.

Roxanne's two loves—arts and wilderness—came together with a new East Branch purchase in April 2011. She acquired the historic Lunksoos Camps on the east side of the Penobscot East Branch in T3R7 for $334,539 from a Florida couple. The purchase was a tactical move, assuring that no one else would buy the 13-acre property and turn it into a commercial business that would be incompatible with her wishes for the proposed park area. Roxanne also wanted the property, with its rustic lodge and four cabins, as a retreat for artists and writers. In January, 2014, she paid Lakeville Shores Inc. $350,000 for a small piece of land adjoining her 11,512 acres in T5R7 bought in 2011; the acquisition provided waterfront access to Lower Shin Pond.

Some months after the Lunksoos purchase, Roxanne was filmed by the New England Outdoor Center, based outside Millinocket, talking about wilderness. She reflected that wilderness teaches us humility and helps us learn how to treat each other and how to treat our planet. "To me," she said, "looking at the stars, I remind myself that I am just this little tiny, tiny speck in the universe. It fills me with awe that I was put here for some reason … it's very humbling and very inspiring."

Roxanne meanwhile was keeping her eye on another tract adjoining Lunksoos Camps. The parcel, about 900 acres, was owned by East Branch Land Company and included Whetstone Bridge, the key access point to her lands, to public lands, and to other tracts on the east side of Baxter State Park. Besides controlling bridge access, it was a pivotal piece of land that could fill out the boundaries of the property she intended to donate on the west side of the East Branch for a national park.

More Controversy

With Democrat Barack Obama in the White House, Roxanne's national park supporters deemed her chances of getting congressional approval for a federal designation far better than they had been during the administration of George W. Bush. Before the 2008 presidential election, Roxanne had met with National Park Service director Mary Bomar, a Bush appointee, to discuss the path to federal designation for her East Branch lands. It was a chilly session. Bomar did not dismiss all possibilities, but she tried to discourage Roxanne by saying that a gift of land would have to be accompanied by an endowment of at least $40 million to pay for long-term management costs.

In 2010, Roxanne again traveled to Washington to discuss donating her lands for a new national park, this time meeting with Interior Secretary Ken Salazar and National Park Service director Jon Jarvis, Obama appointees. She also began a relationship with the National Parks Conservation Association, an independent nonprofit dedicated to supporting and enhancing federal parks.* On October 25, 2010, President Obama appointed her to the National Parks Foundation board of directors. Chartered by Congress, the foundation was "the official charity of America's national parks" and aimed to "strengthen the connection between American people and their national parks" and ensure that parks were preserved for future generations. The foundation was a coveted platform, with well-connected and wealthy board members, from which to promote Roxanne's proposed park. To help inspire the public to support America's national parks, Roxanne agreed to match contributions of up to $50,000 made to the foundation during the 2010 holiday season, between November 12 and December 31.

Her National Parks Foundation appointment provided more grist for critics. Outdoor Internet blogger Tom Remington commented that "this political appointment puts Quimby into an influential position along with other enviros in the Obama Administration to promote the agenda for a federal takeover of rural Maine to replace private ownership and local government with federally forced wilderness preservation." On November 14, 2010, Paul Reynolds, publisher of the *Northwoods Sporting Journal* and a persistent critic of Roxanne,

*In September 2010, the National Parks Conservation Association announced the results of a poll it had commissioned from Zogby International two months previously. According to the poll, 78 percent of the 502 Mainers contacted preferred "parkland" and sustainable forestry to development of vacation homes in the north woods.

told readers that "clearly [she] will not rest until she sees her wealth turned into a federalized national park in Maine."

Personal Challenges

Almost everything Roxanne did garnered state and national headlines. But one important event was kept private. In 2010, to mark her sixtieth birthday, Roxanne hiked up Mt. Katahdin for the first time. It was the highest mountain summit she had ever climbed. The idea was hatched by her twins, but due to conflicting schedules, Hannah and Lucas couldn't make it happen on July 11, their mom's birthday. The following month, however, the family was staying at Matt Libby's sporting camps near Ashland in far northern Maine, and the bagging of Katahdin occurred spontaneously on August 25.

Hannah made the climb with Roxanne while Lucas stayed behind to fish, one of his favorite pastimes. Matt Libby Jr. offered to fly Hannah, Roxanne, Lucas's wife Yemaya, and a friend close to Baxter State Park to start the hike. They started up the steep, exposed Abol Trail at about 9 a.m. Having spent months pursuing a healthy diet, working out in a gym, and losing weight, Roxanne was in better shape than she'd enjoyed for years.

Roxanne joked that she might not make it up Abol's scree slopes, but she completed the climb in fine spirits. Hannah snapped her photo on the summit with a red ribbon in her hair, flashing a thumbs-up and a smile at the Baxter Peak sign.

The party descended via the boulder-strewn Gateway down the Hunt Trail, the northernmost five miles of the Appalachian Trail. Darkness was falling as they reached the end of the rocky path at Katahdin Stream Campground and tumbled into a car for the two-hour drive back to the Libby Camps. Too late for a big celebration, the weary hikers shared a beer with Lucas and enjoyed the photos they had taken that exciting day.

Back in Portland on August 29, Roxanne learned that her sister Renee was terminally ill. Until then, 59-year-old Renee had kept her ovarian cancer confidential from everyone but her husband and continued to work as Burt's Bees' marketing and sales manager almost to the end. She died on August 30 in Tampa, Florida.

Renee's death was heartbreaking for Roxanne. She and Renee had been the closest of the Quimby siblings growing up; Renee was Roxanne's confidante and had been critical to the development of Burt's Bees. Just before losing Renee, Roxanne had been talking about wanting a personal assistant, and Renee was the first person she had planned to ask. 🐝

Millinocket's fiftieth-anniversary parade in 1951.

End of an Era: 2011

I n the 1990s, RESTORE's leaders had dreamed of cutting a ribbon at the entrance to a Maine Woods National Park on August 25, 2016, the centenary of the day when legislation authorizing the National Park Service was signed by President Woodrow Wilson. As she pieced together parcels of land along the Penobscot East Branch, that date became Roxanne's target as well.

After splitting from RESTORE in April 2004, Roxanne had concentrated on buying land to place under federal protection in order that it might revert to wilderness. At times she considered asking for national monument designation. "It is the perfect solution: less than a park, but still protected, and it requires only the order of a president, not an act of Congress," she mused in Edward Humes's 2009 book *Eco Barons.* "We're not ready for a park. A monument or a national wilderness area is less threatening. It's doable. And it will protect nature. And once it's there, and people find they can live with it, enjoy it, and prosper because of it, then turning it into a park becomes no big deal. That's what I'm gunning for. And that's what will save the Maine Woods."*

*To sidestep inaction by a gridlocked or recalcitrant Congress, a president can invoke the 1906 Antiquities Act and issues an executive order conferring national monument status on a site. Teddy Roosevelt did just that in 1908, declaring the Grand Canyon a national monument to protect it from mining and logging interethat had opposed a national park there for decades. In 1918, Woodrow Wilson signed the legislation that elevated the Grand Canyon to a national park. Similarly, Maine's Acadia National Park first achieved federally protected status upon being designated as Sieur de Monts National Monument by President Wilson on July 8, 1916, then was elevated to Lafayette National Park (in honor of the Marquis de Lafayette) in 1919. The name was changed to Acadia a decade later to reflect the broader French history of the region. Today, George Dorr is celebrated as the "father of Acadia" for his gifts of land and his persistent, unfailingly tactful advocacy for the park in the face of concerted opposition.

By the spring of 2011, however, she had dropped the monument or national wilderness idea and began advocating for a national park, using the phrase *gold standard* to define that coveted classification.* After discussions with National Park Service and National Parks and Conservation Association officials and staff in Washington, she had come to see that national parks were "relevant to the largest number of [Americans]. Even kids who are brought up watching TV and shopping at Kmart usually make it to a national park."

An Associated Press story on March 27, 2011, reported that Roxanne wanted to donate more than 70,000 acres next to Baxter State Park to the federal government for a Maine Woods National Park. It was the first time Roxanne had floated an acreage figure. Her proposed park was just one-fiftieth the size of RESTORE's—an easier pill to swallow for those concerned about loss of logging opportunities and recreational access.

A national park designation was "an initial, rough balloon," confided an advisor to Roxanne. "There will be lots of adjustment over what is expected to be a multi-year effort." Hers would be the first full national park to be created since 1971 from lands not already in the national park system.† In other words, it would be created from scratch, just as Roxanne had created Burt's Bees. She visualized a visitors' center at one of the park entrances dedicated to Henry David Thoreau, to honor the inspiration he had provided to her and the nation.

"The parks are so loved, we assume that they were handed down by a benevolent Congress," said Dayton Duncan, coproducer and coauthor with Ken Burns of *The National Parks: America's Best Idea*. "But when you start to turn over the rock of any national park, you find the opposite—that Congress was the last one to the table."

Into the Lion's Den

Following the recommendations of the Pew Environmental Group, Roxanne ventured into hostile territory—the town of Millinocket—on May 5, 2011, for a public meeting of the working group to discuss the Millinocket

*National parks have been called the "gold standard" of land conservation for years, although the origin of the term is undocumented. In 2006, Tom Kiernan, former president of the National Parks Conservation Association, used it in his editorial in the NPCA summer newsletter, and it has since caught on as the way to distinguish national parks from other holdings in the National Park Service ownership.

†American Samoa National Park, created in 1988, is leased from the Samoan government.

town forest initiative and the preservation of the ITS85 snowmobile trail corridor. In the course of this meeting, she presented her vision for a 70,000-acre Maine Woods National Park. A standing-room-only crowd packed the Northern Timber Cruisers snowmobilers' clubhouse to hear what she had to say and to grill her with questions. The East Millinocket paper mill had shut down completely the previous month, putting 415 employees out of work. The Millinocket mill was still closed as well. Unemployment in the area had shot up to 22 percent. People were moving away to find work.

Roxanne was prepared with maps, facts, and confidence. Dressed in a dark blue suit for the occasion, she appeared relaxed and open. She told the audience that she had had no idea when she undertook the park project that it would take so long and generate so much conflict. "I completely was shocked and taken by surprise," she said. "It has been an arduous and difficult journey that we've taken together."

She pointed to the "good dialogue" she had had with the "working group," including Millinocket town manager Eugene Conlogue, who appeared nervous as he sat with her at a table at the front of the room. He and other working group members had been able to bring to her attention important needs that had not previously been "clearly defined," such as the need for permanent, protected snowmobile trails, she said. She noted that most of the north woods snowmobile trails were unprotected—allowed to continue only by the good graces of landowners.

Roxanne affirmed that "sobering, conflicting priorities" existed between her and opponents of a national park, but she was optimistic that solutions were possible. In any negotiation, she said, "everybody has three things they absolutely need and three they'd like to have. But you're lucky to get one or two things you absolutely need."

She emphasized the potential economic benefits of creating a new national park near Baxter State Park, noting that Acadia National Park contributed $191 million a year to the Mt. Desert Island–area economy and supported 3,150 jobs. The feasibility study she advocated was the way to get beyond arguing about the economic impact of a park. "Let's see if the ideas and the vision I have are anchored in truth and [are] practical or not," she said. "I may be off-base. I'd like to see a study because up to this point it's just opinions. I believe this area deserves a feasibility study to put this matter to bed."

Roxanne took questions from the audience relating to public access, timber cutting, and camp leases, handling the grilling competently and calmly for more than two hours. On the matter of camp leases, she was forthright, calling them "a thorn in my side." She said she didn't feel much sympathy for those who "slammed [her] and tore her down limb from limb without ever having met [her] or without ever having discussed the situation with [her]." She didn't want to cooperate when "under attack," she told the group. People nodded sympathetically.

The leased lot arrangement with the paper companies had, over the decades, created the "illusion that [the camps sat on] public lands," not private lands. "People are suffering from the notion [that] ... they are entitled to unfettered access," she said. But unfettered access "is not the reality of 2011," she advised. "The days of the $200-a-year lease are over. As a private property owner, I have a different plan than the previous owner. I have a right to that plan." On the other hand, she said, "almost unfettered access" could be created through a national park that "will be to the benefit of all Americans."

She retold the story of her family's flight from Russia and China to America, saying that America saved their lives. America was "the land of opportunity, freedom and democracy, where they couldn't be murdered for their beliefs," she said. "America is what we believe in as a family... and the national parks symbolize what America has meant to my family. They [provide] the most democratic enjoyment this country has."

A national park, she told the audience, was the gold standard of public lands, and she presented it as a proven, valuable asset to people and communities, one from which Mainers could only benefit.

Roxanne emphasized again that a national park could only be created by Congress. "I can't create a national park," she noted. "This is not a monarchy." As for the fear that she would buy land for a much larger park, she acknowledged that, in her view, no national park could be too big, but she added, "I'm not Bill Gates. I couldn't buy it all if I wanted to. But I'm proud to be part of the [land conservation] process."

George Smith stood up then, retelling his story of how he once considered Roxanne his "enemy." Now he liked, admired, respected, and appreciated "her extensive effort to accommodate" other interests without giving up her national park dream.

Roxanne waited until the end of the meeting to make a surprise offer to her opponents. "I will do a deal if you will," she said, explaining that she would buy an equal amount of land for a multiple-use recreation area if her adversaries would support her proposed 70,000-acre national park. Her purchases for the recreation area would be "in recognition [that she and her opponents] could live amicably," she said. When she asked, "Is that a deal you like?" the audience yelled, "Yeah," applauding.

Jym St. Pierre, who attended the session, remarked, "I'd seen her in many different contexts, and this was by far her best presentation." She had accepted the significant compromises that would be needed to bring the East Branch project into reality via congressional involvement.

The evening ended on a high note, but the afterglow soon dimmed. Roxanne remained untrustworthy to the diehards who saw her creation of a multiple-use area as trickery and figured that if the federal government got its hands on that land they would impose onerous restrictions, such as no bear baiting or trapping. (At the meeting, Roxanne suggested that the multiple-use land could be turned over to the federal, state, or municipal government, but later she talked about it strictly as a federally owned area.) Also, it was hard to convince adversaries that any stated acreage would be the final figure. They argued that a park, once established, would be like a black hole absorbing the land around it. Acadia National Park provided a nearby example of the history of federal park expansions.*

Roxanne revealed at the meeting that she hoped to have her lands designated as a national park in 2016, and she said that U.S. Senator Susan Collins was demanding significant local support as a prerequisite for reversing her long-standing opposition to a national park in the Maine woods. That information empowered Roxanne's opponents in the Millinocket area with the urgency of a deadline and the knowledge that at least one politician, her finger in the wind, was granting them veto power.

The first skirmish came a few weeks after Roxanne's tour de force in Millinocket in the form of a sneak attack in the Maine Legislature. Senate President Kevin Raye, Susan Collins's former chief of staff and a politician

*Acadia National Park had no set boundaries until the mid-1980s. Until then, the park expanded slowly through fee purchases and easement gifts. Some residents of Mount Desert Island, like some people in the Katahdin area, opposed a national park in their backyards. The most bitter opponents were those who had been displaced from shorefront lands by the park's expansion and felt their lives and culture being marginalized. In 1986, when the National Park Service proposed a modest expansion to clean up boundaries and protect key features, the initiative met a storm of local opposition. Senator George Mitchell wrote the law that set the boundaries. Next came a battle over visitor entrance fees. When Sheridan Steele became park superintendent in 2003, he made it clear that his top priority was to acquire as many in-holdings as possible within the park boundaries. Behind the scenes, Roxanne came to his aid.

with congressional aspirations, rammed through an anti-park resolution asking Congress to deny consideration of any national park or even a park feasibility study. There was no meaningful public notice of the resolution, no public hearing, and no opportunity for public debate. It appeared suddenly on the legislative calendar and was rushed through in the crush of business during the final hours of the legislative session in June 2011.

The resolution had been written by Bob Meyers of the Maine Snowmobile Association with help from the Maine Forest Products Council. Meyers, a member of the working group convened by Roxanne in 2006, had sat at the head table during Roxanne's talk in Millinocket at the snowmobilers' clubhouse and witnessed the impressive momentum she generated there. He left that meeting knowing he needed a symbolic act to slow her progress, and a resolution carrying the weight of the elected representatives of the people of Maine was a convincing roadblock.

Armed with statistics about the influx of new jobs and revenues to the gateway communities of existing national parks, Roxanne returned to Millinocket on July 18 to meet with citizens in an open forum at Stearns High School.* That same day, the school committee in the small nearby community of Medway voted 3–0 to support a feasibility study. Medway, the closest exit off Interstate 95 to Roxanne's proposed park, stood to benefit as a potential park gateway.

Roxanne continued to meet with conservation groups as well, appearing at a board meeting of the Friends of Baxter State Park on July 11, 2011. She informed the group that she had placed under contract the last parcel she wanted between Baxter State Park and the East Branch of the Penobscot, and she was negotiating another purchase for the multiple-use recreation area she was piecing together. Roxanne expressed optimism that Bob Meyers and Eugene Conlogue would be willing to suspend their criticism of a feasibility study if she gave their constituencies what they wanted. Following the meeting, the Friends' board of directors voted to send a letter of support for a study to Maine's congressional delegation, and individual directors offered to appeal to Maine legislators for support. This was the first official request for consideration of her proposed park from any conservation group in the state.

---

*A flyer passed out at that forum by park opponents stated, "Roxanne has shown no willingness to date to limit her land acquisitions either here or elsewhere. There is an urgent need to protect the wood basket from preservationists who seek to take forest land out of production and disrupt the livelihoods of thousands of Maine workers."

On July 28, the Millinocket Town Council again voted to oppose a national park feasibility study, calling a park "an economic disaster for Northern Maine." This time, however, the council's action met resistance from some in the local business community. The Katahdin Area Chamber of Commerce and the Millinocket Downtown Revitalization Committee (MDRC) both publicly announced their support of a feasibility study. Alice Morgan, MDRC president and owner of a downtown retail shop, told the council that she saw no conflict between tourism and the wood products industry and did not believe that merely gathering information would pose a threat to the mills, forest industry, or local way of life. Matt Polstein, owner of the River Driver's Restaurant and a former town council member, said it would be "unconscionable not to explore a feasibility study." Their arguments fell on deaf ears. The council's vote against the study was unanimous. The split between the Millinocket Town Council and downtown businesses provoked reactions from new and old voices on both sides, but the heart of the arguments didn't change.

Roxanne's efforts suffered negative publicity in early August when her land agent, Mark Leathers of the James W. Sewall Company, told gatherings of the Brownville and Medway snowmobile clubs that they could use trails on Roxanne's lands for another year in exchange for letters supporting a park feasibility study. Bob Meyers of the Maine Snowmobile Association called the tactic implied coercion, saying, "[W]e are taking exception to … her using [trail access] as a wedge to force people to do something that they didn't necessarily want to do." Recapitulating his views in a news release, he said, "It's ironic that while Ms. Quimby speaks of her desire to spark economic activity in the region at public meetings, behind the scenes she and her representatives are threatening the livelihoods of dozens of small family-owned businesses in towns like Medway, Mount Chase, Patten, and Brownville."

Despite years of conciliatory meetings and concessions by Roxanne, the snowmobile association's board voted unanimously to reaffirm their opposition to a national park in the north woods. Meyers said the board didn't buy Roxanne's "branding argument" any more than they believed she and RESTORE had separate agendas.

A National Visitation to Maine

Against this background, a much publicized visit to Millinocket by U.S. Interior Secretary Ken Salazar and National Park Service director Jon Jarvis acquired heightened importance to both sides. On the morning of August 18, 2011, the two officials joined Senator Susan Collins at L.L. Bean's main retail store in Freeport to celebrate the 5,000 jobs the company supported. Talking to reporters, Collins praised private landowners, who, she said, had traditionally been "good stewards" of the Maine woods and had long allowed public access to their forestlands. Salazar, who had worked across the aisle with Collins during his time in Congress, remained outwardly neutral, emphasizing that "strong community support" would be necessary to create a new national park in northern Maine. Jarvis added that the park service did not yet have a position on the matter.

Salazar and Jarvis then flew to Millinocket, where park opponents waited outside Stearns High School carrying "No Park" signs. Inside the school, opponents had set up tables with "No Park" stickers and sign-up cards. "We became expert at sizing up people as they came through the door," wrote park opponent Mary Adams in her online *Adams Report*. "The pro-park, professional environmentalists" from southern Maine contrasted sharply with those who were "dependent on earning their living from the Maine woods." The male park advocates "wore immaculate hiking boots," and the women had "stone faces, graying hair and [wore] no bras."

About 300 people packed the hot auditorium for a spirited exchange. Several vocal park opponents expressed concerns ranging from fear that the proposed park would grow beyond Roxanne's 70,000 acres to accusations that a feasibility study would be rigged to favor her goals. State Senator Doug Thomas, a Republican from Ripley, and Millinocket councilman Mike Madore pelted Salazar with questions about who had invited him to Millinocket, intimating that it must have been Roxanne. "Nobody invited me," Salazar stated. "It was my decision to come here because I wanted to listen to the people of this area."

Supporters of a park or at least a feasibility study were also outspoken, although in quieter tones. An equal number of people spoke on both sides of the issue. Salazar, dressed casually in jeans and a baseball cap, was nonplused by the intensity of many of the comments. He assured the audience that Mainers, not federal officials, would determine the park parameters should they choose to create a national park.

The secretary described the two studies his agency could conduct on Roxanne's park proposal. The quicker, less expensive option was a reconnaissance survey that would cost $25,000 and provide a basic assessment of the benefits and costs of the proposed park. A full-blown feasibility study would cost an estimated $250,000, require an act of Congress, and take years to complete. He wouldn't say whether he favored either option.

After the meeting, dozens in the crowd drove to neighboring Medway, where Roxanne again presented her case for a park to local selectmen. At one point, as the now-familiar arguments flew back and forth, former Baxter State Park director Buzz Caverly stood to address the audience on the issue of a feasibility study: "What are you people afraid of? To ask a question, to get an answer that it will be feasible or not?"

The two-hour meeting concluded with Medway citizens voting 46–6 in favor of a feasibility study. Senator Collins, who had previously suggested that she might support a park study if there were local support for one, remained unmoved. That same day she told a Maine Public Broadcasting reporter that she was "worried about the effect of a national park on Maine's forest products industry and the wood supply, even though Roxanne Quimby and other landowners can choose to restrict timber harvesting whether a park is created or not."

Maine's other U.S. Senator, Olympia Snowe, continued to oppose both a national park and a feasibility study, although she said it should be up to area residents to decide what would be best for their region. (She seemed unaware of the built-in contradictions of her position.) Second District Congressman Mike Michaud's position on the proposed park was unclear. In a statement issued on October 28, 2011, he said he didn't support a study by the National Park Service and thought "an independent economic analysis" of the issues ought to be done first. (He didn't say by whom.) Roxanne did have one member of the congressional delegation on her side: First District Democrat Chellie Pingree, who had replaced Tom Allen in 2008. Pingree told Maine Public Radio, "I would say the majority of people who live in my district would probably travel to a northern woods national park and ... I think it is well worth a feasibility study."

Momentum

The Medway citizens' vote spurred more park-positive news in the following months. The Medway-based National Park Regional Citizen Evaluation Committee, organized in August, announced on October 5 that sixteen area groups now supported a feasibility study, among them five snowmobilers' clubs. Statewide polls continued to find that a majority of Mainers favored a study.* State Senator Cynthia Dill, an outspoken progressive from southern Maine and one of the few members of the Maine Legislature who supported Roxanne's efforts, started a nonprofit called Friends of the Maine Woods in late summer to drum up support for a park feasibility study. With funding from Roxanne, she printed tee-shirts, launched a website and Facebook page, and collected thousands of petition signatures urging the Interior Department to have the National Park Service undertake a study.

The *Bangor Daily News* weighed in with several editorials recommending that people "hold [their] fire on the North Woods park" idea and listen with an open mind to what Roxanne was proposing. Her offer of 70,000 acres for a multiple recreation use area and the compromises she had made "far exceed what residents of the region could have expected ... from the board of directors of a multinational corporation that owned the land. Rather than suspect the worst of her, residents should take her up on her offer to achieve mutual goals," the *News* wrote.†

Jon Lund, columnist/owner of *The Maine Sportsman* magazine, dryly observed that, after leaving office, former Governor Angus King had taken his family in an RV to national parks across the country. King didn't "visit places with industrial forest easements," Lund wrote, "nor did he aim for state parks," making the point that national parks are undeniable attractions for Americans. In his book, King exuded enthusiasm and appreciation for national parks and national monuments, Lund noted.‡ At the same time, another surprise rocked the Millinocket region. Cate Street Capital, an investment firm based in New Hampshire, announced that it was buying the two shuttered pulp and paper mills in Millinocket and East Millinocket (for $1) and creating a new subsidiary to be called Great Northern Paper Company

*On October 11, 2011, 60 percent of 600 interviewees told Critical Insights of Portland, an independent, nonpartisan polling and market research firm, that they backed a study. "Support [for the park] is most likely to be observed among the college-educated, younger (18–24 years of age) residents of the Southern or Central regions and registered Democrats," the firm reported. "Opposition is most prominent among northern or coastal residents and registered Republicans."

†George Smith of the Sportsman's Alliance of Maine pointed out that conservation-minded landowners like Roxanne might not be the only or even the chief threat to traditions of public use in the north woods, citing as one example that wealthy groups might lease large swaths of land for private hunting reserves, as was common in other states.

‡Back in Maine from his park tour, when he decided to run for major political office again, King reverted to opposing any new national parks in Maine.

LLC after the original Great Northern Paper Company. A month later the Great Northern mill in East Millinocket reopened, putting 250 or so people back to work and stoking hopes that the company could revive prosperity in the Magic City (Millinocket's nickname, referring to the speed with which it had been hacked from the wilderness more than a century before). According to Cate Street, a torrefied wood pellet manufacturing facility was planned for Millinocket.*

Park opponents seized on this news to argue more fervently than ever against the economic need for a national park—and there could be serious consequences to anyone who disagreed. In December, Peter Hanson, president of the resuscitated Great Northern Paper, told the Katahdin Area Chamber of Commerce that Roxanne's park proposal did not threaten the supply of wood for his mills and that the mills and park could coexist. Within 24 hours, the company "clarified" Hanson's comments, stating that he had meant to say the mills and park could not coexist. Five days later, Hanson was gone from Great Northern.†

On September 26, 2011, Roxanne purchased another 11,512 acres south of Shin Pond in T4R7 and T5R7. The deal with Herb Haynes's company included acreages on both sides of the Seboeis River, as well as 2,220-foot Peaked Mountain. The Seboeis was notable for its whitewater rapids and wild brook trout. The land along the river, east of the Penobscot East Branch, was intended to be part of the multiple-use recreation area Roxanne was offering as a sweetener to national park opponents.

Blunder

After all her hard work to gain support for a park, Roxanne shot herself in the foot in a telephone interview for an October 1, 2011, online article in *Forbes* magazine, making an offhand comment that fell like tinder in a dry brush pile on a windy Maine day. "I don't get it," reporter Michael Tobias said to her, referring to the resistance to donating land for a national park. "In

---

*The torrefied wood pellet facility was never developed, and the East Millinocket mill would be closed again in early 2014. Cate Street Capital was placed in Chapter 7 bankruptcy in September 2014.

†Another prominent figure in the forest products industry, Tom Colgan, president and CEO of Wagner Forest Management, would affirm two years later that a national park could fit in with the economic diversity the Katahdin region needed, stating that it "would not have a deleterious effect on the forest products industry."

an earlier interview you've remarked that 'there's enough land that we can all get what we want.' So what's the problem?" Roxanne explained that the forestlands north of Bangor had once been owned by seven large owners, and even now, 100 years or so later, had maybe fourteen owners. "It's a very tight-knit group of industry people who own, manage, and call the shots over 10 million acres of land. And they have, I would politely call it, aggressively harvested those forests for the last hundred years to the point where the mills in the area have been unable to stay competitive.... A hundred years later, there isn't enough to make a living." Area residents "still have not accepted that the old paradigm isn't working," she continued. "They're in complete denial.... We have the most aged population in the country.... I believe we have one of the highest adult obesity rates in New England. We have ... oxycontin abuse ... [and] Maine's the largest net receiver of federal funds, even though we supposedly hate the feds.... [I]t's a welfare state."

Roxanne also told Tobias that "ownership and private property were the beginning of the end in this country. Once the Europeans came in, drawing lines and dividing things up, things started getting exploited and over-consumed."

The *Bangor Daily News* dubbed Roxanne's remarks "inflammatory," adding that "one could conclude ... she was patronizing and condescending of rural residents." The editorial also took exception to her assertions about the forest being overcut, claiming that it was actually under-harvested.

In an op-ed piece in the same *News* issue, Peter Triandafillou, vice president of woodlands for Huber Resources, wrote that "Ms. Quimby would have us believe that the large land holdings of northern Maine are mismanaged and unable to support the forest products industry.... Maine's forests support a diverse and healthy forest-products economy.... Perhaps the most astonishing aspect of the [*Forbes*] interview, one that has been promulgated elsewhere, is that Ms. Quimby is a reasonable person." He declared himself "insulted but no longer surprised by [Roxanne's] accusations. The interview was full of hyperbole and falsehoods which seem to escalate in tone and scope with each interview." She had gone out of her way, he said, to dump on Mainers. "I have no idea what this has to do with her plan to donate land to the National Park Service. She seems to be telling Maine that we are too old, fat, drugged up and stupid to know what is good for us, and that we should simply accept her vision and thank her for her largesse." Millinocket town manager Eugene Conlogue told the *Bangor Daily News* that Roxanne's "welfare" remark was "a blatantly false claim that ... should infuriate [all Mainers]" and her statements "denigrate the people of Maine." Town councilor Jimmy Busque called Roxanne "the enemy of the North Woods," and councilor Mike Madore remarked that "every time she opens her mouth, she does more good for our side than theirs."

Seeing an opportunity to score political points, Senator Snowe stepped into the fray, commenting in the *News* on October 11 that Roxanne's welfare remark wasn't a true representation of Maine. Snowe chose this moment to comment through a spokesperson that a feasibility study for a national park "would be a misdirection." The focus, she said, should be on assessing how to improve the region's economic potential and create jobs.

The Sportsman's Alliance of Maine, the Maine Snowmobile Association, and the Maine Forest Products Council held a joint news conference to announce that they would collaborate to stop a park feasibility study. David Trahan, who had replaced George Smith as head of the Maine Sportsman's Alliance, declared with apparent disregard for the facts, "Whether it's the original proposal of RESTORE: The North Woods, which actually talked about clearing out everything north of Dover and returning it to a pre-colonial state, or the Roxanne Quimby proposal to anchor a national park around Baxter State Park, we cannot support any proposal which ends traditional uses in order to create a playground for the 'non-consumptive' users. We believe Roxanne Quimby's real goal is to create a 3 million acre national park. Such a park would guarantee that a culture steeped in decades of hunting and outdoor tradition passed through generations of Maine families would vanish." The Sportsman's Alliance's board of directors adopted a resolution saying that its 15,000 members opposed a north woods national park and were resolved to "stand in defense of our sporting heritage ... and oppose efforts to sweep away our economic independence and traditional cultural heritage."

The rash of angry comments and letters prompted Roxanne to submit a public apology to the October 11 issue of the *Bangor Daily News*. "I would like to convey my heartfelt and very sincere apology to BDN readers and the residents of Maine for the unkind remarks expressed toward them in my recent interview with *Forbes* magazine," she wrote. "I do not consider Maine a welfare state—in truth, Maine can boast an impressive population of people who work tirelessly and show brave Yankee independence. My goal in the interview ... was to emphasize my hopes for helping Maine to build its future by adding jobs and creating economic growth." She concluded, "I am mindful of what Abraham Lincoln said: 'Better to remain silent and be thought a fool than speak out and remove all doubt.'" She apologized a second time at an October 20 meeting in East Millinocket. Mainers were not "old and fat and stupid," she said. "I have a great deal of respect for the people of Maine."

On November 5, Roxanne made her park proposal official by sending Interior Secretary Salazar a cover letter, a 30-page project outline, maps, a plan for a $40 million endowment, and 406 letters of support from Mainers. According to the proposal, the land could encompass up to 75,000 acres, including 13,000 acres of lynx foraging habitat and 4,000 acres "critical for biodiversity conservation." An additional 43,000 acres would be set aside for multiple-use recreation east of the Penobscot East Branch and south near Sebec Lake. The 10,559 acres she had acquired to buffer the Appalachian Trail in the Hundred Mile Wilderness would become part of the national scenic trail overseen by the National Park Service. Conservation easements on the latter lands would provide for sustainable forestry, public access for hunting and fishing, and permanent snowmobile and ATV rights-of-way. The document projected a park operating budget of $2.5 million and about 25 park employees, with the costs to be paid by user fees and the annual income from the $40 million endowment. Vehicular access to the park's edge would be via a right of way near Sherman; foot access would be from the north through Baxter State Park and from logging roads near Stacyville.

"Rarely has an opportunity arisen that would so effectively strengthen the economic vitality of a region while simultaneously preserving its natural beauty," she said in the correspondence. She asserted that "a growing alliance of thousands of individuals demonstrated broad support from neighboring communities, including participation by 205 residents of Millinocket, 137 from Medway, and 49 from East Millinocket—the three communities in closest proximity [to the planned park]."*

Shortly after Roxanne made her submission to Salazar, East Millinocket residents voted 513 to 132 against the park proposal. Town selectman Mark Scally, chairman of the board, said Roxanne lost in his town because she "says and does things that are contrary to the people of this area. I feel sad about it because a park could be a viable jobs producer ... but when she says the things she does, you have to question her motives."

---

*In her proposal, Roxanne stated that her total East Branch area ownership was 59,188 acres.

The following weeks brought another setback. In a badly timed move, Roxanne's land manager at Sewall Company sent letters to a dozen snowmobile clubs in the region saying that snowmobilers could have access to Roxanne's lands for five years if they endorsed her park plan. Several snowmobile groups went along, but Bob Meyers of the Maine Snowmobile Association pulled some of them back in line, declaring that he did not like local clubs being given an ultimatum.

Nor did Roxanne's opponents stop with words. The *Bangor Daily News* reported on November 15 that someone had "yanked out" a gate on one of her properties in Elliotsville Township, and another tug of war ensued over whether the gated road was public or private. Ultimately, Roxanne approved a compromise that created a parking area outside the gate and converted the road and trails to a public recreational easement given to Piscataquis County.

In early January 2012, the Great Northern members of United Steelworkers Local 37 voted against the park idea. The following month, the Medway-based National Park Regional Citizen Evaluation Committee, which had formed months earlier to look open-mindedly at Roxanne's park proposal, decided to become "inactive," saying that a path forward wasn't clear.

Also in February, Interior Secretary Salazar was called to Capitol Hill for an Appropriations Subcommittee meeting on his department's budget. During an exchange with Senator Collins, who sat on the committee, he delivered another blow to Roxanne's park effort.

Collins initiated the exchange, saying that "[the harder park advocates] have pushed, the stronger the resistance has become." She named more than a dozen groups "and many small communities in the area." Ignoring statewide polls showing majority support in Maine for a national park, Collins said that only a minority of the public was behind it—and even those numbers had "declined significantly," she claimed, adding, "I hope you'll reassure me that the National Park Service, which has so many demands on its funds, will not be looking into funding a reconnaissance study of this region."

Collins was trying to score political points with park opponents back home, and Salazar, who was planning to leave his Interior post soon, did not want to engage in a fight. He gave her the assurance she wanted, saying, "We have no plans to move ahead on a reconnaissance study of any kind."

Retreat from the Public Eye

It was at this point that the board of directors of the Natural Resources Council of Maine (NRCM), which had remained quiet about Roxanne's project for years, finally endorsed a park feasibility study. A change in NRCM leadership and the proposal Roxanne submitted to the Department of the Interior spurred the influential organization to get behind the project. NRCM president Lisa Pohlmann and senior staff attorney and long-time North Woods Project director Cathy Johnson met with Roxanne to express an interest in working with her, and NRCM took the lead among Maine's environmental organizations in supporting the project.* With funding from Roxanne, Johnson began meetings with Millinocket business owners and residents to try to build regional support.

In 2012, the *Land Report* named Roxanne for the second time as one of the top 100 private landowners in the United States. Her 119,000 acres made her number 86 on the list, up from 100 in 2007. (She would maintain the same ranking in 2013 but would drop to number 88 in 2014.) Number one for the second year in a row was John Malone, who in 2011 purchased 1,004,346 acres of timberland in Maine and New Hampshire (most of it the old International Paper holdings), thus besting his rival and friend Ted Turner's acreage in the West. Malone had told *Forbes* magazine in 2010 that his Maine lands would be managed for sustainable forestry and would be open to traditional public recreation, as property owners in the state were protected from liability claims.† Asked about the proposed national park and donating land to that cause, he responded that he wasn't "an extreme tree-hugger" and believed private ownership was better than public "because you care about the land more, and it doesn't get trashed."

On December 10, 2012, Roxanne signed papers with Heartwood Forestland Fund V Limited Partnership to acquire the missing parcel she had been trying to buy for almost a decade. For the 8,315 acres in T4R8, bordering Baxter

*In 2012, Roxanne and Lucas invited NRCM to join a campaign steering committee. "[The council] doesn't support big proposals lightly," said Pohlmann. "[We] know how to conduct policy campaigns in Maine…. [W]e became the on-the-ground force for this committee, bringing our strategic advice, grassroots organizing, and long-standing relationships to the campaign. We also brought our deep expertise in land conservation and wildlife habitat for Maine's north woods as the committee continued to reshape the [park] proposal."

†Malone's land entity in Maine is called BBC Land LLC. The principal legal bulwark of landowner protection in Maine is Title 14, Section 159-A of the Maine Revised Statutes.

State Park and connecting her T5R8 and T4R7 properties, she paid $5,737,500, or $690 an acre. This tract featured a knob called "The Lookout" that was accessed by a signed trail from Bowlin Camps. Popular with snowmobilers, the knob provided a beautiful view into Wassataquoik Valley and Norway Falls.

Roxanne now owned all the private land on the east side of Baxter State Park except for the 6,011-acre Katahdin Lake tract owned by Baxter State Park and the Maine Bureau of Parks and Lands. Her land encompassed the lower 13 miles of Wassataquoik Stream and bordered 22 miles of the Penobscot East Branch. The forestland that had been logged would now have time to restore itself to wilderness. The eastern border of Baxter State Park had been given a priceless buffer of protection. All of her land, as it turned out, was within the geographical map of RESTORE's proposed 3.2 million-acre park.

Figures from the Sewall Company as of March 21, 2013, and from EPI's 990 tax form for the calendar year 2013 showed that Roxanne had spent approximately $74 million to purchase 127,593 acres of land. This included more than 87,000 acres in the East Branch region, most of it for her proposed national park and recreation area; 38,520 acres in the Elliotsville Township region; and 466 acres of in-holdings in Acadia National Park.* Some observers found it unsettling that Roxanne had kept the ownership of her property in Elliotsville Plantation Inc., not in a binding conservation trust, but EPI gave her options, such as selling or trading some or all of the tracts.†

In 2013, the centennial of the National Park Service founding was only three years away, and there was another reason Roxanne wanted to fulfill her vision as soon as possible. With three members of her immediate family having passed away, her own mortality was on her mind. "I don't want to leave [the park effort] in the hands of a board of directors or my children or a custodian," she said. She had seen the Libra Foundation sell the Portland Farmers Market after the death of its creator, philanthropist Betty Noyce. "The justification made by the person who decided to make that sale was that it was costing them $1 million to maintain it. But the foundation was a $200 million entity.

---

*The figures don't include 57 acres on Kineo and three properties in Monson, and she had spent almost $4 million more in Pennsylvania, Colorado, Montana, and Arizona to purchase in-holdings in existing national parks or property for national monuments. These properties, along with others on her to-buy list, were to be turned over to the National Park Service on its hundredth anniversary.

†After purchasing her various Maine tracts, Roxanne named them "sanctuaries." The names identified their geographic locations, such as East Branch Sanctuary, Wassataquoik and Valley Sanctuaries, Three Rivers Sanctuaries, and Kineo Sanctuary.

To spend $1 million in upkeep shouldn't have been a problem," Roxanne said. "I don't think that was a reason to override the intentions of the person who created the project. I thought it was very cavalier to just dismiss it like that and not even give it a good long try. I don't want somebody to look at my [land] and say, 'She would have wanted this or she didn't really need that, we'll just sell it.' I'm really worried about that, so I kind of want to rip through [the process]."

Having met privately with supporters to discuss how to carry on after the *Forbes* interview fallout, Roxanne realized she couldn't continue to be the face of her campaign and a lightning rod for park opponents. Her son, Lucas, worried that "she would just stop … 'cause when she's done with something, she's done." He believed that if he didn't offer to take over the project, the national park effort would fizzle.

In 2012, while Roxanne avoided the spotlight, Lucas moved his wife and daughter from Seattle to Portland, Maine. He had much in common with park adversaries. A Maine native, an expert fly fisherman and fishing guide, Lucas was also a hunter and snowmobiler. He set about becoming the new face of the national park campaign.

Lucas soon learned how easy it was to be misconstrued in an emotional debate. In remarks the *Bangor Daily News* printed on December 11, 2012, he surprised opponents and disconcerted proponents by conveying the impression that Roxanne had withdrawn her park proposal in September. In fact, she had merely withdrawn her paperwork submission to the Department of Interior and was starting over to see if a widely acceptable plan could evolve. It took another day or so for Lucas to get this clarification across.

It didn't take him long to become adept at talking to the media, and he demonstrated a gift for working with people and engaging their trust. With the help of hired consultants, he generated considerable news coverage, sending a message that a new day was dawning for his mother's north woods conservation goals. Roxanne would not give up her national park effort, Lucas affirmed, but he made it clear that forthcoming concessions on the lands proposed for multiple-use recreation would please her adversaries. His graciousness and friendly demeanor impressed both sides, and Roxanne had faith in his ability to bond with opponents. She described him as "a real blender … a real all-round guy and in a way [north woods people] don't feel about me. He's low key and never blasts people."

In February 2013, two economic reports that had been long awaited by Roxanne were finally released. One study, by Montana-based Headwaters Economics, assessed the impacts of a national park and a national multiple-use recreation area in the Piscataquis-Penobscot region; the other compiled a comparative analysis of sixteen peer communities that were gateways to existing national parks or recreation areas.

The analyses concluded that the two East Branch projects for a national park and a multiple-use recreation area—encompassing up to 150,000 acres altogether*—would increase jobs, tourism, and personal income in the region. Between 450 and 1,000 jobs could be created over time. Headwaters concluded that the impact on forest products industry employment would be minimal. Even if fully stocked with timber, the land in question could produce only one percent of the state's yearly wood basket needs, and growing market size timber would take years given how hard the forest had been cut by previous owners. Withholding the lands from logging would mean forgoing up to 21 timber cutters' jobs and up to 29 support jobs in other sectors, the report estimated. Forestry jobs in Maine were already in freefall. In 2011, according to the report, there were 1,324 wood and paper manufacturing jobs in Piscataquis and Penobscot counties compared with 16,463 jobs in health care.

Several prominent Maine economists at the University of Maine, the University of Southern Maine, and Bowdoin College deemed the studies well done and concluded that Roxanne's park plan was worthy of greater consideration. Predictably, park opponents were unimpressed. The Maine Snowmobile Association's Bob Meyers noted that the reports were paid for by Roxanne, but he and other critics did not commission independent assessments of the Headwaters reports or the earlier Thomas Power economic study commissioned by RESTORE.†

Seeking to counter the public perception that the Maine paper industry was on the skids, the Maine Forest Products Council followed the Headwaters study with a report of its own, concluding that the forest products industry had generated a total economic impact of $8 billion in 2011 while employing 38,789 full and part-time workers.‡ The council's report noted that paper manufacturing

*The acreages proposed for the park and the recreation area had both increased from 70,000 to 75,000 (a total of 150,000 acres) to ensure enough protected land.

†The Headwaters reports for Roxanne (and the earlier Power report for RESTORE) did not go through the rigorous peer-review process required by academic journals as a condition of publication. Still, the validation of the Headwaters study by academics argued for a serious discussion of its conclusions based on their merit.

‡The components of the 38,789 full- and part-time jobs included: paper, 6,798; forestry and logging, 4,741; wood products manufacturing, 3,909; other forest-sector jobs, 1,627; wholesale trade, 2,006; scientific and technical services, 1,658; miscellaneous other categories, 11,156; and "industries not listed," 10,558.

was the largest moneymaker ($4 billion) and accounted for the most jobs (6,798) in the forest-products sector. The council put the number of forest jobs in Piscataquis County at 1,867; and in Penobscot County, 5,152.

Tourism, by contrast, generated nearly $10 billion in sales in 2011 and at least 88,000 jobs—more than 12 times as many jobs as the paper industry.

The Headwaters findings sparked editorials in *Bangor Daily News* and the *Maine Sunday Telegram* challenging park opponents. "If not [the park], then what?" the editorial in the *News* asked. "More manufacturing jobs would clearly be welcome, but they are not certain. And it's very unlikely, considering industry trends, that the area will return to the booming economy that sprang from the mills a few decades ago." The *News* concluded, based on the Headwaters study, that a national park and national recreation area would likely create 450 jobs if it attracted as little as 15 percent of the 2.5 million people that visit Acadia National Park annually. The *Telegram* editorial had more bite. It interpreted the Headwaters Economics report as recasting the park debate from different "views of preservation" of the north woods and its culture to "competing visions of growth." "If critics dispute the questions these economists asked or the conclusions they have reached, they should challenge them," the *Telegram* opined. "But they should challenge them with data and not just gut feelings, regional prejudices, or personal attacks." The *Telegram* favored a "neutral, well-designed feasibility study"—the kind park advocates had been promoting unsuccessfully for years. The pressure was now on "park opponents to show what they think would be better for the economy of rural Maine," the editorial concluded. To date, the adversaries had not presented factual evidence proving that the proposed park and recreation area would be detrimental and had not mapped out an alternative plan to improve the Katahdin area economy.

In September 2013, Lucas St. Clair announced that sportsmen could immediately start hunting, snowmobiling, and using ATVs on the proposed 40,000-acre multiple-use recreation area—making good on a promise to accommodate those cherished recreational uses in the Katahdin region. He said logging roads would be improved to help hunters and ATV riders get around. And he reassured skeptics that the language drafted for an eventual bill to create the national park and recreation area would constrain federal planners from changing assurances made to residents of the park region. Longtime adversary Ray "Bucky" Owen, wildlife educator and former commissioner of the Maine Department of Inland Fisheries and Wildlife, wrote in the November 2013 issue of *North Woods Journal* that "the East Branch watershed is special and needs some protection. The more I think about [Roxanne's proposed park], the more I believe it can work; all this while also supporting the needs of the nearby forest industries." Owen agreed with the Headwaters Economics conclusion that a park would help businesses in nearby towns. "From an economic standpoint, the status quo is not an option," he said.

In December 2013, Roger Milliken Jr., a respected, progressive forest landowner and conservationist, went public with his support for a study of the park proposal that would have credibility with both sides. If the study concluded that Roxanne's lands are "national park worthy," he would be in favor of the transfer to the federal government. Milliken, president of a commercial forest ownership called Baskahegan Company and former chairman of the state and national boards of The Nature Conservancy, had held back from taking a public position on the park until after the annual meeting of the Maine Forest Products Council in September 2012. "I was appalled at what I saw," he said, referring to "how reactive" the council members were, passing what was in his mind "an unnecessary" resolution against Roxanne's project. Milliken cast the only negative vote.

In years past, recalled Milliken, when his "brothers and sisters" in the forest industry were upset about forest practices and clear-cutting restrictions in-the-making, they would rant at meetings against environmentalists and regulators, but after having their say, they could "think rationally" about how to respond. "But looking at the whole arc of conversation, I see how polarized we are now ... and they want to fight." He viewed the council's vote against Roxanne's proposal as a reflection of their belief that they were up against a wall and fighting for their own "survival." With the Katahdin area economy in such poor shape, people need "to start looking forward to the future," Milliken said. "It's the only direction we have."

More support from Maine's business community developed in 2014. The Katahdin Area Chamber of Commerce moved from supporting a feasibility study to backing the national park and recreation proposal outright. The Katahdin Rotary Club and the Maine Innkeepers Association joined the "yes" side, too. Near the end of the year, the Penobscot Indian Nation announced that it too was on board. Penobscot Nation president Kirk Francis said that all Katahdin residents, including tribal members, would benefit from the protection of lands along the rivers in the East Branch area and from the new economic activity a national park and recreation area would generate. About

25 miles of the East Branch, along with stretches of Wassataquoik Stream and the Sebois River, have been major travel corridors for the Penobscots for generations, Francis pointed out.

Opponents began claiming that a national park would result in tougher Clean Air Act standards for the region that might negatively impact business and forest products industry activities. They also raised the possibility that the federal government would want to take more forestland out of commercial harvesting in order to create a buffer of some kind to the national park and recreation area. In response, Lucas offered to support such conditions for establishing the park as exempting regional business and forest industry activities from new Clean Air Act requirements and prohibiting the National Park Service from establishing a buffer or regulating logging outside the park boundary.

The end of the paper mill era was driven home in 2014 with the sudden shutdown of the Verso Paper mill in Bucksport and the razing of the shuttered Millinocket mill. At the end of the year, another drama developed over the fate of the closed East Millinocket mill, still structurally intact. After Cate Street Capital filed for Chapter 7 bankruptcy in September, a federal court trustee auctioned off the mill on December 2.* Hackman Capital Partners of Los Angeles outbid four others, paying $5.4 million for the property. The trustee set aside funds to pay secured and unsecured creditors, and the town of East Millinocket was assured $686,000 to settle all but $81,392 of the mill's unpaid taxes. Whether Hackman would repurpose the mill for manufacturing or sell off the physical assets and demolish the structures was a question that remained unanswered in early 2015, but one thing was clear: Hackman didn't operate paper mills.

The Millinocket and East Millinocket paper mills, woodland camps, engineering and other support operations, and the Pinkham sawmill had once employed as many as 4,700 workers.† Those in the mills, especially, were in lifetime jobs that paid wages and benefits ranking among the best in Maine.

---

*The shabby ending of the Cate Street Capital chapter became an issue in the 2014 governor's race. "The story of Cate Street Capital, its investors, and Maine's governor is a massive scandal—a story of corporate welfare and crony capitalism at its worst," Independent candidate Eliot Cutler declared. Noting that Cate Street had benefited from $50 million of tax credits promoted by Governor Paul LePage, Cutler said, "The people of Maine have been victimized in a financial shell game because no one—especially the governor—was asking the hard questions. Now we're left with the question, 'where's the money?'"

†Great Northern's workers in its peak years lived in more than 30 towns and cities. Only one in three employees lived in one of the mill towns. Baxter State Park, with a staff of 61 (full time and seasonal), and the Millinocket Regional Hospital, with 240 (full time and part time).

As 2015 dawned, the largest employers left in the Katahdin region were Baxter State Park, with a staff of 61 (full time and seasonal), and the Millinocket Regional Hospital, with 240 (full time and part time).

The appearance of Millinocket and East Millinocket changed noticeably with the demise of the two mills. Traffic along the 10½-mile stretch of Route 11/157 from the Medway exit off Interstate 95 through East Millinocket to Millinocket dropped off as business plunged. The town centers faded. Dozens of vehicles once parked around the East Millinocket mill disappeared, except for a few belonging to maintenance employees, as did the smoke and vapor from the mill stacks. The piles of logs in the yard disappeared, and railroad lines sat empty of cars that once carried newsprint and specialty papers to market. Everyone knew their towns would never look the same.

A drive along the north woods' best-known haul road, Great Northern's 96-mile Golden Road, would never be the same either. The first mile had once been occupied by contractors that moved wood and material down the road to the mills, but the contractors left for other work. The next 2.5-mile stretch had formerly been an awesome and reassuring indication of prosperity with tree-length wood for the Millinocket mill piled along the road up to 30 feet high. Over the course of "a 60-day 'spring' season there could be from 100,000 to 150,000 cords" sitting along the road, and now "the pile-down areas are overgrown with brush and small trees," said former Millinocket mill manager Jim Giffune. The Golden Road, which follows the Penobscot West Branch for awhile, continued to provide vehicular access from Millinocket west to Greenville on Moosehead Lake, to the St. Zacharie crossing into Quebec, and to many connector haul roads, beloved lakes, and woods camps. The wood once cut for the paper mills was still being harvested, but it was going mostly to Canada.

The toppling of the old Millinocket mill's smoke stacks before Christmas 2014 caused anti-park organizer Kathy Gagnon to throw in the towel. She called the sight of the iconic stacks crashing to the ground "both epic and devastatingly sad." Her *Bangor Daily News* op-ed asked the citizens of Millinocket, East Millinocket, and Medway to face the music: "[I]t's no longer a matter of having a national park here or not, it's a matter of saving our towns. No one entity, be it industry or tourism, can 'fix' what the loss of our mills has done to the area," wrote Gagnon.

She said that those who had fought the proposed park because it wouldn't pay the high wages of a paper mill needed to accept that times had changed. "[W]e need to start with whatever is going to get things moving," she wrote. "The alternative is to continue fighting until there is nothing left to save."

Preserving the Land

Roxanne had spent more than $74 million on land conservation acquisition by the end of 2013, about two-thirds of it for her proposed national park and recreation area. In reality, the park was already rooted in the ground, even if the land didn't yet have the national designation she had pursued for years. A new 15-mile scenic loop road in the southern end of the proposed park land had been stitched together mostly from existing former logging roads. The public was invited to drive, hike, bike, or ride horses on the road. Signs painted brown like those in national parks and Baxter State Park had been installed to guide visitors to several high lookout points from which they could view Millinocket Lake, Mount Katahdin, and other nearby scenic places. A new trail was completed to the summit of 1,616-foot Barnard Mountain, the peak on Roxanne's proposed park land closest to Katahdin. Providing visitors with an opportunity to stand on the ground of the proposed park took the proposal off the paper and rooted it in the soil.

More than 650 cars traveled the loop road in 2014, and more than 40 groups visited the park-in-waiting. The caretakers at Lunksoos Camps welcomed visitors, gave tours of Roxanne's lands, led special events, and worked on trails.

The proposed national park and national recreation area lands were rebranded as Katahdin Woods and Waters, replicating the name used for the 89-mile Scenic Byway to and around Baxter State Park and the East Branch lands. The name change (and redesign of the web page) marked the rebooting of the beleaguered fourteen-year struggle to create Roxanne's park. The question of where the major access gate to the park and recreation area would be located was not yet settled.

Roxanne and Lucas had hoped that Second District Congressman Mike Michaud, a Democrat and former paper mill worker from East Millinocket, would be elected governor of Maine in 2014 and would get behind the park effort. Instead, incumbent Republican Governor Paul LePage won reelection, defeating Michaud and Independent Eliot Cutler, the only candidate in the three-way race who was in favor of federalizing the East Branch lands.

Representative Chellie Pingree, a Democrat, remained the only member of Maine's congressional delegation to favor a national park in the north woods.

With Republicans gaining control of the U.S. Senate, there seemed no chance of a stand-alone Katahdin Woods and Waters park bill getting through Congress by 2016. However, as support increased in the Katahdin region, so did the guarded optimism of those who had pursued the vision for so long.

After Percival Baxter purchased 4,500 acres in June 1935 to add to his budding park, the *Maine Sunday Telegram* wrote that it was "of course appreciated now, but not to the extent that it will be later, as so-called civilization presses further into the primeval forests of the north." Eighty years later, Roxanne too believed that time would reveal to all Americans—but especially to local residents—the value of a public park in the once-private land they considered "theirs."

The creation of national and state parks in America has almost always been difficult. Behind most successful park projects have been deeply inspired, courageous individuals who, despite years or decades of daunting opposition, refused to give up. Many of them have been women, including Mardy Murie (Alaska's Arctic National Wildlife Refuge); Marjorie Stoneman Douglas (Everglades National Park); Virginia McClurg (Colorado's Mesa Verde National Park); Katharine Ordway (the Tallgrass Prairie state preserves in the Midwest); and Dr. Mary Wharton (Kentucky's Floracliff Preserve in the Inner Bluegrass region). As Roxanne Quimby tries to achieve a national designation for her land, she can be heartened by these women's historic successes. If she holds her ground as they did, she may join their ranks in the future, and the legacy she has fought so hard for will be secured. 🐝

Messer Pond. (Bill Duffy photo)

EPILOGUE

"Philanthropy is as humble as it is generous. It expresses itself across the wealth continuum no matter the giver's means. It inspires always."

—W. Kent Olson, "The Geography of Philanthropy"

As I write this in April 2015, a mosaic of conservation easements and acquisitions is developing and shifting in the Maine woods. Plum Creek's 363,000-acre Moosehead Forest conservation easement on both sides of Moosehead Lake north of Greenville, completed in 2012, was the key to state approval of the company's planned 16,900-acre shorefront resort and residential development. (Opponents of the development took the company to court, and the case went all the way to the Maine Supreme Court, which affirmed the legality of state regulators' approval.) In a complex deal, Plum Creek received $10 million from The Nature Conservancy and the Appalachian Mountain Club to protect the land, which will be held by the Forest Society of Maine.* It will be working forest on which hunting, fishing, hiking, and snowmobiling will be permitted—a concept that should sound very familiar to Katahdin-area residents.

* In addition, The Nature Conservancy and the Appalachian Mountain Club paid Plum Creek $15 million to acquire 45,000 acres of conservation land west and east of the Moosehead Forest project (see map page 368).

According to Plum Creek's website, "These lands connect to already-conserved properties, resulting in a network of conserved lands totaling nearly 2.25 million acres—three times the size of Rhode Island—stretching from the Canadian border, across the Moosehead Lake region to Mount Katahdin." A map shows the necklace of lands anchored in the north and west by other conservation easements and The Nature Conservancy's Upper St. John River lands, and in the east by Baxter State Park. Extending the necklace to include Roxanne's proposed East Branch national park would give it the most brand-powerful eastern terminus possible.

Bowdoin College economics professor and tourism expert David Vail believes the Moosehead region is a more powerful tourist magnet than the East Branch. He noted that a major Moosehead destination branding is underway and backed by substantial private and public resources. In the best of future worlds, he said, "a potent Maine woods tourism destination would be built and branded around an 'emerald necklace' of protected lands stretching from Moosehead Lake (plus the Forks and the Moose River corridor) all the way to the Elliotsville Plantation lands bordering the East Branch of the Penobscot. For the near term, however, the best economic bet is the greater Moosehead region, prominently featuring Plum Creek's conserved and developable lands and the Appalachian Mountain Club's 67,000-acre Maine Woods Initiative."*

But there is no more powerful brand in American landscapes than a national park. The problem with most conserved land is the lack of public knowledge of its accessibility and recreational opportunities. Those who live nearby may know all about it, but vacationers seldom do. A national park, Baxter State Park, the Moosehead region, and the Appalachian Trail would together comprise an enticing package for any outdoor-oriented tourist.

It has been many years since Millinocket's sobriquet, The Magic City, was based in reality. East Millinocket, the so-called Town that Paper Made, has fallen almost as far into the pit of hard times as its sister community. The first two-thirds of the twentieth century were the best of times. Mill jobs making paper were among the best in the state, offering high wages and secure retirements. Sons worked alongside fathers. The future looked like the past, stretching ahead for generations. But that future was an illusion. Millinocket's

*Dr. Vail wrote an analysis for Plum Creek on the historic appropriateness and economic importance of anchor resorts in the Moosehead region. He also provided a baseline analysis of the local, regional, and state economic contributions of AMC's Maine Woods Initiative.

population declined from 8,500 in 1970 to 4,500 in 2014 and is projected to drop to 2,500 by 2030 if nothing changes. East Millinocket dropped from 2,200 people to 1,600 in the same span of time.

When Great Northern Paper ruled over two million acres of Maine, Dan Corcoran worked in the company's forestry operations department. He was the lead surveyor laying out the Golden Road to truck timber from the north woods when the river log drives stopped. Back then the paper mills overshadowed tourism and recreation, which had been little more than afterthoughts in the northern Maine economy since the mid-1800s.

But when Great Northern filed for bankruptcy in 2003, Corcoran, a thirty-year employee, went into real estate in the Millinocket region. In 2012, Katahdin Forest Management (the remnant of the old Great Northern Paper) threw on the market its leased camp lots on Millinocket, Ambejejus, Pemadumcook, and North and South Twin lakes, and Corcoran's North Woods Real Estate found a ready market among out-of-towners. While single-family homes in down-and-out Millinocket were available for as little as $15,000 to $30,000 in 2015, lakeside camps with views of Katahdin were selling for six figures.

Corcoran believes the area economy will shift from a major dependence on paper manufacturing to a mixed dependence on tourism, recreation, and forest-products manufacturing. He sees Roxanne's park as part of the mix. He thinks the Katahdin region can offer a unique quality of place, attracting and nourishing a variety of enterprises from hiking and rafting to wood pellets and sawmills.

He thinks more local citizens are buying into that vision since the mills closed and the stacks came crashing down. People are finally accepting that there will be no mills making paper anymore. Residents may look back at 2014 as "the turning point for the future," he says.

Matt Polstein, a former Millinocket town councilor, has operated an outdoor guide service, the area's best restaurant, and a sporting camp for years. A proponent of Roxanne's park, he started getting ready for the new economy by adding cabins to his Twin Pines sporting camp. He bought a downtown building for $5,000 to house a new bike shop, and he is planning a mountain bike trail on his 1,200-acre property outside town. National Park Service lands are proven drivers of local economies throughout America, he says.

A national park will not provide the number of jobs or levels of pay and benefits that paper manufacturing once provided to generations of

Katahdin-area families. But it can be a key component of a new, more diversi-
fied, sustainable economic future based partly on tourism. Reports published
in 1996, 2001, and 2011 provided compelling evidence of the economic benefits that a national park would confer on the Katahdin region, including jobs,
sales and property taxes, and an in-migration of entrepreneurs wanting to live
and work in an area rich in natural beauty and outdoor opportunities.

The idea that public land ownership "is somehow either an encroachment
on local autonomy or the removal of access historically enjoyed by locals is a
canard pedaled by irresponsible people," consultant Charles Buki said in early
2015. "The rights that accompany private property ownership are a far greater
threat to loss of access than public ownership. Public ownership is, in fact, the
only way to both preserve access and steward the land."

After seeing an August 2014 article in the *New York Times* about Millinocket's plight, Buki offered the services of his Alexandria, Virginia, company CZB
Associates—dedicated to neighborhood revitalization and urban planning—to
the town on a pro bono basis. When his offer was reported in the *Bangor Daily
News* in September, "the online vitriol was right away harsh and without factual
standing," he said. Internet posts and anonymous e-mails to Buki linked him to
Roxanne Quimby, whom he didn't know and had never heard of.

Buki led his team to Millinocket anyway. They met with town officials,
business owners, and residents, evaluated the town's demographics and
market conditions, and gathered 500 responses to an extensive survey.

CZB's website touts a philosophy of "urban truth telling," and Buki's
report to the town council did just that. While not speaking directly to Roxanne's proposed national park and recreation area or even mentioning her
name, the findings implied strongly that local leaders had let the town hit
bottom while expending a lot of time and energy fighting Roxanne's park.

Other communities in America have struggled with similar and even
more difficult situations than Millinocket's and have reinvented themselves
successfully, said Buki. He mentioned Moab, Utah, once a uranium mining
center and now the mountain biking capital of the world, and Saxapahaw,
North Carolina (population 1,648 in 2010), a mill town that had fallen on
hard times and today is a thriving culinary and arts center.

He advised officials to raise taxes, beautify the town center and its main
gateway thoroughfare, push for regional school consolidation, clean up old
industrial sites, remove or rebuild falling-down or vacant houses and commercial properties, and get over their resentment of outsiders. "[A]s long as

the five-hour trek from Boston doesn't adequately reward those who make the trip with gifts of a beautiful town and broader access to the wilderness," he wrote, "there's near zero probability of significant outside investment."

He advised that Millinocket should be a leader in state and regional discussions "about the nature of land ownership and the role that natural resources play in your economy and your future.... Private ownership of lands is not working, so it's time to be the leading voice for a balanced portfolio of private and public trusts" in the Katahdin region. Buki pointed out that the town "has a disproportionate degree of informal authority on this subject, but has only used it to petition for the status quo in small-minded ways."

Buki's effort, a gift worth $23,000 in billable time, received no thank you from Millinocket. The town council, whose majority has opposed Roxanne's park project since the beginning, was considering how to respond to the report at the time of this writing. Buki's blunt words stirred East Millinocket town leaders to call for a new vote by local residents on the proposed park and to let the congressional delegation know what the community's requirements would be to accept Roxanne's offer, but the Millinocket town council wasn't budging, at least not yet. However, the Bangor City Council voted 7–2 to support the concept of a national park and recreation area, believing the municipality could see positive economic gains from the project. By April 2015, 200 regional business owners had pledged to back Roxanne's project.

Roxanne Quimby is a unique presence in the north woods. As a former back-to-the-lander, she knows from experience how vital nature can be in people's lives. As a businesswoman, she knows what jobs mean to communities. As an artist she is stirred by the beauty of the northern forest. As a Thoreau acolyte, she wants to pay her dues to nature for having made her money manufacturing consumer goods.

She scraped and clawed for years to build a successful company from nothing except her creative imagination. She pulled herself up by her bootstraps. Hers is the quintessential American success story, and now she wants to do something—for free—to protect forever a landmark swath of the beloved north woods. She spent tens of millions of dollars buying land on both sides of the Penobscot East Branch, and she wants to give that land to the nation as a 150,000-acre public park and recreation area, accessible to all in perpetuity. She has pledged $40 million to pay for most of the operational and key infrastructure costs of the new park. She has proposed that half the land, 75,000 acres, be open for snowmobiling and hunting so that area residents can continue to enjoy the traditional activities the paper companies allowed.

There is not enough time remaining before the National Park Service's 2016 centennial for a federal feasibility study of Roxanne's park proposal. However, the natural values of Roxanne's East Branch lands have been inventoried as they were added to her holdings by Dr. Bart DeWolf (her science director) and an assistant and college student interns.

In letters to Maine's congressional delegation in early December 2014, DeWolf said his firsthand knowledge of the East Branch lands' ecological treasures supports his belief that "they merit consideration" for national park designation "first and foremost, because of the great rivers that are found there: the Penobscot East Branch river system, including its major tributaries, the Seboeis River and Wassataquoik Stream.... This complex has been identified as one of the least-developed watersheds in the Northeast, eligible for inclusion in the National Wild and Scenic Rivers system."

DeWolf went on to note the important wildlife species that depend on the East Branch waters and land, the "spectacular rapids and waterfalls ... the magnificent mountains and mountain views ... the fascinating human history," and other significant features. He asked the delegation members to "think favorably about the potential of creating a new national park, one that complements Acadia National Park along Maine's scenic coast by celebrating Maine's great interior forest."*

While never having met Roxanne, Charles Buki considers her "a hero," given the lengths to which she has gone for public land stewardship. "It's too uncommon an act," he said. 🐝

---

*DeWolf did not declare outright that Roxanne's East Branch lands are park-worthy because, he said, "the criteria for 'ecologically significantly enough to merit national park status' are not very well defined."

Sources

Roxanne Quimby was the primary source for much of this book. As explained in the prologue, the book began with her cooperation, and she granted numerous interviews and access to documents and other interviewees for two years before declining further involvement with the project. Parts of her story have been chronicled in many newspaper and magazine articles as well as a few business case studies and books, some of which I drew on. Some people I interviewed did not want to be identified and thus are not named as sources. Some who worked for Roxanne at Burt's Bees in Maine did not want to be interviewed; others could not be located.

Burt Shavitz did not acknowledge several faxed requests for an interview, nor did he answer his telephone, which was listed in the name of his dog. The last denial for access to him came from a public relations spokesperson for Burt's Bees in October 2014. Most of the information about Burt that appears in this book came from Roxanne Quimby. Bits and pieces of his life relayed to me by Roxanne and reported in various media articles over the years were augmented and verified in a 2013 documentary by Canadian filmmaker Jody Shapiro—the only significant portrait allowed by Burt and by Burt's Bees, now owned by the Clorox Company. Shapiro's documentary, *Burt's Buzz*, was released on DVD in 2014, and the sprinkling of quotes from Burt in Chapter 5 and elsewhere in this book come from the film. After the film's release, Burt became the subject of numerous articles. I also retrieved information about Burt from people who worked for Burt's Bees in Maine and North Carolina and people who knew him in Guilford, Maine.

Since Burt's Bees had been sold twice by the time I began interviews with Roxanne in early 2009, there were only a small number of documents available to me for this book, most of them from Roxanne. Burt's Bees' former employee Brooks Juhring visited the Edes Building in Guilford after the company moved to North Carolina and found documents scattered around. He boxed some of them up and allowed me to use whatever I needed. The catalogs and supplements (some originals) were invaluable for tracing the evolution of Burt's Bees' products and packaging and for the stories Roxanne wrote in them about the early years of the company.

A number of libraries, historical societies, county registries of deeds, and archives helped with some of the most hard-to-find information on the Quimby family: the Maine State Library in Augusta; the Maine Historical Society in Portland; the St. Louis Central Library in St. Louis, Missouri; the Lewiston Public Library in Lewiston, Maine; the Brunswick Public Library in Brunswick, Maine; the Portland Public Library in Portland, Maine; the Piscataquis County Register of Deeds in Dover-Foxcroft, Maine; the Penobscot County Register of Deeds in Bangor, Maine; the Thompson Free Library in Dover-Foxcroft; the Sebec (Maine) Historical Society; the Abbot (Maine) Historical Society; the Central and Brighton branches of the Boston Public Library; the Newton Free Library in Newton, Massachusetts; the Bethlehem Area Public Library in Bethlehem, Tennessee; the High Ridge Library of Jefferson County, Missouri; the New England Genealogical Society in Boston, Massachusetts; the Sheboygan Research Center in Sheboygan, Wisconsin; the National Archives and Records Administration in Washington, DC; and the American Civil War Research Database on the Internet.

In addition to the books referenced in chapter-by-chapter source notes, I consulted *Back to The Land: The Enduring Dream of Self-sufficiency in Modern America*, by Dona Brown (University of Wisconsin Press, 2011); *At Home in Nature: Modern Homesteading and Spiritual Practice in America*, by Rebecca Kneale Gould (University of California Press, 2005); *Wildlands Conservation Philanthropy: The Great American Tradition*, by Tom Butler (Earth Aware Editions, 2008); *The Northeast's Changing Forest*, by Lloyd C. Irland (Harvard University Press, 1999); *Aroostook: A Century of Logging in Northern Maine*, by Richard W. Judd (University of Maine Press, 1989); *Outliers*, by Malcolm Gladwell

(Back Bay Books/Little, Brown and Company, 2008); *The Interrupted Forest: A History of Maine's Wildlands*, by Neil Rolde (Tilbury House, 2001); *The Life of the Bee*, by Maurice Maeterlinck (Dover Publications, 2006); *The Wisdom of Bees: What The Hive Can Teach Business About Leadership, Efficiency, and Growth*, by Michael O'Malley (Penguin Group, 2010; Foreword by Roxanne Quimby); *History of Parkman: Mainstream Democracy in Parkman, Maine 1794–1969*, by Roger C. Storms (The Dingley Press, 1969); *Ugly Beauty: Helena Rubinstein, L'Oreal, and the Blemished History of Looking Good*, by Ruth Brandon (Harper-Collins, 2011); *History of Piscataquis County, Maine*, by George J. Varney (B. B. Russell, 1886); and *A Valley White with Mist: Settlers, Nature, and Culture in a North Woods River Valley*, 1800–1870, by Jamie H. Eves (doctoral dissertation, University of Connecticut, 2005).

The *Bangor Daily News* has been the newspaper of record on Roxanne's campaign to create a new national park and recreation area on the Penobscot East Branch. The articles I refer to in the text are available at the *News'* website www.bangordailynews.com. The web, in general, is replete with articles from other newspapers and magazines that a search will turn up. As well, www. youtube.com includes various videos featuring Roxanne.

PROLOGUE

It took some coaxing before Roxanne finally took me on a road trip to see the cabin outside Guilford where she and George St. Clair homesteaded and other places she frequented during that period. In June 2009, she had returned to the cabin for the first time since 1984 with a film crew from France for a documentary on land barons, and it wasn't a pleasant experience for her to see the old place. But the following month we met in Bangor to visit the place. She mentioned that she had to drive her Volvo very slowly because one more traffic ticket meant she would lose her license. Even though ours was her second visit to the cabin in two months, she was visibly disturbed by how the land had been abused (in her eyes) and the cabin gussied up in ways she thought distasteful. Walking the path from Andrews Road to the cabin and seeing the place she and George built and lived in early on was essential to placing Roxanne in context. After our trip, I could see how her homesteading experience still permeated her life long after she'd left the land.

I have been asked many times why I chose to write about Roxanne. There were two main reasons that I knocked on her door. *Maine Times* had closed in 2002, and my subsequent reporting for *Maine Environmental News* (an Internet service) ended when it too succumbed in 2005. I had written about Roxanne for both of those publications, first about her moving Burt's Bees to North Carolina, and then about her land deals starting in 2000. We had talked and exchanged e-mails but had never met. I thought her effort to create a new national park in Maine was an important chapter in north woods history, and I wanted to make sure it was documented. We met a couple of times at her home in Portland to talk about a book. She was not overly enthusiastic, but she agreed. This was not an authorized biography. In retrospect, I could believe that Roxanne consulted her Tarot cards to see if she should let me be the one to tell her story. If not Tarot, it was fate.

Roxanne's quote about the "universe" guiding her came from the raw transcript of an interview she did with David Vinjamuri, author of *Accidental Branding: How Ordinary People Build Extraordinary Brands*. David's offer to share it with me was generous, and it helped illuminate how Roxanne talked in what I considered an unvarnished way about her life, Burt's Bees, and the Maine woods. David titled his chapter on her "The Anarchist."

CHAPTER 1. THE MAINE WOODS

The Maine Woods, by Henry David Thoreau (edited by Joseph J. Moldenhauer; published by Princeton University Press, 1972) is the source for the quotations by Thoreau.

An online map of virgin forest in the U.S. over time (www.endgame.org) provides a quick reference for the disappearance of old-growth forest. An in-depth reference is *The Changing Nature of the Maine Woods*, by Andrew M. Barton, Alan S. White, and Charles V. Cogbill (University of New Hampshire Press, 2012). I also consulted *Modern Maine: Its Historic Background, People and Resources*, Volume 1, by Richard Hebert (Lewis Historical Publishing Company, New York, 1951, pages 497–505); and "Maine's changing landscape to 1820," by David C. Smith (pages 13–23 of *Maine in the Early Republic: From Revolution to Statehood*, edited by Charles E. Clark, James S. Leamon, and Karen Bowden; University Press of New England, 1988). *A History of Lumbering in Maine, 1861–1960*, by David C. Smith (University of Maine Press, 1972) and *A History of Lumbering in Maine, 1820–1861*, by Richard G. Wood (University of Maine Press, 1935) were also useful.

On the sell-off of Maine's public forests to private interests, I used *The Maine Book*, by Henry E. Dunnack (privately printed, Augusta, page 221).

The primary reference for Katahdin history was *Legacy of a Lifetime: The Story of Baxter State Park*, by Dr. John W. Hakola (TBW Books, University of Maine Press, 1981), which I turned to multiple times for information on people, politicians, and organizations that advocated for a preserve around Katahdin. I used *Sprague's Journal of Maine History*, by John Sprague (June 1916 issue, "Shall We Have a Forest Sanctuary in Maine," page 37, accessed online) for his quote on "what a wonderful national park" could be created in the Katahdin region.

Katahdin: An Historic Journey, by John Neff (AMC Books, 2006) provided guidance on the first proposal for a carriage road and hotel at Chimney Pond below Katahdin's summit.

Jym St. Pierre of RESTORE: The North Woods has spent many hours compiling quotes about the Maine woods going back to the 1730s. His unpublished manuscript, called "Preserving Our Maine Woods Legacy: Excerpts from the Literature" (2010), was a valuable guide (along with Hakola's book) to references for such personalities as George Kimball, Congressman Frank Guernsey, and Lucius Merrill.

I was guided by John Hakola's book (see above) and *The Baxters of Maine: Downeast Visionaries*, by Neil Rolde (Tilbury House Publishers, 1997) for my commentary on Percival P. Baxter's efforts to preserve the Katahdin area as a state park and the years he spent building the preserve. Additional details were gleaned from "Baxter State Park at 50 and the Baxters at Bowdoin," compiled by Earle G. Shettleworth Jr., Maine State Historian (*Bowdoin Daily Sun*, August 22, 2012, accessed online). Federal interest in the Katahdin area for a national park was outlined in the National Park Service's report, *Proposed Mount Katahdin National Park, Maine*, summer 1937; and in the National Park and Conservation Association's Investing in Park Futures: A Blueprint for Tomorrow, Vol. 8 (New Parks, New Promise, 1988). The Reagan era opposition to national parks is described in *Protecting the Wild* (Foundation for Deep Ecology, 2015), pg. 201.

The Wilderness Society proposed "A New Maine Woods Reserve" in 1989, laying out options to protect Maine's northern wildlands. Publications calling for large-scale protection of the Maine woods include *The Big Outside*, by Dave Foreman and Howie Wolke (Ned Ludd Books, 1989); "A North Woods Conservation Area" (The Natural Resources Council, 1991); and the Northern

Forest Forum's Spring Equinox issue of 1994. "The Diamond Legacy" (*Maine Times*, March 13–19, 1997) reported on the fallout from the sale of the Diamond International lands and subsequent major paper company land sales, as did "Changing Timberland Ownership in the Northern Forest and Implications for Biodiversity" (Manomet Center for Conservation Sciences, 2005); and *Forestland Ownership in Maine: Recent Trends and Issues*, by Karen S. Nadeau (Report to a Maine legislative committee, March 2000). Helpful too was "Effects of forest ownership and change on forest harvest rates, types and trends in northern Maine," by Suming Jin and Steven A. Sader (Department of Forest Management, University of Maine at Orono, 2006).

George Smith's October 1995 fundraising letter to Sportsman's Alliance of Maine members was the call to arms to the sporting community to fight RESTORE: The North Woods' proposed park. My sources for the struggle over RESTORE's proposed national park include RESTORE's own published materials; "National park bid divides Maine" (*Boston Globe*, July 30, 1995, pages 79–80); "Clearcutting: A Cloudy Issues in Maine" (*Christian Science Monitor*, October 15, 1996, page 14). Also: *Maine Times*, May 24, 2001, pages. 4–6; *Bangor Daily News*, January 12, 2001, page A1; and *Wild Earth* magazine, Summer 2000, page 64.

Two books that provided paper company information from opposite points of view were *Timber: The Fall of Maine's Paper Giant*, by Paul McCann (*Ellsworth American*, page 65); and *Beyond the Beauty Strip: Saving What's Left of Our Forests*, by Mitch Lansky (Tilbury House Publishers, 1992, pages 6–8 and 139–40). Other sources were George Neavoll's op-ed article in the *Maine Sunday Telegram* (June 12, 1994, page 4C); the Maine Woods Coalition's press release of December 21, 2003, about the potential negative effects of RESTORE's proposed national park; and "How Maine Ended Up With a $12 Million a Year Habit" (*Maine Times*, November 15, 1976, pages 1–4) on the era of clearcutting and the two unsuccessful attempts to change clearcutting practices in the mid-1990s.

CHAPTER 2. ORIGINS

My account of Roxanne's Russian ancestors was almost solely from Liliane Willens's book *Stateless in Shanghai* (Earnshaw Books, 2010). Dr. Willens taught French language and literature at Boston College and the Massachusetts Institute of Technology and later worked for the U.S. Agency for

International Development and the Peace Corps. She taped interviews with her mother about her memories of growing up in Shanghai amid political and military turmoil. I interviewed Dr. Willens (of Washington, DC) a few times by phone in 2009 and talked once with her sister, Jacqueline Arons, in Massachusetts. For an understanding of the political events of the time, I interviewed an associate history professor at Bowdoin College in Brunswick, Maine (who asked not to be identified) and referenced Nathaniel Deutsch's *The Jewish Dark Continent: Life and Death in the Russian Pale* (Harvard University Press, 2011, pages 3–4 and 315). I was further helped by *History of Russia*, by Nicholas Riasanovsky (Oxford University Press, 2010, pages 394–397, 389, 398, 401, 415, 452, 481–483, 401, and 512–515).

Genealogical history of the Quinby (Quimby) Family in England and America, by Henry Cole Quinby (no publishing company cited, 1910) is the essential ancestral history of Roxanne's paternal origins in England starting in 686 A.D. By phone and via e-mail, Salem State University history professor and author Emerson Baker provided perspective of Massachusetts and New England before the arrival of the Pilgrims and when the first Quimby on Roxanne's American family tree arrived in Plymouth, Massachusetts. The National Archives Trust Fund in Washington and the American Civil War Research Database provided records of John Colby Quimby in the Civil War. For the life and times of John Colby Quimby, I consulted two books by James H. Mundy: *Hard Times, Hard Men: Maine and the Irish* and *Second to None: The Story of the 2nd Maine Volunteer Infantry, "The Bangor Regiment"* (Harp Publications, 1990 and 1992, respectively).

Quimby family records were made available to me from the Jefferson County Library in High Ridge, Missouri, on John Colby Quimby's sojourn there to be near his brother for a short time. Other information about his life and that of his family was in the Piscataquis County Registry of Deeds, Dover-Foxcroft, Maine, and the Lewiston (Maine) Public Library's city directories and annual reports of 1880–81. The sawmills on the Penobscot River were noted in the 1860 town report of Old Town, Maine. The Boston Central Public Library provided the obituary of Benjamin Willens published in the *Boston Globe* on May 13, 1998. Katie Dippel, executive assistant at the Sheboygan County Historical Research Center in Sheboygan Falls, Wisconsin, sent news articles and obituaries of the Quimby family, among them photos of John Alvan and Frank Quimby in their World War I uniforms. The story of John and Anne Quimby's relocation from Maine to Wisconsin was published in the *Sheboygan Press*, May 3, 1998, page C1; the obituary of John Colby Quimby on May 27, 1941, page 1. The obituaries of Carroll Quimby and Carrie Quimby were carried in the *Sheboygan Press* on May 27, 1941, and April 13, 1963, respectively, and provided background details on their lives. Roxanne's father, John Arthur Quimby, wrote a 20-page retrospective of his life that provided information about Roxanne's family life and her childhood and youth. Rachelle Quimby shared some of her family memories during two phone conversations. Hannah Quimby provided letters from Thais Willens and Margaret Genter written during the year their children became engaged, married, and relocated from Shanghai to the U.S. My thanks to Hannah Quimby and Lucas St. Clair for interviews and e-mails regarding events and descriptions in this chapter.

CHAPTER 3. HEADING WEST: SAN FRANCISCO, 1970

Roxanne Quimby's personal account of leaving her family with George St. Clair, moving to San Francisco, and attending the San Francisco Art Institute was the paramount source for her life in those years. A friend of the couple, John Knox, provided additional perspective. The Bethlehem Area Public Library in Bethlehem, Pennsylvania, provided obituaries of George St. Clair Jr.'s parents that carried background information on the couple. The library sent copies of the obituary of George W. St. Clair from the *Express of Bethlehem* (December 5, 1995, page B6) and the obituary of Gena St. Clair from the *Morning Call* (September 24, 2010). Documentation of Wilda Quimby's role in creating a Children's Forest in the Nicolet National Forest came from "Racine Points Way Toward Children's Forest" (*Racine Journal Times*, February 22, 1936) and Nicolet National Forest records on Wilda Quimby (file with author).

CHAPTER 4. BACK TO THE LAND: MAINE, 1975

I thank Roxanne Quimby, her friends from the homesteading years, and her children, Hannah Quimby and Lucas St. Clair, for stories from Guilford and Parkman, Maine. Other contributing sources included Rita Corbin, Tom Staley, Virginia Anderson, Ellie Daniels, Lee Ann Berry, Alan Bray, Allen Bell, Wynona Boothroyd Randall, Richard Garrett, Bob Littlefield, Paul Davis, and

Bruce Tibbets. Cynthia Hall told me about Roxanne's employment at Hall's Christmas Tree Farm. George Frangolis talked about starting *Farmstead*, his alternative "how-to" magazine for homesteaders, in 1974.

For a description of the pulp and paper company lands and the political power the industry wielded at the time, I used the Maine classic, *The Paper Plantation*, by William C. Osborn (Grossman Publishers, 1974). The town valuation and property taxes for Roxanne and George's 30 acres off Andrews Road came from the Guilford town office. The quote by Thoreau is in *Writings of Henry David Thoreau*, Vol. 3 (Houghton Mifflin, 1906, page 77). The U.S. Census Bureau estimated the population of Piscataquis County in 1975 as 16,667. The U.S. Bureau of Economic Analysis reported the per capita personal income for Piscataquis County at $4,555 in 1979 (both figures accessed online). Mildred Mauthe's quote was from *Down East* magazine, July 2005, page 73.

CHAPTER 5. BURT AND THE BEES: 1984

Roxanne Quimby and her essay in the 1987 Burt's Bees catalog guided me through the history of the early days of creating the little company that could. Other sources for this chapter included Guilford and Parkman area people who knew Roxanne and Burt Shavitz: Ellsworth "Junior" Perkins, Bob Eagan, Patti Dowse, Bev Crockett, Susan Blaisdell, Tony Kulik, Bob Littlefield, Bruce Tibbets, Hannah Quimby, Lucas St. Clair, and Chitanya York. The first newspaper article about Burt's Bees appeared in the *Bangor Daily News* on March 31, 1992, page B1. *People* magazine first discovered Burt's Bees in 1998, publishing the article "Minding His Beeswax" on July 13, page 98. The story provided background information on Burt from his early years in Long Island to an Army stint, settling into work as a freelance photographer, and the move from Manhattan to upper New York State and then to Dexter, Maine. Roxanne was the source for how she met Burt, their budding relationship, and learning how to be a beekeeper. Chitanya York reflected on the Common Ground Fair's creation and popularity. Tony Kulik attended numerous crafts fairs with Roxanne and Burt and became acquainted with their first handmade products and her dislike of rules and control by others. He was one of the first people to spot her unusual entrepreneurial instincts.

The Parkman, Maine, town office provided information on Roxanne's property taxes and values on the 40 acres she purchased in 1986. The July 1,

1997, issue of *Business North Carolina* is the source for how much Burt paid in property taxes when he moved to Roxanne's land in Parkman and built a new Cape-style house. Boomer Career.com carried an article on June 10, 2003, on Burt as "quite the local color." Roxanne's comment about not being able to get a loan from a bank to finance Burt's Bees was on page 121 in *The Entrepreneurial Mind*, by Jeffry Timmons (Brick House, 1989). Burt's decision to stop keeping bees was related by Roxanne in the transcript of her interview for "The Anarchist" chapter in *Accidental Branding*, by David Vinjamuri (Wiley, 2008). Burt's quotes come from the 2013 documentary *Burt's Buzz*, by filmmaker Jody Shapiro.

CHAPTER 6. BACKWOODS ENTREPRENEUR

Contributing sources for this chapter of Burt's Bees in Parkman, Maine, are Roxanne Quimby, Wyonana Boothroyd Randall, Bev Crockett, Joanie Slamm, Joanie White, Hilde Beinsheimer, Frances Webber, Linda Luellen, Sharon Cloud, Paul Dochen, Hil Artman, Bruce Tibbets, Alan LaValle, Ralph Lazotte, Sol Solomon, Danielle Smith Bouthot, and Hannah Quimby. An evaluation of Burt's Bees' first years of operation done at Roxanne's request in 1989 by John Sanders, associate professor of accounting at the University of South Maine, was a valuable source of details on the company's financial metrics in 1987, 1988, and 1989. Roxanne provided documents on employee salaries; recipes for the first crème products, such as Royal Jelly Eye Crème; sales by product; and customer details.

Mention of Roxanne's hands freezing while taking an order from Bloomingdale's was in the September 1, 2000, report of *Fortune Small Business* online. The *Allston-Brighton Journal* in Brighton, Massachusetts, published the obituary of Benjamin Willens on May 12, 1988. Louis Sagar still sold Burt's Bees products in his Zona stores in New York, Tokyo, and Florence in 2003, according to the December 6, 2003, issue of *Forbes* magazine, page 89.

CHAPTER 7. BURT'S BEES MOVES TO MAIN STREET

Burt's Bees' history in Guilford, Maine, 1989–93, was told by Roxanne Quimby, Bev Crockett, Paul Daigle, Patti Dowse, Stu Kauder, Bob Littlefield, Mary Thackery, Burt Isaac, Angel Ginn, Dusty Trembley, Linda Frederichs, Larch Hanson, Peter Martell, Alvin McDonald, Mark Smith, Bill Teague,

Michael Aube, Tom White, Tom Goulette, Robert Shaffer, Barry Ellis, and Shirley Ellis. Sol Solomon and Joe Marks provided additional perspectives.

The history of the Edes Building came from the Maine Historical Society, the Maine Historical Preservation Commission, and Barry Ellis. Roxanne tried to help save the dilapidated building from demolition in 2006 with an offer of $80,000, but Guilford selectmen didn't want to spend the $750,000 to $1.1 million it would have cost to restore the structure. The reference to Maine Chance Farm is in the August 8, 2002, issue of the *Bangor Daily News*, page A7. Stu Kauder said he kept a diary of his work at Burt's Bees but declined a request to use it for this book. The U. S. Department of Labor investigations are laid out in a report from March 24, 1992, and a July 10, 1992, letter. The dismissal of sex discrimination charges against Burt's Bees was confirmed in an e-mail communication from Maine Human Rights commission director Pat Ryan on February 23, 2011. The first story ever written about Burt's Bees was in the *Bangor Daily News* on March 31, 1992, on page B1. The *Inc.* magazine story *"The Secrets of Bootstrapping"* was published in the September 1992 issue on page 78. *Maine Times* put Burt's Bees on the cover of its June 3, 1994, issue (pages 2–5), explaining why the company moved south. The "Dear Dad" article in *Forbes* magazine appeared on pages 98–99 of the December 1993 issue. The *Lear's* magazine article on Burt's Bees, entitled "Enterprise," ran in the March 1994 issue on pages 20–21. The reference to Burt's Bees having only $2,500 in uncollected debts came from the *Lear's* article.

CHAPTER 8. GOODBYE MAINE, HELLO NORTH CAROLINA: 1994

The tale of Burt's Bees moving to North Carolina and starting over was told by Roxanne Quimby and four of those who helped her transform the business: Frank Baldwin, Mark Smith, Bob Kingery, and Chuck Friedman. Danielle Smith Bruce also contributed.

Roxanne's statement about Burt having minimal involvement appeared in *Lear's* magazine, March 1994, page 21. An article in the *News & Observer* on April 20, 1996, quoted Roxanne saying Burt had not yet seen the company's new facilities in Raleigh and hadn't been in North Carolina for a year and a half. "The last time he was here he lost his rental car at Crabtree Valley Mall and had to have a cop drive him up and down the parking lot. That was the end. He has never been back. He can't handle it." A story on April 20, 1999, in the *News & Observer* online reported that Roxanne ordered the outlets closed.

Business Journal wrote an article about Roxanne on November 8, 2002, that revealed how much of Burt's Bees business was through the company Web site. Roxanne was quoted as saying, "When the guys in my art department recommended a Web site, I was very skeptical. To my amazement, they soon reported that 70 percent of our business was coming in by the Web site."

Roxanne disclosed the slip in not taking into account labor costs in North Carolina in *MORE* magazine, March 2005, page 113. Her statement about lip balm carrying Burt's Bees through its struggles is in the *Accidental Branding* transcription of David Vinjamuri's interview with Roxanne.

CHAPTER 9. BURT'S BEES REINCARNATED

Key sources were Roxanne Quimby, Chuck Friedman, Mark Smith, Sunne Justice, Donna Hollenbach, and Frank Baldwin. I relied on Sunne Justice's training DVD for store owners and the 1996 and 1998 Burt's Bees catalogs and supplemental catalogs for store buyers. Chuck Friedman's memo on microorganisms in Burt's Bees products was given to Roxanne "during the 1995–96 period," he wrote in an e-mail dated July 21, 2010. The article in the Drug Store News about the buzz Burt's Bees created at the 1997 trade show in San Diego was in the August 30, 1999, issue on page 99. Burt's salary of $25,000 in 1998 was reported in *Forbes*, December 28, 1998, page 91. Renee Quimby's employee training letter was dated May 30, 1992.

The July 13, 1998, *People* magazine article on Burt's Bees, page 98, quoted Roxanne on why customers were attracted to Burt's face on the product packaging, saying, "They say, 'oh boy, this is a funky brand. It must be *really* natural.'" The same article on the same page said that Burt's mother came to visit once and told Roxanne that "she didn't raise him that way," referring to his hermit-like lifestyle and unkempt looks. The *Forbes* article of December, 28, 1998, pages 90–91, theorized that if Burt's Bees had been willing to take "outside money," Roxanne and Burt "would long since have diluted their ownership and would have wasted time talking to bankers that could be better spent selling candles and soap."

CHAPTER 10. THE TIGER ROARS
CHAPTER 11. LEAVING BURT'S BEES

These chapters were built on interviews with Roxanne Quimby, Mike Abramson, Larry Groseclose, Sheila Clark, Sunne Justice, Andrew Schlindler, Chuck Friedman, Donna Hollenbach, Mark Smith, Bill Whyte, Darrin Duber-Smith, Jamies Trimble, Rachelle Quimby, Brooks Juhring, Hannah Quimby, Charles Alley, Margie McDaniel, Gail Zauder, and John Replogle. The 2000 Burt's Bees catalog and the March 2003 confidential document for potential buyers of the company were indispensable.

The value of Burt's one-third share of the company had he been able to keep it would have been $59 million, according to the *New York Times* online January 6, 2008, but calculates as $77 million from the sale price reported by elixirAdvisors. The difference might be accounted for by the investment banker's fees. Information about Clorox writing down the value of Burt's Bees, is on Reuters online, February 4, 2011, with the headline "Clorox moves on after sting of Burt's Bees charge."

Roxanne's comment of having a "tiger by the tail" was often repeated in the media. It was in *Forbes*, September 2000, page 84. "Once I got a measure of success, I was captivated," said Roxanne. "I had a tiger by the tail. It was incredibly challenging. And it was a gradual transition. One day I realized, 'Hey, I'm not cutting my own firewood anymore.' I felt nostalgic about leaving that simplicity behind. But it's all an evolution. Back then, I worked incredibly long hours every single day of the week. I went years without a weekend off or a vacation."

The recyclable materials used in the first lipsticks that Burt's Bees produced was touted in *Women's Wear Daily* online, February 12, 1999. The deal with Starbucks to sell Burt's Bees lip balm during the Christmas holidays was noted in *Women's Wear Daily* online on September 24, 1999. Roxanne's discovery of a Manhattan drugstore selling knockoffs of Burt's Bees soaps was mentioned in *Inc.* magazine, September 2000, page 109. The September 2000 *Entrepreneur* magazine online had the story of the actor in the bee costume handing out lip balm to passersby in Manhattan.

The *Charlotte Observer* reported on August 27, 2001, page 3D, that Roxanne and Burt's Bees were named Entrepreneur of the Year in 2001 by Ernest & Young. The *New York Times* of February 16, 2003, reported on why Roxanne didn't use professional models and mentioned that Burt's Bees had 144 products sold in 6,000 outlets. Roxanne called her father "a despot" in *Inc.* magazine's January 1, 2004, issue. *Hope* magazine carried a story on Roxanne and Burt's Bees in its March/April 2004 issue, and on page 32 Roxanne said, "There's more important things to be than pretty." Knight Ridder's *Tribune Business News* online on February 11, 2005, said Burt's Bees employee numbers had climbed from 130 to 400. Roxanne had not abandoned plans for running for governor of Maine, according to the *Palm Beach Post* on May 10, 2004. The more than 10,000 calls to Burt's Bees' toll-free number as the result of an ad for Baby Bee skin care products in *Women's Day* magazine was reported in the *News & Observer*, April 30, 1999, page D1.

"Burt's Bees: Leaving the Hive" was a March 19, 2007, Harvard Business School case study that reported on page 3 that the company manufactured more than 150 personal care items sold in 9,000 natural foods and specialty stores in the U.S. and Canada. A Burt's Bees case study in *DATAMONITOR* of April 2008, page 4, reported on the $5.2 billion value of the U.S. personal care products market. The way Roxanne liked to jazz up her Burt's Bees staff when she arrived from out-of-town was taken from the transcribed manuscript of the 2008 book *Accidental Branding* by David Vinjamuri. Roxanne's praise of Mike Abramson, her human resources director, was also in the transcript, as well as her discussion of manufacturing problems.

CHAPTER 12. FAMILY MATTERS

Roxanne Quimby, Hannah Quimby, and Lucas St. Clair provided most of the material for this chapter. Other contributors were Rabbi Moshe Wilansky, Danielle Smith Bruce, and Larry Smith Sr., Larry Smith Jr., Barbara Prudhommeaux, David Marshall, Bob Keyes, Jessica Tomlinson, and Nat May.

The *JUMP* magazine article about Hannah Quimby's Appalachian Trail thru-hike was on pages 57–58 in the April 2000 issue. A story about Mama's Boy Bistro was in the *Bangor Daily News* on June 25, 2003, pages C1–2. The *News* reported on June 9, 2004, pages C1 and 3, about Gerrish's reopening under Lucas St. Clair and Jennifer Amara's management.

After purchasing Gerrish's Restaurant, Roxanne tried to create a town park on the lot she bought beside it to provide a green space downtown and provide public toilet facilities, which were not available anywhere else in Winter Harbor. The town "has world-class possibilities, with its views, its village atmosphere and its people," Roxanne told columnist Bill Nemitz in his column in the *Portland Press Herald* on August 31, 2005. The *Bangor Daily News* reported on August 21, 2006, about Roxanne spending time baking at Gerrish's Provisions, and her cooking school plans for Winter Harbor were revealed in a September 21, 2006, article. Roxanne's effort to open a cooking school was reported in the *Ellsworth American* online on September 21, 2006.

The Raleigh *News & Observer* online announced that Roxanne had opened a new company called Happy Green Bee, maker of organic baby clothes. "I'm going to see if lightning can strike twice," Roxanne said. "I'm still young [56]. I felt I needed an active daily challenge."

The beginning of Roxanne's purchase of a number of properties in Portland was announced on the *Sun-Journal* website on February 11, 2007. The *American Online* reported on November 18, 2010, that Roxanne had put Gerrish's Provisions up for sale. *Successful Living*'s winter issue, pages 33–35, carried a story about Roxanne's business ventures.

Roxanne's plan to reopen the former Mama's Boy Bistro as a cafe and visitors' center was reported in the *Ellsworth American* online on June 20, 2012. The demolition of Winter Harbor's old gas station on property newly purchased by Roxanne was filed online by the *Ellsworth American* in October 2014 (day unavailable).

CHAPTER 13. IMAGINING A NATIONAL PARK: 2000

The chapter was pieced together from interviews with Roxanne Quimby, Jym St. Pierre, Sam Hodder, Ralph Knoll, Chuck Gadzik, John Cochrane, Roger Milliken, Karen Woodsum, Mimi McConnell, Angus King, Rudy Engholm, David Soucy, Bob Meyers, George Smith, Michael Kellett, Ken Olson, Bud Fackleman, Cathy Johnson, Matt Polstein, Marsha Donahue, Pat McGowan, Ted Koffman, Mark Leathers, Michael Weymouth, Ray Campbell, and Jimmy Busque.

The paper industry discussion at the beginning of the chapter came from "The Pulp and Paper Industry, 1865–1930," by Richard W. Judd, a chapter in *Maine: The Pine Tree State from Prehistory to the Present* (University of Maine Press, 1995, pages 426–431); from "Maine's Forest Industry from One Era to Another" by Lloyd C. Irland, a chapter in Changing Maine 1960–2010 (edited by Richard Barringer; Tilbury House, 2004, page 369); and from "The Northern Forest: Our Last Best Chance," by Carl Reidel (Gale Group, 1990, accessed online February 14, 2015).

The background on Diamond International, Sir James Goldsmith, and Al Dunlap was sourced from "Al Dunlap: The Chainsaw Capitalist," by David Plotz (*Slate*, August 1997; accessed online 2/14/15); "Who Is the Real Chainsaw Al?," by John A. Byrne (*Businessweek*, December 1, 1996; accessed online 2/14/15); "Corporate Blitzkrieg Brings a Rapid Turnaround," by James Flanigan (*Los Angeles Times*, March 19, 1995; accessed online 2/14/15); *The Forewarned Investor: Don't Get Fooled Again by Corporate Fraud*, by Brett Messing and Steven Sugarman (Career Press, Inc., 2006, pages 168–170; accessed online 2/14/15); and "How Al Dunlap Self-Destructed," by John A. Byrne (*BusinessWeek*, June 25, 1998; accessed online 2/14/15).

Sources for Plum Creek's transformation from timberland owner to real estate investment trust and its development plans for Moosehead Lake included *Eco Barons*, by Edward Humes (Ecco, 2009, pages 178-179). The Diamond Occidental divestiture was covered in "The Diamond Legacy" (*Maine Times*, March 13, 1997, pages 4–7). Plum Creek's initial development plan at First Roach Pond was reported by *Maine Times* on June 12, 2002. The *Maine Times* issue of February 10, 2004, was the source for Plum Creek's development proposal for Moosehead Lake.

Roxanne's initial conservation land purchase on Kineo was reported in the *Moosehead Messenger*, June 20, 2001, page 1. Her effort to build a visitor's center in Monson was reported in the *Bangor Daily News*, February 6, 2003, page B3. Bill McKibben's quote about RESTORE's national park proposal came from his essay called "The Maine Woods" in Patagonia's 2002 holiday issue. Tom Allen, at the time Maine's First District Congressman, told the *Moosehead Messenger* on September 5, 2001, page 13, that he wouldn't back RESTORE's park plan. Bob Kimber's essay, "The Case for a North Woods Park," appeared in *Down East* magazine's July 2001 issue, pages 47–49. John Malone's first two purchases of Maine land are available on *Maine Times* online. The Associated Press story of his 900,000-acre purchase in 2011 is on boston.com and available from various newspaper websites.

Roxanne's statement that her "philanthropy-environmentalist career will be my last one" was in *HOPE* magazine, March/April 2004, page 35. Discussions with national park officials about her proposed park plan were reported in *Backpacker* magazine, February 2005, page 88. The Pingress heirs' conservation easement project was reported in the *New York Times* (March 21, 2001; accessed online). The increasing number of conservation easements was detailed in "From Diamond International to Plum Creek: The era of large landscape conservation in the northern forest," by Sara A. Clark and Peter Howell (*Maine Policy Review*, Volume 16, Issue 2, pages 55–65, 2007). The interview with Angus King by phone was on December 6, 2010.

People magazine's "Green Acres" article about Roxanne's national park proposal was in its October 15, 2001, article on pages 73–74. The reason wilderness had become a "dirty word" in Maine politics was in a chapter of *On Wilderness: Voices from Maine*, edited by Phyllis Austin, Dean Bennett, and Robert Kimber (Tilbury House, 2003, pages 56–65). The St. John River protection campaign was the subject of a *Down East* magazine article, May 1999, pages 38–41.

The formation of the Maine Woods Coalition was reported in the *Bangor Daily News*, January 5, 2001 (page unavailable). Governor John Baldacci's opposition to the proposed national park was noted in the *Moosehead Messenger*, January 11, 2001, page 7. Public polling information on the proposed park by RESTORE: The North Woods was reported in the Forest Ecology Network's Winter 2001 issue (accessed online). The vote by Greenville selectmen to oppose Roxanne's planned visitor's center in Monson was reported in the *Bangor Daily News* on October 4, 2002 (accessed online).

CHAPTER 14. A NEW VISION: 2004

Roxanne's shift from the national park project of RESTORE: The North Woods to one of her own design came from many memos, e-mails, and interviews. Among those I consulted were Roxanne Quimby, Jym St. Pierre, Rudy Engholm, Michael Kellett, Mimi McConnell. Other key sources for this chapter were Sam Hodder, Charles FitzGerald, Chuck Gadzik, Ralph Knoll, Pat McGowan, David Soucy, George Smith, Bob Meyers, Don Hudson, Chris Drew, and Loren Goode. The Pew Charitable Foundation report of February 2011 with recommendations to Roxanne on how to move forward with her park project was insightful. Americans for a Maine Woods National Park issued a news release on May 7, 2003, about their formation as a group composed of numerous national celebrities. An e-mail from Roxanne and Will LaPage to RESTORE board members set the stage for their attempted spin-off of "Americans" as an autonomous entity. In the author's possession is an April 10, 2004, e-mail from Rudy Engholm to Michael Kellett laying out the best scenario he envisioned for dealing with the split between RESTORE and Roxanne.

The Irving land sale on the border of Baxter State Park was written by the author for *Maine Environmental News* online on November 22, 2002. The author published another article on *Maine Environmental News* on May 23, 2002, about Roxanne's land purchases making her the second-largest individual landowner in Maine. Charles FitzGerald's purchase of Katahdin Lake Camps was an article by the author that appeared on the *Maine Environmental News* website on May 30, 2003. Herb Haynes's purchase of 12,500 acres of Irving land was noted on June 20, 2003 on the *Maine Environmental News* website.

Roxanne's appearance on December 3, 2003, at the Industrial Forestry Forum in Brewer was attended by the author. Roxanne's plans to cancel camp leases and the impact on Bowlin sporting camp was in the *Bangor Daily News* on November 26, 2003, pages A1-2. Muriel Fortier's determination to fight eviction from Roxanne's land (Township 5, Range 8), was in the *Bangor Daily News* on May 13, 204, pages 1 and C9. Paul Reynolds's column mentioning Roxanne being named by President Obama to the National Park Foundation board was in the *Ellsworth American* on November 18, 2010 (page number unavailable).

Roxanne's separation from RESTORE is documented in files with the author and was noted in the *Community Press* on June 22, 2004, page 3. The RESTORE newsletter reported that Roxanne had received a restoration leadership award on January 24, 2002. Roxanne's comment that "it's bad news when I buy [land]" was in the *Wall Street Journal* on December 2, 2006, page1.

CHAPTER 15. END OF AN ERA: 2011

My account of the increasing conflict and deal-making over the Penobscot East Branch lands came from Roxanne Quimby, Roger Milliken, Chuck Gadzik, Jym St. Pierre, Charles FitzGerald, Ralph Knoll, Pat McGowan, David Soucy, Sam Hodder, William T. Gardner, and others who wished not to be mentioned. Also contributing were Marsha Donahue, George McLaughlin, Bob Meyers, Matt Polstein, Anita Meuller, Peggy Daigle, Mark Scally, Cathy Johnson, Lucas St. Clair, and Charles Buki. I consulted the Thomas Power report, the Headwaters Economics reports, and the Maine Forest Council forest report for data and projections about the forest industry, tourism. and potential jobs from a national park. Much of the information in Chapters 13–15 was gathered from public meetings the author attended in which

Roxanne made presentations, and I attended the Millinocket meeting led by U.S. Secretary of the Interior Ken Salazar and National Park Service director Jon Jarvis. The land purchases Roxanne made, with acreage and dollar figures, came from a list provided by the James S. Sewall Company.

In the wake of Roxanne's departure from the public scene in 2011, news about the continuing park campaign from multiple sources was available primarily in the *Bangor Daily News*. (There are many more articles at the newspaper's website about the park project and local responses than I have sourced here.) Lucas St. Clair, Cathy Johnson, and Lisa Polhmann also held many events in communities to discuss their evolving national park and recreation area plans in efforts to gain citizen support. Printed material was available at these meetings explaining the proposed park vision.

Roxanne's remark about consideration of a national monument was in Edward Humes's book *Eco Barons*, page 218. The Associated Press article on Roxanne's plan to buy 70,000 acres for a national park was carried by several Maine newspapers and was in the *Bangor Daily News* March 28, 2001, online edition. Dayton Duncan's quote was given to the author in an e-mail on February 11, 2015. The 2011 figures for Acadia National Park's financial impact in neighboring communities and the number of jobs produced came from the National Park Service's report, *Economic Benefits to Local Communities from National Park Visitation* for 2011, released on February 21, 2013.

Senate president Kevin Raye introduced the anti-national park resolution on June 15, 2011, and it was passed by a Republican majority in the state legislature that same day. The Millinocket town council's vote on July 28, 2011, against a national park feasibility study was carried online by the *Bangor Daily News* that same day. The visit to Freeport by U.S. Interior Secretary Ken Salazar and National Park Service director Jon Jarvis was reported online by the *Portland Press Herald*. Jon Lund's remarks about Governor Angus King were in his "Jottings" column on May 2, 2011 (page unavailable). The announcement that Cate Street Capital was buying the two closed pulp and paper mills in Millinocket and East Millinocket was carried in *New Hampshire Business Review* online on August 31, 2011. Michael Tobias's interview with Roxanne was carried on *Forbes* online on October 3, 2011. The congressional budget hearing on October 5, 2011, where Interior Secretary Salazar told Maine Senator Susan Collins that the National Park Service had no plans to do a reconnaissance study for Roxanne's proposed national park was covered by C-Span television and was reported by *National Parks Traveler* online on March 5, 2012. The

Bangor Daily News editorial and Peter Triandafillou's op-ed piece against the proposed national park were available online on October 11, 2011. Roxanne's letter of apology was in the *Bangor Daily News* online on October 18, 2011.

Maine Biz's interview with Roger Milliken was online on December 9, 2013. The reference to the deaths of anti-park stalwarts referred to Vern Haines of Millinocket on September 25, 2008, Ray Campbell of Millinocket on June 14, 2013, and William T. Gardner on June 15, 2014. The purchase of the East Millinocket mill by Hackman Capital Partners was announced in the *Portland Press Herald* online on December 14, 2015. The number of the largest employers left in the Katahdin region came from the Baxter State Park website and the Millinocket Regional Hospital human resources manager. (An account of the lands that Roxanne has bought and how much she paid is available to the public on the web at GuideStar.com.) The conditions on which the 200 business owners based their support of the proposed national park and recreation area were posted on the *Bangor Daily News* website on March 28, 2015.

EPILOGUE

W. Kent Olson's quote in the Epilogue is from "The Geography of Philanthropy," a chapter in a forthcoming book from Rizzoli and the Friends of Acadia celebrating the 2015 centennial of Acadia National Park.

Acknowledgments

I am grateful for Roxanne Quimby for her cooperation in the launch of this project. Without that encouragement, the book would not have come to pass. I also greatly appreciate the help I received from Hannah Quimby and Lucas St. Clair, who shared memories of their early years. Liliane Willens provided assistance with ancestral information about the maternal side of Roxanne's family.

I have been extremely fortunate to work with Jon Eaton, who, with Tris Coburn, had just purchased Tilbury House Publishers when I sought a publisher for this book. The book might not have come to fruition without his unwavering support and his guidance around and over numerous obstacles. As editor, Jon contributed much to the accuracy, organization, and readability of the text. I felt great joy in the collaboration.

Among the many invaluable sources of information about Burt's Bees' early years in North Carolina, Mark Smith, Chuck Friedman, Frank Baldwin, Bob Kingery, Mike Abramson, and Sunne Justice are due special thanks. Numerous people involved in Burt's Bees or in Roxanne's national park project spoke to me off the record. They know who they are, and this book is better because of them. To all who stuck with me to the end, I send a joyful "wow."

Unofficial north woods historian Jym St. Pierre, the Maine director of RESTORE: The North Woods, shared with endless generosity and patience his knowledge of the upheaval in land ownership in the Maine woods during the 1990s and Roxanne's entry to the scene. His insights into events, personalities, and relationships were vital. His suggestions for improving my early manuscript drafts helped me over one hump after another in the long process of writing this multifaceted tale. Jym lived the history of the north country for almost 30 years through his work with the Maine Land Use Regulation Commission, and, since 1992, with RESTORE. He provided a frontline view of the land conservation fight, and his perspective was always balanced despite his desire for a national park 50 times larger than the one proposed by Roxanne.

David Vinjamuri, who writes for *Forbes* and teaches branding and social media at New York University, generously shared the transcripts of his interviews with Roxanne for his 2008 book *Accidental Branding*. Former *Wild Earth* editor and author Tom Butler offered guidance in placing Roxanne in the context of American land conservation philanthropists, the subject of his book *Wildlands Philanthropy: The Great American Tradition*.

Three others to whom I am indebted for help with the first draft are Debora Price, Ann Logan, and Kim Ridley. Besides improving the manuscript with editing corrections and suggestions, all three encouraged me without reservation. Those who provided invaluable feedback on later drafts include Lloyd Irland, David Vail, Paul Mills, and George Smith.

Research staff at numerous libraries and historical and genealogical societies sent me essential ancestral material. I thank those who answered my requests for records from the National Archives Trust; the Massachusetts National Guard Military Museum and Archives (Worcester); the New England Historical Genealogical Society (Boston); the Sheboygan County Research Center (Wisconsin); the Jefferson County Library (High Ridge, Missouri); the Maine State Library (Augusta); the Lewiston (Maine) Public Library; the Curtis Memorial Library (Brunswick, Maine); the Bethlehem (Pennsylvania) Public Library; the Boston Public Library; the Salem (Massachusetts) Public Library; the Stratford (Connecticut) Historical Society, the Maine Historical Society (Portland); the Sebec (Maine) Historical Society; and newspapers in Sheboygan and Racine, Wisconsin. Applause to the staff at Chequamegon-Nicolet National Forest in Wisconsin for finding records confirming the work of Wilda Quimby to establish a Children's Forest in the late 1930s.

The managers and staff at Maine town offices in Parkman, Guilford, Monson, Abbott, Willimantic, Dover-Foxcroft, Livermore, and Winter Harbor were repeatedly generous with their time and help. Special thanks go to volunteer archivists Betty Ellis in Sebec and Kay Sakahara in Abbot for efforts to find local Quimby ancestor records. The late Bob Littlefield, longtime Guilford town manager, always picked up the phone to answer more questions. Thanks to Bill Teague in North Carolina, ever enthusiastic about recounting how he hosted Roxanne and Burt during their scouting trips for a new location for Burt's Bees. And the team at BEK, Inc. in Brunswick rescued me many times from my computer deficiencies.

The love, steadfastness, and rational perspectives of my closest friends helped me enormously when unexpected obstacles cropped up. Debora Price, Anne Dellenbaugh, Judy McLamb, and Bunny McBride endured it all. Libbet Cone and Nancy Coleman were godsends.

I never yearned for or expected the life of a writer. It arose out of thin air, as if my assignment were handed to me by design, and remarkable people showed up to guide me. North Carolina newspaper publishers Tom and Janet David induced me to work for them after college in the 1960s, strangely sure that I should have a career in journalism on the weak basis of having edited my high school paper. Rob Wood, an Associated Press correspondent in Raleigh, perplexed me with an offer of a political reporting job that, years later, led me to actualize my yearning to live in New England. Maine was the place with an AP opening, and putting down roots here changed my life. *Maine Times* cofounder John Cole told me over and over that I should work for the statewide weekly. But it was Cole's partner, newspaper editor Peter Cox, who gave me the alternative journalism job-to-die-for in the mid-1970s, when *Maine Times* was entering its most influential years. My gratitude to them goes deep.

My 45-year interest in the Maine woods came from many directions. The *Maine Times* provided a platform from which to write continuously about the environment and major forest issues. After I interviewed National Audubon field editor Frank Graham Jr. about his book *Since Silent Spring,* he and his wife, Ada, introduced me to hiking, snowshoeing, and cross-country skiing. Expeditions with the Grahams excited a passion in me for an outdoor life that became my primary personal commitment.

I have been hugely inspired by wilderness writers who were irresistibly driven to hike: Bob Marshall, Guy and Laura Waterman, and, most recently, Robert Macfarlane. Marshall's writings led me to Alaska's Arctic, my first encounter with an extreme, heart-stopping wildland that launched me into more adventures in the far north. In 1994, I was drawn to the Watermans to write about their homesteading life in Vermont, where they typewrote their outdoor classics. My day with these homesteading and wilderness icons was a profoundly moving experience; they have remained a potent influence through the subsequent years in my writing and mountain explorations. Robert Macfarlane, a fellow of Emmanuel College, Cambridge, dropped into my life on the wings of his trilogy of books on wild places, mostly in Britain. His writings took my breath away with their lyricism, imagery, and power to alter my thinking and experience of wildness. They provide insistent encouragement to continue my journeys to high peaks and secluded valleys, no matter what.

To these fellow travelers, I am spiritually indebted.

The 3.2-million-acre national park and preserve proposed by RESTORE: The North Woods.
(Courtesy Jym St. Pierre, RESTORE: The North Woods)

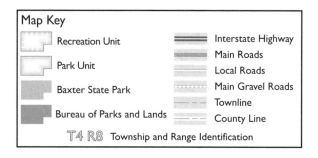

Opposite page: Roxanne Quimby's proposed 75,000-acre national park (between Baxter State Park and the East Branch) and parcels for the accompanying national recreation area, also projected to be 75,000 acres. (Courtesy Bill Duffy)

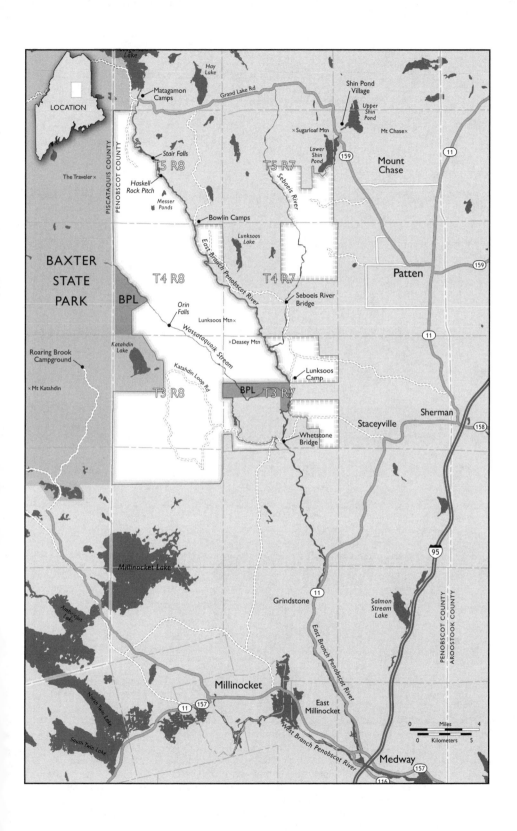

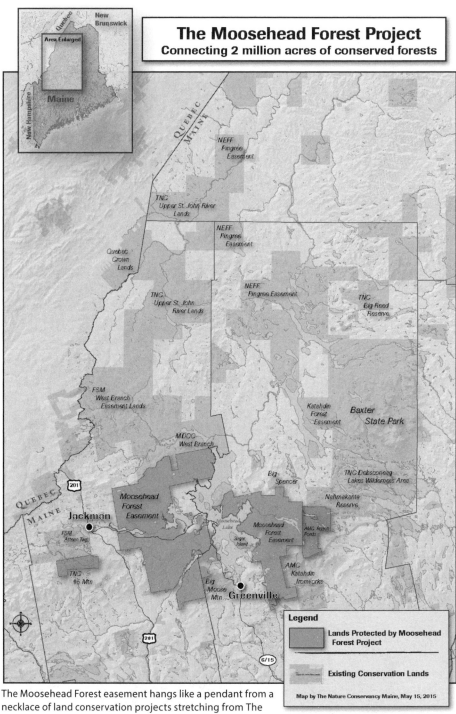

The Moosehead Forest Project
Connecting 2 million acres of conserved forests

New Brunswick

Area Enlarged

Maine

New Hampshire

QUEBEC MAINE

NEFF Pingree Easement

TNC Upper St. John River Lands

NEFF Pingree Easement

Quebec Crown Lands

TNC Upper St. John River Lands

NEFF Pingree Easement

TNC Big Reed Reserve

FSM West Branch Easement Lands

Katahdin Forest Easement

Baxter State Park

MDOC West Branch

Big Spencer

TNC Debsconeag Lakes Wilderness Area

QUEBEC MAINE

201

Moosehead Forest Easement

Nahmakanta Reserve

Jackman

FSM Attean Twp

Moosehead Forest Easement

Sugar Island

Moosehead Forest Easement

AMC Roach Ponds

AMC Katahdin Ironworks

TNC #5 Mtn

Big Moose Mtn

Greenville

201

6/15

Legend

Lands Protected by Moosehead Forest Project

Existing Conservation Lands

Map by The Nature Conservancy Maine, May 15, 2015

The Moosehead Forest easement hangs like a pendant from a necklace of land conservation projects stretching from The Nature Conservancy's Upper St. John holdings in the northwest to Baxter State Park in the east. Roxanne's proposed national park would anchor the eastern end of the necklace. Also shown here are the 45,000 acres in two parcels acquired from Plum Creek for $15 million by TNC and the Appalachian Mountain Club: "TNC #5 Mtn" (south of Jackman) and "AMC Roach Ponds" (east of Moosehead Forest). (Illustrated by Daniel Coker, courtesy The Nature Conservancy)

INDEX